Pro Python System Administration

Rytis Sileika

Pro Python System Administration

ISBN-13 (pbk): 978-1-4302-2605-5

ISBN-13 (electronic): 978-1-4302-2606-2

Printed and bound in the United States of America 9 8 7 6 5 4 3 2 1

President and Publisher: Paul Manning
Lead Editors: Duncan Parkes and Michelle Lowman
Technical Reviewer: Patrick Engebretson
Editorial Board: Clay Andres, Steve Anglin, Mark Beckner, Ewan Buckingham, Gary Cornell,
    Jonathan Gennick, Jonathan Hassell, Michelle Lowman, Matthew Moodie, Duncan Parkes,
    Jeffrey Pepper, Frank Pohlmann, Douglas Pundick, Ben Renow-Clarke, Dominic Shakeshaft,
    Matt Wade, Tom Welsh
Coordinating Editors: Mary Tobin and Jennifer L. Blackwell
Copy Editors: Jim Compton, Heather Lang and Marilyn Smith
Compositor: Lynn L'Heureux
Indexer: Julie Grady
Artist: April Milne
Cover Designer: Anna Ishchenko

Distributed to the book trade worldwide by Springer Science+Business Media, LLC.,
233 Spring Street, 6th Floor, New York, NY 10013. Phone 1-800-SPRINGER, fax (201) 348-4505,
e-mail `orders-ny@springer-sbm.com`, or visit `www.springeronline.com`.

For information on translations, please e-mail `rights@apress.com`, or visit `www.apress.com`.

Apress and friends of ED books may be purchased in bulk for academic, corporate, or promotional use. eBook versions and licenses are also available for most titles. For more information, reference our Special Bulk Sales–eBook Licensing web page at `www.apress.com/info/bulksales`.

The source code for this book is available to readers at `www.apress.com`.

I want to dedicate this book to my family—my wife Evelina and daughters Gabija and Milda

Contents at a Glance

Contents

About the Author

Rytis Sileika has over twelve years of experience in the system administration field. Since obtaining his bachelor of science degree in computer science from Kaunas University of Technology, he's been specializing in system integration and deployment automation. His areas of interest and expertise are UNIX-based operating system management and automation tool development. Rytis is also a RedHat Certified Engineer. He lives with his wife and two daughters in London, United Kingdom. His nonprofessional interests are traveling, hiking, and photography.

About the Technical Reviewer

Dr. Patrick Engebreston obtained his doctor of science degree with a specialization in information assurance from Dakota State University. He currently serves as an assistant professor of computer and network security and works as a senior penetration tester for security firm in the Midwest. His research interests include penetration testing, intrusion detection, exploitation, malware, and programming. He teaches courses in security, C programming, and Python. When not hacking or teaching, Dr. Engebretson spends every waking minute with his wife Lori and his two beautiful girls Maggie and Molly.

Acknowledgments

I'd like to express my gratitude to everyone at Apress involved in the development and production of this book. First, I want to thank Duncan Parkes, who helped a lot with the initial proposal, set the general shape and structure of the book, and got the whole project moving forward.

Many thanks go to Michelle Lowman and Dr. Patrick Engebretson for correcting all technical and logical mistakes as well as providing valuable tips.

I would also like to thank Jennifer Blackwell and Mary Tobin for keeping the project and my writing on schedule and gently reminding me about the approaching deadlines.

Last but not least, I'd like to thank the Python development community and Guido van Rossum for creating such a nice and elegant programming language.

Introduction

The scope of the system administrator role has changed dramatically over the years. The number of systems supported by a single engineer has also increased. As such, it is impractical to handcraft each installation, and there is a need to automate as many tasks as possible. The structure of systems varies from organization to organization, therefore system administrators must be able to create their own management tools. Historically, the most popular programming languages for these tasks were UNIX shell and Perl. They served their purpose well, and I doubt they will ever cease to exist. However, the complexity of current systems requires new tools, and the Python programming language is one of them.

Python is an object oriented programming language suitable for developing large-scale applications. Its syntax and structure make is very easy to read, so much so that the language is sometimes referred to as "executable pseudocode." The Python interpreter allows for interactive execution, so in some situations, you can use it instead of a standard UNIX shell. Although Python is primarily an object-oriented language, you can easily adopt it for procedural and functional styles of programming. Given all that, Python makes a perfect fit as a new language for implementing system administration applications. There are a large number of Linux system utilities already written in Python, such as the Yum package manager and Anaconda, the Linux installation program.

Prerequisites for This Book

This book is about using the Python programming language to solve specific system administration tasks. We will look at the four distinctive system administration areas: network management, web server and web application management, database system management, and system monitoring. Although I will explain most of the technologies used in this book in detail, bear in mind that the main goal of this book is to show you the practical application of the Python libraries to solve rather specific issues. Therefore, I'm assuming that you are a seasoned system administrator.

As we go along with the examples, you will be asked to install additional packages and libraries. In most cases, I provide the commands and instructions to perform these tasks on a Fedora system, but you should be ready to adopt these instructions to the Linux distribution that you are going to use. Most of the examples work without many modifications on a recent OS X release (10.6.X) too.

I also assume that you have a background in the Python programming language. I will be focusing on introducing the specific libraries that are used in system administration tasks as well as some lesser known or less-often-discussed language functionality, such as the generator functions or the class internal methods, but the basic language syntax is not explained. If you want to refresh your Python skills I would recommend *Beginning Python: From Novice to Professional, Second Edition* by Magnus Lie Hetland (Apress, 2008).

All examples presented in this book assume the Python version 2.6 and will not work correctly with the latest Python 3 without additional modifications. Most of the examples rely on additional modules that have not yet been ported to this version of Python.

■**Note** Because of the line length limitations of the printed page, some lines of the code had to be split into two lines. This is indicated by the backslash character (\) at the end of the split line. When you use the code examples, you can either leave the structure as it is (i.e., with the wrapped lines), or you can join the two lines together, in which case you'll have to remove the backslash character from the code.

Structure of This Book

This book contains 13 chapters, and each chapter solves a distinctive problem. Some examples span multiple chapters, but even then, each chapter deals with a specific aspect of the particular problem.

In addition to the chapters, several other organizational layers span this book. First, I grouped the chapters by the problem type. Chapters 1 to 4 deal with network management issues; Chapters 5 to 7 talk about the Apache web server and web application management; Chapters 8 to 11 are dedicated to monitoring and statistical calculations; and finally, Chapters 12 and 13 focus on database management issues.

Second, I am maintaining a common pattern in all chapters. I start with the problem statement and then move on to gather requirements and through the design phase before going into the implementation section.

Third, each chapter focuses on one or more technologies and the Python libraries that provide the language interface to the particular technology. Examples of such technologies could be the SOAP protocol, application plug-in architecture, or cloud computing concepts.

Chapter 1: Reading and Collecting Performance Data Using SNMP

Most network attached devices expose the internal counters via the Simple Network Management Protocol (SNMP). This chapter explains basic SNMP principles and the data structure. We then look at the Python libraries that provide the interface to SNMP–enabled devices. We also investigate the Round Robin database, which is the *de facto* standard for storing the statistical data. Finally, we'll look at the Jinja2 template framework, which allows us to generate simple web pages.

Chapter 2: Managing Devices Using the SOAP API

Complicated tasks, such as managing the device configuration, cannot be easily done by using SNMP, because the protocol is too simplistic. Therefore, advanced devices, such as the Citrix Netscaler load balanacers, provide the SOAP API interface to the device management system. In this chapter, we'll investigate the SOAP API structure and the libraries that enable the SOAP–based communication from the Python programming language. We'll also look at the basic logging functionality using the built-in libraries.

Chapter 3: Creating a Web Application for IP Address Accountancy

In this chapter, we will build a web application that maintains the list of the assigned IP addresses and the address ranges. We will learn how to create web application using the Django framework. I'll show you the way Django application should be structured, how to create and configure the application settings and the URL structure. We'll also investigate how to deploy the Django application using the Apache web server.

Chapter 4: Integrating the IP Address Application with DHCP

This chapter expands on the previous chapter, and we will implement the DHCP address range support. We will also look at some advanced Django programming techniques such as customizing the response MIME type as well as serving AJAX calls.

Chapter 5: Maintaining a List of Virtual Hosts in an Apache Configuration File

This is another Django application that we are going to develop, but this time, our focus will be the Django administration interface. While building the Apache configuration management application, you'll learn how to customize the default Django administration interface with your own views and functions.

Chapter 6: Gathering and Presenting Statistical Data from Apache Log Files

In this chapter, our goal is to build an application that parses and analyses the Apache web server log files. Instead of taking the straightforward but inflexible approach of building a monolithic application, we'll look at the design principles of building plug-in based applications. You will learn how to use the object and class type discovery functions and how to perform a dynamic module loading.

Chapter 7: Performing Complex Searches and Reporting on Application Log Files

This chapter also deals with the log file parsing, but this time I'll show you how to parse complex, multiline log file entries. We are going to investigate the functionality of the open source log file parser tool called Exctractor, which you can download from `http://exctractor.sourceforge.net/`.

Chapter 8: A Web Site Availability Check Script for Nagios

Nagios is one of the most popular open source monitoring systems, because its modular structure allows users to implement their own check scripts and thus customize the monitoring tool to their needs. In this chapter, we are going to create two scripts that check the functionality of a web site. We're going to investigate how to use the Beautiful Soup HTML parsing library to extract the information from the HTML web pages.

Chapter 9: Management and Monitoring Subsystem

This chapter starts a three chapter series in which we'll build a complete monitoring system. The goal of this chapter is not to replace mature monitoring systems such as Nagios or Zenoss but to show you the basic principles of the distributed application programming. We'll look at database design principles such as data normalization. We're also going to investigate how to implement the communication mechanisms between network services using the RPC calls.

Chapter 10: Remote Monitoring Agents

This is the second chapter in the series where we'll implement the remote monitoring agent components. In this chapter, I also describe how to decouple the application from its configuration using the ConfigParser module.

Chapter 11: Statistics Gathering and Reporting

This is the last part of the monitoring series, where I'll show you how to perform basic statistical analysis on the collected performance data. We're going to use scientific libraries—NumPy to perform the calculations and matplotlib to create the graphs. You'll learn how to find which performance readings fall into the comfort zone and how to calculate the boundaries of that zone. We'll also do the basic trend detection, which provides a good insight for the capacity planning.

Chapter 12: Automatic MySQL Database Performance Tuning

In this chapter, I'll show you how to obtain the MySQL database configuration variables and the internal status indicators. We'll build an application that makes a suggestion on how to improve the database engine performance based on the obtained data.

Chapter 13: Amazon EC2/S3 as a Data Warehouse Solution

This chapter shows you how to utilize the Amazon Elastic Compute Cloud (EC2) and offload the infrequent computation tasks to it. We're going to build an application that automatically creates a database server where you can transfer data for further analysis. You can use this example as a basis to build an on-demand data warehouse solution.

The Example Source Code

The source code of all the examples in this book, along with any applicable sample data, can be downloaded from the Apress web site at `http://apress.com/book/view/1430226056`. The source code stored at this location contains the same code that is described in the book.

Most of the prototypes described in this book are also available as open source projects. You can find these projects at the author's web site `http://www.sysadminpy.com/`.

CHAPTER 1

■ ■ ■

Reading and Collecting Performance Data Using SNMP

Most devices that are connected to a network report their status using SNMP (the Simple Network Management Protocol). This protocol was designed primarily for managing and monitoring network-attached hardware devices, but some applications also expose their statistical data using this protocol. In this chapter we will look at how to access this information from your Python applications. We are going to store the obtained data in an RRD (round robin database), using RRDTool—a widely known and popular application and library, which is used to store and plot the performance data. Finally we'll investigate the Jinja2 template system, which we'll use to generate simple web pages for our application.

Application Requirements and Design

The topic of system monitoring is very broad and usually encompasses many different areas. A complete monitoring system is a rather complex system and often is made up of multiple components working together. We are not going to develop a complete, self sufficient system here, but we'll look into two important areas of a typical monitoring system: information gathering and representation. In this chapter we'll implement a system that queries devices using an SNMP protocol and then stores the data using the RRDTool library, which is also used to generate the graphs for visual data representation. All this is tied together into simple web pages using the Jinja2 templating library. We'll look at each of these components in more detail as we go along through the chapter.

Specifying the Requirements

Before we start designing our application we need to come up with some requirements for our system. First of all we need to understand the functionality we expect our system to provide. This will help us to create an effective (and we hope easy-to-implement) system design. In this chapter we are going to create a system that monitors network-attached devices, such as network switches and routers, using the SNMP protocol. So the first requirement is that the system needs to be able to query any device using SNMP.

The information gathered from the devices needs to be stored for future reference and analysis. Let's make some assumptions about the use of this information. First, we don't need to store it indefinitely. (I'll talk more about permanent information storage in Chapters 9–11). This means that the information is stored only for a predefined period of time, and once it becomes obsolete it will be erased. This defines our second requirement: the information needs to be deleted after it's "expired."

Second, the information needs to be stored so that graphs can be produced. We are not going to use it for anything else, and therefore the data store should be optimized for the data representation tasks.

Finally, we need to generate the graphs and represent this information on easily accessible web pages. The information needs to be structured by the device names only. For example, if we are monitoring several devices for CPU and network interface utilization, this information needs to be presented on a single page. We don't need to present this information on multiple time scales; by default the graphs should show the performance indicators for the last 24 hours.

High-Level Design Specification

Now that we have some ideas about the functionality of our system, let's create a simple design, which we'll use as a guide in the development phase. The basic approach is that each of the requirements we specified earlier should be covered by one or more design decisions.

The first requirement is that we need to monitor the network-attached devices, and we need to do so using the SNMP protocol. This means that we have to use appropriate Python library that deals with the SNMP objects. The SNMP module is not included in the default Python installation, so we'll have to use one of the external modules. I recommend using the PySNMP library (available at `http://pysnmp.sourceforge.net/`), which is readily available on most of the popular Linux distributions.

The perfect candidate for the data store engine is RRDTool (available at `http://oss.oetiker.ch/rrdtool/index.en.html`). The Round Robin Database means that the database is structured in such a way that each "table" has a limited length, and once the limit is reached, the oldest entries are dropped. In fact they are not dropped; the new ones are simply written into their position.

The RRDTool library provides two distinct functionalities: the database service and the graph-generation toolkit. There is no native support for RRD databases in Python, but there is an external library available that provides an interface to the RRDTool library.

Finally, to generate the web page we will use the Jinja2 templating library (available at `http://jinja.pocoo.org/2/`), which lets us create sophisticated templates and decouple the design and development tasks.

We are going to use a simple Windows INI-style configuration file to store the information about the devices we will be monitoring. This information will include details such as the device address, SNMP object reference, and access control details.

The application will be split into two parts: the first part is the information-gathering tool that queries all configured devices and stores the data in the RRDTool database, and the second part is the report generator, which generates the web site structure along with all required images. Both components will be instantiated from the standard UNIX scheduler application—cron. These two scripts will be named snmp-manager.py and snmp-pages.py respectively.

Introduction to SNMP

SNMP (Simple Network Management Protocol) is a UDP-based protocol used mostly for managing network-attached devices, such as routers, switches, computers, printers, video cameras, and so on. Some applications also allow access to internal counters via the SNMP protocol.

SNMP not only allows you to read performance statistics from the devices, it can also send control messages to instruct a device to perform some action—for example, you can restart a router remotely by using SNMP commands.

There are three main components in a system managed by SNMP:

- The management system, which is responsible for managing all devices

- The managed devices, which are all devices managed by the management system

- The SNMP agent, which is an application that runs on each of the managed devices and interacts with the management system

This relationship is illustrated in Figure 1-1.

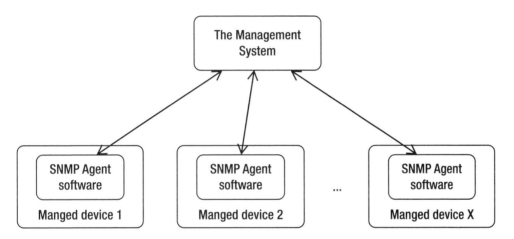

Figure 1-1. *The SNMP network components*

This approach is rather generic. The protocol defines seven basic commands, of which the most interesting to us are get, get bulk, and response. As you may have guessed, the former two are the commands that the management system issues to the agent, and the latter is a response from the agent software.

How does the management system know what to look for? The protocol does not define a way of exchanging this information, and therefore the management system has no way to interrogate the agents to obtain the list of available variables.

The issue is resolved by using a Management Information Base (or MIB). Each device usually has an associated MIB, which describes the structure of the management data on that system. Such a MIB would list in hierarchical order all object identifiers (OIDs) that are available on the managed device. The OID effectively represents a node in the object tree. It contains numerical identifiers of all nodes leading to the current OID starting from the node at the top of the tree. The node IDs are assigned and regulated by the IANA (Internet Assigned Numbers Authority). An organization can apply for an OID node and when assigned is responsible for managing the OID structure below the allocated node.

Figure 1-2 illustrates a portion of the OID tree.

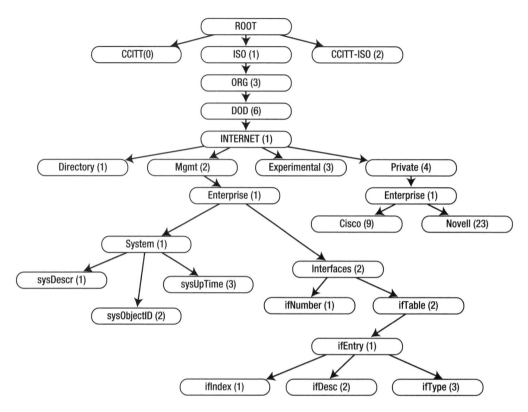

Figure 1-2. *The SNMP OID tree*

Let's look at some example OIDs. The OID tree node that is assigned to the Cisco organization has a value of 1.3.6.1.4.1.9, which means that all *proprietary* OIDs that are associated with the Cisco manufactured devices will start with these numbers. Similarly, the Novell devices will have their OIDs starting with 1.3.6.1.4.1.23.

I deliberately emphasized proprietary OIDs because some properties are expected to be present (if and where available) on all devices. These are under the 1.3.6.1.2.1.1 (System SNMP Variables) node, which is defined by RFC1213. For more details on the OID tree and its elements, please visit http://www.alvestrand.no/objectid/top.html. This web site allows you to browse the OID tree and contains quite a large collection of the various OIDs.

The System SNMP Variables Node

In most cases the basic information about a device will be available under the System SNMP Variables OID node subtree. Therefore let's have a close look at what you can find there.

This OID node contains several additional OID nodes. Table 1-1 provides a description for most of the sub nodes.

Table 1-1. *System SNMP OIDs*

OID String	OID Name	Description
1.3.6.1.2.1.1.1	`sysDescr`	A string containing a short description of the system or device. Usually contains the hardware type and operating system details.
1.3.6.1.2.1.1.2	`sysObjectID`	A string containing the vendor-specific device OID node. For example, if the organization has been assigned an OID node 1.3.6.1.4.1.8888 and this specific device has been assigned a .1.1 OID space under the organization's space, this field would contain a value of 1.3.6.1.4.1.8888.1.1.
1.3.6.1.2.1.1.3	`sysUpTime`	A number representing the time in hundreds of a second from the time when the system was initialized.
1.3.6.1.2.1.1.4	`sysContact`	An arbitrary string containing information about the contact person who is responsible for this system.
1.3.6.1.2.1.1.5	`sysName`	A name that has been assigned to the system. Usually this field contains a fully qualified domain name.
1.3.6.1.2.1.1.6	`sysLocation`	A string describing the physical location of the system.
1.3.6.1.2.1.1.7	`sysServices`	A number that indicates which services are offered by this system. The number is a bitmap representation of all OSI protocols, with the lowest bit representing the first OSI layer. For example, a switching device (operating on layer 2) would have this number set to $2^2 = 4$. This field is rarely used now.
1.3.6.1.2.1.1.8	`sysLastChange`	A number containing the value of `sysUpTime` at the time of a change to any of the system SNMP objects.
1.3.6.1.2.1.1.9	`sysTable`	A node containing multiple `sysEntry` elements. Each element represents a distinct capability and the corresponding OID node value.

The Interfaces SNMP Variables Node

Similarly, the basic interface statistics can be obtained from the Interfaces SNMP Variables OID node subtree. The OID for the interfaces variables is 1.3.6.1.2.1.2 and contains two subnodes:

- An OID containing the total number of network interfaces. The OID value for this entry is 1.3.6.1.2.1.2.1; and it is usually referenced as `ifNumber`. There are no subnodes available under this OID.

- An OID node that contains all interface entries. Its OID is 1.3.6.1.2.1.2.2 and it is usually referenced as `ifTable`. This node contains one or more entry nodes. An entry node (1.3.6.1.2.1.2.2.1, also known as `ifEntry`) contains the detailed information about that particular interface. The number of entries in the list is defined by the `ifNumber` node value.

You can find detailed information about all ifEntry subnodes in Table 1-2.

Table 1-2. *Interface entry SNMP OIDs*

OID String	OID Name	Description
1.3.6.1.2.1.2.2.1.1	ifIndex	A unique sequence number assigned to the interface.
1.3.6.1.2.1.2.2.1.2	ifDescr	A string containing the interface name and other available information, such as the hardware manufacturer's name.
1.3.6.1.2.1.2.2.1.3	ifType	A number representing the interface type, depending on the interface's physical link and protocol.
1.3.6.1.2.1.2.2.1.4	ifMtu	The largest network datagram that this interface can transmit.
1.3.6.1.2.1.2.2.1.5	ifSpeed	The estimated current bandwidth of the interface. If the current bandwidth cannot be calculated, this number should contain the maximum possible bandwidth for the interface.
1.3.6.1.2.1.2.2.1.6	ifPhysAddress	The physical address of the interface, usually a MAC address on Ethernet interfaces.
1.3.6.1.2.1.2.2.1.7	ifAdminStatus	This OID allows setting the new state of the interface. Usually limited to the following values: 1 (Up), 2 (Down), 3 (Testing).
1.3.6.1.2.1.2.2.1.8	ifOperStatus	The current state of the interface. Usually limited to the following values: 1 (Up), 2 (Down), 3 (Testing).
1.3.6.1.2.1.2.2.1.9	ifLastChange	The value containing the system uptime (sysUpTime) reading when this interface entered its current state. May be set to zero if the interface entered this state before the last system reinitialization.
1.3.6.1.2.1.2.2.1.10	ifInOctets	The total number of bytes (octets) received on the interface.
1.3.6.1.2.1.2.2.1.11	ifInUcastPkts	The number of unicast packets forwarded to the device's network stack.
1.3.6.1.2.1.2.2.1.12	ifInNUcastPkts	The number of non-unicast packets delivered to the device's network stack. Non-unicast packets are usually either broadcast or multicast packets.
1.3.6.1.2.1.2.2.1.13	ifInDiscards	The number of dropped packets. This does not indicate a packet error, but may indicate that the receive buffer was too small to accept the packets.

OID String	OID Name	Description
1.3.6.1.2.1.2.2.1.14	ifInErrors	The number of received invalid packets.
1.3.6.1.2.1.2.2.1.15	ifInUnknownProtos	The number of packets that were dropped because the protocol is not supported on the device interface.
1.3.6.1.2.1.2.2.1.16	ifOutOctets	The number of bytes (octets) transmitted out of the interface.
1.3.6.1.2.1.2.2.1.17	ifOutUcastPkts	The number of unicast packets received from the device's network stack. This number also includes the packets that were discarded or not sent.
1.3.6.1.2.1.2.2.1.18	ifNUcastPkts	The number of non-unicast - packets received from the device's network stack. This number also includes the packets that were discarded or not sent.
1.3.6.1.2.1.2.2.1.19	ifOutDiscards	The number of valid packets that were discarded. It's not an error but may indicate that the send buffer is too small to accept all packets.
1.3.6.1.2.1.2.2.1.20	ifOutErrors	The number of outgoing packets that couldn't be transmitted because of the errors.
1.3.6.1.2.1.2.2.1.21	ifOutQLen	The length of the outbound packet queue.
1.3.6.1.2.1.2.2.1.22	ifSpecific	Usually contains a reference to the vendor-specific OID describing this interface. If such information is not available the value is set to an OID 0.0, which is syntactically valid, but is not pointing to anything.

Authentication in SNMP

Authentication in earlier SNMP implementations is somewhat primitive and is prone to attacks. An SNMP agent defines two community strings—one for read-only access and the other for read/write access. When the management system connects to the agent, it must authenticate with one of those two strings. The agent accepts commands only from a management system that has authenticated with valid community strings.

Querying SNMP from the Command Line

Before we start writing our application, let's quickly look at how to query SNMP from the command line. This is particularly useful if you want to check whether the information returned by the SNMP agent is correctly accepted by your application.

The command-line tools are provided by the Net-SNMP-Utils package, which is available for most Linux distributions. This package includes the tools to query and set SNMP objects. Consult your Linux distribution documentation for the details on installing this package.

The command-line tools are provided by the Net-SNMP-Utils package, which is available for most Linux distributions. This package includes the tools to query and set SNMP objects. Consult your Linux distribution documentation for the details on installing this package.

The most useful command from this package is snmpwalk, which takes an OID node as an argument and tries to discover all subnode OIDs. This command uses the SNMP operation getnext, which returns the next node in the tree and effectively allows you to traverse the whole subtree from the indicated node. If no OID has been specified, snmpwalk will use the default SNMP system OID (1.3.6.1.2.1) as the starting point. Listing 1-1 demonstrates the snmpwalk command issued against a laptop running Fedora Linux.

Listing 1-1. *An example of the snmpwalk command*

```
$ snmpwalk -c public -On 192.168.1.68
.1.3.6.1.2.1.1.1.0 = STRING: Linux fedolin.example.com 2.6.32.11-99.fc12.i686 #1↵
SMP Mon Apr 5 16:32:08 EDT 2010 i686
.1.3.6.1.2.1.1.2.0 = OID: .1.3.6.1.4.1.8072.3.2.10
.1.3.6.1.2.1.1.3.0 = Timeticks: (110723) 0:18:27.23
.1.3.6.1.2.1.1.4.0 = STRING: Administrator (admin@example.com)
.1.3.6.1.2.1.1.5.0 = STRING: fedolin.example.com
.1.3.6.1.2.1.1.6.0 = STRING: MyLocation, MyOrganization, MyStreet, MyCity, MyCountry
.1.3.6.1.2.1.1.8.0 = Timeticks: (3) 0:00:00.03
.1.3.6.1.2.1.1.9.1.2.1 = OID: .1.3.6.1.6.3.10.3.1.1
.1.3.6.1.2.1.1.9.1.2.2 = OID: .1.3.6.1.6.3.11.3.1.1
.1.3.6.1.2.1.1.9.1.2.3 = OID: .1.3.6.1.6.3.15.2.1.1
.1.3.6.1.2.1.1.9.1.2.4 = OID: .1.3.6.1.6.3.1
.1.3.6.1.2.1.1.9.1.2.5 = OID: .1.3.6.1.2.1.49
.1.3.6.1.2.1.1.9.1.2.6 = OID: .1.3.6.1.2.1.4
.1.3.6.1.2.1.1.9.1.2.7 = OID: .1.3.6.1.2.1.50
.1.3.6.1.2.1.1.9.1.2.8 = OID: .1.3.6.1.6.3.16.2.2.1
.1.3.6.1.2.1.1.9.1.3.1 = STRING: The SNMP Management Architecture MIB.
.1.3.6.1.2.1.1.9.1.3.2 = STRING: The MIB for Message Processing and Dispatching.
.1.3.6.1.2.1.1.9.1.3.3 = STRING: The management information definitions for the↵
SNMP User-based Security Model.
.1.3.6.1.2.1.1.9.1.3.4 = STRING: The MIB module for SNMPv2 entities
.1.3.6.1.2.1.1.9.1.3.5 = STRING: The MIB module for managing TCP implementations
.1.3.6.1.2.1.1.9.1.3.6 = STRING: The MIB module for managing IP and ICMP↵
implementations
.1.3.6.1.2.1.1.9.1.3.7 = STRING: The MIB module for managing UDP implementations
.1.3.6.1.2.1.1.9.1.3.8 = STRING: View-based Access Control Model for SNMP.
.1.3.6.1.2.1.1.9.1.4.1 = Timeticks: (3) 0:00:00.03
.1.3.6.1.2.1.1.9.1.4.2 = Timeticks: (3) 0:00:00.03
.1.3.6.1.2.1.1.9.1.4.3 = Timeticks: (3) 0:00:00.03
.1.3.6.1.2.1.1.9.1.4.4 = Timeticks: (3) 0:00:00.03
.1.3.6.1.2.1.1.9.1.4.5 = Timeticks: (3) 0:00:00.03
.1.3.6.1.2.1.1.9.1.4.6 = Timeticks: (3) 0:00:00.03
.1.3.6.1.2.1.1.9.1.4.7 = Timeticks: (3) 0:00:00.03
.1.3.6.1.2.1.1.9.1.4.8 = Timeticks: (3) 0:00:00.03
.1.3.6.1.2.1.2.1.0 = INTEGER: 5
```

```
.1.3.6.1.2.1.2.2.1.1.1 = INTEGER: 1
.1.3.6.1.2.1.2.2.1.1.2 = INTEGER: 2
.1.3.6.1.2.1.2.2.1.1.3 = INTEGER: 3
.1.3.6.1.2.1.2.2.1.1.4 = INTEGER: 4
.1.3.6.1.2.1.2.2.1.1.5 = INTEGER: 5
.1.3.6.1.2.1.2.2.1.2.1 = STRING: lo
.1.3.6.1.2.1.2.2.1.2.2 = STRING: eth0
.1.3.6.1.2.1.2.2.1.2.3 = STRING: wlan1
.1.3.6.1.2.1.2.2.1.2.4 = STRING: pan0
.1.3.6.1.2.1.2.2.1.2.5 = STRING: virbr0
.1.3.6.1.2.1.2.2.1.3.1 = INTEGER: softwareLoopback(24)
.1.3.6.1.2.1.2.2.1.3.2 = INTEGER: ethernetCsmacd(6)
.1.3.6.1.2.1.2.2.1.3.3 = INTEGER: ethernetCsmacd(6)
.1.3.6.1.2.1.2.2.1.3.4 = INTEGER: ethernetCsmacd(6)
.1.3.6.1.2.1.2.2.1.3.5 = INTEGER: ethernetCsmacd(6)
.1.3.6.1.2.1.2.2.1.4.1 = INTEGER: 16436
.1.3.6.1.2.1.2.2.1.4.2 = INTEGER: 1500
.1.3.6.1.2.1.2.2.1.4.3 = INTEGER: 1500
.1.3.6.1.2.1.2.2.1.4.4 = INTEGER: 1500
.1.3.6.1.2.1.2.2.1.4.5 = INTEGER: 1500
.1.3.6.1.2.1.2.2.1.5.1 = Gauge32: 10000000
.1.3.6.1.2.1.2.2.1.5.2 = Gauge32: 0
.1.3.6.1.2.1.2.2.1.5.3 = Gauge32: 10000000
.1.3.6.1.2.1.2.2.1.5.4 = Gauge32: 10000000
.1.3.6.1.2.1.2.2.1.5.5 = Gauge32: 10000000
.1.3.6.1.2.1.2.2.1.6.1 = STRING:
.1.3.6.1.2.1.2.2.1.6.2 = STRING: 0:d:56:7d:68:b0
.1.3.6.1.2.1.2.2.1.6.3 = STRING: 0:90:4b:64:7b:4d
.1.3.6.1.2.1.2.2.1.6.4 = STRING: 4e:e:b8:9:81:3b
.1.3.6.1.2.1.2.2.1.6.5 = STRING: d6:f9:7c:2c:17:28
.1.3.6.1.2.1.2.2.1.7.1 = INTEGER: up(1)
.1.3.6.1.2.1.2.2.1.7.2 = INTEGER: up(1)
.1.3.6.1.2.1.2.2.1.7.3 = INTEGER: up(1)
.1.3.6.1.2.1.2.2.1.7.4 = INTEGER: down(2)
.1.3.6.1.2.1.2.2.1.7.5 = INTEGER: up(1)
.1.3.6.1.2.1.2.2.1.8.1 = INTEGER: up(1)
.1.3.6.1.2.1.2.2.1.8.2 = INTEGER: down(2)
.1.3.6.1.2.1.2.2.1.8.3 = INTEGER: up(1)
.1.3.6.1.2.1.2.2.1.8.4 = INTEGER: down(2)
.1.3.6.1.2.1.2.2.1.8.5 = INTEGER: up(1)
.1.3.6.1.2.1.2.2.1.9.1 = Timeticks: (0) 0:00:00.00
.1.3.6.1.2.1.2.2.1.9.2 = Timeticks: (0) 0:00:00.00
.1.3.6.1.2.1.2.2.1.9.3 = Timeticks: (0) 0:00:00.00
.1.3.6.1.2.1.2.2.1.9.4 = Timeticks: (0) 0:00:00.00
.1.3.6.1.2.1.2.2.1.9.5 = Timeticks: (0) 0:00:00.00
.1.3.6.1.2.1.2.2.1.10.1 = Counter32: 89275
.1.3.6.1.2.1.2.2.1.10.2 = Counter32: 0
```

```
.1.3.6.1.2.1.2.2.1.10.3 = Counter32: 11649462
.1.3.6.1.2.1.2.2.1.10.4 = Counter32: 0
.1.3.6.1.2.1.2.2.1.10.5 = Counter32: 0
.1.3.6.1.2.1.2.2.1.11.1 = Counter32: 1092
.1.3.6.1.2.1.2.2.1.11.2 = Counter32: 0
.1.3.6.1.2.1.2.2.1.11.3 = Counter32: 49636
.1.3.6.1.2.1.2.2.1.11.4 = Counter32: 0
.1.3.6.1.2.1.2.2.1.11.5 = Counter32: 0
.1.3.6.1.2.1.2.2.1.12.1 = Counter32: 0
.1.3.6.1.2.1.2.2.1.12.2 = Counter32: 0
.1.3.6.1.2.1.2.2.1.12.3 = Counter32: 0
.1.3.6.1.2.1.2.2.1.12.4 = Counter32: 0
.1.3.6.1.2.1.2.2.1.12.5 = Counter32: 0
.1.3.6.1.2.1.2.2.1.13.1 = Counter32: 0
.1.3.6.1.2.1.2.2.1.13.2 = Counter32: 0
.1.3.6.1.2.1.2.2.1.13.3 = Counter32: 0
.1.3.6.1.2.1.2.2.1.13.4 = Counter32: 0
.1.3.6.1.2.1.2.2.1.13.5 = Counter32: 0
.1.3.6.1.2.1.2.2.1.14.1 = Counter32: 0
.1.3.6.1.2.1.2.2.1.14.2 = Counter32: 0
.1.3.6.1.2.1.2.2.1.14.3 = Counter32: 0
.1.3.6.1.2.1.2.2.1.14.4 = Counter32: 0
.1.3.6.1.2.1.2.2.1.14.5 = Counter32: 0
.1.3.6.1.2.1.2.2.1.15.1 = Counter32: 0
.1.3.6.1.2.1.2.2.1.15.2 = Counter32: 0
.1.3.6.1.2.1.2.2.1.15.3 = Counter32: 0
.1.3.6.1.2.1.2.2.1.15.4 = Counter32: 0
.1.3.6.1.2.1.2.2.1.15.5 = Counter32: 0
.1.3.6.1.2.1.2.2.1.16.1 = Counter32: 89275
.1.3.6.1.2.1.2.2.1.16.2 = Counter32: 0
.1.3.6.1.2.1.2.2.1.16.3 = Counter32: 922277
.1.3.6.1.2.1.2.2.1.16.4 = Counter32: 0
.1.3.6.1.2.1.2.2.1.16.5 = Counter32: 3648
.1.3.6.1.2.1.2.2.1.17.1 = Counter32: 1092
.1.3.6.1.2.1.2.2.1.17.2 = Counter32: 0
.1.3.6.1.2.1.2.2.1.17.3 = Counter32: 7540
.1.3.6.1.2.1.2.2.1.17.4 = Counter32: 0
.1.3.6.1.2.1.2.2.1.17.5 = Counter32: 17
.1.3.6.1.2.1.2.2.1.18.1 = Counter32: 0
.1.3.6.1.2.1.2.2.1.18.2 = Counter32: 0
.1.3.6.1.2.1.2.2.1.18.3 = Counter32: 0
.1.3.6.1.2.1.2.2.1.18.4 = Counter32: 0
.1.3.6.1.2.1.2.2.1.18.5 = Counter32: 0
.1.3.6.1.2.1.2.2.1.19.1 = Counter32: 0
.1.3.6.1.2.1.2.2.1.19.2 = Counter32: 0
.1.3.6.1.2.1.2.2.1.19.3 = Counter32: 0
.1.3.6.1.2.1.2.2.1.19.4 = Counter32: 0
```

```
.1.3.6.1.2.1.2.2.1.19.5 = Counter32: 0
.1.3.6.1.2.1.2.2.1.20.1 = Counter32: 0
.1.3.6.1.2.1.2.2.1.20.2 = Counter32: 0
.1.3.6.1.2.1.2.2.1.20.3 = Counter32: 0
.1.3.6.1.2.1.2.2.1.20.4 = Counter32: 0
.1.3.6.1.2.1.2.2.1.20.5 = Counter32: 0
.1.3.6.1.2.1.2.2.1.21.1 = Gauge32: 0
.1.3.6.1.2.1.2.2.1.21.2 = Gauge32: 0
.1.3.6.1.2.1.2.2.1.21.3 = Gauge32: 0
.1.3.6.1.2.1.2.2.1.21.4 = Gauge32: 0
.1.3.6.1.2.1.2.2.1.21.5 = Gauge32: 0
.1.3.6.1.2.1.2.2.1.22.1 = OID: .0.0
.1.3.6.1.2.1.2.2.1.22.2 = OID: .0.0
.1.3.6.1.2.1.2.2.1.22.3 = OID: .0.0
.1.3.6.1.2.1.2.2.1.22.4 = OID: .0.0
.1.3.6.1.2.1.2.2.1.22.5 = OID: .0.0
.1.3.6.1.2.1.25.1.1.0 = Timeticks: (8232423) 22:52:04.23
.1.3.6.1.2.1.25.1.1.0 = No more variables left in this MIB View (It is past the end⏎
of the MIB tree)
```

As an exercise, try to identify some of the listed OIDs using Tables 1-1 and 1-2 and find out what they mean.

Querying SNMP Devices from Python

Now we know enough about SNMP to start working on our own management system, which will be querying the configured systems on regular intervals. First let's specify the configuration that we will be using in the application.

Configuring the Application

As we already know, we need the following information available for every check:

- An IP address or resolvable domain name of the system that runs the SNMP agent software

- The read-only community string that will be used to authenticate with the agent software

- The OID node's numerical representation

We are going to use the Windows INI-style configuration file, because of its simplicity. Python includes a configuration parsing module by default, so it is also convenient to use. Chapter 9 discusses the ConfigParser module in great detail; please refer to that chapter for more information about the module.

Let's go back to the configuration file for our application. There is no need to repeat the system information for every SNMP object that we're going to query, so we can define each system parameter once in a separate section and then refer to the system ID in each check section. The check section defines the OID node identifier string and a short description, as shown in Listing 1-2.

Listing 1-2. *The management system configuration file*

```
[system_1]
description=My Laptop
address=192.168.1.68
port=161
communityro=public

[check_1]
description=WLAN incoming traffic
oid=1.3.6.1.2.1.2.2.1.10.3
system=system_1

[check_2]
description=WLAN incoming traffic
oid=1.3.6.1.2.1.2.2.1.16.3
system=system_1
```

Make sure that the system and check section IDs are unique, or you may get unpredictable results.

We're going to create an SnmpManager class with two methods, one to add a system and the other to add a check. As the check contains the system ID string, it will automatically be assigned to that particular system. In Listing 1-3 you can see the class definition and also the initialization part that reads in the configuration and iterates through the sections and updates the class object accordingly.

Listing 1-3. *Reading and storing the configuration*

```
import sys
from ConfigParser import SafeConfigParser


class SnmpManager:
    def __init__(self):
        self.systems = {}

    def add_system(self, id, descr, addr, port, comm_ro):
        self.systems[id] = {'description' : descr,
                            'address'     : addr,
                            'port'        : int(port),
                            'communityro' : comm_ro,
                            'checks'      : {}
                           }

    def add_check(self, id, oid, descr, system):
        oid_tuple = tuple([int(i) for i in oid.split('.')])
        self.systems[system]['checks'][id] = {'description': descr,
                                              'oid'         : oid_tuple,
                                             }
```

```python
def main(conf_file=""):
    if not conf_file:
        sys.exit(-1)
    config = SafeConfigParser()
    config.read(conf_file)
    snmp_manager = SnmpManager()
    for system in [s for s in config.sections() if s.startswith('system')]:
        snmp_manager.add_system(system,
                                config.get(system, 'description'),
                                config.get(system, 'address'),
                                config.get(system, 'port'),
                                config.get(system, 'communityro'))
    for check in [c for c in config.sections() if c.startswith('check')]:
        snmp_manager.add_check(check,
                               config.get(check, 'oid'),
                               config.get(check, 'description'),
                               config.get(check, 'system'))
```

As you see in the example, we first have to iterate through the system sections and update the object before proceeding with the check sections.

▓**Note** This order is important, because if we try to add a check for a system that hasn't been inserted yet, we'll get a dictionary index error.

Also note that we are converting the OID string to a tuple of integers. You'll see why we have to do this later in this section. The configuration file is loaded and we're ready to run SNMP queries against the configured devices.

Using the PySNMP Library

In this project we are going to use the PySNMP library, which is implemented in pure Python and doesn't depend on any precompiled libraries. The pysnmp package is available for most Linux distributions and can be installed using the standard distribution package manager. In addition to pysnmp you will also need the ASN.1 library, which is used by pysnmp and is also available as part of the Linux distribution package selection. For example, on a Fedora system you can install the pysnmp module with the following commands:

```
$ sudo yum install pysnmp
$ sudo yum install python-pyasn1
```

Alternatively, you can use the Python Package manager (PiP) to install this library for you:

```
$ sudo pip install pysnmp
$ sudo pip install pyasn1
```

If you don't have the `pip` command available, you can download and install this tool from `http://pypi.python.org/pypi/pip`. We will use it in later chapters as well.

The PySNMP library hides all the complexity of SNMP processing behind a single class with a simple API. All you have to do is create an instance of the `CommandGenerator` class. This class is available from the `pysnmp.entity.rfc3413.oneliner.cmdgen` module and implements most of the standard SNMP protocol commands: `getCmd()`, `setCmd()` and `nextCmd()`. Let's look at each of those in more detail.

The SNMP GET Command

All the commands we are going to discuss follow the same invocation pattern: import the module, create an instance of the CommandGenerator class, create three required parameters (an authentication object, a transport target object, and a list of arguments), and finally invoke the appropriate method. The method returns a tuple containing the error indicators (if there was an error) and the result object.

In Listing 1-4, we query a remote Linux machine using the standard SNMP OID (1.3.6.1.2.1.1.1.0).

Listing 1-4. *An example of the SNMP GET command*

```
>>> from pysnmp.entity.rfc3413.oneliner import cmdgen
>>> cg = cmdgen.CommandGenerator()
>>> comm_data = cmdgen.CommunityData('my-manager', 'public')
>>> transport = cmdgen.UdpTransportTarget(('192.168.1.68', 161))
>>> variables = (1, 3, 6, 1, 2, 1, 1, 1, 0)
>>> errIndication, errStatus, errIndex, result = cg.getCmd(comm_data, transport,
variables)
>>> print errIndication
None
>>> print errStatus
0
>>> print errIndex
0
>>> print result
[(ObjectName('1.3.6.1.2.1.1.1.0'), OctetString('Linux fedolin.example.com↵
 2.6.32.11-99.fc12.i686 #1 SMP Mon Apr 5 16:32:08 EDT 2010 i686'))]
>>>
```

Let's look at some steps more closely. When we initiate the community data object, we have provided two strings—the community string (the second argument) and the agent or manager security name string; in most cases this can be any string. An optional parameter specifies the SNMP version to be used (it defaults to SNMP v2c). If you must query version 1 devices, use the following command:

```
>>> comm_data = cmdgen.CommunityData('my-manager', 'public', mpModel=0)
```

The transport object is initiated with the tuple containing either the fully qualified domain name or the IP address string and the integer port number.

The last argument is the OID expressed as a tuple of all node IDs that make up the OID we are querying. Therefore, we had to convert the dot-separated string into a tuple earlier when we were reading the configuration items.

Finally, we call the API command getCmd(), which implements the SNMP GET command, and pass these three objects as its arguments. The command returns a tuple, each element of which is described in Table 1-3.

Table 1-3. *CommandGenerator Return Objects*

Tuple Element	Description
errIndication	If this string is not empty, it indicates the SNMP engine error.
errStatus	If this element evaluates to True, it indicates an error in the SNMP communication; the object that generated the error is indicated by the errIndex element.
errIndex	If the errStatus indicates that an error has occurred, this field can be used to find the SNMP object that caused the error. The object position in the result array is errIndex-1.
result	This element contains a list of all returned SNMP object elements. Each element is a tuple that contains the name of the object and the object value.

The SNMP SET Command

The SNMP SET command is mapped in PySNMP to the setCmd() method call. All parameters are the same; the only difference is that the variables section now contains a tuple: the OID and the new value. Let's try to use this command to change a read-only object; Listing 1-5 shows the command-line sequence.

Listing 1-5. *An example of the SNMP SET command*

```
>>> from pysnmp.entity.rfc3413.oneliner import cmdgen
>>> from pysnmp.proto import rfc1902
>>> cg = cmdgen.CommandGenerator()
>>> comm_data = cmdgen.CommunityData('my-manager', 'public')
>>> transport = cmdgen.UdpTransportTarget(('192.168.1.68', 161))
>>> variables = ((1, 3, 6, 1, 2, 1, 1, 1, 0), rfc1902.OctetString('new system
description'))
>>> errIndication, errStatus, errIndex, result = cg.setCmd(comm_data, transport,↵
variables)
>>> print errIndication
None
>>> print errStatus
6
>>> print errIndex
```

```
1
>>> print errStatus.prettyPrint()
noAccess(6)
>>> print result
[(ObjectName('1.3.6.1.2.1.1.1.0'), OctetString('new system description'))]
>>>
```

What happened here is that we tried to write to a read-only object, and that resulted in an error. What's interesting in this example is how we format the parameters. You have to convert strings to SNMP object types; otherwise; they won't pass as valid arguments. Therefore the string had to be encapsulated in an instance of the OctetString class. You can use other methods of the rfc1902 module if you need to convert to other SNMP types; the methods include Bits(), Counter32(), Counter64(), Gauge32(), Integer(), Integer32(), IpAddress(), OctetString(), Opaque(), TimeTicks(), and Unsigned32(). These are all class names that you can use if you need to convert a string to an object of a specific type.

The SNMP GETNEXT Command

The SNMP GETNEXT command is implemented as the nextCmd() method. The syntax and usage are identical to getCmd(); the only difference is that the result is a list of objects that are immediate child nodes of the specified OID node.

Let's use this command to query all objects that are immediate child nodes of the SNMP system OID (1.3.6.1.2.1.1); Listing 1-6 shows the nextCmd() method in action.

Listing 1-6. *An example of the SNMP GETNEXT command*

```
>>> from pysnmp.entity.rfc3413.oneliner import cmdgen
>>> cg = cmdgen.CommandGenerator()
>>> comm_data = cmdgen.CommunityData('my-manager', 'public')
>>> transport = cmdgen.UdpTransportTarget(('192.168.1.68', 161))
>>> variables = (1, 3, 6, 1, 2, 1, 1)
>>> errIndication, errStatus, errIndex, result = cg.nextCmd(comm_data, transport,
variables)
>>> print errIndication
requestTimedOut
>>> errIndication, errStatus, errIndex, result = cg.nextCmd(comm_data, transport,
variables)
>>> print errIndication
None
>>> print errStatus
0
>>> print errIndex
0
>>> for object in result:
...   print object
...
```

```
[(ObjectName('1.3.6.1.2.1.1.1.0'), OctetString('Linux fedolin.example.com⏎
 2.6.32.11-99.fc12.i686 #1 SMP Mon Apr 5 16:32:08 EDT 2010 i686')))]
[(ObjectName('1.3.6.1.2.1.1.2.0'), ObjectIdentifier('1.3.6.1.4.1.8072.3.2.10')))]
[(ObjectName('1.3.6.1.2.1.1.3.0'), TimeTicks('340496')))]
[(ObjectName('1.3.6.1.2.1.1.4.0'), OctetString('Administrator
(admin@example.com)')))]
[(ObjectName('1.3.6.1.2.1.1.5.0'), OctetString('fedolin.example.com')))]
[(ObjectName('1.3.6.1.2.1.1.6.0'), OctetString('MyLocation, MyOrganization,⏎
MyStreet, MyCity, MyCountry')))]
[(ObjectName('1.3.6.1.2.1.1.8.0'), TimeTicks('3')))]
[(ObjectName('1.3.6.1.2.1.1.9.1.2.1'), ObjectIdentifier('1.3.6.1.6.3.10.3.1.1')))]
[(ObjectName('1.3.6.1.2.1.1.9.1.2.2'), ObjectIdentifier('1.3.6.1.6.3.11.3.1.1')))]
[(ObjectName('1.3.6.1.2.1.1.9.1.2.3'), ObjectIdentifier('1.3.6.1.6.3.15.2.1.1')))]
[(ObjectName('1.3.6.1.2.1.1.9.1.2.4'), ObjectIdentifier('1.3.6.1.6.3.1')))]
[(ObjectName('1.3.6.1.2.1.1.9.1.2.5'), ObjectIdentifier('1.3.6.1.2.1.49')))]
[(ObjectName('1.3.6.1.2.1.1.9.1.2.6'), ObjectIdentifier('1.3.6.1.2.1.4')))]
[(ObjectName('1.3.6.1.2.1.1.9.1.2.7'), ObjectIdentifier('1.3.6.1.2.1.50')))]
[(ObjectName('1.3.6.1.2.1.1.9.1.2.8'), ObjectIdentifier('1.3.6.1.6.3.16.2.2.1')))]
[(ObjectName('1.3.6.1.2.1.1.9.1.3.1'), OctetString('The SNMP Management⏎
Architecture MIB.')))]
[(ObjectName('1.3.6.1.2.1.1.9.1.3.2'), OctetString('The MIB for Message Processing⏎
and Dispatching.')))]
[(ObjectName('1.3.6.1.2.1.1.9.1.3.3'), OctetString('The management information⏎
 definitions for the SNMP User-based Security Model.')))]
[(ObjectName('1.3.6.1.2.1.1.9.1.3.4'), OctetString('The MIB module for SNMPv2⏎
entities')))]
[(ObjectName('1.3.6.1.2.1.1.9.1.3.5'), OctetString('The MIB module for managing TCP⏎
 implementations')))]
[(ObjectName('1.3.6.1.2.1.1.9.1.3.6'), OctetString('The MIB module for managing IP⏎
 and ICMP implementations')))]
[(ObjectName('1.3.6.1.2.1.1.9.1.3.7'), OctetString('The MIB module for managing UDP⏎
 implementations')))]
[(ObjectName('1.3.6.1.2.1.1.9.1.3.8'), OctetString('View-based Access Control Model⏎
for SNMP.')))]
[(ObjectName('1.3.6.1.2.1.1.9.1.4.1'), TimeTicks('3')))]
[(ObjectName('1.3.6.1.2.1.1.9.1.4.2'), TimeTicks('3')))]
[(ObjectName('1.3.6.1.2.1.1.9.1.4.3'), TimeTicks('3')))]
[(ObjectName('1.3.6.1.2.1.1.9.1.4.4'), TimeTicks('3')))]
[(ObjectName('1.3.6.1.2.1.1.9.1.4.5'), TimeTicks('3')))]
[(ObjectName('1.3.6.1.2.1.1.9.1.4.6'), TimeTicks('3')))]
[(ObjectName('1.3.6.1.2.1.1.9.1.4.7'), TimeTicks('3')))]
[(ObjectName('1.3.6.1.2.1.1.9.1.4.8'), TimeTicks('3')))]
>>>
```

As you can see, the result is identical to that produced by the command-line tool snmpwalk, which uses the same technique to retrieve the SNMP OID subtree.

Implementing the SNMP Read Functionality

Let's implement the read functionality in our application. The workflow will be as follows: we need to iterate through all systems in the list, and for each system we iterate through all defined checks. For each check we are going to perform the SNMP GET command and store the result in the same data structure.

For debugging and testing purposes we will add some print statements to verify that the application is working as expected. Later we'll replace those print statements with the RRDTool database store commands. I'm going to call this method `query_all_systems()`. Listing 1-7 shows the code.

Listing 1-7. *Querying all defined SNMP objects*

```
def query_all_systems(self):
    cg = cmdgen.CommandGenerator()
    for system in self.systems.values():
        comm_data = cmdgen.CommunityData('my-manager', system['communityro'])
        transport = cmdgen.UdpTransportTarget((system['address'], system['port']))
        for check in system['checks'].values():
            oid = check['oid']
            errInd, errStatus, errIdx, result = cg.getCmd(comm_data, transport, oid)
            if not errInd and not errStatus:
                print "%s/%s -> %s" % (system['description'],
                                       check['description'],
                                       str(result[0][1]))
```

If you run the tool you'll get results similar to these (assuming you correctly pointed your configuration to the working devices that respond to the SNMP queries):

```
$ ./snmp-manager.py
My Laptop/WLAN outgoing traffic -> 1060698
My Laptop/WLAN incoming traffic -> 14305766
```

Now we're ready to write all this data to the RRDTool database.

Storing Data with RRDTool

RRDTool is an application developed by Tobias Oetiker, which has become a de-facto standard for graphing monitoring data. The graphs produced by RRDTool are used in many different monitoring tools, such as Nagios, Cacti, and so on. In this section we'll look at the structure of the RRTool database and the application itself. We'll discuss the specifics of the round-robin database, how to add new data to it, and how to retrieve it later on. We will also look at the data-plotting commands and techniques. And finally we'll integrate the RRDTool database with our application.

Introduction to RRDTool

As I have noted, RRDTool provides three distinct functions. First, it serves as a database management system, by allowing you to store and retrieve data from its own database format. It also performs complex data-manipulation tasks, such as data-resampling and rate calculations. And finally, it allows you to create sophisticated graphs incorporating data from various source databases.

Let's start by looking at the round robin database structure. I must apologize for the number of acronyms that you'll come across in this section, but it is important to mention them here, as they all are used in the configuration of RRDTool, so it is vital to become familiar with them.

The first property that makes an RRD different from conventional databases is that the database has a limited size. This means that the database size is known at the time it is initialized, and the size never changes. New records overwrite old data, and that process is repeated over and over again. Figure 1-3 shows a simplified version of the RRD, to help you to visualize the structure.

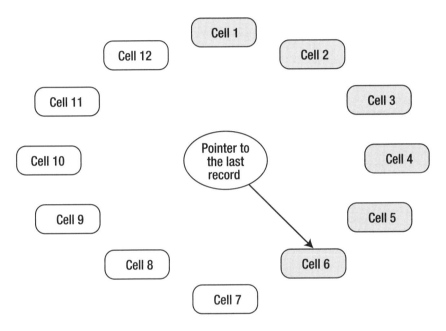

Figure 1-3. *The RRD structure*

Let's assume that we have initialized a database that is capable of holding 12 records, each in its own cell. When the database is empty, we start by writing data to cell number 1. We also update the pointer with the ID of the last cell we've written the data to. Figure 1-3 shows that 6 records have already been written to the database (as represented by the grayed-out boxes). The pointer is on cell 6, and so when the next write instruction is received, the database will write it to the next cell (cell 7) and update the pointer accordingly. Once the last cell (cell 12) is reached, the process starts again, from cell number 1.

The RRD data store's only purpose is to store performance data, and therefore it does not require maintaining complex relations between different data tables. In fact, there are no tables in the RRD, only the individual data sources (DSs).

The last important property of the RRD is that the database engine is designed to store the time series data, and therefore each record needs to be marked with a timestamp. Furthermore, when you create a new database you are required to specify the sampling rate, the rate at which entries are being written to the database. The default value is 300 seconds, or 5 minutes, but this can be overridden if required.

The data that is stored in the RDD is called a RoundRobin Archive (RRA). The RRA is what makes the RRD so useful. It allows you to consolidate the data gathered from the DS by applying an available consolidation function (CF). You can specify one of the four CFs (average, min, max and last) that will be applied to a number of the actual data records. The result is stored in a round-robin "table". You can store multiple RRAs in your database with different granularity. For example, one RRA stores average values of the last 10 records, and the other one stores an average of the last 100.

This will all come together when we look at the usage scenarios in the next sections.

Using RRDTool from a Python Program

Before we start creating the RRDTool databases, let's look at the Python module that provides the API to RRDTool. The module we are going to use in this chapter is called the Python RRDTool and is available to download at http://sourceforge.net/projects/py-rrdtool/.

However, most Linux distributions have this already prepackaged and available to install using the standard package management tool. For example, on a Fedora system you would run the following command to install the Python RRDTool module:

```
$ sudo yum install rrdtool-python
```

Once the package is installed, you can validate that the installation was successful:

```
$ python
Python 2.6.2 (r262:71600, Jan 25 2010, 18:46:45)
[GCC 4.4.2 20091222 (Red Hat 4.4.2-20)] on linux2
Type "help", "copyright", "credits" or "license" for more information.
>>> import rrdtool
>>> rrdtool.__version__
'$Revision: 1.14 $'
>>>
```

Creating a RoundRobin Database

Let's start by creating a simple database. The database we are going to create will have one data source, which is a simple increasing counter. The counter value increases over time. A classical example of such a counter is bytes transmitted over the interface. The readings are performed every 5 minutes.

We also are going to define two RRAs. One is to average over a single reading, which effectively instructs RRDTool to store the actual values, and the other will average over 6 measurements. Following is an example of the command-line tool syntax for creating this database:

```
$ rrdtool create interface.rrd \
> DS:packets:COUNTER:600:U:U \
> RRA:AVERAGE:0.5:1:288 \
> RRA:AVERAGE:0.5:6:336
```

Similarly, you can use the Python module to create the same database:

```
>>> import rrdtool
>>> rrdtool.create('interface.rrd',
...                'DS:packets:COUNTER:600:U:U',
...                'RRA:AVERAGE:0.5:1:288',
...                'RRA:AVERAGE:0.5:6:336')
>>>
```

The structure of the DS (data source) definition line is

DS:*<name>*:*<DS type>*:*<heartbeat>*:*<lower limit>*:*<upper limit>*

The *name* field is what you name this particular data source. Since RRD allows you to store the data from multiple data sources you must provide a unique name to each so that you can access them later. If you need to define more than one data source, simply add another DS line.

The DS type (or data source type) field indicates what type of data will be supplied to this data source. There are four types available: COUNTER, GAUGE, DERIVE and ABSOLUTE:

- The COUNTER type means that the measurement value is increasing over time. To calculate a rate, RRDTool subtracts the last value from the current and divides by the measurement step (or sampling rate) to obtain the rate figure. If the result is a negative number, it needs to compensate for the counter rollover. A typical use is monitoring ever-increasing counters, such as total number of bytes transmitted through the interface.

- The DERIVE type is similar to COUNTER, but it also allows for a negative rate. You can use this type to check the rate of incoming HTTP requests to your site. If the graph is above the zero line, this means you are getting more and more requests. If it drops below the zero line, it means your web site is becoming less popular.

- The ABSOLUTE type indicates that the counter is reset every time you read the measurement. Whereas with the COUNTER and DERIVE types, RRDTool subtracted the last measurement from the current one before dividing by the time period, ABSOLUTE tells it not to perform the subtraction operation. Use this on counters that are reset at the same rate that you do the measurements. For example, you could measure the system average load (over the last 15 minutes) reading every 15 minutes. This would represent the rate of change of the average system load.

- The GAUGE type means that the measurement is the rate value, and no calculations need to be performed. For example, current CPU usage and temperature sensor readings are good candidates for the GAUGE type.

The *heartbeat* value indicates how much time to allow for the reading to come in before resetting it to the unknown state. RRDTool allows for data misses, but it does not make any assumptions and uses the special value unknown if the data is not received. In our example we have the heartbeat set to 600, which means that the database waits for two readings (remember, the step is 300) before it declares the next measurement to be unknown.

The last two fields indicate the minimum and maximum values that can be received from the data source. If you specify those, anything falling outside that range will be automatically marked as unknown.

The RRA definition structure is

```
RRA:<consolidation function>:<XFiles factor>:<dataset>:<samples>
```

The *consolidation function* defines what mathematical function will be applied to the *dataset* values. The *dataset* is the last dataset measurements received from the data source. In our example we have two RRAs, one with just a single reading in the dataset and the other with six measurements in the dataset. The available consolidation functions are AVERAGE, MIN, MAX and LAST:

- AVERAGE instructs RRDTool to calculate the average value of the dataset and store it.

- MIN and MAX selects either the minimum or maximum value from the dataset and stores it.

- LAST indicates to use the last entry from the dataset.

The *XFiles factor* value shows what percentage of the dataset can have unknown values and still the consolidation function calculation will be performed. For example, if the setting is 0.5 (50%), then three out of six measurements can be unknown and still the average value for the dataset will be calculated. If four readings are missed, the calculation is not performed and the unknown value is stored in the RRA. Set this to 0 (0% miss allowance) and the calculation will be performed only if all data points in the data set are available. It seems to be a common practice to keep this setting at 0.5.

As already discussed, the *dataset* parameter indicates how many records are going to participate in the consolidation function calculation.

And finally, *samples* tells RRDTool how many CF results should be kept. So, going back to our example, the number 288 tells RRDTool to keep 288 records. Because we're measuring every 5 minutes, this is 24 hours of data (288/(60/5)). Similarly, the number 336 means that we are storing 7 days worth of data (336/(60/30)/24) at the 30 minute sampling rate. As you can see, the data in the second RRA is resampled; we've changed the sampling rate from 5 minutes to 30 minutes by consolidating data of every six (5 minute) samples.

Writing and Reading Data from the RoundRobin Database

Writing data to the RRD data file is very simple. You just call the update command and, assuming you have defined multiple data sources, supply it a list of data source readings in the same order that you specified when you created the database file.. Each entry must be preceded by the current (or desired) timestamp, expressed in seconds since the epoch (1970-01-01). Alternatively, instead of using the actual number to express the timestamp, you can use the character N, which means the current time. It is possible to supply multiple readings in one command:

```
$ date +"%s"
1273008486
$ rrdtool update interface.rrd 1273008486:10
$ rrdtool update interface.rrd 1273008786:15
$ rrdtool update interface.rrd 1273009086:25
$ rrdtool update interface.rrd 1273009386:40 1273009686:60 1273009986:66
$ rrdtool update interface.rrd 1273010286:100 1273010586:160 1273010886:166
```

The Python alternative looks very similar. In the following code, we will insert another 20 records, specifying regular intervals (of 300 seconds) and supplying generated measurements:

```
>>> import rrdtool
>>> for i in range(20):
...   rrdtool.update('interface.rrd',
...                  '%d:%d' % (1273010886 + (1+i)*300, i*10+200))
...
>>>
```

Now let's fetch the data back from the RRDTool database:

```
$ rrdtool fetch interface.rrd AVERAGE
                       packets

1272983100: -nan
[...]
1273008600: -nan
1273008900: 2.3000000000e-02
1273009200: 3.9666666667e-02
1273009500: 5.6333333333e-02
1273009800: 4.8933333333e-02
1273010100: 5.5466666667e-02
1273010400: 1.4626666667e-01
1273010700: 1.3160000000e-01
1273011000: 5.5466666667e-02
1273011300: 8.2933333333e-02
1273011600: 3.3333333333e-02
1273011900: 3.3333333333e-02
1273012200: 3.3333333333e-02
1273012500: 3.3333333333e-02
1273012800: 3.3333333333e-02
1273013100: 3.3333333333e-02
1273013400: 3.3333333333e-02
1273013700: 3.3333333333e-02
1273014000: 3.3333333333e-02
1273014300: 3.3333333333e-02
1273014600: 3.3333333333e-02
1273014900: 3.3333333333e-02
1273015200: 3.3333333333e-02
1273015500: 3.3333333333e-02
1273015800: 3.3333333333e-02
1273016100: 3.3333333333e-02
1273016400: 3.3333333333e-02
1273016700: 3.3333333333e-02
1273017000: -nan
[...]
1273069500: -nan
```

23

If you count the number of entries, you'll see that it matches the number of updates we've performed on the database. This means that we are seeing results at the maximum resolution, in our case a sample per record. Showing results at the maximum resolution is the default behavior, but you can select another resolution (provided that it has a matching RRA) by specifying the `resolution` flag. Bear in mind that the resolution must be expressed in the number of seconds and not the number of samples in the RRA definition. Therefore in our example the next available resolution is 6 (samples) * 300 (seconds/sample) = 1800 (seconds):

```
$ rrdtool fetch interface.rrd AVERAGE -r 1800
                        packets

[...]
1273010400: 6.1611111111e-02
1273012200: 6.1666666667e-02
1273014000: 3.3333333333e-02
1273015800: 3.3333333333e-02
1273017600: 3.3333333333e-02
[...]
```

Now, you may have noticed that the records inserted by our Python application result in the same number stored in the database. Why is that? Is the counter definitely increasing? Remember, RRDTool always stores the *rate* and not the actual values. So the figures you see in the result dataset show how fast the values are *changing*. And because the Python application generates new measurements at a steady rate (the difference between values is always the same), the rate figure is always the same.

What does this number exactly mean? We know that generated values are increasing by 10 every time we insert a new record, but the value printed by the `fetch` command is 3.3333333333e-02. (For many people this may look slightly confusing, but it's just another notation for the value 0.0333(3).) Where did that come from? In discussing the different data source types, I mentioned that RRDTool takes the difference between two data point values and divides that by the number of seconds in the sampling interval. The default sampling interval is 300 seconds, so the rate has been calculated as $10/300 = 0.0333(3)$, which is what is written to the RRDTool database. In other words, this means that our counter on average increases by 0.0333(3) every second. Remember that all rate measurements are stored as a change per second. We'll look at converting this value to something more readable later in the section.

Here's is how you retrieve the data using the Python module method call:

```
>>> for i in rrdtool.fetch('interface.rrd', 'AVERAGE'): print i
...
(1272984300, 1273071000, 300)
('packets',)
[(None,), [...], (None,), (0.023,), (0.03966666666666667,),
(0.056333333333333339,),↵
 (0.048933333333333336,), (0.055466666666666671,), (0.14626666666666666,),
 (0.13160000000000002,), (0.055466666666666671,), (0.082933333333333331,),
 (0.033333333333333333,), (0.033333333333333333,), (0.033333333333333333,),
 (0.033333333333333333,), (0.033333333333333333,), (0.033333333333333333,),
 (0.033333333333333333,), (0.033333333333333333,), (0.033333333333333333,),
 (0.033333333333333333,), (0.033333333333333333,), (0.033333333333333333,),
```

```
 (0.033333333333333333,), (0.033333333333333333,), (0.033333333333333333,),
 (0.033333333333333333,), (0.033333333333333333,), (0.033333333333333333,),
 (None,), [...] (None,)]
>>>
```

The result is a tuple of three elements: *dataset information*, *list of datasources*, and *result array*:

- *Dataset information* is another tuple that has three values: start and end timestamps and the sampling rate.

- *List of datasources* simply lists all variables that were stored in the RRDTool database and that were returned by your query.

- *Result array* contains the actual values that are stored in the RRD. Each entry is a tuple, containing values for every variable that was queried. In our example database we had only one variable; therefore the tuple contains only one element. If the value could not be calculated (is unknown), Python's None object is returned.

You can also change the sampling rate if you need to:

```
>>> rrdtool.fetch('interface.rrd', 'AVERAGE', '-r', '1800')
((1272983400, 1273071600, 1800), ('packets',), [(None,), [...] (None,),
 (0.06161111111111111,), (0.061666666666666668,), (0.033333333333333333,),
 (0.033333333333333333,), (0.033333333333333333,), (None,), [...] (None,)])
```

■**Note** By now you should have an idea of how the command-line tool syntax is mapped to the Python module calls. You always call the module method, which is always named after the RRDTool function name, such as fetch, update, and so on. The argument to the function is an arbitrary list of values. A value in this case is whatever string is separated by spaces on the command line. Basically, you can take the command line and copy it to the function as an argument list. Obviously, you need to enclose each individual string with quote symbols and separate them with a comma symbol. To save space and avoid confusion, in further examples I'm only going to provide the command-line syntax, which you should be able to map to the Python syntax quite easily.

Plotting Graphs with RRDTool

Plotting graphs with RRDTool is really easy, and graphing is one reason this tool has become so popular. In its simplest form, the graph generating command is quite similar to the data-fetching command:

```
$ rrdtool graph packets.png --start 1273008600 --end 1273016400 --step 300\
> DEF:packetrate=interface.rrd:packets:AVERAGE \
> LINE2:packetrate#c0c0c0
```

Even without any additional modification, the result is a quite professional-looking performance graph, as you can see in Figure 1-4.

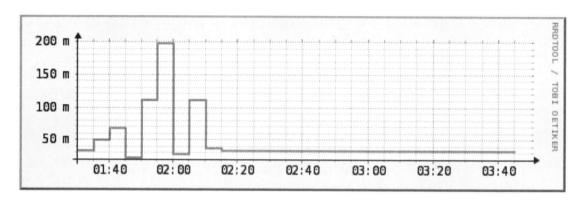

Figure 1-4. *A simple graph generated by RRDTool*

First of all, let's look at the command parameters. All the plotting commands start with a file name for the resulting image and optionally the time scale values. You can also provide a resolution setting, which will default to the most detailed resolution if not specified. This is similar to the -r option in the fetch command. The resolution is expressed in seconds.

The next line (although you can type the whole graph command in one line) is the selector line, which selects the dataset from an RRDTool database. The format of the selector statement is

```
DEF:<selector name>=<rrd file>:<data source>:<consolidation function>
```

The *selector name* argument is an arbitrary string, which you use to name the resulting dataset. Look at it as an array variable that stores the result from the RRDTool database. You can use as many selector statements as you need, but you need to have at least one to produce any output.

The combination of the *rrd file*, *data source*, and *consolidation function* variables defines exactly what data needs to be selected. As you can see, this syntax completely decouples the data storage and data representation functions. You can include results from different RRDTool databases on the same graph and combine them in any way you like. The data for the graphs can be collected on different monitoring servers and yet combined and presented on a single image.

This selector statement can be extended with optional parameters that specify the start, stop, and resolution values for each data source. The format would be as follows, and this string should be appended at the end of the selector statement. Each element is optional, and you can use any combination of them.

```
:step=<step value>:start=<start time value>:end=<end time value>
```

So we can rewrite the previous plotting command as

```
$ rrdtool graph packets.png \
> DEF:packetrate=interface.rrd:packets:AVERAGE:step=300:↵
start=1273008600:end=1273016400 \
> LINE2:packetrate#c0c0c0
```

The last element on the command line is the statement that tells RRDTool how to plot the data. The basic syntax for the data plotting command is

```
<PLOT TYPE>:<selector name><#color>:<legend>
```

The most widely used plot types are LINE and AREA. The LINE keyword can be followed by a floating-point number to indicate the width of the line. The AREA keyword instructs RRDTool to draw the line and also fill in the area between the x-axis and the graph line.

Both commands are followed by the *selector name*, which provides the data for the plotting function. The *color* value is written as an HTML color format string. You can also specify an optional argument *legend*, which tells RRDTool that a small rectangle of a matching color needs to be displayed at the bottom of the graph, followed by the legend string.

As you could with the data selector statement, you can have as many of the graphing statements as you need, but you need to define at least one to produce a graph.

Let's take a second look at the graph we produced. RRDTool conveniently printed the time stamps on the x-axis, but what is displayed on the y-axis? It may look like measurements in meters, but in fact the *m* stands for milli, or one thousandth of the value. So the values printed there are exactly what has been stored in the RRDTool database. This is, however, not really intuitive. We don't really see the packet size, and the data transfer rate can be either really low or high, depending on the transmitted packet size. Let's assume that we're working with 4KB packets. In this case the logical solution would be to represent the information as bits per second. What do we have to do to convert the packets per second into bits per second? Because the rate interval doesn't change (in both cases we measure the amount per second), only the packets value needs to be multiplied, first by 4096 (the number of bytes in a packet) and then by 8 (the number of bits in a byte).

The RRDTool graph command allows defining the data conversion function that will be applied to any *data selector* variable. In our example we would use the following statement to convert packets per second into bytes per second:

```
$ rrdtool graph kbps.png --step 300 --start 1273105800 --end 1273114200 \
DEF:packetrate=interface.rrd:packets:AVERAGE \
CDEF:kbps=packetrate,4096,\*,8,\* \
LINE2:kbps#c0c0c0
```

If you look at the image produced by this command, you'll see that its shape is identical to Figure 1-4, but the y-axis labels have changed. They are not indicating a "milli" value anymore—all numbers are labeled as *k*. This makes more sense, as most people feel more comfortable seeing 3kbps rather than 100 milli packets per second.

■**Note** You may be wondering why the calculation string looks rather odd. First of all, I had to escape the * characters so they are passed to the rrdtool application without being processed by the shell. And the formula itself has to be written in Reverse Polish Notation, in which you specify the first argument, then the second argument, and then the function that you want to perform. The result can then be used as a first argument. In my example I effectively tell the application to "take the *packetrate* and 4096 and multiply them, take the result and 8 and multiply them". It takes some time to adjust, but once you get a handle on it, expressing formulas in RPN is really pretty easy.

Finally, we need to make the graph even more presentable by adding a label to the y-axis, a legend for the value that we are plotting, and the title for the graph itself. This example also demonstrates how to change the size of the generated image:

```
$ rrdtool graph packets.png --step 300 --start 1273105800 --end 1273114200 \
--width 500 --height 200 \
--title "Primary Interface" --vertical-label "Kbp/s" \
DEF:packetrate=interface.rrd:packets:AVERAGE \
CDEF:kbps=packetrate,4096,\*,8,\* \
AREA:kbps#c0c0c0:"Data transfer rate"
```

The result is shown in Figure 1-5.

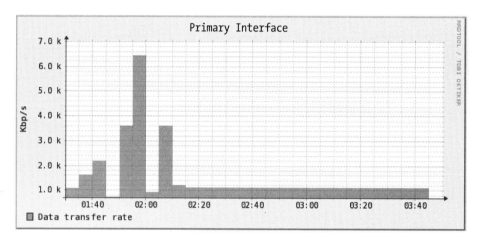

Figure 1-5. *Formatting the RRDTool- generated graph*

This introduction to RRDTool has covered only its basic uses. The application, however, comes with a really extensive API, which allows you to change pretty much every aspect of a graph. I recommend reading the RRDTool documentation, which is available at `http://oss.oetiker.ch/rrdtool/doc/`.

Integrating RRDTool with the Monitoring Solution

We're now ready to integrate RRDTool calls into our monitoring application, so that the information we gather from the SNMP-enabled devices is recorded and readily available for reporting. Although it is possible to maintain multiple data sources in one RRDTool database, it is advisable to do so only for measurements that are closely related. For example, if you're monitoring a multiprocessor system and want to store interrupt counts of every single CPU, it would make perfect sense to store them all in one data file. Mixing memory utilization and temperature sensor readings, by contrast, probably is not a very good idea, because you may decide that you need a greater sampling rate for one measurement, and you can't easily change that without affecting other data sources.

In our system the SNMP OIDs are provided in the configuration file and the application has absolutely no idea whether they are related or not. Therefore we will store every reading in a separate data file. Each data file will get the same name as the check section name (for example, `check_1.rrd`), so make sure to keep them unique.

We will also have to extend the configuration file, so that each check defines the desired sampling rate. And finally, every time the application is invoked, it will check for the presence of the data store files and create any that are missing. This removes the burden from application users to create the files manually for every new check. You can see the updated script in Listing 1-8.

Listing 1-8. *Updating the RRDs with the SNMP data*

```python
#!/usr/bin/env python

import sys, os.path, time
from ConfigParser import SafeConfigParser
from pysnmp.entity.rfc3413.oneliner import cmdgen
import rrdtool


class SnmpManager:
    def __init__(self):
        self.systems = {}
        self.databases_initialised = False

    def add_system(self, id, descr, addr, port, comm_ro):
        self.systems[id] = {'description' : descr,
                            'address'     : addr,
                            'port'        : int(port),
                            'communityro' : comm_ro,
                            'checks'      : {}
                           }

    def add_check(self, id, oid, descr, system, sampling_rate):
        oid_tuple = tuple([int(i) for i in oid.split('.')])
        self.systems[system]['checks'][id] = {'description': descr,
                                              'oid'          : oid_tuple,
                                              'result'       : None,
                                              'sampling_rate' : sampling_rate
                                             }

    def query_all_systems(self):
        if not self.databases_initialised:
            self.initialise_databases()
            self.databases_initialised = True
        cg = cmdgen.CommandGenerator()
        for system in self.systems.values():
            comm_data = cmdgen.CommunityData('my-manager', system['communityro'])
            transport = cmdgen.UdpTransportTarget((system['address'],
            system['port']))
            for key, check in system['checks'].iteritems():
                oid = check['oid']
                errInd, errStatus, errIdx, result = cg.getCmd(comm_data, transport,
                oid)
```

```
if not errInd and not errStatus:
                    file_name = "%s.rrd" % key
                    rrdtool.update(file_name,
                                "%d:%d" % (int(time.time()),),
                                        float(result[0][1]),)
                            )

    def initialise_databases(self):
        for system in self.systems.values():
            for check in system['checks']:
                data_file = "%s.rrd" % check
                if not os.path.isfile(data_file):
                    print data_file, 'does not exist'
                    rrdtool.create(data_file,
                                "DS:%s:COUNTER:%s:U:U" % (check,
                                 system['checks'][check]['sampling_rate']),
                                "RRA:AVERAGE:0.5:1:288",)


def main(conf_file=""):
    if not conf_file:
        sys.exit(-1)
    config = SafeConfigParser()
    config.read(conf_file)
    snmp_manager = SnmpManager()
    for system in [s for s in config.sections() if s.startswith('system')]:
        snmp_manager.add_system(system,
                                config.get(system, 'description'),
                                config.get(system, 'address'),
                                config.get(system, 'port'),
                                config.get(system, 'communityro'))
    for check in [c for c in config.sections() if c.startswith('check')]:
        snmp_manager.add_check(check,
                                config.get(check, 'oid'),
                                config.get(check, 'description'),
                                config.get(check, 'system'),
                                config.get(check, 'sampling_rate'))
    snmp_manager.query_all_systems()

if __name__ == '__main__':
    main(conf_file='snmp-manager.cfg')
```

The script is now ready for monitoring. You can add it to the Linux cron scheduler and have it executed every 5 minutes. Don't worry if you configure some checks with a sampling rate greater than 5 minutes; RRDTool is clever enough to store the measurements at the sampling rate that has been specified at the database creation time. Here's a sample cronjob entry that I used to produce sample results, which we'll be using in the next section:

```
$ crontab -l
*/5 * * * * (cd /home/rytis/snmp-monitor/; ./snmp-manager.py > log.txt)
```

Creating Web Pages with the Jinja2 Templating System

In the last section of this chapter we are going to create another script, this one generating a simple structure of web pages containing the graphs. The main entry page lists all available checks grouped by the system and links to the check details page. When a user navigates to that page, she will see the graph generated by RRDTool and some details about the check itself (such as the check description and OID). Now, this looks relatively easy to implement, and most people would simply start writing a Python script that would use `print` statements to produce the HTML pages. Although this approach may seem to work, in most cases it soon becomes unmanageable. The functional code often becomes intermingled with the content-producing code, and adding new functionality usually breaks everything, which in turn leads to hours spent debugging the application.

The solution to this problem is to use one of the templating frameworks, which allow decoupling the application logic from the presentation. The basic principle of a templating system is simple: you write code that performs calculations and other tasks that are not content-specific, such as retrieving data from the databases or other sources. Then you pass this information to the templating framework, along with the name of the template that uses this information. In the template code you put all HTML formatting text together with the dynamic data (which was generated earlier). The framework then parses the template for simple processing statements (like iteration loops and logical test statements) and generates the result. You can see the basic flow of this processing in Figure 1-6.

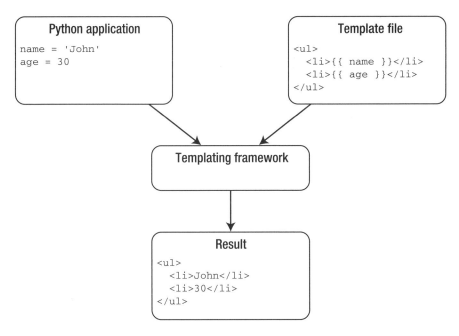

Figure 1-6. *Data flow in the templating framework*

This way, your application code is clean from all content-generation statements and is much easier to maintain. The template can access all variables presented to it, but it looks more like an HTML page, and loading it in a web browser usually produces acceptable results. So you can even ask a dedicated web developer to create the templates for you, as there is no need to know any Python to modify them.

I'm going to use a templating framework called *Jinja*, which has syntax very similar to that used by the Django web framework. We're also going to talk about the Django framework in this book, so it makes sense to use a similar templating language. The Jinja framework is also widely used, and most Linux distributions include the Jinja package. On a Fedora system you can install it with the following command:

```
$ sudo yum install python-jinja2
```

Alternatively, you can use the PiP application to install it:

```
$ sudo pip install Jinja2
```

You can also get the latest development version of the Jinja2 framework from the official web site: `http://jinja.pocoo.org/2/`.

▓**Tip** Make sure to install Jinja2 and not the earlier release—Jinja. Jinja2 provides an extended templating language and is actively developed for and supported.

Loading Template Files with Jinja2

Jinja2 is designed to be used in the web framework and therefore has a very extensive API. Most of its functionality is not used in simple applications that only generate a few pages, so I'm going to skip those functions, as they could be a topic for a book of their own. In this section I'll show you how to load a template, pass some variables to it, and save the result. These three functions are what you will use most of the time in your applications. For more extensive documentation on the Jinja2 API, please refer to `http://jinja.pocoo.org/2/documentation/api`.

The Jinja2 framework uses so called *loader* classes to load the template files. These can be loaded from various sources, but most likely they are stored on a file system. The loader class, which is responsible for loading the templates stored on a file system, is called `jinja2.FileSystemLoader`. It accepts one string or a list of strings that are the pathnames on a file system where the template files can be found:

```
from jinja2 import FileSystemLoader

loader1 = FileSystemLoader('/path/to/your/templates')
loader2 = FileSystemLoader(['/templates1/', '/teamplates2/'])
```

Once you initialized the loader class, you create an instance of the `jinja2.Environment` class. This class is the central part of the framework and is used to store the configuration variables, access the templates (via the loader instance), and pass the variables to the template objects. When initializing the environment, you must pass the loader object if you want to access externally stored templates:

```
from jinja2 import Environment, FileSystemLoader

loader = FileSystemLoader('/path/to/your/templates')
env = Environment(loader=loader)
```

When the environment has been created, you can then load the templates and render the output. First you call the get_template method, which returns a template object associated with the template file. Next you call the template object's method render, which processes the template contents (loaded by the previously initialized loader class). The result is the processed template code, which can be written to a file. You have to pass all variables to the template as a dictionary. The dictionary keys are the names of the variables available from within the template. The dictionary values can be any Python objects that you want to pass to the template.

```
from jinja2 import Environment, FileSystemLoader

loader = FileSystemLoader('/path/to/your/templates')
env = Environment(loader=loader)
template = env.get_template('template.tpl')
r_file = open('index.html', 'w')
name = 'John'
age = 30
result = template.render({'name': name, 'age': age})
r_file.write(result)
r_file.close()
```

The Jinja2 Template Language

The Jinja2 templating language is quite extensive and feature-rich. The basic concepts, however, are quite simple and the language closely resembles Python. For a full language description, please check the official Jinja2 template language definition at
http://jinja.pocoo.org/2/documentation/templates.
The template statements have to be escaped; anything that is not escaped is not processed and will be returned verbatim after the rendering process.
There are two types of language delimiters:

- The variable access delimiter, which indicates a reference to a variable: {{ ... }}

- The statement execution delimiter, which tells the framework that the statement inside the delimiter is a functional instruction: {% ... %}

Accessing Variables

As you already know, the template knows the variables by the names they were given as dictionary keys. So if the dictionary passed to the render function was this:

```
{'name': name, 'age': age}
```

The following statements in the template can access these variables as shown here:
{{ name }} / {{ age }}

The object passed to the template can be any Python object, and the template can access it using the same Python syntax. For example, you can access the dictionary or array elements. Assume the following render call:

```
person = {'name': 'John', 'age': 30}
r = t.render({'person': person})
```

Then you can use the following syntax to access the dictionary elements in the template:

```
{{ person.name }} / {{ person.age }}
```

Flow Control Statements

The flow control statements allow you to perform check on the variables and select different parts of the template that will be rendered accordingly. You can also use these statements to repeat a piece of the template when generating structures such as tables or lists.

The for ...in loop statement can iterate through these *iterable* Python objects, returning one element at a time:

```
<h1>Available products</h1>
<ul>
{% for item in products %}
  <li>{{ item }}</li>
{% endfor %}
</ul>
```

Once in the loop, the following special variables are defined. You can use them to check exactly where you are in the loop.

Table 1-4. *The loop property variables*

Variable	Description
loop.index	The current iteration of the loop. The index starts with 1; use loop.index0 for a count indexed from 0 .
loop.revindex	Similar to loop.index, but counts iterations from the end of the loop.
loop.first	Set to True if the first iteration.
loop.last	Set to True if the last iteration.
loop.length	The total number of elements in the sequence.

The logical test function `if` is used as a Boolean check, similar to the use of the Python `if` statement:

```
{% if items %}
  <ul>
  {% for item in items %}
    {% if item.for_sale %}
      <li>{{ item.description }}</li>
    {% endif %}
  {% endfor %}
  </ul>
{% else %}
  There are no items
{% endif %}
```

The Jinja2 framework also allows for template inheritance. That is, you can define a base template and then inherit from it. Each child template then redefines the blocks from the main template file with appropriate content. For example, the parent template (`parent.tpl`) may look like this:

```
<head>
  <title> MyCompany - {% block title %}Default title{% endblock %}</title>
</head>
<html>
{% block content %}
There is no content
{% endblock %}
</html>
```

The child template then inherits from the base template and extends the blocks with its own content:

```
{% extends 'parent.tpl' %}
{% block title %}My Title{%endblock %}
{% block content %}
My content %}
{% endblock %}
```

Generating Web Site Pages

The script that generates the pages and the images uses the same configuration file used by the check script. It iterates through all system and check sections and builds a dictionary tree. The whole tree is passed to the index generation function, which in turn passes it to the index template.

The detailed information for each check is generated by a separate function. The same function also calls the `rrdtool` method to plot the graph. All files are saved in the web site root directory, which is defined in the global variable but can be overruled in the function call. You can see the whole script in Listing 1-9.

Listing 1-9. *Generating the web site pages*

```python
#!/usr/bin/env python

from jinja2 import Environment, FileSystemLoader
from ConfigParser import SafeConfigParser
import rrdtool
import sys

WEBSITE_ROOT = '/home/rytis/public_html/snmp-monitor/'

def generate_index(systems, env, website_root):
    template = env.get_template('index.tpl')
    f = open("%s/index.html" % website_root, 'w')
    f.write(template.render({'systems': systems}))
    f.close()

def generate_details(system, env, website_root):
    template = env.get_template('details.tpl')
    for check_name, check_obj in system['checks'].iteritems():
        rrdtool.graph ("%s/%s.png" % (website_root, check_name),
                       '--title', "%s" % check_obj['description'],
                       "DEF:data=%(name)s.rrd:%(name)s:AVERAGE" % {'name':
                                                            check_name},
                       'AREA:data#0c0c0c')
        f = open("%s/%s.html" % (website_root, str(check_name)), 'w')
        f.write(template.render({'check': check_obj, 'name': check_name}))
        f.close()

def generate_website(conf_file="", website_root=WEBSITE_ROOT):
    if not conf_file:
        sys.exit(-1)
    config = SafeConfigParser()
    config.read(conf_file)
    loader = FileSystemLoader('.')
    env = Environment(loader=loader)
    systems = {}
    for system in [s for s in config.sections() if s.startswith('system')]:
        systems[system] = {'description': config.get(system, 'description'),
                           'address'    : config.get(system, 'address'),
                           'port'       : config.get(system, 'port'),
                           'checks'     : {}
                          }
```

```
    for check in [c for c in config.sections() if c.startswith('check')]:
        systems[config.get(check, 'system')]['checks'][check] = {
                                         'oid'        : config.get(check, 'oid'),
                                         'description': config.get(check,
                                                            'description'),
                                         }


    generate_index(systems, env, website_root)
    for system in systems.values():
        generate_details(system, env, website_root)


if __name__ == '__main__':
    generate_website(conf_file='snmp-manager.cfg')
```

Most of the presentation logic, such as checking whether a variable is defined and iterating through the list items, is implemented in the templates. In Listing 1-10, we first define the index template, which is responsible for generating the contents of the index.html page. As you know, in this page we're going to list all defined systems with a complete list of checks available for each system.

Listing 1-10. *The index template*

```
<h1>System checks</h1>
{% if systems %}
  {% for system in systems %}
    <h2>{{ systems[system].description }}</h2>
    <p>{{ systems[system].address }}:{{ systems[system].port }}</p>
    {% if systems[system].checks %}
      The following checks are available:
      <ul>
        {% for check in systems[system].checks %}
          <li><a href="{{ check }}.html">
              {{ systems[system].checks[check].description }}</a></li>
        {% endfor %}
      </ul>
    {% else %}
      There are no checks defined for this system
    {% endif %}
  {% endfor %}
{% else %}
  No system configuration available
{% endif %}
```

The web page generated by this template is rendered as shown in Figure 1-7.

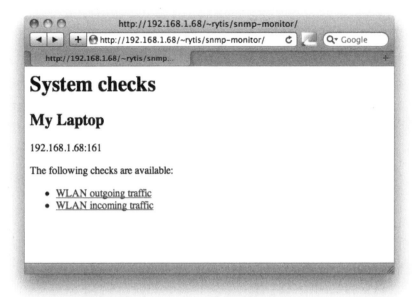

Figure 1-7. *The index web page in the browser window*

The link for each list item points to an individual check details web page. Each such web page has a check section name, such as check_1.html. These pages are generated from the details.tpl template:

```
<h1>{{ check.description }}</h1>
<p>OID: {{ check.oid }}</p>
<img src="{{ name }}.png" />
```

This template links to a graph image, which has been generated by the RRDTool graph method. Figure 1-8 shows the resulting page.

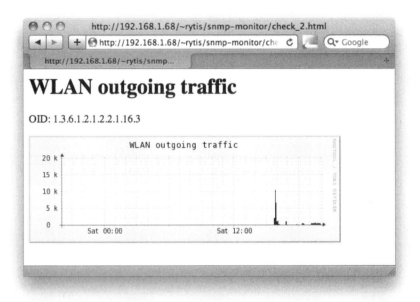

Figure 1-8. *SNMP detail information with graph*

Summary

In this chapter we've built a simple device monitoring system. In doing so you learned about the SNMP protocol, as well as the data collecting and plotting libraries used with Python—RRDTool and the Jinja2 templating system. Important points to keep in mind:

- The majority of network-attached devices expose their internal counters using the SNMP protocol.
- Each such counter has a dedicated object ID assigned to it.
- The object IDs are organized in a tree-like structure, where tree branches are allocated to various organizations.
- RRDTool is a library that allows you to store, retrieve, and plot network statistical data.
- The RRD database is a round-robin database, which means it has a constant size, and new records push old records out when inserted.
- If you generate web pages, make use of the Jinja2 templating system, which allows you to decouple the functional code from the representation.

## CHAPTER 2

Managing Devices Using the SOAP API

In this chapter we are going to build a command line tool to query and manage the Citrix Netscaler load balancer devices. These devices expose the management services via the SOAP API, which is one of the standard ways of communicating between the web services.

What Is the SOAP API?

SOAP stands for Simple Object Access Protocol. This protocol has been developed and created to be used as a mechanism for exchanging structured information between various web services. Many well-known companies expose their services via the SOAP API interface; for example, Amazon allows controlling their Elastic Compute Cloud (EC2) and Simple Storage System (S3) services using the SOAP API calls.

Using SOAP queries, users can create virtual machines, start and stop services, manipulate data on a remote distributed file system, or perform product searches. SOAP-enabled applications exchange information by sending SOAP "messages." Each message is an XML-formatted document. The SOAP protocol sits on top of other transmission protocols, such as HTTP, HTTPS, SMTP, and so on. In theory you can send a SOAP request encapsulated in an email message (SMTP), but most widely used transport mechanisms for SOAP are either plain HTTP or HTTPS (SSL encrypted HTTP).

SOAP is not the most efficient way of communicating, because of the XML verbosity, so even the smallest and the simplest messages become quite large and cryptic.

SOAP defines a set of rules for structuring messages of the application-level protocols. One of the most commonly used protocols is RPC (Remote Procedure Call). Therefore, what is normally referenced as the SOAP API in fact is a SOAP-encoded RPC API.

RPC defines how web services communicate and interact with each other. When used with RPC, SOAP is used to perform request-response dialogues.

The greatest strength of SOAP is that it is not language- or platform-specific, so applications that are written in different languages and are running on different platforms can easily communicate with each other. It is also an open-standard protocol, which means there are numerous libraries that provide support for developing SOAP-enabled applications and services.

The Structure of a SOAP Message

Each SOAP message contains the following elements:

- *Envelope.* This element identifies the XML document as a SOAP message. It also defines namespaces that are used within the SOAP message.

- *Message Header.* This element resides within the Envelope element and contains application-specific information. For example, authentication details are usually stored in the Header element. This element may also contain data that is not intended for the recipient of the message, but addresses the intermediate devices that retransmit SOAP communication.

- *Message Body.* This element resides within the SOAP Envelope element and contains request and response information. The Message Body element is a required field and cannot be omitted. This element contains the actual data that is intended for the recipient of the message.

- *Fault Element.* This optional element resides within Message Body. If present, it contains an error code, a human-readable error description, the reason the error occurred, and any application-specific details.

Listing 2-1 is an example of a skeleton SOAP message.

Listing 2-1. *The skeleton of a simple SOAP message*

```
<?xml version="1.0"?>
<soap:Envelope
    xmlns:soap="http://www.w3.org/2001/12/soap-envelope"
    soap:encodingStyle="http://www.w3.org/2001/12/soap-encoding">

    <soap:Header>
        [...]
    </soap:Header>

    <soap:Body>
        [...]
        <soap:Fault>
            [...]
        </soap:Fault>
    </soap:Body>

</soap:Envelope>
```

Requesting Services with SOAP

Let's assume we have two web services: Web Service A and Web Service B. Each web service is an application running on a dedicated server. Let's also assume that Service B implements a simple customer lookup service, which accepts an integer number that represents the customer identifier and returns two fields in an array: the name of the customer and the contact telephone number. Service A is an application that acts as a client and requests details from Service B.

When Service A (wants to find out details about the customer. it constructs the SOAP message shown in Listing 2-2 and sends it to Service B as an HTTP POST request.

Listing 2-2. *A SOAP request message*

```
<?xml version="1.0" encoding="UTF-8" ?>
  <SOAP-ENV:Envelope
   SOAP-ENV:encodingStyle="http://schemas.xmlsoap.org/soap/encoding/"
   xmlns:SOAP-ENV="http://schemas.xmlsoap.org/soap/envelope/"
   xmlns:SOAP-ENC="http://schemas.xmlsoap.org/soap/encoding/"
   xmlns:xsi="http://www.w3.org/1999/XMLSchema-instance"
   xmlns:xsd="http://www.w3.org/1999/XMLSchema">
   <SOAP-ENV:Body>
      <ns1:getCustomerDetails
       xmlns:ns1="urn:CustomerSoapServices">
         <param1 xsi:type="xsd:int">213307</param1>
      </ns1:getCustomerDetails>
   </SOAP-ENV:Body>
  </SOAP-ENV:Envelope>
```

Next, Service B (server) would perform the lookup, encapsulate the result in an SOAP message and send it back. The response message (Listing 2-3) would be served as an HTTP response to the original POST request.

Listing 2-3. *A SOAP response message*

```
<?xml version="1.0" encoding="UTF-8" ?>
  <SOAP-ENV:Envelope
   xmlns:xsi="http://www.w3.org/1999/XMLSchema-instance"
   xmlns:xsd="http://www.w3.org/1999/XMLSchema"
   xmlns:SOAP-ENV="http://schemas.xmlsoap.org/soap/envelope/">
   <SOAP-ENV:Body>
      <ns1: getCustomerDetailsResponse
      xmlns:ns1="urn:CustomerSoapServices"
      SOAP-ENV:encodingStyle="http://schemas.xmlsoap.org/soap/encoding/">
         <return
         xmlns:ns2="http://schemas.xmlsoap.org/soap/encoding/"
         xsi:type="ns2:Array"
         ns2:arrayType="xsd:string[2]">
            <item xsi:type="xsd:string">John Palmer</item>
            <item xsi:type="xsd:string">+44-(0)306-999-0033</item>
         </return>
      </ns1:getCustomerDetailsResponse>
   </SOAP-ENV:Body>
  </SOAP-ENV:Envelope>
```

As you can see from the example, SOAP conversation is very chatty. All that extra information (including namespace definitions and field data types) is required so that both client and server know how to parse and validate data.

Finding Information about Available Services with WSDL

If you look carefully at the previous example, you will notice that the client requested the following method: getCustomerDetails. How do we know what methods or services are available to use? Furthermore, how do we find out what arguments the method requires and what the method will return in its response message?

The easiest way to find this information is from the web service's WSDL (Web Services Description Language) document. This XML-formatted document describes various details related to the web service we are interested in, such as

- Communication protocols used by the service (the <bindings> section)

- Messages that the service accepts and sends (the <messages> section)

- Methods exposed by the web service (the <portType> section)

- Data types used by the service (the <types> section)

Each of those sections may contain multiple entries, depending on what the web service is doing. For example, Listing 2-4 is a simplified WSDL definition for a translation service. In this example, our imaginary automated translator accepts a text string as input parameter, and returns a translated string as result. We have two remote methods that are called translateEnglishToFrench and translateFrenchToEnglish. They both use the same request and response data types.

Listing 2-4. *An example WSDL definition*

```
<message name="translateRequest">
   <part name="term" type="xs:string"/>
</message>

<message name="translateResponse">
   <part name="value" type="xs:string"/>
</message>

<portType name="languageTranslations">
   <operation name="translateEnglishToFrench">
      <input message="translateRequest"/>
      <output message="translateRequest"/>
   </operation>
   <operation name="translateFrenchToEnglish">
      <input message="translateRequest"/>
      <output message="translateRequest"/>
   </operation>
</portType>
```

```
<binding type="languageTranslations" name="bn">
    <soap:binding style="document" transport="http://schemas.xmlsoap.org/soap/http"/>
    <operation>
        <soap:operation soapAction="http://example.com/translateEnglishToFrench"
                        name="trEn2Fr"/>
        <input><soap:body use="literal"/></input>
        <output><soap:body use="literal"/></output>
    </operation>
    <operation>



        <soap:operation soapAction="http://example.com/translateFrenchToEnglish"↲
 name="trFr2En"/>
        <input><soap:body use="literal"/></input>
        <output><soap:body use="literal"/></output>
    </operation>
</binding>
```

The binding section defines access URLs for accessing each method that is exposed. Each operation also has a name that is used to reference it.

SOAP Support in Python

Python is not as fortunate as other languages when it comes to supporting the SOAP protocol. In the past, there were a few initiatives and projects that attempted to implement SOAP libraries into Python, but most were abandoned. Currently the most active and mature project is the Zolera SOAP Infrastructure (ZSI).

In most Linux distributions, this package is named python-ZSI and is available to install from the distribution's default package manager. If you choose to install the ZSI package from source, it can be found at http://pywebsvcs.sourceforge.net/.

There are two ways to access SOAP services from Python using ZSI:

- Service methods can be accessed through the ServiceProxy class, which is part of the ZSI library. When you create an object of this class all remote functions are available as methods of this object instance. This is a convenient way of accessing all services, but it requires you to generate type codes and define namespaces manually, which is a lot of work.

- Another way of accessing the SOAP interface is to use the wsdl2py tool. This tool reads the WSDL definition of the service and generates two modules: one with typecode information and another containing service methods.

I prefer using the second method, because it relieves me from having to define type codes and memorize namespaces. When using the ServiceProxy class , the user must explicitly define the namespace of the procedure. Furthermore, the type code of the request object must be compatible with the type defined in the WSDL, and this type code has to be crafted manually, which can become a real pain with services that use complicated data structures.

Converting WSDL Schema to Python Helper Module

So far you have learned about the SOAP protocol (an XML-based protocol that defines how messages are encapsulated), RPC's way of communication (the client sends a message that tells what function it wants the server to execute, and the server responds with a message that contains the data generated by the remote function) and WSDL (the language that defines what methods are available and what data types are used in requests/responses).

We also decided that we are going to generate two helper modules: one that contains remote methods and another that defines data structures, and that we are going to use wsdl2py tool that is available from ZSI library.

I am going to write a tool to manage Citrix Netscaler load balancer devices. These devices provide two web service interfaces:

- *The Statistics Web Service.* This service provides methods to query statistical information about all functional aspects of the loadbalancer, such as virtual servers, services, VLAN configuration and so on. In version 8.1 of Netscaler OS there are 44 objects that you can gather performance information from.

- *The Configuration Web Service.* This service allows you to change device configuration and perform maintenance tasks, such as enable/disable servers and services. In the same 8.1 NS OS there are 2364 configurable parameters that are accessible via SOAP interface.

Links to WSDL locations and other useful information, such as API documentation and SNMP object definitions, can be found by visiting http://192.168.1.1/ws/download.pl, where 192.168.1.1 needs to be replaced with the IP address of the Netscaler load balancer that you are using. In this chapter I will assume and use 192.168.1.1 as the IP of my Netscaler device. A link to the downloads page is also available from the main management screen.

I have provided the following WSDL URLs, as it is unlikely they will change:

- WSDL for the statistics SOAP interface: http://192.168.1.1/api/NSStat.wsdl

- WSDL for the configuration SOAP interface: http://192.168.1.1/api/NSConfig.wsdl

Using the wsdl2py script is very simple; if no special configuration is required, all you need to do is provide the location of a WSDL document and it will generate both method and data type modules automatically. No additional user input is required. Either the wsdl2py tool can fetch the WSDL document from the web location, or you can provide a filename and it will parse the file.

In the example shown in Listing 2-5, we will point the wsdl2py script directly at the WSDL URL on the Netscaler load balancer.

Listing 2-5. *A Command to convert Python modules from a WSDL file*

```
$ wsdl2py --url http://192.168.1.1/api/NSStat.wsdl
```

If the script can contact the destination server and the XML document it receives contains no errors, it will not produce any messages and will silently create two Python packages.

■**Note** If you have retrieved a WSDL file and stored it locally, you can use the --file flag and supply the filename of the WSDL document. This will instruct wsdl2py to parse the locally stored file.

At this point we've run the script and `wsdl2py` has produced the following two modules:

> `NSStat_services.py`: This module contains the Locator class, which is used to connect to the service and classes for each remotely available method.

> `NSStat_services_types.py`: This file is rarely used directly. It is imported from the previous module and contains class definitions for every data type used by our web service. It does contain useful information that you will need later when creating requests and inspecting responses from the web service.

There are other options for the `wsdl2py` tool, which could be used to produce server helper modules. With these modules you can then implement your own version of the web service that exposes the same interface and understands same protocols as defined by our WSDL file, but this goes beyond the scope of our project.

Defining Requirements for Our Load Balancer Tool

So far we have only been investigating the SOAP protocol and Python libraries that provide SOAP support, which created helper modules that we will use to access the Netscaler web services.

We have yet to write the actual code that performs SOAP calls and does something useful with the information it receives, but before we dive into the interesting stuff (that is, writing the code), let's step back and decide a few important things:

- What do we want our tool to do?

- How are we going to structure our code?

Because these questions sound simple and appear obvious they are often overlooked. This usually leads to poorly written and unmanageable code.

If we do not know precisely what we want our code to do, we risk either oversimplifying or over-complicating our code. In other words, we might write a few simple lines of code, where in fact we wanted it to be something more generic and reusable for others or in other projects. So we'll keep on adding new functions and creating various workarounds, and so the code grows into an unmaintainable monster. Overcomplicating is also dangerous, because we might find ourselves spending days and weeks (and, if we're really creative, months) coding complicated data structures, when a few lines of throw-away prototyped code would be more efficient.

So give careful thought to what you want to do before you start, but do not spend too much time on it either, as in most cases system administrators are not expected to develop full scale applications, and so things are easier for them.

Before starting, I find that considering the following points and writing a simple few paragraphs for each is sufficient to perform well as a rough guideline and requirements specification document:

- Define the basic requirements

- Define the code structure

- Decide on configurable and changeable items

- Define error handling and logging

Basic Requirements

Make a bullet point list of what you want this tool to do, simple statements like "I want ... to do ..." are very effective as we're not after formal requirement specifications. The following example illustrates this point:

- I want my application to gather statistical information about:

  - CPU and memory utilization

  - System overview: requests rate, data rate, established connections

  - Overview of all virtual servers: up/down and what services are down within each

- I want my application to be able to:

  - Disable/enable all services for any of the available virtual servers

  - Disable/enable any individual service

  - Disable/enable any set of services (may span across multiple virtual servers)

- I want to reuse defined functions in other scripts.

- The code should be easy to modify and add new functionality.

Code Structure

Now that we have defined our requirements for the tool, we can clearly see how to organize our script:

- All functions that make SOAP calls need to be defined in a separate module. This module can be imported by various scripts, which could make use of the same functions.

- It would be good to define one class containing methods for accessing web services, so that anyone could simply inherit from this class and extend with additional functionality.

- The tool will consist of two distinct parts—one to read statistical data and the other to control services..

Mapping this to source code, we are going to have the following files and modules:

1. Our own library `NSLib.py`, which is going to contain definitions for the following:

    - The `NSLibError` exception class. Whenever we encounter any unrecoverable issues, we will raise this exception.

    - The `NSSoapApi` class. This is the root class and implements methods common to all Netscaler SOAP API objects: initialization and login.

    - The `NSStatApi` class, which inherits the `NSSoapApi` class. This class implements all methods that deal with statistics gathering and monitoring. It only performs calls defined by Statistics WSDL.

    - The `NSConfigApi` class which inherits `NSSoapApi` class. This class implements all methods that deal with loadbalancer configuration and calls methods defined by Configuration WSDL.

2. `ns_stat.py`. This file uses NSStatApi from NSLib and in the actual script that implements our statistic gathering tasks. This is the script we will be calling from the command line.

3. `ns_conf.py`. This file uses NSConfigApi from NSLib and is the actual script that implements our load balancer configuration tasks. This is the script we will be calling from the command line.

4. `ns_config.py`. This is our configuration script that contains all definitions we need to establish communication with the load balancer. See detailed description below.

Configuration

We might have more than one load balancer that we would like to manage and monitor. Therefore we'll create a simple configuration file that identifies every one of them and would also contain login details and service groups.

Since it's going to be used by people who are reasonably comfortable with scripting and is not a script targeting simple users, we can create a Python file with statically defined variables and import it.

Listing 2-6 is the example I will be using throughout this chapter.

Listing 2-6. *A configuration file with load balancer details*

```
#!/usr/bin/env python

netscalers = {
            'default': 'primary',

            'primary':    {
                        'USERNAME': 'nstest',
                        'PASSWORD': 'nstest',
                        'NS_ADDR' : '192.168.1.1',
                        'groups': {},
                    },

            'secondary': {
                        'USERNAME': 'nstest',
                        'PASSWORD': 'nstest',
                        'NS_ADDR' : '192.168.1.2',
                        'groups': {},
                    },
        }
```

As you can see, we have two `netscalers` here, primary and secondary, with different IP addresses (you can have different users and passwords as well). No service groups are defined yet; we can add those later when we need to.

Within our tools, if we need to access this configuration data we would retrieve it as shown in Listing 2-7.

Listing 2-7. *Accessing configuration data*

```
import ns_config as config

# to access configuration of the 'primary' loadbalancer
username_pri = config.netscalers['primary']['USERNAME']

# to access configuration of the default loadbalancer
default_lb = config.netscalers['default']
username_def = config.netscalers[default_lb]['USERNAME']
```

Accessing Citrix Netscaler Load Balancer with the SOAP API

First we need to find the service location. With web services it is almost always a URL. However, we do not really need to know the URL, as we have the special Locator class, which once initiated creates a binding object we use to access the SOAP service.

Before we continue, we need to resolve one minor issue with Netscaler's WSDL.

Fixing Issues with Citrix Netscaler WSDL

The locator class in our generated service access helper module (NSStat_services.py) is defined as shown in Listing 2-8.

Listing 2-8. *The Locator class definition*

```
# Locator
class NSStatServiceLocator:
    NSStatPort_address = "http://netscaler_ip/soap/"
    def getNSStatPortAddress(self):
        return NSStatServiceLocator.NSStatPort_address
    def getNSStatPort(self, url=None, **kw):
        return NSStatBindingSOAP(url or NSStatServiceLocator.NSStatPort_address,⏎
**kw)
```

This is obviously wrong, because the service host name netscaler_ip is not a valid IP address (it should have been 192.168.1.1), nor is a valid domain name. Citrix Netscaler has always been exposing its endpoint this way, so we can only assume this is done by design.

One possible reason it is done this way is that you may want to use the same WSDL information along with your software to manage multiple load-balancing devices, and therefore it would be impractical to retrieve and compile WSDL from every single device you are going to manage. Therefore it is left to the API user/developer to replace this address with the correct one. All examples from Netscaler SOAP API manual behave the same way, and ignore this variable instead of passing their own settings.

Therefore you have to modify the NSStatPort_address variable by replacing netscaler_ip with the IP address of your device. Fortunately this has to be done only once; WSDL is not going to change very often (usually only during the major OS upgrades). Listing 2-9 shows the modification.

Listing 2-9. *Manually modifying the Locator class*

```
# Locator
class NSStatServiceLocator:
    NSStatPort_address = "http://192.168.1.1/soap/"
    def getNSStatPortAddress(self):
        return NSStatServiceLocator.NSStatPort_address
    def getNSStatPort(self, url=None, **kw):
        return NSStatBindingSOAP(url or NSStatServiceLocator.NSStatPort_address,↩
**kw)
```

If you do not wish to modify the module, you will see another way of fixing the issue later in the chapter, where you can specify the service end point during the initialization of the Locator object.

Creating a Connection Object

We have the helper modules ready and fixed, so finally we are going to actually communicate with our load balancer via SOAP API.

Before we can continue, we need to import all our methods that we generated with wsdl2py:

```
import NSStat_services
```

Initializing the locator and service access objects is very simple and can be achieved with only two lines of code. First we're creating the actual Locator object, which contains information about the web service location:

```
locator = NSStat_services.NSStatServiceLocator()
```

Then we call the method that will return us the binding object, already initialized with service URL:

```
soap = locator.getNSStatPort()
```

The locator object has only two methods, one to read the URL from WSDL and another to initialize and return a binding object.

The binding object (in our example initialized as the variable soap) contains all methods that are available on our web service (in this instance Citrix Netscaler Statistics API). It acts like a proxy, mapping object methods to API functions.

Before we continue let's see how we can fix the Netscaler invalid URL issue. As you already know, you can interrogate the Locator object and request an endpoint URL. You can also force getNSStatPort to use a custom URL instead of the generated one. So what we are going to do is to get the URL, replace the bogus string with the IP of our load balancer, and then generate a binding object with the correct URL. Listing 2-10 shows the code.

Listing 2-10. *Substituting the load balancer address*

```
MY_NS_IP = '192.168.1.1'
locator = NSStat_services.NSStatServiceLocator()
bad_url = locator.getNSStatPortAddress()
```

```
good_url = re.sub('netscaler_ip', MY_NS_IP, bad_url)
soap = locator.getNSStatPort(url=good_url)
```

As you can see, here I used the getNSStatPortAddress Locator method to retrieve the URL string, which I then modified using a regular expression and replaced the netscaler_ip string with the load balancer's IP. Finally I asked the Locator to create my SOAP binding object with my new (correct) URL.

This approach is more flexible than changing automatically generated module. If for whatever reason (an NS OS upgrade would be one example) you decide to generate a new module, you will lose the changes that you have made. That other approach also requires you to remember that you have to change the code. Overriding the IP in the code that makes a request is more obvious, and will not interfere with other tools that might reuse the same helper modules.

So this was a quick way of creating our connection object, but how are we going to fit this into our required structure that we have defined earlier? Remember, we decided to have one generic class with initialization and logging facilities, and then derive two different classes from it: one for statistics and monitoring module and one for management and configuration module. You can see the class inheritance in the Figure 2-1 below.

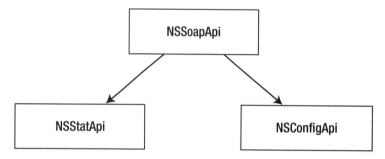

Figure 2-1. *Class inheritance diagram.*

This poses an immediate problem, because we will need to use different Locator objects for each service, so we cannot initialize them in the NSSoapApi class, because we do not know what type of Locator object, Stat or Config, we will need to use.

The generic class needs to be able to identify which module it is supposed to use as a service locator, so I will pass a module object from NSStatApi or NSConfigApi as a parameter to NSSoapApi, which will then use this parameter to initialize the appropriate Locator and perform the login call using the specific module call. It may sound complicated, but it really isn't at all. Listing 2-11 shows the code that implements this.

Listing 2-11. *Defining a generic class*

```
class NSSoapApi(object):

    def __init__(self, module=None,
                       hostname=None,
                       username=None,
                       password=None):
        [...]
```

```
        self.username = username
        self.password = password
        self.hostname = hostname
        self.module   = module

        if self.module.__name__ == 'NSStat_services':
            [...]
            self.locator = self.module.NSStatServiceLocator()
            bad_url = self.locator.getNSStatPortAddress()
            good_url = re.sub('netscaler_ip', self.hostname, bad_url)
            self.soap = self.locator.getNSStatPort(url=good_url)
        elif self.module.__name__ == 'NSConfig_services':
            [...]
            self.locator = self.module.NSConfigServiceLocator()
            bad_url = self.locator.getNSConfigPortAddress()
            good_url = re.sub('netscaler_ip', self.hostname, bad_url)
            self.soap = self.locator.getNSConfigPort(url=good_url)
        else:
            [...]
        self.login()

    def login(self):
        [...]
        req = self.module.login()
        req._username = self.username
        req._password = self.password
        [...]
        res = self.soap.login(req)._return
        [...]
```

This generic class expects a module object to be passed into it, so it can

- Call generic methods such as login directly from whichever module is passed

- Depending on the module, call specific methods or refer to module-specific classes, such as NSStatServiceLocator vs NSConfigServiceLocator

Our subclasses will pass the module object on to the superclass, as shown in Listing 2-12.

Listing 2-12. *Passing a module object to a generic class*

```
class NSStatApi(NSSoapApi):

    def __init__(self, hostname=None, username=None, password=None):
        super(NSStatApi, self).__init__(hostname=hostname,
                                        username=username,
                                        password=password,
                                        module=NSStat_services)
```

```
class NSConfigApi(NSSoapApi):

    def __init__(self, hostname=None, username=None, password=None):
        super(NSConfigApi, self).__init__(hostname=hostname,
                                          username=username,
                                          password=password,
                                          module=NSConfig_services)
```

Logging In: Our First SOAP Call

At this point, no actual API calls have been made yet; what we've done was just preparation and initialization work. The first thing we need to do before we can start requesting performance data or making configuration changes is to authenticate with the load balancer. So our first API call is going to be the login method.

Performing SOAP requests with a generated helper library always follows the same pattern:

1. Create a request object.

2. Initialize the request object with parameters; this is your argument list to the SOAP function.

3. Call the binder method representing the appropriate SOAP method and pass the request object to it.

4. The binder method returns an API response (or raises an exception if it fails to contact the web service).

As we have already seen, the binding object returned by the Locator is of NSStatBindingSOAP class. Methods of this class represent all functions available on the web service. One of them is the login function, shown in Listing 2-13, which we are going to use to identify ourselves to the load balancer.

Listing 2-13. *The definition of a login method*

```
# op: login
def login(self, request):
    if isinstance(request, login) is False:
        raise TypeError, "%s incorrect request type" % (request.__class__)
    kw = {}
    # no input wsaction
    self.binding.Send(None, None, request, soapaction="urn:NSConfigAction",
                      encodingStyle="http://schemas.xmlsoap.org/soap/encoding/",
                      **kw)
    # no output wsaction
    typecode = Struct(pname=None, ofwhat=loginResponse.typecode.ofwhat,
                      pyclass=loginResponse.typecode.pyclass)
    response = self.binding.Receive(typecode)
    return response
```

like other methods of the `NSStatBindingSOAP` class, the `login` method accepts only one parameter, the request object.

A request object must be constructed from the `login` class, which is available from the same helper module. The easiest way to find out what the request object must contain is to look at its definition; Listing 2-14 shows what we have in our instance.

Listing 2-14. *The login request class*

```
class login:
    def __init__(self):
        self._username = None
        self._password = None
        return
```

So when initializing the new request object, we must set both _username and _password before we pass it to our binding object.

Now let's create these objects and make a login SOAP call. Listing 2-15 shows the code.

Listing 2-15. *A wrapper around the default login method*

```
class NSSoapApi(object):
    [...]
    def login(self):
        # create request object and assign default values
        req = self.module.login()
        req._username = self.username
        req._password = self.password
        [...]
        res = self.soap.login(req)._return
        if res._rc != 0:
            # an error has occurred
```

Just as with all other requests, making the SOAP login call is a two-step process:

1. Create and initialize the request object; this object contains data we are going to send to the web service. In the following example, `req` is our `login` request object, which we are initializing by setting a username and password for the `login` call:

```
req = self.module.login()
req._username = self.username
req._password = self.password
```

2. Call the appropriate proxy function from the Binding object and pass the request object to it. The following steps are condensed into a single line of code:

   1. Call the login method of our Binding object.

   2. Pass the request object constructed in the previous step.

   3. Read the response.

When all steps are complete, res will contain the return object, with variables as defined in the NSStat_services_types.py module (or the WSDL datatype section):

```
res = self.soap.login(req)._return
```

Finding What Is Being Returned in the Response from a Web Service

We already know that to find out what we're expected to send in a request to a web service, we need to look in the service's helper module, which contains classes for all request objects, but how do we know what we are receiving as a response?

If we look again at the login method in the Binding class, we will find that it returns an object of the loginResponse type, as shown in Listing 2-16.

Listing 2-16. *The return value from the Binding class*

```
def login(self, request):
    [...]
    typecode = Struct(pname=None, ofwhat=loginResponse.typecode.ofwhat,
                      pyclass=loginResponse.typecode.pyclass)
    response = self.binding.Receive(typecode)
    return response
```

From the loginResponse class (Listing 2-17), we find that it contains only one variable, _return.

Listing 2-17. *The contents of the loginResponse class*

```
class loginResponse:
    def __init__(self):
        self._return = None
        returnloginResponse.typecode =↵
Struct(pname=("urn:NSConfig","loginResponse"),↵
 ofwhat=[ns0.simpleResult_Def(pname="return", aname="_return", typed=False,
encoded=None,↵
 minOccurs=1, maxOccurs=1, nillable=True)], pyclass=loginResponse,
encoded="urn:NSConfig")
```

Yet this is not enough, as _return is the object that contains the information we require, and we need to find out how to reference it. Since loginResponse is very simple (only two fields returned), it uses a generic response object, and we find that from the typecode setting for the loginResponse class, by looking at the ofwhat setting in the class' typecode definition. In the following example it is the highlighted string:

```
class loginResponse:
    def __init__(self):
        self._return = None
        return
```

```
loginResponse.typecode = Struct(pname=("urn:NSConfig","loginResponse"),
  ofwhat=[ns0.simpleResult_Def(pname="return",
                               aname="_return",
                               typed=False,
                               encoded=None,
                               minOccurs=1,
                               maxOccurs=1,
                               nillable=True)],
  pyclass=loginResponse, encoded="urn:NSConfig")
```

More complex structures have Result objects named after them, so it is easier to find them, but with login we need to look for the simpleResult class in the types definition module (NSStat_services_types.py). This class definition, shown in Listing 2-18, may look a bit cryptic, but we do not really need to know the details of its functioning; just look for the Holder class definition.

Listing 2-18. *The class definition for* simpleResult

```
class simpleResult_Def(ZSI.TCcompound.ComplexType, TypeDefinition):
    [...]
        class Holder:
            typecode = self
            def __init__(self):
                # pyclass
                self._rc = None
                self._message = None
                return
    [...]
```

I will explain in more detail how to find references and definitions of the objects for complex data types later in this chapter in the "Reading System Health Data" section.

How Is the Session Maintained After We Have Logged In?

You might be wondering what happens next after we successfully log on to our web service. How does the load balancer know that we are authorized to make other calls, when other calls do not require a username and password to be sent along with other parameters?

Some web services send back a special token, which is generated on the server and is associated with the account that is using the API. If that was the case, we would have to incorporate this token with every request that we send to the web service.

Things are much simpler with the Netscaler load balancer. After we send our login request, and if our authentication details are correct, the load balancer will respond with a simple "OK" message. It will also respond with a special cookie in the HTTP header, which acts as our token. Instead of incorporating token details into every SOAP request, we simply need to make sure that we have this cookie set in our HTTP header when we're sending subsequent requests to our web service. Listing 2-19 shows the output from the tcpdump command, which clearly demonstrates this in action (I have omitted other TCP packets and removed irrelevant binary data, so only HTTP and SOAP protocols are shown).

Listing 2-19. *HTTP encapsulated SOAP login request and login response messages*

```
11:11:35.283170 IP 192.168.1.10.40494 > 192.168.1.1.http: P 1:166(165) ack 1 win
5488
[...]
POST /soap/ HTTP/1.1
Host: 192.168.1.1
Accept-Encoding: identity
Content-Length: 540
Content-Type: text/xml; charset=utf-8
SOAPAction: "urn:NSConfigAction"
[...]
<SOAP-ENV:Envelope xmlns:SOAP-ENC="http://schemas.xmlsoap.org/soap/encoding/"
xmlns:↵
SOAP-ENV="http://schemas.xmlsoap.org/soap/envelope/"↵
 xmlns:ZSI="http://www.zolera.com/schemas/ZSI/" xmlns:xsd=↵
"http://www.w3.org/2001/XMLSchema" xmlns:xsi=↵
"http://www.w3.org/2001/XMLSchema-instance" SOAP-ENV:encodingStyle=↵
"http://schemas.xmlsoap.org/soap/encoding/"><SOAP-ENV:Header></SOAP-ENV:↵
Header><SOAP-ENV:Body
xmlns:ns1="urn:NSConfig"><ns1:login><username>nstest</username>↵
<password>nstest</password></ns1:login></SOAP-ENV:Body></SOAP-ENV:Envelope>

11:11:35.567226 IP 192.168.1.1.http > 192.168.1.10.40494: P 1:949(948) ack 706 win
57620
[...]
HTTP/1.1 200 OK
Date: Mon, 29 Jun 2009 11:13:08 GMT
Server: Apache
Last-Modified: Mon, 29 Jun 2009 11:13:08 GMT
Status: 200 OK
Content-Length: 622
Connection: closeSet-Cookie:↵
NSAPI=##F0F402A6574084DB4956184C6443FEE54DD5FC1E1953E3730A5A307BBEC3;Domain=↵
192.168.1.1; Path=/soapContent-Type: text/xml; charset=utf-8
<?xml version="1.0" encoding="UTF-8"?><SOAP-ENV:Envelope xmlns:SOAP-ENV=↵
"http://schemas.xmlsoap.org/soap/envelope/" xmlns:SOAP-ENC=↵
"http://schemas.xmlsoap.org/soap/encoding/" xmlns:xsi=↵
"http://www.w3.org/2001/XMLSchema-instance" xmlns:xsd=↵
"http://www.w3.org/2001/XMLSchema" xmlns:ns=↵
"urn:NSConfig"><SOAP-ENV:Header></SOAP-ENV:Header><SOAP-ENV:Body SOAP-ENV:↵
encodingStyle="http://schemas.xmlsoap.org/soap/encoding/" id=↵
"_0"><ns:loginResponse><return xsi:type=↵
"ns:simpleResult"><rc xsi:type="xsd:unsignedInt">0</rc><message xsi:type=↵
"xsd:string">Done</message></return></ns:loginResponse></SOAP-ENV:Body></SOAP-
ENV:Envelope>
```

We can see that with our initial request for login action we send a SOAP message with our credentials encapsulated as HTTP POST request.

The response is also a SOAP message, encapsulated into an HTTP response. The SOAP response does not carry much useful information; it contains only two pieces of data: a numeric return code (`rc`) and an alphanumeric string (`message`). When everything is OK, `rc` is set to `0` and `message` is set to `Done`.

The HTTP header carries more important information—it sets a cookie that we need to use with other requests:

```
Set-Cookie: NSAPI=##F0F402A6574084DB4956184C6443FEE54DD5FC1E1953E3730A5A307BBEC3;↵
Domain=192.168.1.1;Path=/soap
```

This cookie value is associated with our account on NS, and so the web service knows that whoever sends this cookie has already been authenticated.

Gathering Performance Statistics Data

We have already established the following requirements for the statistic gathering and monitoring tool:

- I want my tool to gather statistical information about:
    - CPU and memory utilization
    - System overview: requests rate, data rate, established connections
    - Overview of all virtual servers: up/down and what services are down within each
- These can be split into two groups:
    - System status (CPU, memory and request rate readings)
    - Virtual server status (virtual server states)

We can now split our implementation into two parts, which is easier to code and test.

SOAP Methods for Reading Statistical Data and Their Return Values

Table 2-1 lists the methods that are used in our statistics gathering tool, along with the name and a brief description of each one's return object. We are going to use some of them in our code. You should be able to modify the code quite easily and add more items for the tool to query. If you find yourself needing more details about more specific items, such as AAA, GSLB or Compression, please refer to Netscaler API documentation, which is available to download from the Netscaler management web page.

Table 2-1. *Statistic Web Service Methods and Their Return Values Used in Our Example*

Method	Return Variable	Description
statsystem	_internaltemp	The internal system temperature in C.
	_rescpuusage	The combined CPU usage expressed as a percentage.
	_memusagepcnt	The memory usage expressed as a percentage.
statprotocolhttp	_httprequestsrate	The total HTTP(S) request rate (per second).
statlbvserver	_primaryipaddress	The IP address of the virtual server.
	_primaryport	The port number of the virtual server
	_state	The state of the virtual server: UP: The Virtual server is running. DOWN: All services failed in the virtual server. OUT OF SERVICE: The virtual server is disabled.
	_vslbhealth	The health of the virtual server. Expressed as the percentage of services that are in the UP state.
	_requestsrate	The rate of requests per second the virtual server is receiving.
statservice	_primaryipaddress	The IP address of the virtual server.
	_primaryport	The port number of the virtual server.
	_state	The state of the virtual server: UP: The service is running. DOWN: The service is not running on the physical server. OUT OF SERVICE: The service is disabled.
	_requestsrate	The rate of requests per second the service is receiving.

Reading System Health Data

Reading system status data is pretty straightforward; all we need to do is call two methods: one to retrieve readings about hardware and memory status, and another to check the total HTTP and HTTPS requests served by our load balancer.

So as we can see from Table 2-1, we will be calling the statsystem and statprotocolhttp methods. Neither of these methods requires any input parameters. Listing 2-20 shows a simplified version of the statistics gathering method in our NSStatApi class.

Listing 2-20. *Obtaining system health data*

```
def system_health_check(self):
    results = {}
    [...]
    req = self.module.statsystem()
    res = self.soap.statsystem(req)._return
    results['temp'] = res._List[0]._internaltemp
    results['cpu'] = res._List[0]._rescpuusage
    results['mem'] = res._List[0]._memusagepcnt
    [...]
    req = self.module.statprotocolhttp()
    res = self.soap.statprotocolhttp(req)._return
    results['http_req_rate'] = res._List[0]._httprequestsrate
    [...]
    return results
```

This looks very similar to the login request we performed earlier; however, there is one important thing to notice. This time we need to use the _List variable to access the details we are interested in. The reason for this is that all response _return objects contain two required and one optional variable: _rc, _message, and _List. We already know that _rc and _message contain a request return code and a message that provides more details about the request status.

_List is optional and is an array that may contain one or more instances of the return object(s). Even if the method will always return a single instance, it is still contained in the array. This is one of the options to provide a standard way of communication: every request is always going to return the same set of variables, so if we needed to, we could write a standard SOAP request dispatcher/response handler.

How do we find out what structure objects are returned in the list? This is very simple. First you need to look for the methodname response class in the NSStat_services_types.py module that contains all datatypes used in SOAP communication. So in our case we would be searching for statsystemResult_Def class.

Once we have found it, we need to look for the type definition, similar to the following:

```
TClist = [ZSI.TCnumbers.IunsignedInt(pname="rc", aname="_rc", minOccurs=1,
maxOccurs=1, nillable=False, typed=False, encoded=kw.get("encoded")),
ZSI.TC.String(pname="message", aname="_message", minOccurs=1, maxOccurs=1,
nillable=False, typed=False, encoded=kw.get("encoded")),
GTD("urn:NSConfig","systemstatsList",lazy=False)(pname="List",
aname="_List", minOccurs=0, maxOccurs=1, nillable=False, typed=False,
encoded=kw.get("encoded"))]
```

Now we will look for the systemstatsList class definition, shown in Listing 2-21.

Listing 2-21. *The systemstatsList class definition*

```
class systemstatsList_Def(ZSI.TC.Array, TypeDefinition):
    #complexType/complexContent base="SOAP-ENC:Array"
    schema = "urn:NSConfig"
    type = (schema, "systemstatsList")
    def __init__(self, pname, ofwhat=(), extend=False, restrict=False,
                 attributes=None, **kw):
        ofwhat = ns0.systemstats_Def(None, typed=False)
        atype = (u'urn:NSConfig', u'systemstats[]')
        ZSI.TCcompound.Array.__init__(self, atype, ofwhat, pname=pname,
                                      childnames='item', **kw)
```

In this class definition we are going to find a reference to the actual class, which is going to contain all the variables we will receive in the response from SOAP.

So finally, in Listing 2-22, we search for systemstats_Def class, where the subclass Holder contains all available variables.

Listing 2-22. *The definition of the systemstats return type*

```
class systemstats_Def(ZSI.TCcompound.ComplexType, TypeDefinition):
    [...]
    class Holder:
        typecode = self
        def __init__(self):
            # pyclass
            self._rescpuusage = None
            self._memusagepcnt = None
            self._internaltemp = None
            [...]
```

This may look really complicated, but for automated systems it is always the same pattern in accessing the information, which helps to simplify the process.

Reading Service Status Data

Retrieving information about services is very similar; it just involves more steps:

1. First we need to retrieve a list of all virtual servers on the Netscaler. This can be achieved with the statlbvserver method, which accepts an optional *name* parameter. If that is specified, only information about that virtual server will be returned. If *name* is not specified or is set to blank, information about all virtual servers will be returned.

2. For each virtual server on the list, we create a list of services attached to it. This actually requires using a different SOAP service—the Netscaler configuration SOAP. The Statistics API does not provide functionality to query dependencies between configuration entities, so we are going to use the getlbvserver method from the Configuration API.

3. Finally we check whether the virtual server health score is not 100%. If the server is not on the ignore list, we will list unhealthy services that are attached to it. We will use the statservice method to retrieve statistics about each service, and if the service is not in the UP state we will indicate that.

■**Note** In the Citrix load balancer, the virtual server has a number of services attached to it that serve user requests. The health score for a virtual server is calculated as a percentage of active services in the virtual server pool. So if a virtual server contained ten services in its pool and two of them were not responding to the health checks, the score for that virtual server would be 80%.

In the following code listings I will show classes and methods that implement health and service statistic gathering. In order to keep the code simple, these examples will not have any error handling. The full source code, which is available to download from the book's page at www.apress.com, contains additional error handling and reporting functionality.

First, in Listing 2-23, we define a new Statistics API wrapper class, which implements two methods: get_vservers_list and get_service_details. The class inherits all functions from the base NSSoapApi class, which we defined earlier.

The get_vservers_list method calls the statlbvserver SOAP method and passes an optional name parameter. If the name string is empty, a list of all virtual servers will be returned. When the list is returned we create our own dictionary with just few items from the complete list.

The get_service_details method calls the statservice SOAP method and passes a service name as an argument. The SOAP response consists of detailed information about the service. We will extract only the information that is interesting for us and return it as a Python dictionary.

Listing 2-23. *The Statistics API wrapper class*

```
class NSStatApi(NSSoapApi):
    [...]
    def get_vservers_list(self, name=''):
        result = {}
        req = self.module.statlbvserver()
        req._name = name
        res = self.soap.statlbvserver(req)._return
        for e in res._List:
            result[e._name.strip('"')] = { 'ip':          e._primaryipaddress,
                                           'port':         e._primaryport,
                                           'status':       e._state,
                                           'health':       e._vslbhealth,
                                           'requestsrate': e._requestsrate, }
        return result

    def get_service_details(self, service):
        result = {}
        req = self.module.statservice()
        req._name = service
```

```
    res = self.soap.statservice(req)._return
    result = { 'ip': res._List[0]._primaryipaddress,
               'port': res._List[0]._primaryport,
               'status': res._List[0]._state,
               'requestsrate': res._List[0]._requestsrate, }
    return result
```

The second class we are going to define, in Listing 2-24, is a Configuration API wrapper class. This class should mainly be used for functions that deal with load balancer configuration, but we need to call one function from this service: getlbvserver, which returns (among other details about the virtual server) a list of all services that are bound to a particular virtual server. Our method is called get_services_list and simply returns the result as a Python list with service names as elements.

Listing 2-24. *A configuration API wrapper class*

```
class NSConfigApi(NSSoapApi):
    def get_services_list(self, vserver):
        req = self.module.getlbvserver()
        req._name = vserver
        res = self.soap.getlbvserver(req)._return
        result = [e.strip('"') for e in res._List[0]._servicename]
        return result
```

Finally, in Listing 2-25, we are going to implement our query function, which performs the following steps:

- Initiates instances of both classes.

- Retrieves a list of all virtual servers.

- If the virtual server health is not 100%, gets a list of services bound to it.

- Prints out all unhealthy services.

Listing 2-25. *Retrieving service status data*

```
ns = NSStatApi([...])
ns_c = NSConfigApi([...])


for (vs, data) in ns.get_vservers_list(name=OPTS.vserver_query).iteritems():
        if (data['status'] != 'UP' or data['health'] != 100) and
            vs not in config.netscalers['primary']['vserver_ignore_list'] or
            OPTS.verbose:
            print " SERVICE: %s (%s:%s)" % (vs, data['ip'], data['port'])
            print "    LOAD: %s req/s" % data['requestsrate']
            print "  HEALTH: %s%%" % data['health']
```

```
for srv in sorted(ns_c.get_services_list(vs)):
    service = ns.get_service_details(srv)
    if service['status'] != 'UP' or OPTS.vserver_query or OPTS.verbose:
        print ' * %s (%s:%s) - %s (%s req/sec)' % (srv, service['ip'],
                                                    service['port'],
                                                    service['status'],
                                                    service['requestsrate'])
```

Following is the sample output from the tool. Depending on your load balancer configuration and the operational status of the virtual servers and services, you obviously will get different results.

In this example, the first section displays basic health information about the load balancers: memory usage, CPU usage, temperature, and total HTTP requests. The second section displays information about a service that is not completely healthy. This service is supposed to have 30 services running, but two of them are marked as DOWN

```
$ ./ns_stat.py
**************************************************
Health check for loadbalancer: 192.168.1.1
 Memory usage: 6.434952%
    CPU usage: 15%
  Temperature: 47C
     Requests: 4926/sec
-------------------------------
SERVICE: main_web_server (192.168.0.5:80)
    LOAD: 1140 req/s
  HEALTH: 92%
 * web_farm_service-13 (192.168.2.13:80) - DOWN (0 req/sec)
 * web_farm_service-14 (192.168.2.14:80) - DOWN (0 req/sec)
-------------------------------
$
```

Automating Administration Tasks

The second part of our exercise is to create a management tool for our load balancer. Going back to our original requirements, we know that we want the configuration tool to perform the following tasks:

1. Disable/enable all services for any of the available virtual servers.

2. Disable/enable any individual service.

3. Disable/enable any set of services (may span across multiple virtual servers).

Device Configuration SOAP Methods

The Configuration API provides over 2500 different methods to alter load balancer configuration. Configuring a load balancer is usually a complicated task and goes far beyond the scope of this book. In this section I am going to show how to get a list of services, and then you will learn how to enable and disable them. Other functions behave in a very similar fashion, so if you need to create a new virtual server you would just call appropriate functions.

Table 2-2 lists the methods we will be using in the configuration tool, along with each one's return variable and a description.

Table 2-2. *Methods Used to Enable and Disable Servers*

Method	Return Variable	Description
disableservice	_rc	The return code of the operation (simpleResult type); 0 if successful.
	_message	A detailed explanation of the result (simpleResult type). Done" if successful; otherwise a meaningful explanation is provided.
enableservice	_rc	The return code of the operation (simpleResult type); 0 if successful.
	_message	A detailed explanation of the result (simpleResult type). "Done" if successful; otherwise a meaningful explanation is provided.
getlbvserver	_servicename	A list of all services bound to a particular virtual server.

As you can see, the first two methods for enabling and disabling services are really simple in their responses; they either succeed or fail. Just like the login method, they return a datastructure simpleResponse, which contains only a return code and a detailed description of the error in case of failure.

The last method is getlbvserver, which we used in previous section to retrieve a list of all services that are bound to a virtual server. The same method wrapper will be reused here as well.

Setting a Service State

Setting the state of a service is as simple as calling either enableservice or disableservice with a service name as a parameter to the method call. Citrix Netscaler load balancer service and virtual server names are not case-sensitive, so when calling either method you do not need to care about setting a correct case for the name parameter.

We are going to define another function in our NSConfigApi class that will implement switching between the states and wrap two SOAP functions into one convenient, easy-to-use class method. We will call this method set_service_state, and it will accept two required arguments: a new state and a

Python array that contains the names of all the services whose state we want to change. Listing 2-26 shows the code.

Listing 2-26. *The wrapper for the SOAP* enableservice *and* disableservice *functions*

```
def set_service_state(self, state, service_list, verbose=False):
    [...]
        for service in service_list:
            if verbose:
                print 'Changing state of %s to %sd... ' % (service, state)
            req = getattr(self.module, '%sservice' % state)()
            req._name = service
            res = getattr(self.soap, '%sservice' % state)(req)._return
    [...]
    return
```

As you can see, it is a very simple function; however, it contains one thing that's worth a bit more attention: we do not explicitly specify the name of the method we are calling—it is automatically constructed during runtime from the argument value that we receive in the state variable.

To achieve this, we use the Python getattr function, which allows us to get a reference to an object's property at runtime without knowing the property name in advance. When we call getattr, we provide two arguments: a reference to an object and the name of the property we are addressing. Therefore, our explicit call to a method looks like this:

```
result = some_object.some_function()
```

would be equivalent to:

```
result = getattr(some_object, "some_function")()
```

It is important to note the () after the getattr call. The getattr return value is a reference to an object, and as such does not execute a function. If we are accessing an object variable, it will return the value of the variable, but if we are accessing a function we would only get a reference to it:

```
>>> class C():
...    var = 'test'
...    def func(self):
...      print 'hello'
...
>>> o = C()
>>> getattr(o, 'var')
'test'
>>> getattr(o, 'func')
<bound method C.func of <__main__.C instance at 0xb7fe038c>>
>>> getattr(o, 'func')()
hello
>>>
```

This method is often used to implement dispatcher functionality, which we use in our code as well, instead of explicitly testing for the state parameter, as shown here:

```
if state == 'enable':
    req = self.module.enableservice()
    req._name = service
    res = self.soap.enableservice(req)._return
elif state == 'disable':
    req = self.module.disableservice()
    req._name = service
    res = self.soap.disableservice(req)._return
```

At this point we construct the name of our function and call it automatically:

```
req = getattr(self.module, '%sservice' % state)()
req._name = service
res = getattr(self.soap, '%sservice' % state)(req)._return
```

This is a very powerful technique that makes your code much more readable and easier to maintain. In the previous example we reduced the number of lines from eight to only three. There are some caveats to watch for; the biggest problem is that we might reference a property that does not exist. In our example we must make sure that state is set to either 'enable' or 'disable'; otherwise, getattr will return None as a result.

A Word About Logging and Error Handling

Although they do not affect the functionality of our tools or API access library, it is very important to implement basic logging, error reporting, and error handling. At every stage of writing code we need to anticipate all possible outcomes, especially if we are using external libraries and/or external services, such as the SOAP API.

Using the Python logging Module

Regardless of the size of our project, it is a good practice to report as many details as possible of what is happening in the code. Python comes with a built-in logging module, which is very flexible and configurable yet is easy and simple to use.

Logging Levels and Scope

The Python logging module provides five levels of detail. Table 2-3 provides details on when to use each level.

Table 2-3. *Logging Levels and When You Should Use Each*

Level	When to Use
DEBUG	As the name suggests, this logging level is for debugging purpose. Use DEBUG to log as much information as possible; messages at this level should contain enough detail for you to identify possible problems with the code.
INFO	This is a less detailed level, and it's usually used to log key events in the system's life cycle, such as contacting an external service or calling a rather complicated subsystem.
WARNING	Report all unexpected events with this logging level. Everything that is not harmful but is out of the ordinary should be reported here. For example, if a configuration file is not found, but we have default settings, we should raise a warning.
ERROR	Use this level to log any event that prevents us from completing a given task, but still allows us to proceed with the remaining tasks. For example, if we need to check the status of five virtual servers, but one of them cannot be found, report this as an error, and proceed with checking other servers.
CRITICAL	If you cannot proceed any further, log the error with this logging level and exit. There is no need to provide detailed information at this point; when it comes to troubleshooting, you will switch to lower level, such as DEBUG.

It is very important to think about the scope and purpose of your logging. You must differentiate between regular output from the tool and logging. Regular output and reporting are the primary functions of the tool and thus must not mix with the logging message from the application. You might choose to use the logging module to write application output messages as well, but they need to go to a different stream. Application logging is purely for reporting the status of the application.

For example, if we are not able to connect to the load balancer, we must log that as a critical event and quit. In other words, something happened to our tool that prevented it from finishing its operation. However, if we get the temperature reading and decided that it is too far from normal, we must not log this as critical in our log stream, because high system temperature has nothing to do with our application. Regardless of the load balancer health, our tool behaves and functions correctly. Continuing with this example, we might decide either to simply print the warning message or to log it in some other stream, possibly called loadbalancers_health.log.

Configuring and Using the Logger

Depending on what you want to achieve, the logger configuration can be very simple or very complex. I tend not to overcomplicate it and keep it as simple as possible. At the end of the day, there are only a handful of things you need in your logger configuration:

- The logging level. How much output do I want my logger to produce? If the tool is mature, well tested and stable, realistically I would set the log level to ERROR, but if I'm developing, I'd probably stick to DEBUG.

- The log destination. Do I want log messages on screen or in the file? It is best to write it to a file, especially if you are using multiple loggers, one for application status messages and another for systems that you are managing or monitoring.

- The logging message format. The default logger message format is not very informative, so you might want to add additional fields to it, which is very simple to achieve.

Fortunately, the logging module provides a basicConfig method, which allows you to set all of these with one function call:

```
import logging
logging.basicConfig(level=logging.DEBUG, filename='NSLib.log',
format="%(asctime)s [%(levelname)s] (%(funcName)s() (%(filename)s:%(lineno)d))
%(message)s")
```

As you might have already guessed, setting the logging level is trivial; you just need to use one of the defined internal variables, whose names match the log level names we used previously: DEBUG, INFO, WARNING, ERROR or CRITICAL. The log output destination is just a filename. If you do not specify any filename, the logging module will use standard output (stdout) to write all messages.

The logging format is a bit more complicated. The format must be defined following Python string formatting rules, assuming that right argument is a dictionary. The standard convention of formatting a string in Python with parameters in a hash array is as follows:

```
>>> string = "%(var1)s %(var2)d %(var3)s" % {'var1': 'I bought', 'var2': 3, 'var3':↵
 'sausages'}
>>> print string
I bought 3 sausages
>>>
```

Just as in our example, the logging module expects a formatted string on the left of the % operator and provides a standard prepopulated dictionary as the right argument. Table 2-4 lists the most useful parameters that you might want to use in the logging format string.

Table 2-4. *Predefined Dictionary Fields That Can Be Used in a* logging *Format String*

Level	Description
%(asctime)s	The time when the log message was presented, in human-readable form, such as 2009-07-07 14:04:39,462. The number after the comma is the time portion in milliseconds.
%(levelname)s	A string representing the log level. Possible default values: DEBUG, INFO, WARNING, ERROR or CRITICAL.
%(funcName)s	The name of the function where the logging message was generated.
%(filename)s	The name of the file where the logging call was made. This does not contain the full path to the file, just the filename portion.
%(module)s	The name of the module that generated the logging call. This is same as the filename with extension stripped out.
%(lineno)d	The line number in the file that issued the logging call. Not always available.
%(message)s	The actual logging message processed as msg % args in the following format: logging.debug(msg, args)

Once you have configured the logging module, using it is extremely simple—all you have to do is initialize a new instance of the logger and call its methods to write appropriate log messages:

Listing 2-27. *Initialising a new logger instance*

```
logging.basicConfig(level=logging.DEBUG, filename='NSLib.log',
format="%(asctime)s [%(levelname)s] (%(funcName)s() (%(filename)s:%(lineno)d))
%(message)s")

logger = logging.getLogger()

logger.critical('Simple message...')
logger.error('Message with one argument: %s', str1)
logger.warning('Message with two arguments. String %s and digit: %d', (msg, val))
try:
    not_possible = 1 / 0
except:
    logger.critical('An exception has occurred! Stack trace below:', exc_info=True)
```

As you can see, the logging module is very flexible, yet easy to configure. Use it as much as possible and try to avoid old-style logging using print statements.

Handling Exceptions

Exceptions are errors that prevent your code (or the code of modules that your code is calling) from executing properly and cause execution to terminate. In our previous example in the Listing 2-27, the code fails because we included a statement that instructs Python to execute division by zero, which is not possible. This raised a `ZeroDivisionError` exception and execution of the code is terminated there. Unless we used the `try: ... except: ...` statement, our program would terminate at this point. Python allows us to act on the exceptions, so we can decide how |to handle them appropriately. For example, if we try to establish communication with a remote web service, but the service is not responding, we will get a "connection timed out" exception. If we have more than one service to query, we might just report this as an error and proceed with other services.

Catching exceptions is easy:

```
try:
    call_to_some_function()
except:
    do_something_about_it()
```

As you saw in the previous section, you can log a full exception stack trace just by indicating that you want to log exception details to the logger function call. In my code example I use the following construction to detect an exception, log it and pass it on. If you are writing a module, and you cannot really decide what to do with exceptions that occur, this is one of the ways to deal with them:

```
try:
    module.function()
except:
    logger.error('An exception has occurred while executing module.function()',
                 exc_info=True)
    raise
```

It is also possible to catch specific exceptions and perform different actions for each:

```
try:
    result = divide_two_numbers(arg1, arg2)
except ZeroDivisionError:
    # if this happens, we will return 0
    logger.error('We attempted to divide by zero, setting result to 0')
    result = 0
except:
    # something else has happened, so we reraise it
    logger.critical('An exception has occurred while executing module.function()',
                    exc_info=True)
    raise
```

If you're writing your own module, you might decide to introduce exceptions specific to this module, so they can be caught and dealt with accordingly. I use this technique in the `NSLib.py` module. Custom exceptions must be derived from the generic `Exception` class. If you do not require any specific functionality, you could define new exception as the following class:

```
class NSLibError(Exception):
    def __init__(self, error_message):
        self.error_message = error_message

    def __str__(self):
        return repr(self.error_message)
```

Once the exception class is defined, you would raise it by calling the raise operator and passing an object instance of this exception class:

```
class NSSoapApi(object):
    def __init__(self, module=None, hostname=None, username=None, password=None):
        [...]
        if not (hostname and username and password):
            self.logger.critical('One or more from the following: hostname, username
and password, are undefined')
            raise NSLibError('hostname, username and password must be defined')
```

Although it is not required, it is a good practice to follow the exception class convention, which states that all exception class names should end with Error. Unless the module is huge and implements distinctively different functionality, you might just define one exception per module or group of omodules.

Summary

In this chapter you have learned how to use Python for accessing the SOAP API to monitor and manage Citrix Netscaler load balancers. You also learned how to organize your own project, how to structure your code, and how to handle errors and report the functional status of your module.

- The SOAP API is a method to call procedures on a remote server, also called a web service.

- The SOAP protocol defines a message structure for information exchange between service provider and consumer.

- SOAP messages use the XML language to structure data.

- The underlying or carrier protocol is HTTP.

- WSDL is used to describe all services available on a web service and the data structures used in call/response messages.

- The WSDL definition can be converted to Python helper modules with the wsdl2py tool.

- It is important to define requirements before you start coding.

- Handle errors and exceptions appropriately.

- Use the logging module to log messages and group them by severity.

■■■

## CHAPTER 3

Creating a Web Application for IP Address Accountancy

In this chapter, we are going to build a simple application that will keep track of all IP addresses allocated on the internal network. The chapter covers all phases of developing this application—starting with gathering and setting the requirements to design the application and going through the implementation phase.

Designing the Application

Ideally, application design should not be based on the technology that is going to be used to implement it. Having said that, this kind of independence is rarely achievable and in most cases is not practical, as each technology implies its own implementation patterns and best practices.

In this chapter, we will define requirements and application design before explaining what technology is going to be used. This way it will be easier for you to understand how to reuse the design phase even if in your own work you will be using different technologies.

Setting Out the Requirements

The most important thing in developing any application is to understand exactly what we want from it. Step away from the images of user interfaces you have seen somewhere else, or the functionality of some other (possible similar) application that you may have used in the past. Take a piece of paper and write down in short sentences what you want your application to do.

Our imaginary organization is a rather large enterprise with reasonably complicated network infrastructure, so it is very important to assign and use IP address space effectively. In the past. addresses were recorded in a simple spreadsheet and different teams used different structures to represent the same information. There is no authority that would be assigning IP address ranges, and so effective and clear communication between teams is important. New systems are being introduced as well as old ones being decommissioned. Group policy prevents servers from using dynamic IP allocation; only user machines can obtain address information from DHCP.

Based on that brief description, let's write down the following list of requirements:

- This system must be centralized, but accessible by many different users.

- The application must be able to store IP ranges as well as individual IP addresses.

- The application must provide a means to create a hierarchical organization of ranges and individual IP addresses.

- Users must be able to add, remove, and modify entries.

- Users must be able to search for information.

- The system must be able to check whether the machines that use IP addresses are responsive.

- For all IP addresses, the system should attempt to obtain name records.

- Users must be required to enter a description for any IP reservation they make.

- It should be easy to extend the system to use DHCP.

Now that we have defined all our requirements, we can go back to them at any time during the development phase and verify that our application does exactly what it is expected to do. We will not be implementing unnecessary functionality; and by comparing the actual implementation against the set of requirements, we will always know how much progress we have made and how much work is still left to do. Going forward, we can even delegate individual tasks to other people if there is a need to do so. If at some point we discover that we have left out some important functionality, we can always go back to our list and modify it accordingly, but that will always be a conscious decision and will prevent us from implementing new functionality "as we go along" with our development.

Making Design Decisions

Once we have the requirements written down we can proceed to make some design decisions about how to implement them. Each design decision must attempt to solve some problem stated in the requirements list.

Because this is not a massive project, there is no need to create a formal design document; the same informal list of statements should suffice here.

So based on the requirements we can make the following decisions about the application development and structure:

- The application is going to be web based.

- It will run on a dedicated web server and will be accessible by anyone in the organization from their web browser.

- The application will be written in Python and will use the Django framework.

- Implementation is split into two phases: basic IP allocation and reservation functionality, and integration with DHCP. We'll tackle the first phase in this chapter and move on to DHCP integration in Chapter 4.

This is it; even as short as this list is, it ensures that we're not going to deviate from the decisions we made initially, and if we really need to make some variation, that will be recorded. The list here mainly represents the nonfunctional aspects of design; we'll get to more specific details in the following sections. Formally this should constitute a detailed design document, but I am only going to describe two things: what data our application is going to operate on, and what the application will do with that data.

Defining the Database Schema

From the requirements just stated, we know that we need to record the following data:

- The IP range and/or individual IP addresses
- The parent range that the current range belongs to
- For each record, whether it is allowed to be empty

HOW IP ADDRESSES WORK

Before proceeding, I need to explain how IP addressing works, so you will better understand some specific database layout and structure decisions we're going to make. The description provided here is somewhat simplified; if you want to learn more about IP networks and specifically IP addressing, I recommend the Wikipedia entry on CIDR:: http://en.wikipedia.org/wiki/Classless_Inter-Domain_Routing.

Briefly, each IP address has two parts: the network address part, which identifies the network this particular address belongs to, and the host address within that network. A full IP address in IPV4 is always 32 bits long. Before CIDR was introduced, there were only three available network blocks or classes: class A (8 bits to define the network address, allowing over 16 million unique host addresses), class B (16 bits for the network address, and over 65,000 unique host addresses) and class C (24 bits for the network address with 256 unique host addresses). This was very inefficient as it did not allow for fine-grained address and range allocation, so CIDR or Classless Inter-Domain Routing scheme was introduced, which allows us to use a network address of any length. In CIDR notation, each IP address is followed by the number that defines how many bits the network part comprises. So the address 192.168.1.1/24 tells us that this is an IP from a class C network whose first 24 first bits are a network address.

This image illustrates various configurations of an IP address, which I'll explain following it. The example uses a network address range that is much smaller than a default class C, so you can see how that works.

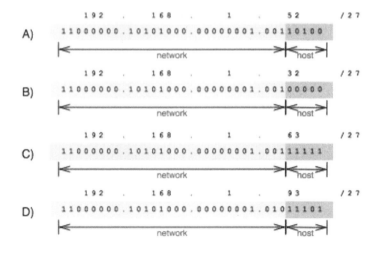

- A shows an IP number 192.168.1.52 and how it is split into two parts—network and host addresses.

- In B the host address is set to 0, thus effectively defining a network. So if you want to refer to a network range that 192.168.1.52 address belongs to, you would write it as 192.168.1.32/27.

- If we set the host address to all 1s, we will get the last possible IP address in that range, which is also called the *broadcast IP*. In the example in C it is the address 192.168.1.63.

- Finally, in D you can see how 192.168.1.93/27 falls out of the range and thus is on a different IP network range than 192.168.1.52/27; its network part is different. In fact, it is in an adjacent network range, 192.168.1.64/27

This should have shed some light on the IP numbering scheme, and you can see how understanding this helps us to define our database schema more efficiently.

When you look at how IP addresses are constructed, you might notice that larger network ranges encompass smaller ones, so a 24 bit network may contain two 25 bit networks, or four 26 bit networks and so on; this purely depends on the network infrastructure. This structure lets us easily check parent-child relationships between them.

Now we need to decide how we are going to store this information. Storing it as four separate decimal numbers (four octets) and a number of bits is an obvious choice, but as you might have guessed, that not going to help any database system. Searches such as "give me all IPs that fall into this range" would be very computation-heavy on the client side. Therefore we will convert all IP numbers to 32-bit integers and store them as such. We will also separately store the network size in bits, so calculating first and last addresses in the range will be very simple.

Let me explain this by example. If we take the previously used IP address 192.168.1.52/27 and express it in bitwise notation, we will get the following binary number: 11000000101010000000000100110100. This number can be represented as a 32-bit integer (in decimal notation): 3232235828. Now we can find its network address. We know that the network range is defined by the first 27 bits, so all we need to do is apply a binary AND operation to this number and a number that consists of 27 1s and five 0s (11111111111111111111111111100000B = 4294967264D):

3232235828D AND 4294967264D = 3232235808D

Or in binary representation:

11000000101010000000000100100000B

Compare this result with the example in the "How IP Addresses Work" sidebar and you'll see that the results match.

Finding the upper boundary is equally easy; we need to add the maximum number of available addresses to the result from our previous calculation. Because 27-bit network space leaves 5 bits to define the host address, the largest (or broadcast) address is $2^5=32$.

Therefore the network for our given address is represented as 3232235808D and the last address in it is 3232235808D + 32D = 3232235840D. From here we can easily find all addresses that are in the same network range.

Based on that information above we are ready to define our database schema, which is very simple and consists of only one table. Table 3-1 describes each column in the schema.

Table 3-1. *Fields in the Network's Definition Schema*

Column	Datatype	Comments
Record ID	Integer	The primary key, it is unique and automatically increments with each new record.
Address	Integer	A key, it must be defined and is an integer that represents a 32-bit network address.
Network size	Integer	A key, it must be defined and determines the number of bits in the network part of the address.
Description	Text	Must be defined, a description of what this IP is for.

Creating the Application Workflow

Because of the relative simplicity of this application, we don't need to use formal specification languages, such as UML (Unified Modeling Language) to define application behavior and workflow. The main goal at this stage is to write down the ideas and lay out the structure, so we can always refer to the document while implementing and confirm that the implementation is not different from what was initially designed. I find it useful to write only few statements that describe briefly what is going to happen and how information will be presented to the end user for every functional requirement in our list of requirements. *Functional requirements* are those functions our application is expected to perform. Do not confuse them with nonfunctional requirements, such as for performance or availability, which do not influence application workflow.

The Search and Display Functions

One of the common functions that we need is search functionality. Even if we do not intend to search and merely want to see all addresses and network ranges listed, this is a broad search request that asks the system to display all available information.

Since we have already decided to create a hierarchical structure for the information, the search function is going to look for either IP addresses or substrings in the description and return a list of matching entries.

The display function will display information about the current selected address (the address, number of network bits, and beginning and end addresses of the range) and also list all child entries, that is, all addresses or networks that are part of the selected entry. Clicking any of them would result in a search and display call, which would go down the tree. The display function should also provide a link to the parent entry, so users can move in both directions. If the search query is empty or matches the topmost node in the tree, there should be no option to move one level up. The topmost node in the network tree (or super network) is always 0.0.0.0/0. For every child entry, the view function should call a health check function to see if the address is responding. Also, a name-resolution procedure is called to obtain a DNS name. This information should be displayed accordingly.

If the currently selected tree node is a network address, users should be presented with a link to an Add New Entry form.

The Add Function

The Add function allows users to add new child entries. The form asks for details for the new entry, such as IP address and description, and creates a corresponding database entry. If completed successfully it should return to the previous view.

When adding a new entry, this function must confirm that the entry is valid and the provided IP address exists. We also need to check whether the address is a subset of any current parent network.

The Delete Function

The Delete option should be presented in the address list next to each entry. Clicking on it should yield a simple JavaScript confirm dialog, and if deletion is confirmed, the corresponding entry must be removed from the database.

If the entry is a network address, all child entries should be removed recursively. For example, if I have a Network A that contains Network B, which in turn contains Address C, when I delete Network A, the Network B and Address C entries should also be removed.

The Modify Function

A Modify option should be available for all entries in the current address listing. Clicking Modify should display a form similar to adding a new entry, with all fields populated with the current information.

If the entry is a network address, only the description should be changeable. If the entry is a host IP address, sanity checks (such as whether the address is not duplicated or is within the valid network range) should be performed before the database row is updated with the new settings.

The System Health Check Function

When listing all child entries, the view function should call a system health check for every address that is not a network address. The health check function performs a simple ICMP check (ping) and returns True if it has received the response or False if not.

The Name Resolution Function

As we did with the health check function, we will create another procedure, which will call name resolution for all addresses outside the network. Name resolution will perform a reverse DNS lookup and return the DNS name if available. If no DNS records are present, an empty string will be returned.

The Basic Concepts of the Django Framework

As I mentioned earlier, we are going to use the Django web framework to develop the application. I chose Django because it is a very versatile tool that greatly simplifies web application development.

What Is Django?

Briefly, Django is a high-level web development framework. Django provides tools for rapid web application development. It is designed in a way that encourages developers to write cleaner and more consistent code; at the same time it also allows them to write less code. Developers are provided with a wide variety of high-level functions that are commonly used in web development, so they do not need to rewrite something that has been already developed by someone else. Django also enforces modularity, enabling us to write a module that can be used in many different projects without or with little change.

Following are some highlights of the Django framework.

The Object-to-Relation Database Mapper

You use Python classes to define your data models, and Django automatically converts them to database tables and relations. In addition to that, Django provides a database access API directly from Python, so you rarely will need to write any SQL code yourself. Furthermore, you can switch between various database systems (MySQL, SQLite, and others) without any changes to your code.

The Administration Interface

When you define your data scheme, Django not only automatically creates the database and all required tables, it, also generates a fully functional administration interface to manage your data.

A Flexible Template System

All displayable components or views are separated into templates, so you will never find yourself generating HTML code in your program. Instead, the code and HTML design are separated. The template language is very simple to learn yet flexible and designer-friendly, so you can offload the design work to someone else.

Open Source Community Support

Last but not least on my list is the fact that Django is open source and receives support from a very active community of developers. Django is evolving quite rapidly, with several major upgrades a year, and has been on the scene for quite some time now to prove itself as mature and reliable product.

The Model/View/Controller Pattern

Before diving into its implementation details, I need to explain the most important design pattern that Django is based on: MVC or Model-View-Controller. Any web application that follows this pattern is divided into three distinctive parts: the data model, the view, and the controller.

The Data Model Component

The data model (or just model) part defines the data that the application is using or operating on. This is usually a database data structure, but it also can be data access methods and functions. In Django all data structures are defined as Python classes, and the framework automatically creates a corresponding data schema on the database.

The View Component

The view component in most web frameworks is responsible for displaying the data to the end user. It is a set of functions that generate HTML code, which is sent back to the web browser. Django goes a step further and separates what conventionally is called the view component into two distinct entities: view and template. The view in Django terms is the code that decides *which* data is going to be displayed, and the template is the component that defines *how* data is displayed.

The Controller Component

Conventionally, the controller component is responsible for retrieving data from the database (or accessing the model), operating on the data, and passing it to the view component. In Django the controller component is not so obvious or separated from the other components—the whole framework acts as a controller component. Because in Django the data model is defined as a set of Python classes, it is more intelligent and knows how to perform basic operation on the data. Views (but not templates!) also incorporate some application logic, and all that is controlled by the framework.

Installing the Django Framework

I recommend that you download and use the latest Django code release from www.djangoproject.com. As of this writing, the latest version is 1.2, and all examples and code you'll find here are based upon this version of Django. The framework already went through a major upgrade from version 0.9x to 1.x, and I do not expect too many further changes, but if you are going to use a version other than 1.2, please read the release notes for any changes that might affect the functionality. Usually there are clear instructions provided on how to adapt your code to the newer version of Django. From my experience this task is usually pretty straightforward and does not require major work from the developer.

I am going to assume that you already have Python 2.5+ installed on your system. The database engine this chapter's example will use is SQLite, so the corresponding packages and Python bindings must be installed as well. In most modern Linux distributions this comes as standard set and most likely will be present on your system. If in doubt, you can check it with the following commands:

```
$ python
Python 2.6 (r26:66714, Jun  8 2009, 16:07:26)
[GCC 4.4.0 20090506 (Red Hat 4.4.0-4)] on linux2
Type "help", "copyright", "credits" or "license" for more information.
>>> import sqlite3
>>> sqlite3.version
'2.4.1'
>>>
```

If you are using one of the non-mainstream Linux distributions, or if the packages are not installed during the initial installation, please refer to the documentation of your Linux distribution for information on installing the latest Python 2.6.x release and SQLite packages.

■**Note** As of this writing, Django 1.2 does not support the latest Python 3 version. So you will have to use either Python 2.5 or 2.6.

If your packages are already installed, download the latest Django SVN trunk to the location of your choice. We'll use /opt/local/ in this example:

```
svn co http://code.djangoproject.com/svn/django/trunk/ /opt/local/django-trunk
```

Then you need to add this location to the site-packages directory, where Python stores all its libraries, typically found at /usr/lib/python2.x/site-packages/:

```
# SITE_PKG_DIR=`python -c "from distutils.sysconfig import get_python_lib; \
             print get_python_lib()"`
# ln -s /opt/local/django-trunk/django ${SITE_PKG_DIR}/django
```

Test the Django installation by importing its module from the Python command-line interface:

```
$ python
Python 2.5.1 (r251:54863, Jul 31 2008, 23:17:43)
[GCC 4.1.3 20070929 (prerelease) (Ubuntu 4.1.2-16ubuntu2)] on linux2
Type "help", "copyright", "credits" or "license" for more information.
>>> import django
>>> django.get_version()
u'1.2 pre-alpha SVN-11468'
>>>
```

It is also useful to add the Django administration tool to your system path, so you will not need to use absolute paths every time you use this application:

```
ln -s /opt/local/django-trunk/django/bin/django-admin.py /usr/local/bin
```

The Structure of a Django Application

Django treats any web site as a *project*. In Django terms a project is a set of web applications and project- (or site-) specific configuration. You can reuse the same applications in different sites just by deploying them in new projects, and they will automatically use new settings, such as database credentials. A project may contain any number of applications. The term *project* may sound a bit confusing; I find *site* or *web site* more appropriate.

Creating a new project is simple. Assuming you have installed Django correctly, you just need to run the command django-admin.py in the directory where you want the new project directory to be created. Django's administration tool will create a simple project skeleton with basic configuration files. We will use `/var/app/vhosts/www_example_com/` as the base directory for the project that will hold all Django applications:

```
$ mkdir -p /var/app/virtual/
$ cd /var/app/virtual
$ django-admin.py startproject www_example_com
$ ls -l www_example_com
total 12
-rw-r--r-- 1 root root    0 2009-08-24 14:36 __init__.py
-rwxr-xr-x 1 root root  546 2009-08-24 14:36 manage.py
-rw-r--r-- 1 root root 2809 2009-08-24 14:36 settings.py
-rw-r--r-- 1 root root  578 2009-08-24 14:36 urls.py
```

In the project directory you'll find the following files:

manage.py: An automatically generated script that you will use to manage you project. Creating new database tables, validating modes or dumping SQL script all is done using this tool. This tool also allows you to invoke a command prompt interface for accessing data models.

settings.py: A configuration file that holds database information as well as application-specific settings.

urls.py: A configuration file that acts as a URL dispatcher. Here you define which views should respond to which URLs.

■**Note** The configuration file location is specific to your project. In this chapter our project is created in `/var/app/virtual/www_example_com/`, so assume this location when you see references to the `manage.py`, `settings.py` and `urls.py` files.

Once you have created a new project, you need to specify the database engine that Django should use. As mentioned earlier, we are going to use SQLite. To enable this, we need to make two changes in the settings.py configuration file (referenced as *the settings file* later in the chapter): specify the database engine and the absolute filename for the database file:

```
DATABASE_ENGINE = 'sqlite3'
DATABASE_NAME = '/var/app/virtual/www_example_com/database.db'
```

When project and database configuration are finished, you can create your application by issuing the following command in your project directory:

```
$ python manage.py startapp ip_addresses
$ ls -l ip_addresses/
total 12
-rw-r--r-- 1 root root  0 2009-08-24 14:55 __init__.py
-rw-r--r-- 1 root root 57 2009-08-24 14:55 models.py
```

```
-rw-r--r-- 1 root root 514 2009-08-24 14:55 tests.py
-rw-r--r-- 1 root root  26 2009-08-24 14:55 views.py
```

Just like the Django administration tool, the project management script creates a skeleton for your new application. Now that you have your project (or web site) set up and one application configured, what you need to do is define the data model, write view methods, create the URL structure, and finally design the templates. All that I will describe in more detail in the following sections, but first I still need to show you how to make your new site available for others to see.

The application will not be available for immediate use; you need to provision it in the settings file by appending it to the INSTALLED_APPS list:

```
INSTALLED_APPS = (
    'django.contrib.auth',
    'django.contrib.contenttypes',
    'django.contrib.sessions',
    'django.contrib.sites',
    'www_example_com.ip_addresses',
)
```

Using Django with Apache Web Server

Django comes with its own lightweight web server, which is written in Python. This is a great tool for quick testing or during development, but I would strongly advise against using it in a production environment. I have never encountered any problems while using it, but as the developers behind Django say, they are in the web frameworks business and are not here to develop robust web servers.

One of the most obvious choices for a web server is the Apache web service. It is widespread and used on the vast majority of web sites on the Internet. Apache installation packages are included by default on many Linux distributions. It is easy to set up Apache in such a way that it serves both static CSS stylesheets and images and dynamically generated pages (as in a Django application).

Our example will assume the following information:

- Name of the web site: www.example.com

- IP address of the server: 192.168.0.1

- Directory where Django code is stored: /var/app/vhosts/www.example.com/

- Directory where static contents are stored: /var/www/vhosts/www_example_com/

■**Note** You may wonder why the code and contents directories are separate. The reason for separation is that it's an additional security measure. As you will see later in the chapter, we will instruct the web server to call the mod_python module for all requests made to the virtual server. The exception will be all URIs starting with /static/, which will be our static content. Now, if for some reason we make a mistake in the configuration file so that mod_python is not called and the code directory is part of the DocumentRoot directive, all our Python files will become downloadable. So, always keep your code files separate and outside DocumentRoot!

Listing 3-1 shows the VirtualServer definition in the Apache web server configuration file. Depending on your Linux distribution, this section may be included directly in `httpd.conf` or as a separate configuration file alongside other VirtualServer definitions.

Listing 3-1. *The VirtualServer definition for the Django web application*

```
<VirtualHost 192.168.0.1:80>
    ServerName www.example.com
    DocumentRoot /var/www/virtual/www.example.com
    ErrorLog /var/log/apache2/www.example.com-error.log
    CustomLog /var/log/apache2/www.example.com-access.log combined
    SetHandler mod_python
    PythonHandler django.core.handlers.modpython
    PythonPath sys.path+['/var/app/virtual/']
    SetEnv DJANGO_SETTINGS_MODULE www_example_com.settings
    SetEnv PYTHON_EGG_CACHE /tmp
    <Location "/static/">
        SetHandler None
    </Location>
</VirtualHost>
```

The first section of the configuration deals with basic configuration, such as setting server name, base directory for all static contents and log file locations.

This is followed by `mod_python` configuration, where the first line tells Apache to pass execution of each web server phase to the `mod_python` module:

```
SetHandler mod_python
```

This directive is followed by the module configuration settings.

WHAT ARE APACHE HANDLERS?

Every request that is received by an Apache web server is processed in phases. For example, a request to a simple `index.html` file may involve three phases: translate the URI to the absolute location of the file; read the file and send it in an HTTP response; and finally log the event. The phases involved in each request depend on the server configuration. Each phase is processed by a handler. Apache server has only basic handlers; more complicated functions are implemented by handlers that are part of loadable modules, one of them being `mod_python`. The Python module has handlers for all possible Apache phases, but by default no handlers are called. Each phase needs to be associated specifically with the appropriate handler in the configuration file.

Django requires only one handler, the generic `PythonHandler`, which is invoked during the phase when actual content is provided and served to the requestor. The Django framework comes with its own handler and does not require the default `mod_python.publisher` handler. The following statement tells Apache to call Django's handler:

```
PythonHandler django.core.handlers.modpython
```

As you already know, every web site in Django is actually a Python module, with its configuration file. The Django handler requires that information so it can load the configuration and find appropriate functions. This information is provided in the next two lines. The first directive adds our base directory to the default Python path, and the second sets an environment variable identifying which framework will be used to get name of the module for loading.

```
PythonPath sys.path+['/var/app/virtual/']
SetEnv DJANGO_SETTINGS_MODULE ip_accounting.settings
```

You also need to identify where the temporary Python files will be stored. Make sure this directory is writable by the user, which you use to run Apache web server:

```
SetEnv PYTHON_EGG_CACHE /tmp
```

And finally let's define the exception, so that the static contents (everything that starts with /static/) will not be handed to mod_python for processing. Instead the default Apache handler will be called; it will simply serve any requested file:

```
<Location "/static/">
    SetHandler None
</Location>
```

If you were following these instructions to configure Django and have created your first application and instructed Apache to serve it accordingly, you now should be able to fire up your web browser and navigate to the Django web application. At this moment the data models are not created, and even the URL dispatcher is not configured, so Django will only serve the generic "It worked!" page, shown in Figure 3-1.

Figure 3-1. *The Standard Django application greeting page*

■**Tip** If you are seeing a "Server Error" message instead of the standard page, please check the Apache error log file that contains Python exceptions or Apache error messages, which can help you identify the cause of the error.

Implementing Basic Functionality

Once the preparation work that included Django installation and setting up the Apache web server is finished, we can proceed with the development of the web application. This process can be split into the following parts:

- Create models

- Define the URL schema

- Create views

In my experience this process is very iterative—I continue modifying my models, adding new URLs, and creating new views as I go along with the development. This approach allows us to get something working very quickly and test some functionality even if the whole application is not finished yet. Do not assume that this approach is chaotic. Quite the contrary; you only work on the elements that you identified and wrote down in the design phase. Thus, this process merely breaks down a huge piece of work into smaller and more manageable chunks that can be developed and tested separately and in stages.

Defining the Database Model

Before proceeding, please look back at Table 3-1 to review the fields we are going to use in the data model. Because Django maps objects to a relational database and does so automatically, we need to create a class definition for every concept that we are using in the application, which will be mapped to the tables in the database.

We only have one table, so let's define the class for it as shown in Listing 3-2. Add this code to your models.py file just below the default contents.

Listing 3-2. *The data class defining the application's network address model*

```
class NetworkAddress(models.Model):
    address = models.IPAddressField()
    network_size = models.PositiveIntegerField()
    description = models.CharField(max_length=400)
    parent = models.ForeignKey('self')
```

The code is really self-explanatory and straightforward. We start by defining a new class NetworkAddress, which inherits from Django's model.Model class, defined in the django.db module. So the class becomes a custom model, which Django will use to create database tables. This model class will also be used to create the database API dynamically. I will show later how this API can be used.

Within the class we define three fields by initiating class variables with appropriate objects from the models class. Django provides many different types of fields, and Table 3-2 lists the most-used types.

Table 3-2. *Commonly Used Django Field Types*

Field Class Name	Description
BooleanField	This field accepts only `True` or `False` values, except when it's used with a MySQL database, in which case the field stores values `1` or `0` accordingly. Keep that in mind when testing for the field value.
CharField	Use this field to store strings. It requires a `max_length` argument to set the maximum length of the string it can store. Do not use this field to store large amounts of text; use `TextField` instead.
DateField	Stores the date as an instance of the Python `datetime.date` class. This field class accepts two optional parameters: `auto_now`, which if set to `True` sets the field value to the current date every time the object is saved; and `auto_now_add`, which if set to `True` sets the field value to the current date only when created for the first time. Both parameters forces Django to use the current date, and this cannot be overridden.
DateTimeField	Stores the date and time as a Python `datetime.datetime` instance. Uses same optional parameters as DateField.
DecimalField	Used to store fixed-precision decimal numbers. Requires two arguments: `max_digits`, which sets the maximum number of digits in the number, and `decimal_places`, which sets the number of decimal places.
EmailField	Similar to `CharField` but also performs a check for a valid email address.
FileField	Used to store uploaded files. Note that files are stored not in the database but locally on a file system. This field requires an argument `path_to`, which points to a relative to `MEDIA_ROOT` directory. You can use `strftime` variables to construct pathnames and filenames depending on the current date and time. `MEDIA_ROOT` must be set in the settings file for the current project.
FloatField	Stores floating-point numbers.
ImageField	Very similar to `FileField`, but additionally performs a check that the file is a valid image. Also has two optional arguments: `height_field` and `width_field`, which store names of model class variables and will be automatically populated depending on the uploaded image dimensions. Using this field type requires the Python Imaging Library (PIL).
IntegerField	Stores integer values.
PositiveIntegerField	Stores integer values but allows only positive integers.
NullBooleanField	Stores `True` and `False` just like `BooleanField`, but also accepts `None`. Useful where a combination of Yes/No/Undefined choices is required.

Field Class Name	Description
SlugField	Stores text like CharField, but allows only alphanumeric characters, underscores, and hyphens. Useful for storing URLs (without the domain part!). The max_length argument defaults to 50 but can be overridden.
TextField	Used to store large blocks of text.
TimeField	Stores the time as a Python datetime.time instance. Accepts the same optional arguments as DateField.
URLField	Used to store URLs including the domain name. Has an optional parameter verify_exists, which checks that the URL is valid, actually loads, and does not return 404 or any other error.
XMLField	A TextField, which additionally checks whether the text is valid XML and corresponds to the XML schema as defined by RELAX NG (www.relaxng.org). Requires the argument schema_path, which must point to a valid schema definition file.

To create a database table you simply use the manage.py utility with the option syncdb. When you run it for the first time, it will also create tables for other applications listed in the settings file (authentication, Django content type, and session and site management). The built-in authentication application requires an administrator account, so it will ask you few more questions:

```
$ python manage.py syncdb
Creating table auth_permission
Creating table auth_group
Creating table auth_user
Creating table auth_message
Creating table django_content_type
Creating table django_session
Creating table django_site
Creating table ip_addresses_networkaddress

You just installed Django's auth system, which means you don't have any superusers
defined.
Would you like to create one now? (yes/no): yes
Username (Leave blank to use 'rytis'):
E-mail address: rytis@example.com
Password:
Password (again):
Superuser created successfully.
Installing index for auth.Permission model
Installing index for auth.Message model
$
```

This command-line dialog has successfully created all necessary tables in the database. To see exactly how your table has been structured in the database, use the following command:

```
$ python manage.py sql ip_addresses
BEGIN;
CREATE TABLE "ip_addresses_networkaddress" (
    "id" integer NOT NULL PRIMARY KEY,
    "address" char(15) NOT NULL,
    "network_size" integer unsigned NOT NULL,
    "description" varchar(400) NOT NULL
)
;
COMMIT;
$
```

As you can see, Django uses variable names as the names for the fields in the table, and the table name is constructed from application and model class names. This is handy, because it does provide some degree of namespacing, so you don't need to worry that your class name clashes with a class name of another application.

URL Configuration

You will find yourself changing URL configuration quite often in the Django development [AU: OK?]process, as you will be adding new views and functions. In order not to leave the process uncontrolled, you need to set out some basic rules for how you will define new URLs. Although Django gives you full control over the process, be nice to others and especially to yourself by choosing a sensible URL structure and naming convention.

There are no defined rules or guidelines for how to create URLs. And as a system administrator you will probably not be developing web systems available to large audiences, so you can be more relaxed in the way you organize them. However, I would suggest some guidelines that I find quite useful to follow:

- Always start with the name of the application. In the IP address example, all URLs (including the domain name) will be http://www.example.com/ip_address/[...]. If we ever want to use another application in our web site, we will not have to worry about the URL names overlapping. For example, a view function is quite common. If we had not put the application name in front, and we had two applications A and B, we would have an issue if they both wanted to use the URL /view/.

- Put the model name after the application name. If you need a more specific subset of objects of the same type, add the selection criteria after the model name. When possible, avoid using object IDs! So continuing with the example, we would have ip_addresses/ networkaddress/, which lists all top-level networks. If we navigated to /ip_addresses/networkaddress/109.168.0.0/, it would return us either a list of addresses in that particular network, or the details of a specific IP address if that was a host address.

- If you need to operate on any of the objects, add the operation verb after the specific object name. So if we wanted to have a link to the delete function for a network address, we would use /ip_addresses/networkaddress/192.168.0.1/delete.

These guidelines can be summarized by the following example URL:

```
http://www.example.com/<application>/<model>/<object>/<action>/
```

The URL mapping is defined in the `urls.py` module, which has default settings as shown in Listing 3-3.

Listing 3-3. *Default contents of the site-wide urls.py file*

```python
from django.conf.urls.defaults import *

# Uncomment the next two lines to enable the admin:
# from django.contrib import admin
# admin.autodiscover()

urlpatterns = patterns('',
    # Example:
    # (r'^www_example_com/', include('www_example_com.foo.urls')),

    # Uncomment the admin/doc line below and add 'django.contrib.admindocs'
    # to INSTALLED_APPS to enable admin documentation:
    # (r'^admin/doc/', include('django.contrib.admindocs.urls')),

    # Uncomment the next line to enable the admin:
    # (r'^admin/', include(admin.site.urls)),
)
```

The structure of this file is very simple and straightforward. The most important part is the `urlpatterns` variable, which is a list of URL tuples. Each entry (tuple) has three parts:

```
(<regular expression>, <callback function>, <dictionary (optional)>)
```

Here's what happens when the user requests a page from a Django web application: the request is sent to an Apache web server, which in turn will invoke its Django handler. The Django framework will go through all entries in the `urlpatterns` and attempt to match each regular expression against the URL that has been requested. When the match is found, Django will then call a callback function that is coupled with the regular expression. It will pass an `HttpRequest` object (I will discuss this in the views section) and optionally a list of captured parameters from the URL.

I strongly recommend that you do not define any application-specific URL rules in the main `urls.py` file; use configuration local to the application you are developing. This way you decouple application URLs from the web site, which allows you to reuse the same application in different projects. Let me explain how this works. Decoupling is fairly simple; all you need to do is define your application-specific URLs in the application module and reference this file in all requests that start with the name of your application.

So in our example, we would have the following entries in the main project `urls.py`:

```
urlpatterns = ('',
    [...]
    (r'^ip_addresses/', include('www_example_com.ip_addresses.urls')),
    [...]
)
```

whereas application specific configuration file, ip_addresses/urls.py, contains:

```
urlpatterns = patterns('',
    [...]
)
```

As you can see, the main urls.py will capture all URLs that begin with ip_addresses/, and the remainder of the URL is sent to ip_addresses/urls.py for further processing.

Using the Management Interface

We could now go ahead and create some views and forms to display the records, add and remove them, but before we do that, I'd like to show you how to enable the Django administration interface. This is a really handy tool that provides immediate access to your data, with full and rich functionality that allows you to add, remove, modify, search, and filter records stored in the database.

It is also very useful during the development phase, letting you add new records and create display views before you create forms to add new records.

Enabling the Management Interface

There is very little you need to do to enable the administration interface: add it to the applications list in the site configuration, enable URL rules, and finally configure Apache to serve static content for the interface (mostly CSS and JS scripts).

Modify the INSTALLED_APPS list in the settings.py module so that it contains the administration package:

```
INSTALLED_APPS = (
    'django.contrib.auth',
    'django.contrib.contenttypes',
    'django.contrib.sessions',
    'django.contrib.sites',
    'django.contrib.admin',
    'www_example_com.ip_addresses',
)
```

Once you've done that, you need to rerun the syncdb command so that new tables for the administration application are created in the database:

```
$ python manage.py syncdb
Creating table django_admin_log
Installing index for admin.LogEntry model
$
```

93

Uncomment all lines in the `urls.py` module that are related to the administration plug-in. Make sure your `urls.py` looks like Listing 3-4.

Listing 3-4. *Enabling the administration interface in the urls.py module*

```
from django.conf.urls.defaults import *

# Uncomment the next two lines to enable the admin:
from django.contrib import admin
admin.autodiscover()

urlpatterns = patterns('',
    # Uncomment the next line to enable the admin:
    (r'^admin/', include(admin.site.urls)),
    # ip_addresses application
    (r'^ip_addresses/', include('www_example_com.ip_addresses.urls')),
)
```

Create a link in the DocumentRoot directory, so that the contents of `/opt/local/django-trunk/django/contrib/admin/media` are served by Apache from the URL `www.example.com/static/admin`:

```
$ ln -s /usr/share/django/django/contrib/admin/media \
/var/www/virtual/www.example.com/static/admin
```

Once you have done all this preparation work, you should be able to navigate to `www.example.com/admin` and see the administration interface login page, shown in Figure 3-2.

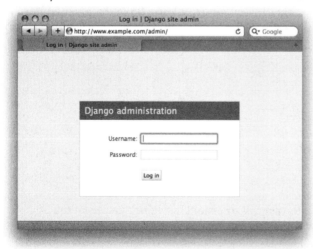

Figure 3-2. *Django administration login page*

You can log in with the administrator's account you created earlier, when you first ran `syncdb`. Once you are logged on, you will be presented with the basic user and site management options shown in Figure 3-3.

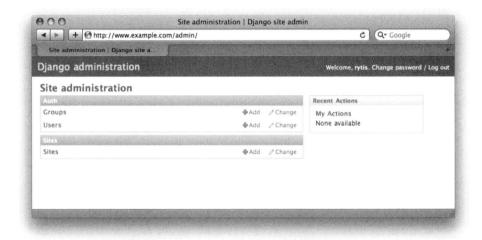

Figure 3-3. *The default view of the Django administration interface*

Allowing the Administration Plug-in to Manage New Models

As you may have noticed, the Django administration interface does not present any options to manage the `NetworkAddress` model yet. This is because it has not found any instructions to do so. Adding any data model class to the administration interface is very easy; all you need to do is create a new Python module in your application directory, `admin.py`, containing the code shown in Listing 3-5.

Listing 3-5. *Adding NetworkAddress class to the administration interface*

```
from www_example_com.ip_addresses.models import NetworkAddress
from django.contrib import admin

class NetworkAddressAdmin(admin.ModelAdmin):
    pass

admin.site.register(NetworkAddress, NetworkAddressAdmin)
```

In this example, we first import the `NetworkAddress` class and the `admin` module from the standard Django package. Then we define an administration class for every model that we want to put under administration module control. The naming convention for the administration classes is `<Model class name>Admin`. This class must inherit from the `admin.ModelAdmin` class, which defines default behavior for the model management interface.

For our simple model there is no need to tweak the default behavior. It does allow for basic functionality such as view/add/delete/modify, and because we are going to create our own interface with additional functionality (such as displaying information in hierarchical order), we do not require anything extra from the Django admin module.

Play around a bit with the automatically generated interface; try adding new entries and modifying existing ones. Also try entering invalid information, such as a malformed IP address, and check how the Django admin interface reacts to the error. You will notice that invalid IP addresses are not accepted; however, there is no logic that would check whether the network size is within the applicable range: 1 – 32. As of this writing, only some of the basic field types have an option to define validation rules. With the 1.2 release of Django, it is expected that validation will be implemented at the model level. So far we will have to use validation at the Form level, which I will describe later.

Viewing Records

Let's start with the simplest view, whose purpose is to represent information about all networks that are defined in the database. For now you will have to use the administration interface, which you created earlier, to add new networks and define relations.

First of all we need to define the URL mapping rules, so the requests are redirected to the appropriate view function:

```
urlpatterns = patterns('www_example_com.ip_addresses.views',
    (r'^networkaddress/$', 'display'),
    (r'^networkaddress/(?P<address>\d{1,3}\.\d{1,3}\.\d{1,3}\.\d{1,3}\/\d{1,2})/$',
     'display'),
)
```

The first rule matches the URL /ip_address/networkaddress/ and calls the display function from the views module. The second rule searches for URLs that look like /ip_address/networkaddress/a.b.c.d/x/. It also calls the display function, but this time it passes the keyword argument address, which is initialized with the string a.b.c.d/x.

Let's quickly test whether this works by defining a simplified version of the view. All we want to know at this stage is whether our two rules work as expected. Listing 3-6 is an example of a simple views.py file that will test our URLs.

Listing 3-6. *A simple view to test the URL dispatcher rules*

```
from www_example_com.ip_addresses.models import *
from django.http import HttpResponse

def display(request, address=None):
    if not address:
        msg = "Top of the address tree"
    else:
        msg = "Top level address: %s" % address
    return HttpResponse(msg)
```

What happens here is pretty straightforward. We import the model class and also the HttpResponse class. The Django framework expects either an instance of HttpResponse or an exception raised as a result from any view function that it calls. Obviously, the view function doesn't do much at this point; it will only display the IP address from the URL or tell you that it's at the top of the address tree if no IP is found in the URL. This is a good technique to sort out your URL mapping regular expressions before you start creating more complex views. When debugging the view functionality, you need to know that your mappings are functioning as expected.

■**Note** The reason for including both the IP address and the network size is that only the pair creates a unique object. If we used only the IP address, in most cases it might be ambiguous. For example, 192.168.0.0 (/24) and 192.168.0.0 (/25) are not the same network, although their IP addresses are the same.

Now, before proceeding let's create some entries in the database. You will have to use the Django administration interface as there are no custom forms for entering the data. Table 3-3 contains sample data you can use to create similar entries and compare the results in this book with what you get as you go along with the implementation.

Table 3-3. *A Sample IP Network and Address Dataset*

Address	Network size	Parent (network)	Description
192.168.0.0	24	none	First top-level network
192.168.1.0	24	none	Second top-level network
192.168.0.0	25	192.168.0.0/25	Subnet 1-1
192.168.0.128	25	192.168.0.0/25	Subnet 1-2
192.168.1.0	26	192.168.1.0/26	Subnet 2-1
192.168.1.64	26	192.168.1.0/26	Subnet 2-2
192.168.1.128	26	192.168.1.0/26	Subnet 2-3
192.168.1.192	26	192.168.1.0/26	Subnet 2-4
192.168.0.1	32	192.168.0.0/25	IP 1 in Subnet 1-1
192.168.0.2	32	192.168.0.0/25	IP 2 in Subnet 1-1
192.168.0.129	32	192.168.0.128/25	IP 1 in Subnet 1-2
192.168.0.130	32	192.168.0.128/25	IP 2 in Subnet 1-2
192.168.1.1	32	192.168.1.0/26	IP 1 in Subnet 2-1
192.168.1.2	32	192.168.1.0/26	IP 2 in Subnet 2-1
192.168.1.65	32	192.168.1.64/26	IP 1 in Subnet 2-2
192.168.1.66	32	192.168.1.64/26	IP 2 in Subnet 2-2

Address	Network size	Parent (network)	Description
192.168.1.129	32	192.168.1.128/26	IP 1 in Subnet 2-3
192.168.1.130	32	192.168.1.128/26	IP 2 in Subnet 2-3
192.168.1.193	32	192.168.1.192/26	IP 1 in Subnet 2-4
192.168.1.194	32	192.168.1.192/26	IP 2 in Subnet 2-4

This might seem to be a lot to add manually. If you feel like creating all records manually, that's fine, but Django has another feature: you can provide initial data as a fixture file. Version 1.1 of Django understands three formats: XML, YAML, and JSON. This is very useful during the development and test phases; you create initial data once, and then re-create your database whenever you need to with the exact set of data. Listing 3-7 shows part of the sample fixtures file we will use to initialize the database. I've chosen to use JSON here, mostly because of its simplicity, readability, and supportability.

Listing 3-7. *An excerpt from the sample_data.json file used to load initial data*

```
[
...
    {
        "model":  "ip_addresses.networkaddress",
        "pk": 1,
        "fields": {
            "address":  "192.168.0.0",
            "network_size": 24,
            "description": "First top level network"
        }
    },
...
    {
        "model":  "ip_addresses.networkaddress",
        "pk": 3,
        "fields": {
            "address":  "192.168.0.0",
            "network_size": 25,
            "description": "Subnet 1-1",
            "parent": 1
        }
    },
...
]
```

The structure of the file is pretty self-explanatory. Each record starts by defining the model class and is followed by the primary key, which is an integer unless you have explicitly redefined it. Finally, all class fields are listed in "key":"value" pairs in the "fields" section. If there are any relationships between records, they are defined by using primary key values, just as in this example, Subnet 1-1 has a parent a parent and references it by setting "parent" to value of 1 (the primary key of the parent record). If the field is optional, you can just skip it. Once you have created the file, load the data with the following command:

```
$ python manage.py loaddata sample_data.json
Installing json fixture 'sample_data' from absolute path.
Installed 20 object(s) from 1 fixture(s)
$
```

Using Templates

Templates play a very important role in the Django framework model. It is the templates that allow developers to separate application logic from presentation. Again, models define data structures, view functions are responsible for data queries and filtering, and finally templates define how data is represented to the end user.

Django comes with a very flexible and sophisticated template language. Let's look at how to use templates with the data obtained by the view functions. First we need to define a view that will query the database and get the information we will then present to the users. Listing 3-8 shows the new display function.

Listing 3-8. *A view function that uses a template to present data*

```
def display(request, address=None):
    if not address:
        parent = None
    else:
        ip, net_size = address.split('/')
        parent = NetworkAddress.objects.get(address=ip, network_size=int(net_size))
    addr_list = NetworkAddress.objects.filter(parent=parent)
    return render_to_response('display.html',
                              {'parent': parent, 'addresses_list': addr_list})
```

As you already know, Django's URL dispatcher calls the display function with either no initial IP address (when users request top-of-the-tree listing) or the initial IP address (a request to display the contents of a subnet). If the address field is empty we will display all tree nodes that have no parents. If the address field is not empty, we need to get the list of tree nodes that have a parent set to the given address. The results are stored in addr_list and are passed to the template.

There are two entities that need to be displayed: information about the current tree node and a list of its children. So we have to pass both as variables to the template rendering procedure. In the example we use a shortcut function called render_to_response, which accepts two parameters: the name of the template file and a dictionary of variables the template will use to render HTML output.

You can import the render_to_response shortcut with the following import statement:

```
from django.shortcuts import render_to_response
```

As you can see, we specify the template name without any preceding directory paths, so how does Django know where to look for the template? By default the following template loaders are enabled in the settings.py configuration file:

```
TEMPLATE_LOADERS = (
                    'django.template.loaders.filesystem.load_template_source',
                    'django.template.loaders.app_directories.load_template_source',
)
```

We are using the functionality provided by the app_directories loader. This loader looks for templates stored in the application directory under templates/ subdirectory. Storing templates with the application is extremely useful, because this allows developers to distribute a set of default templates with each application. So going back to our example, we need to create a subdirectory called templates in the application directory ip_addresses. We then create the template shown in Listing 3-9, which takes care of displaying information passed to it by the display view function.

Listing 3-9. *A template for the display view*

```
{% if parent %}
<h1>Current address: {{ parent.address }}/{{ parent.network_size }}</h1>
<h2><a href="../../{% if parent.parent %}{{ parent.parent.address }}/{{↵
 parent.parent.network_size }}/{% endif %}">Go back</a></h2>
{% else %}
<h1>At the top of the networks tree</h1>
{% endif %}

{% if addresses_list %}
    <ul>
    {% for address in addresses_list %}
        <li><a href="{% if parent %}../../{% endif %}{{ address.address }}/{{↵
 address.network_size }}{% ifequal address.network_size 32 %}/modify/{% endifequal
%}">{{↵
 address.address }}/{{ address.network_size }}
            </a>
             {% ifequal address.network_size 32 %}(host){% else %}(network){%
endifequal %}
             {{ address.description }}
             (<a href="{% if parent %}../../{% endif %}
                        {{ address.address }}/{{ address.network_size
}}/delete/">delete</a> |
             <a href="{% if parent %}../../{% endif %}
                        {{ address.address }}/{{ address.network_size
}}/modify/">modify</a>)
        </li>
    {% endfor %}
    </ul>
{% else %}
{% ifequal parent.network_size 32 %}
This is a node IP
```

```
{% else %}
No addresses or subnets in this range
{% endifequal %}
{% endif %}
<h2><a href="add/">Add new subnet or node IP</a></h2>
```

You might have already guessed that template language tokens are surrounded by {% ... %} or {{ ... }}. The difference between these two is that the former is used to surround command and process control statements, such as comparison and validation operators, while the latter is used to indicate that the contents of a variable need to be displayed at the specified location. All variables follow the same Python convention when referencing object properties. For example, in the template parent is an instance of the NetworkAddress model class, and as such parent has the property address. To display that variable in the template, we need to reference it as parent.address.

Table 3-4 lists the basic command structures that you are going to find yourself using quite often.

Table 3-4. *The Most Common Elements of the Django Templating Language*

Structure	Description
{% if <variable> %} {% else %} {% endif %}	Most commonly used to test whether the variable is defined and the contents are not empty. Depending on the result, you can either display the value of the variable or provide an informational message advising that the value is not found.
{% for <variable> in <list> %} {% endfor %}	Loops through all items in <list> and assigns individual list items to <variable>, which you can use in a for construct.
{% ifequal <variable1> <variable2> %} {% else %} {% endifequal %}	Compares two variables <variable1> and <variable2> and processes one of the two template blocks depending on the result.
{% comment %} {% endcomment %}	Everything between these two operators is ignored.

As you can see from the template, I've already added URL links to delete, modify and add records. All that is possible even at this stage, simply because we initially set the requirements and at any stage of the development process we precisely know what needs to be done. In this instance, the application is not ready yet to perform these actions, but we need to do the layout design and implement that within the template. This is especially useful if you need to hand over the template to somebody else, as they wouldn't have to guess what actions and what links you might require and create them even if the functionality has yet to be implemented.

Figure 3-4 shows how the application web page looks when you have navigated to one of the precreated network addresses.

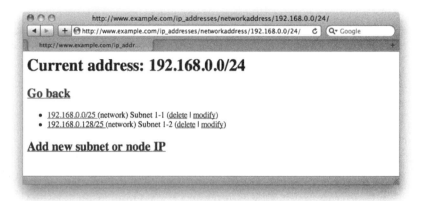

Figure 3-4. *A listing of the network addresses*

Deleting Records

We already have a link to the delete function listed with every IP address, and as you know its base URL is the same as for the listing function, but it also has /delete/ appended to it. So for example here is the delete URL for 192.168.0.0/25 network:

```
http://www.example.com/ip_addresses/networkaddress/192.168.0.0/25/delete/
```

First we need to "teach" Django so it recognizes this URL and call the delete function (or view). Let's do this by adding the following URL rule to the urls.py file:

```
(r'^networkaddress/(?P<address>\d{1,3}\.\d{1,3}\.\d{1,3}\.\d{1,3}\/\d{1,2})/↵
delete/$',

'delete'),
```

Listing 3-10 shows the delete function the Django framework will call whenever it encounters a URL that matches this rule.

Listing 3-10. *The Delete view*

```
def delete(request, address=None):
    ip, net_size = address.split('/')
    parent = NetworkAddress.objects.get(address=ip,
                                         network_size=int(net_size)).parent
    NetworkAddress.objects.get(address=ip, network_size=int(net_size)).delete()
    redirect_to = '../../../'
    if parent:
        redirect_to += '%s/%s/' % (parent.address, int(parent.network_size))
    return HttpResponseRedirect(redirect_to)
```

In this example the address variable is always going to contain an IP address in the format x.x.x.x/y, where x.x.x.x is the IP address and y is the number of network bits. We don't store address information in this format, so we have to split it into two parts before we can use it to find the required record.

Before we delete the object, let's figure out its parent object by running the following object get method:

```
parent = NetworkAddress.objects.get(address=ip, network_size=int(net_size)).parent
```

Once we have the object[Au: OK? CE], let's simply call the delete() method, which is available for any Django model object. You may wonder what happens to objects that are children of the tree node that we just deleted. The Django framework is intelligent enough to run a recursive SQL query that will follow the foreign keys and delete all relevant objects down the tree.

After object deletion is finished, we redirect to the current view by returning the HttpResponseRedirect object with the path as its initialization parameter.

■**Tip** Notice how we use relative paths in the redirect URL? We do this because we don't know what the project or even the application is going to be called if someone reuses the code. What we do know is the URL structure, and so we can work out where we need to redirect and use relative paths. Try to avoid using absolute paths and embedding application names in the generated URLs.

Adding New Records

This is the functionality that requires user input. Since our model is fairly simple, there are only a few fields to fill in, specifically the IP address, network size, and description. A parent tree node will be automatically assigned depending on where the user is when clicking the Add link. For example, if the user navigates to http://www.example.com/ip_addresses/networkaddress/192.168.1.0/24/ and clicks an Add New IP link, the new record will automatically get 192.168.0.1/24 as a parent.

There are two ways of handling data input in Django: the hard way and the Django way. If we were to choose the hard way, we would need to define the form in the template, process request HTTP POST variables manually, perform validation and do data type conversion. Or we can choose to use Django form objects and widgets, which will do all that for us automatically.

So, first we need to define a form model class that will be used to generate HTML form widget. We do this by defining in models.py the class shown in Listing 3-11.

Listing 3-11. *The address add form class*

```
from django.forms import import ModelForm

[...]

class NetworkAddressAddForm(ModelForm):
    class Meta:
        model = NetworkAddress
        exclude = ('parent', )
```

What happens here is that we define a form class which uses a data model class as a prototype. In other words, this tells Django to generate a form to accept data that is defined in the data model. We do have a choice of defining any arbitrary form class, with any set of fields, but in this example all we need is the three fields from our data model. Hold on, we have four fields: one is the parent object. But we don't want users to be able to choose the parent object, simply because it's already known at the time of creation. Another reason is that with large databases, the parent list might become too large to handle. Therefore we have to use the exclude list that indicates what fields do not need to show up in the form.

The second step is to define the form handling the view. This view is slightly different from the normal view function that simply displays data, because it can be called in two different ways: as an HTTP GET, which means the user just navigated to the form page, or as an HTTP POST, which means the user submitted form data.

In the case of HTTP GET, we simply display the empty form. If we receive an HTTP POST, we will have to check whether the form is valid. If the form data is valid, we have to call the form's save() function, which will create a new object in the database. If the form is not valid, it will be displayed again, with the field entries from the request already filled in and the error message explaining what was wrong. How do we validate the form? Very simply—by calling another form method: is_valid(), shown in Listing 3-12. And we don't even need to think about the error messages; these are also automatically created depending on the data type of the model.

Listing 3-12. *The view method for the add function*

```
def add(request, address=None):
    if request.method == 'POST':
        parent = None
        if address:
            ip, net_size = address.split('/')
            parent = NetworkAddress.objects.get(address=ip,
                                                network_size=int(net_size))
        new_address = NetworkAddress(parent=parent)
        form = NetworkAddressAddForm(request.POST, instance=new_address)
        if form.is_valid():
            form.save()
            return HttpResponseRedirect("..")
    else:
        form = NetworkAddressAddForm()
    return render_to_response('add.html', {'form': form,})
```

In this view we also perform the additional step of creating a new object. Usually creating a new form from POST data looks like this:

```
form = NetworkAddressAddForm(request.POST)
```

But remember, in our form there is no parent field, and we need to derive it from the address part in the URL. So we need to find the parent object myself and assign it to the new object:

```
new_address = NetworkAddress(parent=parent)
form = NetworkAddressAddForm(request.POST, instance=new_address)
```

Calling the form initialization function with an instance argument forces Django to use the object assigned to it instead of creating a new one.

You can see that we use template `add.html` and pass the form object to it. Listing 3-13 shows what the template looks like.

Listing 3-13. *The add form template*

```
<form action="." method="POST">
{{ form.as_p }}
<input type="submit" value="Add" />
</form>
```

Yes, it is that short, but it does a lot. First, it will render an HTML form, with appropriate fields and a submit button. If submitted form data was not valid, it will also display error messages. The presentation (shown in Figure 3-5) is fully customizable, but for the sake of simplicity we just use `.as_p` tag, so the fields will be displayed within <p> tags for better alignment.

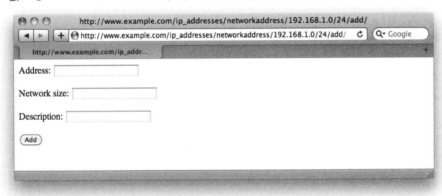

Figure 3-5. *Form widget on HTML page*

Modifying Existing Records

The form and view for object modification are very similar to the add form and view. The only difference is that there will be even fewer fields that users are allowed to edit. Realistically, if the user decides to change an IP, he or she needs to delete the record and recreate it within another network. So we will only allow users to change the description of a record.

Therefore the only field in our form object is the description, as shown in Listing 3-14.

Listing 3-14. *The Modify form class*

```
class NetworkAddressModifyForm(ModelForm):
    class Meta:
        model = NetworkAddress
        fields = ('description',)
```

As you can see, instead of excluding fields we use the `fields` list, which tells Django which fields to include; all other fields are ignored.

The view method is very similar to the one that is used to add new records. In fact everything is the same, with one exception: upon first view the form is prepopulated with the data from the database, because users are changing the existing data instead of creating new records. Saving changes is the same, because Django works out that the record is already present and updates it, instead of adding a new one. As you can see from Listing 3-15, even the template is reused without any changes.

Listing 3-15. *The Modify view method*

```
def modify(request, address=None):
    if request.method == 'POST':
        # submitting changes
        ip, net_size = address.split('/')
        address_obj = NetworkAddress.objects.get(address=ip,
                                             network_size=int(net_size))
        form = NetworkAddressModifyForm(request.POST, instance=address_obj)
        if form.is_valid():
            form.save()
            return HttpResponseRedirect("..")
    else:
        # first time display
        ip, net_size = address.split('/')
        address_obj = NetworkAddress.objects.get(address=ip,
                                             network_size=int(net_size))
        form = NetworkAddressModifyForm(initial={ 'description':
                                             address_obj.description, })
    return render_to_response('add.html', {'form': form,})
```

Summary

In this chapter, you have learned how to design your application and go from the requirement gathering and specification through design to the actual implementation. You learned how to use the Django framework for rapid web application development.

- Always start with the requirements specification. This will act as a reference point and simplify testing. It also helps managing user expectations.

- Design the data model first and make sure the design is in line with requirements.

- Decouple the application from the project (or web site), so it can be reused multiple times.

## CHAPTER 4

Integrating the IP Address Application with DHCP

In the previous chapter, we implemented a simple IP accounting application that allows users to keep track of their IP address estate. I described the full lifecycle of the application, from requirements gathering through the design phase and finally the implementation. The emphasis was on the importance of the requirements and design phases as these allow you as a developer to validate your implementation.

You may have noticed that, although we implemented most of the initial requirements, we did not get all of them! I deliberately left out a few, such as the search function, DNS resolution, and active check. I did that primarily to demonstrate how easy is to validate your implementation and show what's missing in it, but also simply to keep the chapter to a manageable size and not to overwhelm you with information.

So, in this chapter we are going to implement the missing components and extend the original design with new functionality by adding support for DHCP service.

Extending the Design and Requirements

I mentioned "support for DHCP" as a requirement in the previous chapter, but what do we really want from it? Let's take a look at how DHCP is used in a typical organization. I will assume the ISC DHCP service, which is widely available with most Linux distributions.

When assigning addresses on a subnet, we have the following options:

- Assign the IP addresses statically, in which case we configure each device with its own IP address.

- Assign the IP addresses dynamically, depending on a set of rules using the DHCP service.

■ **Tip** Before proceeding with this chapter, you may want to install the ISC DHCP server package. You can do that by using the package manager available with your Linux distribution (on Red Hat Linux it can be done with the command `yum install dhcp`). Alternatively, you can download it from the official ISC DHCP website at `http://www.isc.org/software/dhcp`.

Let's quickly recap what the DHCP can do and how it is configured. The ISC DHCP allows us to define very complicated sets of rules. The simplest set would contain no rule at all, in which case any request for an IP would be granted and a unique address from available pool would be assigned, assuming there are free IPs available in the address pool.

One rule commonly used is to assign IP addresses depending on a hardware MAC address. This method allows you to assign the same IP address always to the same machine, but does not require it to be configured locally on the server. We can use the DHCP group directive to configure such a host:

```
group {
    ...
    host host001 {
        hardware ethernet 00:11:22:33:44:55;
        fixed-address 192.168.0.1;
    }
    ...
}
```

A more advanced use of client grouping is DHCP client class separation, where clients are grouped into classes that satisfy some criteria. The ISC DHCP server provides many options for such separation. For example, you can use various DHCP request fields (or even parts of them) to group the nodes—such as using part of the DHCP hostname to identify what is sending the request. You can see what DHCP options are available by reading the UNIX manual page for dhcp-options. The following example uses the DHCP option vendor-class-identifier to group all Sun Ultra 5 machines into one class:

```
class "sun-ultra-5" {
    match if option vendor-class-identifier "SUNW.Ultra-5_10";
}
```

For a second example, this code matches the beginning of a DHCP hostname and puts into a separate class if it starts with "server":

```
class "server" {
    match if substring (option hostname, 0, 6) = "server";
}
```

For the sake of simplicity, let's assume that all subnets are on the same physical network on the DHCP server, which means we will be using the shared-network directive when defining new subnets.

As you can see, the simple process of investigation is gradually evolving into making certain design decisions. This blurring of tasks should be avoided whenever possible, and I've demonstrated it here just to show how easy is to get carried away and amend your design to accommodate limitations (or features) of any particular product.

So first of all, let's ignore everything we know about the particular DHCP server product and list all the things we want it to do. Our imaginary organization has multiple networks that are subdivided into smaller subnets, which in turn can contain even smaller subnets. Usually, if a subnet is subdivided into smaller networks, it rarely contains IP addresses for physical (or virtual) hosts. The only IPs that will be present in such a network are IP addresses of the networking devices, such as routers, switches, and load balancers—none of which get their IPs from DHCP. Therefore, we will only create DHCP-managed subnets that are right at the bottom of the subnet tree and are not subdivided into smaller networks.

Within the DHCP-managed network, we want to have the following:

- Statically assigned addresses that are completely out of DHCP server control. In other words, the DHCP server should have no knowledge about that range and should not be configured to offer any address from that range. Each IP address is configured manually on the device that uses it.

- Static addresses assigned by the DHCP server. For example, we want IP addresses to be offered depending on the requestor's MAC address.

- IP addresses assigned depending on properties of the client, such as hardware vendor, DHCP parameter values, and so on. Since we do know how many of these IPs we will need, we have to be able to assign a predefined range of addresses. We also don't want to be limited to just a set of DHCP options; we should have full control over all available options.

- IP addresses assigned to all other clients. As in the previous requirement, we need to be able to specify a range of IPs to use here.

As you can see, the listed requirements are very similar to the ones set out earlier, but they do not contain any references to any particular implementation. This approach has two major advantages: you are free to choose any product you think is the best fit for the purpose, and you can outsource implementation to other teams. As long as the result satisfies the requirements, we don't really care about technical implementation details. Also, having this list in hand helps you quickly identify and select the appropriate product.

In addition to the network management and IP allocation requirements, we have some operational ones:

- We need the configuration to be generated, but not immediately applied, so it can be reviewed and changes applied manually.

- We do not require manual changes made to the configuration file to be propagated back to the application database. For example, if we manually add a few hosts into the DHCP configuration, we do not need the application to update the database entries accordingly.

- At this stage we do not want the application to control the DHCP service; this will be done manually using standard OS commands.

Now that we have identified what is required, we can start making basic design decisions:

- We will use ISC DHCP, because it allows us to implement all listed requirements.

- We will use the same web application framework and language, because this project is an extension of another project.

- The configuration file will be generated by the same web application (that is, there are no external tools that read from the database and generate a configuration file).

Just as in the previous example, we now need to do two things: define the extended data model and create an application workflow.

Extending the Database Schema

This time the data model is a lot more complicated than it was when we just had to collect information about the networks and IP addresses. Now we need to store the DHCP server's view of the network topology, consisting of all classification rules and address ranges within each DHCP subnet. Therefore, we are going to break this down into several iterations of defining the DB model class, writing the view functions, and testing. This gradual approach is easier to tackle and we can catch errors more easily.

At this time we have only identified that we are going to have the following data model classes:

- The DHCP Network, which points to its "sponsor" network class. This can only be created for a network that does not have any subnetworks.

- The Address pool model, which defines address ranges within a DHCP network and must have an associated rule.

- The Rules model, which defines rules for classifying DHCP requests. Each rule can be assigned to one or more Address pools.

- The "Static" DHCP address rule model, which allows assigning IPs depending on the requestor's hardware MAC address.

Additions to the Workflow

There are some additions to the workflow as well. First, we need to add a link to create (or delete) a DHCP network for every network that has no subnets. We also need to allow users to add and delete information about the DHCP network pools, rules, and static IP addresses. Each of these options will be available within DHCP network listing.

Adding DHCP Network Data

In the first iteration we are going to add support for the DHCP network definitions. We will use an approach similar to what would do with a larger project: define the data models, define the workflows, and go to the implementation phase.

Defining Data Models

Let's start by adding a new data class that is going to store information about the DHCP network. This class is going to point to its "sponsor" physical network class and contains several DHCP options that are required by the clients, such as router address, DNS server, and domain name. Listing 4-1 shows what we're going to add to the models.py file.

Listing 4-1. *The data model class for the DHCP subnet*

```
class DHCPNetwork(models.Model):
    physical_net = models.OneToOneField(NetworkAddress)
    router = models.IPAddressField()
    dns_server = models.ForeignKey(DNSServer)
    domain_name = models.ForeignKey(DomainName)

    def __unicode__(self):
        return "DHCP subnet for %s" % physical_net
```

In this example we also refer to two new entities: DNSServer and DomainName. Classes for them are also defined in models.py and they only contain information about the IP of the DNS server(s) and domain names with brief comments. The reason for separating them from the DHCPNetwork class is that if we ever want to change the IP address of our DNS server, we won't need to go through each DHCP network entry and change it.

Additional Workflows

What extra workflows does generic DHCP network support require? Obviously we want to add or remove a DHCP network to or from a subnet, assuming the subnet can have a corresponding DHCP network. When a DHCP network is defined, we also want to modify its settings. As in the previous chapter, each workflow action is going to have its own view function, and Add and Modify will have their own data entry forms. As you already know, views don't work unless they are defined in a URL configuration file, so that the Django framework knows what view function to call when it receives a request from a user.

The Add Function

First of all, we need to know if we can provide "Add DHCP network" functionality for a subnet. The easiest and most logical way to do this is to check in the network display view whether there are any address entries that do not have the subnet size set to 32 bits. If so, then this subnet cannot have DHCP enabled; otherwise, provide a link to the DHCP add function. So the network view is going to perform the check and pass a Boolean variable that we will query in the template and will either display a message or provide a link. Here's the quick check in the view code:

```
for address in addr_list:
    if address.network_size != 32:
        has_subnets = True
```

And the additions to the template:

```
<h3><a href="add/">Add new subnet or node IP</a></h3>
<h3>{% if has_subnets %}
DHCP support cannot be enabled for networks with subnets
{% else %}
<a href="dhcp/add/">Enable DHCP support</a>
{% endif %}
</h3>
```

Can you see what the resulting URL is going to be yet? The structure is following the same convention for the URL that we defined earlier:

```
http://www.example.com/<application>/<model>/<object>/<action>/
```

So far the objects have been a pair of IP address and their network sizes, which uniquely identified each object in the database. The object now is a DHCP network within a physical network. The DHCP network as such has nothing that uniquely identifies it. So let's add /dhcp/ to the IP/network size pair, which tells us that this is a DHCP object for this particular network. Assuming the new view for adding DHCP network is called add_dhcp, this is what needs to be added to the URL mapping file:

```
(r'^networkaddress/(?P<address>\d{1,3}\.\d{1,3}\.\d{1,3}\.\d{1,3}\/\d{1,2})/↵
dhcp/add/$', 'add_dhcp'),
```

This view will follow the same form processing pattern, and it looks very similar to the one we used to add new networks. It also requires the form class to generate a form model for the template automatically:

```
class DHCPNetworkAddForm(ModelForm):
    class Meta:
        model = DHCPNetwork
        exclude = ('physical_net',)
```

We exclude the physical network field, because it is already known at the time of creation; it is supplied as a URL argument. Listing 4-2 shows our dhcp_add function, in which we even reuse the same template that was used previously.

Listing 4-2. *A view to handle the add function for DHCP networks*

```
def add_dhcp(request, address=None):
    if request.method == 'POST':
        network_addr = None
        if address:
            ip, net_size = address.split('/')
            network_addr = NetworkAddress.objects.get(address=ip,
                                                      network_size=int(net_size))
        dhcp_net = DHCPNetwork(physical_net=network_addr)
        form = DHCPNetworkAddForm(request.POST, instance=dhcp_net)
        if form.is_valid():
            form.save()
            return HttpResponseRedirect("../..")
    else:
        form = DHCPNetworkAddForm()
    return render_to_response('add.html', {'form': form,})
```

You may wonder what happens to the DNS and Domain Name fields; they are foreign keys in the model definition, so what are users supposed to enter here? In Figure 4-1 you can see what Django is going to display.

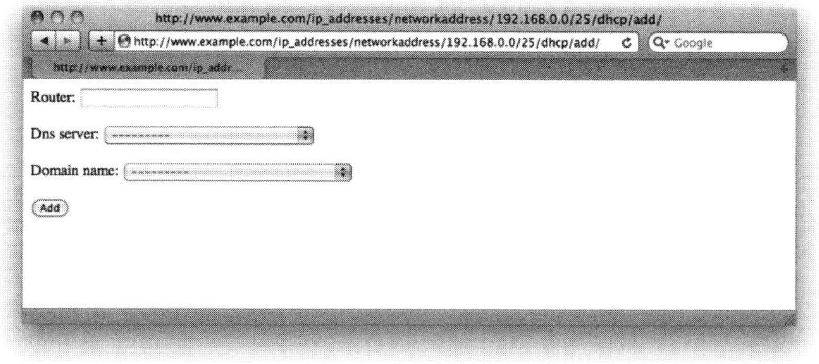

Figure 4-1. *The rendered DHCP add form*

The Django engine was smart enough to figure out that you want to provide users with a selection of the objects from the related table, so it generated a drop-down list of all objects! That is really clever and saved you lots of coding. So all you need to do is enter router details, select the DNS server and domain name from the list, and click the Add button. You can verify that the record has been successfully created by going to the administration interface and selecting the DHCP Networks view.

Try navigating around and enabling DHCP support for other networks as well. Notice that when you navigate up the address tree, you will not be provided with the option to enable DHCP.

At this point we also need to modify the network's display template, so it shows details about the DHCP settings for the network and also provides links to modify and delete the settings.

The Modify Function

The Modify view function is very similar to that of the Add function, except that instead of creating an empty form for the initial view, it retrieves existing data and displays it in the form. So in Listing 4-3 we first search for an existing DHCP network object and pass it to the form class.

Listing 4-3. *The view to handle the Modify function for DHCP networks*

```
def modify_dhcp(request, address=None):
    ip, net_size = address.split('/')
    network_addr = NetworkAddress.objects.get(address=ip,
network_size=int(net_size))
    dhcp_net = DHCPNetwork.objects.get(physical_net=network_addr)
    if request.method == 'POST':
        # submiting changes
        form = DHCPNetworkAddForm(request.POST, instance=dhcp_net)
        if form.is_valid():
            form.save()
            return HttpResponseRedirect("../..")
    else:
        # first time display
        form = DHCPNetworkAddForm(instance=dhcp_net)
    return render_to_response('add.html', {'form': form,})
```

The Delete Function

This is a very simple function that searches for the DHCPNetwork object and deletes it. At this time we have not yet defined any related data structures, such as the DHCP pools or rules, but it's worth mentioning that all related objects would be removed automatically as well.

Extending DHCP Configuration with Address Pools

By now we have decent working code to handle generic DHCP subnet information, such as router, DNS, and Domain server addresses. Should you need any additional fields, you can easily add them by modifying the DHCPNetwork data model class by adding new field instances to it. You may have noticed that none of the view functions have references to the model fields directly. Adding new items would automatically be handled by the Django framework. The template parser will pick them up and generate input fields accordingly.

Now we are going to proceed with the second iteration, where we will add support for the address pool data. As you already know, the address pool is a range of addresses within a subnet that can be allocated to certain set of clients, depending on their class. For example, a class C subnet has 254 available addresses that can be assigned to nodes. We then can instruct the DHCP server to hand out the first 10 addresses to hosts that have a hostname that starts with `server`, another 10 will go to requests that are Sun Microsystems machines, and so on.

The Address Pool Data Model

A typical address pool allows defining additional DHCP options, specific to the pool. For example, you might want to increase the DHCP lease time on certain pools. All servers do not need short-lived DHCP addresses, so you would increase lease time in the pool for those servers. Or you might want all workstations to use different DNS servers. In this example we're not going to allow any additional options. Therefore the model class looks relatively simple and contains only three fields: the pointer to its parent DHCPNetwork object and the two boundary addresses. Listing 4-4 shows the code.

Listing 4-4. *The DHCP pool data model class*

```
class DHCPAddressPool(models.Model):
    DHCPNetwork = models.ForeignKey(DHCPNetwork)
    range_start  = models.IPAddressField()
    range_finish = models.IPAddressField()
```

Once you add this to `models.py`, where you also need to define the form model class, create an appropriate record in the `admins.py` file and run the `syncdb` command, so Django will create a table in the database. Please review the "Defining a Database Model" section in Chapter 3 for the detailed instructions.

Displaying DHCP Network Details

As a first workflow, and therefore a view function, we are going to define the DHCP network view function. We already have some generic information displayed on the physical network listing page, but now we're going to have more items related to DHCP configuration, so it is a good idea to have them displayed on a separate page. This page will contain information about the address pools and the static IP allocation rules as well as classification rules. By now you should be pretty comfortable with adding new views, and you should know that this involves three steps: adding a function rule for mapping URLs to views to the `urls.py` file; defining the view function, and creating a template for the view.

Here's the URL mapping rule we'll be using to call the DHCP display view:

```
(r'^networkaddress/(?P<address>\d{1,3}\.\d{1,3}\.\d{1,3}\.\d{1,3}\/\d{1,2})/dhcp/$',
 'display_dhcp'),
```

For the DHCP display view we are introducing two new functions: one to get the address object from the URL-encoded IP/network_size pair and the other to get the DHCP network object from the same data. As most of the functions require these operations to be performed, it is the time to separate them now, as shown in Listing 4-5.

Listing 4-5. *The DHCP pool display view and helper functions*

```
def display_dhcp(request, address=None):
    dhcp_net = get_dhcp_object_from_address(address)
    dhcp_pools = DHCPAddressPool.objects.filter(dhcp_network=dhcp_net)
    return render_to_response('display_dhcp.html', {'dhcp_net': dhcp_net,
                                                     'dhcp_pools': dhcp_pools,})


def get_network_object_from_address(address):
    ip, net_size = address.split('/')
    return NetworkAddress.objects.get(address=ip, network_size=int(net_size))


def get_dhcp_object_from_address(address):
    return DHCPNetwork.objects.get(physical_net=↵
get_network_object_from_address(address))
```

The DHCP details page (Listing 4-6) displays basic information about the DHCP network and also lists all available pools if they are defined.

Listing 4-6. *The DHCP details display page*

```
<h1>DHCP details for {{ dhcp_net.physical_net.address }}/{{↵
dhcp_net.physical_net.network_size }} network</h1>
<h2><a href="../">Go back to network details</a></h2>
<ul>
<li>Router: {{ dhcp_net.router }}
<li>DNS: {{ dhcp_net.dns_server }}
<li>Domain: {{ dhcp_net.domain_name }}
</ul>
<p>( <a href="modify/">modify</a> | <a href="delete/">delete</a> )</p>
{% if dhcp_pools %}
<p>
<h3>Following DHCP pools are available:</h3>
<ul>
{% for pool in dhcp_pools %}
<li>{{ pool.range_start }} - {{ pool.range_finish }}
( <a href="../dhcp_pool/{{ pool.range_start }}/{{ pool.range_finish↵
}}/delete/">delete</a> )
</li>
{% endfor %}
</ul>
</p>
{% else %}
<h3>There are no DHCP pools defined</h3>
```

```
{% endif %}
<p>
( <a href="../dhcp_pool/add/">add new pool</a> )
</p>
```

Again, another pretty standard view template; there are, however, a few things worth mentioning. The first is that the template parser is quite smart and allows you to reference related objects from the ones that are passed as arguments to the template. As you can see, we do not pass a physical network object directly, only the DHCP network; but because the DHCP network has a foreign key that references its "parent" object, we can simply say `dhcp_net.physical_net.address` and the Django template engine will find the right piece of information to display.

Another thing you might have noticed is the link to the `delete` function. The `object` part of the URL became rather lengthy and is defined as

```
<network_address>/<network_size>/dhcp_pool/<range_start>/<range_finish>
```

Strictly from a data modeling perspective, this key has redundant information in it, because a DHCP pool with given range addresses can belong to only one physical network; therefore there is no need to specify the network address in the URL. However, because we are using relative URLs all over the templates, it is a lot easier to just include it here as well. This is a good example of how strict rules sometimes need compromising to achieve greater effectiveness and simplicity in other areas of the code.

The Add and Delete Functions

Add and Delete in their structure and functionality are almost identical to the equivalent functions in the physical network and DHCP network views. The Add function reuses the same `add.html` template, whereas the Delete function references `DHCPAddressPool` instead.

Reworking the URL Structure

I like to learn by mistakes, as I think that is the most efficient way. Obviously, learning from the mistakes of other people is even better. So I deliberately introduced something that is not really a mistake but could be called a flaw in the design, and left it up to this point in the chapter.

If you've been carefully following all the code examples, you must have noticed one thing: that, although functionally our code is perfect, it just does not feel right. Guessed it yet? Go on, take a second look at all the examples of templates and view functions. What is quite common that you notice there?

Yes! We've been using relative URLs in both the templates and the view functions. It was quite a simple trick to do, and it works perfectly well most of the time, especially in small projects. It even works with decoupled applications, because when you use relative paths address resolution works from the other end, so effectively it doesn't matter at what depth your application URLs start.

The trouble is, with so many class models and functions, it becomes quite difficult to memories the structure of your URLs for each model. We've set very strict rules about formatting the URLs (remember, it's always `<model>/<object>/<method>`), and with a limited number of methods (so far it's only `add`, `delete`, `modify`, and implicit `display'`), we were coping quite easily. However, with a growing number of models and URLs it becomes more difficult to manage and maintain all URLs. Why would you ever need to change the URL structure? There are many reasons—restructuring the site, adding new applications into the hierarchy, or simply fixing a mistake in the development process.

While we're talking about changing URL structure, I need to mention now that I let another "bug" creep in. Remember talking about the `<model>/<object>/<method>` URL structure? Again, I violated it a bit by always using `networkaddress/` at the beginning when referencing DHCP `network` and DHCP `Pool` models. What I should have done is used `dhcpnetwork` and `dhcpaddresspool` prefixes, respectively.

Now that we have a really valid reason for reworking or fixing the code, how should we approach it? It would be ideal if there were a facility or functionality that allowed you to obtain a URL for any object you want to link to.

Generating URLs in the Model Class

The Django framework allows you to define an extra method for each model that returns the absolute URL for an object. So, for example, this is how we could define this method for the `NetworkAddress` class:

```
def get_absolute_url(self):
    return '/networkaddress/%s/%s/' % (self.address, self.network_size)
```

With this defined, we then can use this function in all templates to get the URL of the object:

```
<a href="{{ address.get_absolute_url }}">{{ address }}</a>
```

This allows us to reference object URLs without thinking about the URL structure. All we need is a reference to a URL, and we get that value by referencing the `get_absolute_url` property of the object. If for whatever reason we decide to change the URL structure, we will not need to alter any of the template code, because references are generated outside it.

Reverse Resolution of URLs

There is still a problem with this approach, because if you remember, URLs are now going to be defined in two locations: the URL configuration file and also in the model definition. So even though we do not need to revisit the whole set of templates and view functions, we still need to ensure that whatever `get_absolute_url` returns is also defined in the URLConfig file.

Django has a solution to this problem as well—you can further decouple your models from the URLConfig file with the `permalink` decorator (a decorator is a class that modifies the behavior of the function it decorates). You need to pass a view method name and the view method parameters (either as a list or a dictionary) to the decorator, and it then works out the matching URL for you. Let's look at the example:

```
@models.permalink
def get_absolute_url(self):
    return ('views.networkaddress_display', (),
            {'address': '%s/%s' % (self.address, self.network_size)})
```

Here we're not using a parameter list, but because it is required, we just pass an empty list. My preference is to use a dictionary to pass all arguments that are used in the URL, so we don't need to memorize the number and position of each variable.

Let me remind you what the URL configuration looks like for this view:

```
(r'^networkaddress/(?P<address>\d{1,3}\.\d{1,3}\.\d{1,3}\.\d{1,3}\/\d{1,2})/$',
views.networkaddress_display),
```

Given this combination (the view function and the parameter(s)), the `permalink` is going to find the matching URL and return it.

There is a catch, though; there are situations where the decorator cannot uniquely identify the matching URL:

```
(r'^networkaddress/$', views.networkaddress_display),
(r'^networkaddress/(?P<address>\d{1,3}\.\d{1,3}\.\d{1,3}\.\d{1,3}\/\d{1,2})/$',
                                        views.networkaddress_display),
```

Assigning Names to URL Patterns

In this case there are two URLs that call the same view function, so the reverse URL matcher (which tries to find a matching URL from a view name) gets confused, because more than one URL points to the same view.

If that is the case, you can assign names to your URL patterns, so that they all are uniquely identified:

```
url(r'^networkaddress/$', views.networkaddress_display,
name='networkaddress-displaytop'),
url(r'^networkaddress/(?P<address>\d{1,3}\.\d{1,3}\.\d{1,3}\.\d{1,3}\/\d{1,2})/$',
                    views.networkaddress_display, name='networkaddress-display'),
```

Now, even though both URL pattern are calling the same function, they can be referenced individually using their unique names.

Finally, here's how the model class is going to resolve its objects' URLs:

```
@models.permalink
def get_absolute_url(self):
    return ('networkaddress-display', (),
            {'address': '%s/%s' % (self.address, self.network_size)})
```

Using URL References in the Templates

Obviously the model code can only return one URL for each object. The model class as such has no visibility on the functionality of the application; it is only designed to represent the data upon which the application operates. So usually a model instance returns the URL that is used to display the object, in other words a *representation URL*.

In our application we have multiple functions associated with the data entities, such as `add`, `delete`, and `modify`. Since we have a well-defined URL structure and all action "keywords" are appended at the end, we could use `get_absolute_url` on the object to get its base URL and then append the action word in the template, but this approach isn't proper, as the URL information would be contained in the URLConfig and each of the templates that uses it.

In the previous example we used the {{ object.get_absolute_url }} structure in the templates to refer to the URL. Django also has a URL resolver template tag, which is able to reference URLs by their names. You then need to pass an argument to it so it can match and generate the required URL:

```
{% url networkaddress-display address %}
```

Listing 4-7 shows a more verbose example of how to use the url tag.

Listing 4-7. *An example of a URL resolver template tag*

```
{% if addresses_list %}
    <ul>
    {% for address in addresses_list %}
        <li><a href="{% url networkaddress-display address %}">
                    {{ address.address }}/{{ address.network_size }}</a>
            {% ifequal address.network_size 32 %}(host){% else %}(network){%↵
endifequal %}
            {{ address.description }}
            (<a href="{% url networkaddress-delete address %}">delete</a> |
            <a href="{% url networkaddress-modify address %}">modify</a>)
        </li>
    {% endfor %}
    </ul>
{% else %}
    {% ifequal parent.network_size 32 %}
        This is a node IP
        <ul>
        <li>Description: {{ parent.description }}
            ( <a href="{% url networkaddress-modify parent %}">modify</a> )</li>
        </ul>
    {% else %}
        No addresses or subnets in this range
    {% endifequal %}
{% endif %}
```

All URL pattern names are defined in the URLConfig file, as shown in Listing 4-8.

Listing 4-8. *Networkaddress URL patterns*

```
urlpatterns = patterns('',
    url(r'^networkaddress/$', views.networkaddress_display,
        name='networkaddress-displaytop'),
    url(r'^networkaddress/add/$', views.networkaddress_add,
        name='networkaddress-addtop'),

url(r'^networkaddress/(?P<address>\d{1,3}\.\d{1,3}\.\d{1,3}\.\d{1,3}\/\d{1,2})/$',
        views.networkaddress_display, name='networkaddress-display'),
```

```
url(r'^networkaddress/(?P<address>\d{1,3}\.\d{1,3}\.\d{1,3}\.\d{1,3}\/\d{1,2})/↵
        delete/$', views.networkaddress_delete, name='networkaddress-delete'),

url(r'^networkaddress/(?P<address>\d{1,3}\.\d{1,3}\.\d{1,3}\.\d{1,3}\/\d{1,2})/↵
        add/$', views.networkaddress_add, name='networkaddress-add'),

url(r'^networkaddress/(?P<address>\d{1,3}\.\d{1,3}\.\d{1,3}\.\d{1,3}\/\d{1,2})/↵
        modify/$', views.networkaddress_modify, name='networkaddress-modify'),
```

Finally, all URLs are decoupled and defined in one location—the URLConfig file. Whenever you choose to change them, you only need to do that in one place, and neither models, views, nor templates have to be modified.

Adding Client Classification

To make good use of the address pools, we need to have client classification functionality in place. In other words, we have to define some rules that identify what is sending the requests and then assign IP addresses from the appropriate address pool. Since we're not implementing a "wizard" type of application, all rules need to be plain text in the format that ISC DHCP understands. This would not help people with little knowledge of the configuration file syntax, but it will come in really handy for those who have to manage reasonably large DHCP configurations.

Additions to the Data Model

The class definition for the new data model is fairly simple and contains only two fields: the rule text and the description. We also need to extend the Pool class so that it references the appropriate ClassRule object, as shown in Listing 4-9.

Listing 4-9. *Extending the DHCP pool model and introducing the Rules model*

```
class DHCPAddressPool(models.Model):
    dhcp_network = models.ForeignKey(DHCPNetwork)
    class_rule = models.ForeignKey(ClassRule)
    range_start  = models.IPAddressField()
    range_finish = models.IPAddressField()

    def __unicode__(self):
        return "(%s - %s)" % (self.range_start, self.range_finish)

class ClassRule(models.Model):
    rule = models.TextField()
    description = models.CharField(max_length=400)

    def __unicode__(self):
        return self.id
```

Using Template Inheritance

Since the rules management is going to be generic, we want to make the link to the display and management page available from all our pages, so that the user can jump directly to it. So far we have two display pages to display the physical networks and also DHCP networks, but in the future we may have more. So how do we add a link to all pages? Obviously editing every single page is not an ideal solution.

The Django template management system allows for template inheritance, so you can define a container template and then base the other templates on it. The base template contains placeholders, and each template that inherits from it will provide elements to be placed in those placeholders.

Here is an example. First of all let's define the base template of which all others will inherit; Listing 4-10 shows the code.

Listing 4-10. *The base template*

```
{% block menu %}
<ul>
    <li><a href="{% url networkaddress-displaytop %}">Network address
management</a></li>
    <li><a href="{% url classrule-displaytop %}">Class rule management</a></li>
</ul>
{% endblock %}
<hr/>
{% block contents %}
{% endblock %}
```

Here we define two blocks: a menu block and a block for contents. Since our primary goal is to separate menu template code and reuse it, we do not need to place it in a separate block, but it is a good practice to do so as that allows other templates to replace this menu with something else if there is a need to. Anything that is outside of the {% block %} tag is not accessible from other templates and thus is not changeable. Anything that is contained within the tag is a default value and will be displayed if the inheriting template does not override the block.

The second block is designed to hold the contents of other display pages, so it is left empty. The inheriting templates will substitute their contents for it; optionally they can also override the menu part. Listing 4-11 shows the new display.html template, which now inherits from base.html.

Listing 4-11. *Making display.html inherit from base.html*

```
{% extends "base.html" %}
{% block contents %}
<contents of the original display.html>
{% endblock %}
```

Similarly, we need to change display_dhcp.html as well. Once we've done that, both pages will contain generic menu, allowing application users to switch between the network configuration and class rules configuration.

Class Rules Management

We're going to make the same set of rules available to all DHCP pools in our system. So before we assign a specific rule to any of our DHCP pools, we first need to define this rule. We do this so that the users will be able to reuse existing rules. This approach is good if you have same rules reused in many different subnets. If your rules are very specific and unlikely to be reused, however, this is not the best approach as you will end up with a large number of one-off entries, and the list soon becomes unmanageable.

If that is the case, you might want to think about defining categories for rules and subnets, so that they can be grouped automatically. Then when you create a new DHCP network, you'll pick which categories you want to see.

Previously we created Add, Modify, Delete, and Display views for all models we had in our system. It seems to be a repetitive process, don't you think? It would be nice if there was a way to automatically perform tasks like basic creation, modification, and deletion of the objects. And the Django framework provides this functionality—it is called *generic views*.

Generic Views

The generic views are the views that perform basic and common tasks on any object passed to them. There are four types of generic views shipped with Django:

- Views that redirect to other pages or render any given template, usually static content.

- A view that generates a list of objects or displays details of any specific object.

- Views that list objects based on their creation date. These are more useful if you're creating a blog or news site.

- Views to add, delete, and modify objects.

Generic views can be imported from the `django.views.generic` library. And you normally need them in the URLConfig file, because this is where you are mapping URLs to a view.

Because of the simplicity of the Class Rules model, we're going to use generic views to manage the model's objects. The reason we do not using generic views to manage other models is that we want to leave more flexibility in what the views are doing. At some later stage we might want to extend view functions to perform additional checks and tasks, which we cannot easily do with the generic views.

Displaying a List of Objects

First things first—let's call a generic view to display a list of all available class rule objects. Display views require a *queryset* object passed to them. This object is a dictionary and must contain one entry, which is a list of objects we want to display. Additionally you can specify which template it needs to use and other settings. You may also pass additional lists of related objects. For example we could pass a list of DHCP pools that reference any specific class rule, as shown in Listing 4-12, so that users can have this information displayed along with the class rules listing.

Listing 4-12. *Class rule queryset*

```
classrule_info = {
    'queryset': ClassRule.objects.all(),
    'template_name': 'display_classrule.html',
}
```

The queryset entry here contains all the objects we want to display, and template_name is the name of the template file. If we had chosen not to define the name of a template, Django would have attempted to generate the file name for it automatically and would try to load a file called `<application_name>/<model_name>_detail.html`. We chose to specify template names, so that's just one thing less to worry about if something doesn't work as it should.

You also need to add URL-to-view mapping just as you did with all the other views in previous sections. This time, however, we're going to use a generic view `list_detail.object_list` and pass it the queryset object that contains all the information the generic view requires:

```
url(r'^classrule/$', list_detail.object_list, classrule_info,
name='classrule-displaytop'),
```

And finally you need to create a template that displays all the objects nicely. We have already added links to the Details' Modify, and Delete functions, which we're going to define in the next sections, so the code looks like Listing 4-13.

Listing 4-13. *The class rule list template*

```
{% extends "base.html" %}
{% block contents %}
<h1>List of all Class Rules</h1>
{% if object_list %}
    <ul>
    {% for rule in object_list %}
        <li>{{ rule.description }}
                ( <a href="{% url classrule-display rule.id %}">details</a> |
                  <a href="{% url classrule-modify rule.id %}">modify</a> |
                  <a href="{% url classrule-delete rule.id %}">delete</a> )</li>
    {% endfor %}
    </ul>
{% else %}
No class rules defined yet.
{% endif %}
<h3><a href="{% url classrule-add %}">Add new rule</a></h3>
{% endblock %}
```

This is a much simpler way of quickly displaying a list of any set of objects and doesn't require you to write a single line of view code.

A Detailed View of the Object

Similarly, we're going to use generic views to display details about any specific class rule object. The only difference here is that we need to pass a specific object ID to the generic view, so that the view code can select the appropriate object from the list.

The object's queryset instance is not changing and will be reused. The new URL rule is going to look as shown here; it contains a reference to object_id, which tells the generic view which object it needs to pass to the template:

```
url(r'^classrule/(?P<object_id>\d+)/$', list_detail.object_detail, classrule_info,
    name='classrule-display'),
```

And finally let's update the version of the template as shown in Listing 4-14. It now checks whether the object contains anything, in which case it displays detailed information about it; otherwise it will be displaying a list of class rules.

Listing 4-14. *The updated view to display both lists and object details*

```
{% extends "base.html" %}
{% block contents %}
{% if object %}
    <h1>Class Rules details</h1>
    <ul>
        <li>ID: {{ object.id }}</li>
        <li>Description: {{ object.description }}</li>
        <li>Rule text:
            <pre>
                {{ object.rule }}
            </pre>
        </li>
    </ul>
    ( <a href="{% url classrule-modify object.id %}">modify</a> |
      <a href="{% url classrule-delete object.id %}">delete</a> )
{% else %}
    <h1>List of all Class Rules</h1>
    {% if object_list %}
        <ul>
        {% for rule in object_list %}
            <li>{{ rule.description }}
                ( <a href="{% url classrule-display rule.id %}">details</a> |
                  <a href="{% url classrule-modify rule.id %}">modify</a> |
                  <a href="{% url classrule-delete rule.id %}">delete</a> )</li>
        {% endfor %}
        </ul>
    {% else %}
        No class rules defined yet.
    {% endif %}
    <h3><a href="{% url classrule-add %}">Add new rule</a></h3>
{% endif %}
{% endblock %}
```

■**Note** By default the template object name is `object`. The generic list view appends `_list` to this name. So in a detailed view you would receive `object` as an instance of an individual object or `object_list` as a list of objects. You can always change the template name by setting `template_object_name` to any name you like in the queryset dictionary. Remember, though, that `_list` will still be appended to the name when you use the generic list view.

Adding and Modifying New Objects

Using the generic views to add objects is similarly simple. You need to provide basic information to the view and define URL patterns for those actions. The generic views require the following information:

- The Model Class name, so the view knows what sort of objects it's dealing with.

- The Model Form Class, so the form generation framework knows how to generate form representation.

- The post-action redirect URL, which tells the views where to redirect the user after the data has been submitted. This should be a string representing a URL. If it is not specified, Django will attempt to apply `get_absolute_url` to the object, so make sure the `get_absolute_url` method of the object is defined. The advantage of using `get_absolute_url`, however, is that you don't need to change URL in two places if you modify it.

In Listing 4-15 we define two classes; one is the `Model` class and the other is the `ModelForm` class. Strictly speaking, the `ModelForm` class is not required here as we have a really simple model with only two fields, but I prefer to define them explicitly; this makes it easier should I wish to extend and modify the models later. Note that `get_absolute_url` returns the reverse-resolved URL.

Listing 4-15. *The ClassRule model and form classes*

```
class ClassRule(models.Model):
    rule = models.TextField()
    description = models.CharField(max_length=400)

    def __unicode__(self):
        return self.description[:20]

    @models.permalink
    def get_absolute_url(self):
        return ('classrule-display', (), {'object_id': self.id})

class ClassRuleForm(ModelForm):
    class Meta:
        model = ClassRule
```

Back in the URLConfig file, we define a configuration dictionary with a model name and a form filename:

```
classrule_form = {
    'form_class': ClassRuleForm,
    'template_name': 'add.html',
}
```

We can even reuse the same form we've been using to add or modify other objects. Because we kept the form generic and let the template handler generate all the required fieldsets, it does not require any changes.

Finally, let's add two URL patterns for the Add and Modify functions and make sure the same URL pattern names are used as referenced from the templates:

```
url(r'^classrule/(?P<object_id>\d+)/modify/$', create_update.update_object,
classrule_form,
    name='classrule-modify'),
url(r'^classrule/add/$', create_update.create_object, classrule_form,
    name='classrule-add'),
```

As you can see, the syntax is same as with generic display views—the first argument is a view function and the second argument is the dictionary that contains the view configuration items, such as the form class name and the template file name.

Deleting Objects

Deleting an object involves one intermediate step: the user is required to confirm the action. This is implemented in the generic delete view by using simple logic—if the HTTP request is GET, it means the user clicked the Delete link and thus needs the confirmation page displayed (which points back to the same URL). If the HTTP request is POST, it means the user clicked the Confirm button and the form has been submitted with an HTTP POST call, in which case the view will proceed with deletion of the object.

There is one caveat with the generic Delete view. It requires a post-delete URL; in other words it needs to know where to take the user after the object has been deleted. The obvious solution would be to reverse-lookup the URL and use it, but since that URL is defined in the very same file (URLConfig) where it will be called from, it will not be evaluated at the moment of the function call. So until this is resolved, we need to use a relative URL, as shown in Listing 4-16.

Listing 4-16. *The configuration dictionary for the Delete generic view*

```
classrule_delete = {
    'model': ClassRule,
    'post_delete_redirect': '../..',
    'template_name': 'delete_confirm_classrule.html',
}
```

The confirmation template simply asks for confirmation and resubmits the data to the same URL, but now with the HTTP POST method:

```
<form method="post" action=".">
<p>Are you sure?</p>
<input type="submit" />
</form>
```

And finally, we make another addition to the URL patterns list:

```
url(r'^classrule/(?P<object_id>\d+)/delete/$', create_update.delete_object,
    classrule_delete, name='classrule-delete'),
```

■**Note** As you might have already guessed, both the Modify and Delete views not only require knowledge about the type of objects they are operating on, but must also uniquely identify the object they are modifying or deleting. The object ID is passed to them from the URL pattern as the `object_id` variable.

Generating the DHCP Configuration File

We have all the information we require, but it's not much use in its current form. All data is in the database tables, and although it spells out how the DHCP server should be configured, it cannot be used in this form. We need to write a view that will generate a configuration file, which the DHCP server will be able to understand.

Let's go back and revisit what the DHCP configuration file should look like. Since we're using the ISC DHCP server, the configuration file (including only those elements that we're interested in) has the following structure:

```
<dhcpd configuration items or generic DHCP options>

<class definitions>

<network definition>
    <subnet definition>
        <subnet options>
        <pool definitions>
```

Let's make this configuration file available as a web resource. So we need to approach it very similarly to the way we generated the user interface pages—we need to define a view that supplies data and the template that lays out this data on a page, in this instance a plain text document.

We start with the view, shown in Listing 4-17.

Listing 4-17. *The view that collects data for the DHCP configuration file*

```
def dhcpd_conf_generate(request):
    class_rules = ClassRule.objects.all()
    networks = []
```

```
    for net in DHCPNetwork.objects.all():
        networks.append( { 'dhcp_net': net,
                           'pools': DHCPAddressPool.objects.filter(dhcp_network=net),
                         } )

    return render_to_response('dhcpd.conf.txt',
                              {'class_rules': class_rules,
                               'networks': networks,
                              },
                              mimetype='text/plain')
```

We don't keep the DHCP server configuration items in the database; therefore, we'll put them straight into the template. Class rules are simply listed outside any other structure, so we generate a list of all class rules on the system and pass it as a list.

Each DHCP subnet may have several distinct DHCP pools defined within its range, so those pools need to appear only within the specific DHCP pool definition. We therefore loop through all available DHCP networks and generate a list that contains

- The DHCP address object

- A list of all DHCP pools that are related to given DHCP network

Finally we're telling Django to change the MIME type of the document to 'text/plain'. This doesn't matter much if we're only going to download it. If you tried to open this file in a web browser, you would get the whole document presented on one line, because the web browser would think that it is a valid HTML document. So to preserve the formatting when viewing in a browser we need to format the response to indicate that the document is a flat text file.

Finally, in Listing 4-18 we have a template that puts all the data in a structure that can be used by the DHCP server.

Listing 4-18. *A template for the DHCP configuration file*

```
1 {% autoescape off %}
2 ignore client-updates;
3 ddns-update-style interim;
4
5 {% if class_rules %}
6     {% for cr in class_rules %}
7         # {{cr.description }}
8         class "class_rule_{{ cr.id }}" {
9             {{ cr.rule }};
10        }
11    {% endfor %}
12 {% endif %}
13
14 {% if networks %}
15    {% for net in networks %}
16        shared-network network_{{ net.dhcp_net.id }} {
17            subnet {{ net.dhcp_net.physical_net.address }} netmask {{↩
net.dhcp_net.physical_net.get_netmask }} {
```

```
18              option routers {{ net.dhcp_net.router }};
19              option domain-name-servers {{ net.dhcp_net.dns_server.address }};
20              option domain-name {{ net.dhcp_net.domain_name.name }};
21
22              {% if net.pools %}
23                  {% for pool in net.pools %}
24                      pool {
25                          allow members of "class_rule_{{ pool.class_rule.id↵
}}";
26                          range {{ pool.range_start }} {{ pool.range_finish }};
27                      }
28                  {% endfor %}
29              {% endif %}
30          }
31      }
32  {% endfor %}
33 {% endif %}
34
35 {% endautoescape %}
```

Now let's look in more detail at some of the lines.

Line 1: The Django template engine has a built-in text escaping capability that changes all characters that are not HTML-compliant to their HTML code presentation. For example, the " character would be replaced by the " string. Because we're serving a flat text document, we need to present all characters in their original notation and not HTML encoded. So we turn off autoescape functionality, which is on by default.

Lines 2–3: These are just standard DHCP server configuration items, which you may want to replace with those suitable for your environment.

Lines 5–12: A simple check to see if the class_rules list is not empty, followed by a loop that goes through all elements and displays them.

Lines 14–15: Again, a pre-check to see if the networks list is not empty followed by the loop statement.

Line 17: Here you can see how we refer to related objects. We're not passing any information about the physical network directly to the template, but we can still access it through the DHCP Network object, which has a foreign key to the related Physical Network object. As long as the relation is unambiguous (a DHCP network can only belong to one physical network) you can use this syntax to access relevant information.

Lines 19–20: Similarly we're accessing related Router and DNS objects.

Lines 22–23: Check to see if there are any pools available for the DHCP network and loop through them if there are any.

Lines 25–26: Note that we're generating class and network names based on their object IDs. This is the easiest way to ensure that the names are unique and can also be used to make cross-references within the configuration file.

You might have noticed that we're using the `get_netmask` property of the Physical Network object. This field does not exist, so what is it? Well, the DHCP server expects subnets defined as pairs consisting of a base network address and a netmask. We do not have a netmask field in the model, but it is very simple to derive from the network size, which is expressed in number of bits; Listing 4-19 shows the code.

Listing 4-19. *Calculating the netmask from the network size*

```
def get_netmask(self):
    bit_netmask = 0;
    bit_netmask = pow(2, self.network_size) - 1
    bit_netmask = bit_netmask << (32 - self.network_size)
    nmask_array = []
    for c in range(4):
        dec = bit_netmask & 255
        bit_netmask = bit_netmask >> 8
        nmask_array.insert(0, str(dec))
    return ".".join(nmask_array)
```

The logic of this function is very simple:

- Set the number of bits in an integer variable on (that is, set them to 1). This can be expressed as 2^<number of bits> -1

- Shift the result to the left, filling in the remaining number of bits with 0. The total number of bits in a netmask is always 32.

- For every 8 bits (4 sets in total), convert them to a decimal number string.

- Join all numbers, using the dot symbol to separate individual numbers.
Finally we need to add an additional URL pattern that calls this view:

```
url(r'^dhcpd.conf/$', views.dhcpd_conf_generate, name='dhcp-conf-generate')
```

Following is an example of the DHCP configuration file that was generated from some sample data I entered into my database:

```
ignore client-updates;
ddns-update-style interim;
        # class rule 1
        class "class_rule_1" {
            match if substring (option host-name, 0, 6) = "server";;
        }
        # test rule (gen form)
        class "class_rule_2" {
            test rule - gen form;
        }

        shared-network network_4 {
            subnet 192.168.0.128 netmask 255.255.255.128 {
                option routers 192.168.0.130;
                option domain-name-servers 208.67.222.222;
                option domain-name domain1.example.com;
            }
        }
        shared-network network_5 {
            subnet 192.168.0.0 netmask 255.255.255.128 {
                option routers 192.168.0.113;
                option domain-name-servers 208.67.220.220;
                option domain-name domain2.example.com;
                    pool {
                        allow members of "class_rule_1";
                        range 192.168.0.1 192.168.0.20;
                    }
            }
        }
```

Other Modifications

The majority of the work has already been done, but we still need to add a couple of things to fulfill the initial set of requirements: hostname resolution for node IPs and a status check.

Resolving IPs to Hostnames

To get further information about the IP addresses, let's do a reverse name resolution and print a fully qualified domain name next to each address entry. There are two places where we could implement this lookup: we can either modify the display view and do a host lookup there and pass the information to the template. Or we can extend the Model class with an additional function that returns a hostname for the IP address or an empty string if the hostname cannot be resolved.

Let's go with the second option as it is more elegant and does not require changing the interface between the view and the template. Here's an additional method for the Model class, which uses the gethostbyaddr function from Python's socket library to perform a reverse lookup. The result is a tuple: (<hostname>, <zone>, <address>) and we're using the first entry (hostname) as a result.

```
import socket

...
class NetworkAddress(models.Model):
...
    def get_hostname(self):
        try:
            fqdn = socket.gethostbyaddr(str(self.address))[0]
        except:
            fqdn = ''
        return fqdn
```

And a minor change in the template to display additional property (if available):

```
{% for address in addresses_list %}
  <li><a href="{% url networkaddress-display address %}">{{ address.address }}/
                                               {{ address.network_size↵
}}</a>
    {% ifequal address.network_size 32 %}(host){% else %}(network){% endifequal %}
      {{ address.description }}
      {% if address.get_hostname %} ({{ address.get_hostname }}) {% endif %}
    (<a href="{% url networkaddress-delete address %}">delete</a> |
     <a href="{% url networkaddress-modify address %}">modify</a>)
  </li>
{% endfor %}
```

Checking Whether the Address Is In Use

Let's implement a simple function that checks whether the IP address is in use. To do so, we need to send an ICMP ECHO message to the IP address and wait for the response. Strictly speaking, this is not a valid test to check if address is in use, because there might be few scenarios when the IP address is used but does not respond to a ping request. Firewalls might be preventing ICMP traffic, or that traffic might be blocked at the server level. In most cases, however, this simple test is very effective; just bear in mind that failure indicated by this test may not necessarily mean actual failure of the server or that the address is not used.

The implementation follows the usual pattern of defining a view and adding a new URL pattern to the URLConfig file. Because of a relative complexity of implementing ICMP using the Python socket library (it requires using sockets in raw mode, which in turn requires application to run as root user) we will call the system ping utility and make a decision based on the return code, shown in Listing 4-20.

Listing 4-20. *A view that does an ICMP check for an IP address*

```
def networkaddress_ping(request, address=None):
    if responding_to_ping(address):
        msg = "Ping OK"
    else:
        msg = "No response"
    return HttpResponse(msg)

def responding_to_ping(address, timeout=1):
    import subprocess
    rc = subprocess.call("ping -c 1 -W %d %s" % (timeout, address),
                         shell=True, stdout=open('/dev/null', 'w'),
                         stderr=subprocess.STDOUT)
    if rc == 0:
        return True
    else:
        return False
```

Here we force ping to send only one packet and the timeout is set to 1 second. Although this may reduce accuracy, the response will be much quicker. Most local networks should operate within these constraints, but if you need to have more accuracy you can increase the default timeout and instruct ping to send more than one probe packet.

You also need to add two additional URL patterns:

```
url(r'^networkaddress/(?P<address>\d{1,3}\.\d{1,3}\.\d{1,3}\.\d{1,3})/ping/$',
    views.networkaddress_ping, name='networkaddress-ping'),
url(r'^networkaddress/$', views.networkaddress_ping,
name='networkaddress-ping-url'),
```

The first pattern catches an IP address and also the method (/ping/) that it needs to perform on the given address. The second line is simply for housekeeping—you will find out later why it is required.

Why did we implement this check as a separate call to the web server? Wouldn't it be easier to generate the list of IP addresses to be displayed, ping each one individually, and then pass the ping results along with the IP addresses to the template? Yes, we could have done that, but there is one major issue with that approach—the application response time. In a real-life situation you may have really large networks and may need to perform ping checks on hundreds of servers. Even if you implement this check in a multithreaded manner—in other words attempt to call the ping function simultaneously—you're still going to spend 1, 2 or even more seconds to complete the request. From a usability point of view this is not acceptable; if the system is slow to respond, users are not going to like it.

So what we are going to do here is display the list of all addresses in a subnet and then asynchronously call the ping URL using JavaScript. Users will not get the status report immediately, but at least the page with other information and links to actions will be displayed immediately.

Another good side effect of this approach is that you don't need to make any changes to the display view at all—just some minor modification to the display template (add a placeholder to hold the status information). JavaScript will be placed in the base template, so all pages automatically get this functionality.

Since this book isn't about the JavaScript I'll limit myself to a brief explanation and an example of how it is used. Listing 4-21 uses the jQuery library to perform asynchronous AJAX calls to obtain the results and update the web page accordingly.

Listing 4-21. *Modified address list loop code*

```
{% for address in addresses_list %}
        <li><a href="{% url networkaddress-display address %}">{{ address.address↵
}}/
            {{ address.network_size }}</a>
            {% ifequal address.network_size 32 %}(host){% else %}(network){%↵
endifequal %}
            {{ address.description }}
            {% if address.get_hostname %} ({{ address.get_hostname }}) {% endif %}
            (<a href="{% url networkaddress-delete address %}">delete</a> |
            <a href="{% url networkaddress-modify address %}">modify</a>)
            {% ifequal address.network_size 32 %}
            [Status: <span class="address"
                id="ip_{{ address.get_formated_address }}">Unknown</span> ]
            {% endifequal %}
        </li>
    {% endfor %}
```

The additional line checks whether the address is likely to be a node IP and then inserts an HTML <span> tag, which will be used to update information at this location in the document. This tag has two properties: *class* and *id*. We will use the *class* property to identify what tags contain the IP addresses and need checking, and the *id* property to hold the value of the IP address.

You may wonder what this get_formated_address method is and why we're not using the address directly. The reason is that jQuery expects HTML tag IDs not to have dots in the name, and the ID name also needs to start with a letter; therefore we have to add the ip_ prefix to it. This method simply replaces all occurrences of '.' with '_' in the address field.

Lastly we add some JavaScript that traverses all tags that belong to the same address class and performs an AJAX asynchronous call to the web server. The result will then be used as the HTML content of the tag. The code in Listing 4-22 has been added to the base template, from which all other templates inherit.

Listing 4-22. *JavaScript that performs asynchronous calls and updates the status page*

```
<html>
<head>
<script type="text/javascript" src="/static/js/jquery-1.3.2.min.js"></script>
<script type="text/javascript">
    $(document).ready(function(){
        $(".address").each(function () {
            var curId = $(this).attr('id');
            updateStatus(curId);
        });
    });
```

```
    function updateStatus(attrId) {
        address = attrId.replace('ip_', '');
        address = address.replace(/_/g, '.');
        $.ajax({
            url: '{% url networkaddress-ping-url %}' + address + '/ping/',
            success: function(response) {
                $('#' + attrId).html(response);
            }
        });
    }

</script>
</head>
```

Now you see why we needed to have the placeholder URL pattern. JavaScript is also partially generated by Django—we insert the network address URL using the reverse URL lookup. Because we cannot generate a full URL (with the address part in it), this is a generic URL that will be modified by the JavaScript. WE only use the first part of it, therefore we needed this defined in the URLConfig.

So the logic of this JavaScript code is as follows:

- Remove the ip_ prefix.

- Replace underscores with dots.

- Perform an AJAX asynchronous call

- Update the web page when the results come back.

Now when the user navigates to the listing page it will be displayed immediately and then gradually updated with the status reports for each IP address as the results become available.

Summary

In this chapter we have expanded the functionality of the network address management application by adding support for DHCP and also performing some checks, such as DNS lookups and ICMP pings, to make sure the address is in use.

- Generic views help to reduce the amount of code you need to write; use them to perform generic tasks such as displaying object information and to perform basic manipulations such as delete, modify and add.

- You can modify the response MIME type, allowing Django to be used to generate wide variety of content—HTML, XML, text, and even binary documents.

- Think about the user experience and whether your application will perform various tasks as quickly when the amount of data grows. If you need to, use JavaScript to postpone content loading.

- You don't need to have libraries available or write your own functionality to perform certain tasks. If you need to—you can use system utilities such as ping, to perform these tasks.

## CHAPTER 5

Maintaining a List of Virtual Hosts in an Apache Configuration File

We examined the Django web framework in great detail in Chapters 3 and 4. In this chapter we'll continue exploring the Django framework and in particular the administration application. Instead of writing the views and the forms ourselves, we are going to use the built-in object management application, but we'll customize it to our needs and requirements. The application we will create in this chapter is a web-based application to generate the virtual host configuration for the Apache web server.

Specifying the Design and Requirements for the Application

Why would you want to have an application that generates the Apache configuration files for you? There are pros and cons to this approach. Let me start with the advantages of generating configurations files automatically.

First, although you cannot eliminate it completely, you greatly reduce the error factor. When you automatically generate configuration files, the settings are either available as a selection, so you cannot make any typos, or can be validated. So you have a system that does the basic error checking, and silly mistakes such as "ServreName" are eliminated. Second, this approach to some degree enforces the backup policy. If you accidentally destroy the application configuration, you can always re-create it. Third—and this is the most important aspect in my opinion—you can have a central place to configure multiple clients. For example, let's assume that you have a web farm of ten identical web servers all sitting behind a web load balancer. All servers are running the Apache web server and all should be configured identically. By using an automated configuration system, you generate the configuration file once (or even better, you can create the configuration on demand) and then upload to all servers.

There are some drawbacks as well. Any configuration utility, unless it is natively written for the system that you are configuring, adds another layer between you and the application. Any changes to the configuration structure will immediately have an effect on the configuration tool. New configuration items need to be provisioned in the configuration system. Even the slightest change in the syntax needs to be accounted for. If you want to make the best of your configuration tool, you have to revalidate it against every new software release, to make sure that your tool still produces a valid configuration file.

The choice is obviously yours. For standard configuration, I suggest automating as much as possible, and if you are creating your own tools, you can always account for the extra configuration that is specific to your environment.

Functional Requirements

Let's go back to the Apache web server configuration tool. First of all, this tool should generate only the name-based virtual host configuration. We don't expect this tool to generate the server-specific configuration, only the blocks that are responsible for defining virtual hosts.

In the virtual host definition section you can use the configuration directives from various installed modules. Typically the Apache `core` module is always available; therefore the tool should provide you with the list of all configuration directives from the `core` module. It should be possible to add new configuration directives.

Some configuration directives may be nested inside each other, as in the following example, where the `SetHandler` directive is encapsulated in the `Location` directive section. The tool should allow you to define the relationships between the configuration directives where one is encapsulated by the other:

```
<Location /status>
    SetHandler server-status
</Location>
```

There might be situations where multiple virtual host definition sections have very similar configurations. The application that we're going to build should allow you to clone any existing Virtual Host definition together with all its configuration directives. In addition to the clone operation, the application should allow you to mark any Virtual Host section as a template. The template Virtual Host block should not become a functional part of the configuration file, although it can be included in the form of a comment block.

The most important part of any Virtual Host definition is the server domain name and its aliases. The list of all domain names that the Virtual Host is responding to should be made easily available, and the links to the appropriate web location should be provided.

The configuration file should be made available as a web resource and the server as a plain-text file document.

High-Level Design

As discussed, we will be using the Django web framework to build our application. However, instead of writing all forms manually, we will reuse Django's provided data administration application, which we'll configure to our needs.

It is unlikely that the application will be maintaining the configuration for a great number of Virtual Hosts, so we are going to use the SQLite3 database as the data store for our configuration.

We are going to store two types of data in the database: the virtual host objects and the configuration directives. This allows for expansion and further modification of the application—for example, we could extend the configuration directives model and add an "allowed values" field.

Setting Up the Environment

We've already discussed the Django application structure in great detail in Chapters 3 and 4, so you should be comfortable creating the environment settings for the new application. I'll briefly mention here the key configuration items, so it will be easier for you to follow the examples and code snippets later in the chapter.

Apache Configuration

First we need to instruct the Apache web server how to handle the requests sent to our application. This is a fairly standard configuration that assumes our working directory to be in /srv/app/, and the Django project name is www_example_com. The document root is set to /srv/www/www.example.com, and it's used only to contain a link to the administration web site static files. We'll come to creating the link a bit later. Listing 5-1 shows the code.

Listing 5-1. *The Apache web server configuration*

```
<VirtualHost *:80>
    ServerName www.example.com
    DocumentRoot /srv/www/www.example.com
    ErrorLog /var/log/httpd/www.example.com-error.log
    CustomLog /var/log/httpd/www.example.com-access.log combined
    SetHandler mod_python
    PythonHandler django.core.handlers.modpython
    PythonPath sys.path+['/srv/app/']
    SetEnv DJANGO_SETTINGS_MODULE www_example_com.settings
    SetEnv PYTHON_EGG_CACHE /tmp
    <Location "/static/">
        SetHandler None
    </Location>
</VirtualHost>
```

After creating the configuration, make sure that all directories mentioned in the configuration file (/srv/www/www.example.com/ and /srv/app/) exist. Also make sure that these directories are owned by the user running the Apache daemon. Typically it is the user named *apache* or *httpd*. When you have finished, restart the Apache web server, so it reads the new configuration in.

Creating a Django Project and Application

We'll start off by creating a new Django project called www_example_com. As you already know from Chapters 3 and 4, the project in fact becomes a Python module with its init methods and possibly submodules (the applications within the project). Therefore, the project name has to follow the Python variable naming conventions and cannot contain dots or start with a number. Start a new project first:

```
$ cd /srv/app/
$ django-admin startproject www_example_com
```

At this point you should be able to navigate to the web site URL that you defined earlier (in our example it's http://www.example.com) and you should see the standard Django welcome page.

The next step is to create a new application within the project. You must follow the same naming rules as with the project name when you choose a name for your application. I'll simply call it httpconfig:

```
$ django-admin startapp httpconfig
```

Configuring the Application

Now we need to specify some details about the project, such as the database engine type, and also tell the project about the new application. Even though we have created its skeleton files, the application is not automatically included in the project configuration.

First, change the database configuration in the `settings.py` file in the project directory. Don't worry about the database file, as it will be created automatically:

```
DATABASE_ENGINE = 'sqlite3'
DATABASE_NAME = '/srv/app/www_example_com/database.db'
```

Second, change the default admin media location; we're going to link to it within the existing media directory. In the same `settings.py` file, make sure to have this setting:

```
ADMIN_MEDIA_PREFIX = '/static/admin/'
```

Third, add two new applications to the enabled applications list. We're going to enable the administration application that is part of the standard Django installation, and we'll also add our application to the list:

```
INSTALLED_APPS = (
    'django.contrib.auth',
    'django.contrib.contenttypes',
    'django.contrib.sessions',
    'django.contrib.sites',
    'django.contrib.admin',
    'www_example_com.httpconfig',
)
```

Finally, we have to run a database synchronization script, which will create the database file for us and also create all required database tables as defined in the application model files. To be sure, we don't have any yet in the `httpconfig` application, but we need to do this step so that the administration and other applications have their database tables created. Run the following command to create the database:

```
$ ./manage.py syncdb
Creating table auth_permission
Creating table auth_group
Creating table auth_user
Creating table auth_message
Creating table django_content_type
Creating table django_session
Creating table django_site
Creating table django_admin_log
```

```
You just installed Django's auth system, which means you don't have any superusers
defined.
Would you like to create one now? (yes/no): yes
Username (Leave blank to use 'rytis'):
E-mail address: rytis@example.com
Password: ***
Password (again): ***
Superuser created successfully.
Installing index for auth.Permission model
Installing index for auth.Message model
Installing index for admin.LogEntry model
```

Defining the URL Structure

We've got the application and the database set up, but we still cannot navigate to any of the pages, even the administration interface. This is because the project does not know how to respond to the request URLs and how to map them to appropriate application views.

We need to do two things in the urls.py configuration file: enable the URL routing to the administration interface objects and point to the application-specific urls.py configuration. The project-specific urls.py file is located in the project directory at /srv/app/www_example_com/. Its contents after enabling both settings will be the code shown in Listing 5-2.

Listing 5-2. *Project- (or site-) specific URL mapping*

```
from django.conf.urls.defaults import *

# this is required by the administration appplication
from django.contrib import admin
admin.autodiscover()

urlpatterns = patterns('',
    # route requests to the administration application
    (r'^admin/', include(admin.site.urls)),
    # delegate all other requests to the application specific
    # URL dispatcher
    (r'', include('www_example_com.httpconfig.urls')),
)
```

We have not created any views in our application, but we can already define the URL mapping in the application-specific urls.py, which needs to be created in the application directory httpconfig. The majority of the work is going to be done in the administration interface, so the application's interaction with the outside world is fairly limited. It'll respond to two requests only: if nothing is specified on the URL path, the view should return all virtual hosts in a plain-text format. If an integer is specified, it'll return only the section of the configuration file for that particular Virtual Host. This will be used in the administration interface. In the httpadmin directory, create the urls.py file shown in Listing 5-3.

Listing 5-3. *The application-specific URL mapping*

```
from django.conf.urls.defaults import *

urlpatterns = patterns('www_example_com.httpconfig.views',
    (r'^$', 'full_config'),
    (r'^(?P<object_id>\d+)/$', 'full_config'),
)
```

This configuration means that there is no application-specific part in the URL—all requests to the root location will be forwarded to our application. If you need to "hide" this application behind a certain path in the URL, please refer back to Chapters 3 and 4 for details on how to do that.

In addition to this configuration, you also have to define the view method; otherwise, the Django URL parser may complain about the undefined view. Create the following method in the views.py file in the application directory:

```
def full_config(request):
    return
```

■**Tip** If you get any errors when you navigate to the newly created web site, make sure that all files and directories in the project directory and the project directory itself are owned by the *apache* or *httpd* user. Also note that if you make any changes to the Python files in your project directory, you will need to restart the Apache daemon, so that the requests will be served by the new code rather than the old, which may still be cached in memory.

The Data Model

As we discussed in the requirements and design section, the database model for our application is fairly simple and contains only two entities: the virtual host definition and the configuration directive definition. For the implementation, however, we also need to add a third element into the schema that ties the virtual host and the configuration directive elements. The reason for adding yet another table is that each configuration directive can be part of one or more virtual hosts. Also, there might be one or more directives in each virtual host. Therefore, we have a many-to-many relationship between the objects, and in order to resolve that we need to insert an intermediate table that has a one-to-many relationship with the other tables.

We can represent this relationship model in the entity relationship (ER) diagram shown in Figure 5-1, where you can see the properties of each entity and the relationships between them. ER diagrams are really helpful when coding and sometimes save you from writing complex code just to find information that can be easily obtained with a simple SQL statement if you know the relations between different tables. We'll use this technique again in later chapters.

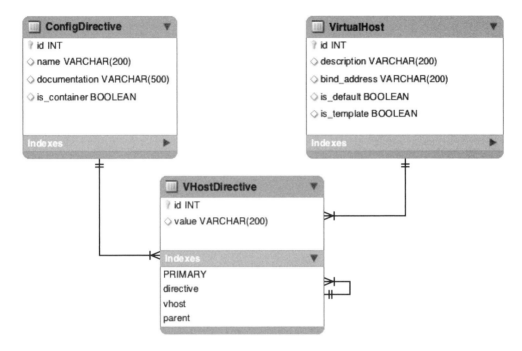

Figure 5-1. *An entity relationship diagram*

■**Note** The diagram in Figure 5-1 was produced using the MySQL Work Bench tool. It follows the convention and structure used to represent the data tables and also the relationships between them (one-to-many links, and so on). The description of those details is beyond the scope of this book, but if you want to learn more about the subject, I recommend *Beginning Database Design: From Novice to Professional,* by Clare Churcher (Apress, 2007), which is a good introduction to database design. A much shorter description of some of the symbols used in the diagram can be found on the Wikipedia page `http://en.wikipedia.org/wiki/Entity-relationship_model`.

You can see that the `ConfigDirective` and the `VirtualHost` tables have a one-to-many relationship with the `VHostDirective` table. This table also holds the value for the configuration directive, which is specific to the particular virtual host. You may also have noticed that the `VHostDirective` has a loop-back relationship to itself. This is to implement the directive encapsulation, where some directives can be the "parent" directives for others.

The Basic Model Structure

We'll go through several iterations while creating the data model. We'll start with the basic model that contains only the object properties and then gradually add functionality as we go along with the administration interface improvements. Listing 5-4 shows the initial code.

Listing 5-4. *The basic model structure*

```python
from django.db import models

# Create your models here.

class ConfigDirective(models.Model):
    name = models.CharField(max_length=200)
    is_container = models.BooleanField(default=False)
    documentation = models.URLField(
                        default='http://httpd.apache.org/docs/2.0/mod/core.html')

    def __unicode__(self):
        return self.name

class VirtualHost(models.Model):
    is_default = models.BooleanField(default=False)
    is_template = models.BooleanField(default=False,
                                    help_text="""Template virtual hosts are
                                        commented out in the configuration
                                        and can be reused as templates""")
    description = models.CharField(max_length=200)
    bind_address = models.CharField(max_length=200)
    directives = models.ManyToManyField(ConfigDirective, through='VHostDirective')

    def __unicode__(self):
        default_mark = ' (*)' if self.is_default else ''
        return self.description + default_mark

class VHostDirective(models.Model):
    directive = models.ForeignKey(ConfigDirective)
    vhost = models.ForeignKey(VirtualHost)
    parent = models.ForeignKey('self', blank=True, null=True,
                            limit_choices_to={'directive__is_container': True})
    value = models.CharField(max_length=200)

    def __unicode__(self):
        fmt_str = "<%s %s>" if self.directive.is_container else "%s %s"
        directive_name = self.directive.name.strip('<>')
        return fmt_str % (directive_name, self.value)
```

If you followed the examples and explanation in Chapters 3 and 4, this model should be reasonably familiar to you. We define the basic properties of each element along with the ForeignKey objects that define the relationship between the classes.

There is one thing, though, that may not look familiar to you—the many-to-many relationship declaration in the VirtualHost class:

```python
directives = models.ManyToManyField(ConfigDirective, through='VHostDirective')
```

Why do we have to define this relationship explicitly, if we already defined the VHostDirective class that joins the two entities together? The reason is that this allows us to find the corresponding ConfigDirectives directly from the VirtualHost, without having to get to the VHostDirective objects first.

We could create the database structure from this model, but it'll be empty at this time and therefore not very useful without at least the list of the core Apache module directives. I have created an initial data JSON file that contains the entries for all core module directives. Here's an example of a few entries; you can get the full set from the book's web page at http://apress.com:

```
[
    <...>
    {
        "model":      "httpconfig.configdirective",
        "pk":         1,
        "fields":     {
                        "name":    "AcceptPathInfo",
                        "documentation":
                      "http://httpd.apache.org/docs/2.0/mod/core.html#AcceptPathInfo",
                        "is_container":     "False"
                      }
    },

    {
        "model":      "httpconfig.configdirective",
        "pk":         2,
        "fields":     {
                        "name":    "AccessFileName",
                        "documentation":
                      "http://httpd.apache.org/docs/2.0/mod/core.html#AccessFileName",
                        "is_container":     "False"
                      }
    },
    <...>
]
```

If you copy this file to the project directory and name it initial_data.json, the data from it will be loaded every time you run the syncdb command. Let's now delete all application-related tables if you have created any in the database and re-create it again with the new model and the initial dataset:

```
$ sqlite3 database.db
SQLite version 3.6.20
Enter ".help" for instructions
Enter SQL statements terminated with a ";"
sqlite> .tables
auth_group                  django_admin_log
auth_group_permissions      django_content_type
auth_message                django_session
```

```
auth_permission              django_site
auth_user                    httpconfig_configdirective
auth_user_groups             httpconfig_vhostdirective
auth_user_user_permissions   httpconfig_virtualhost
sqlite> drop table httpconfig_configdirective;
sqlite> drop table httpconfig_vhostdirective;
sqlite> drop table httpconfig_virtualhost;
sqlite> .exit
$ ./manage.py syncdb
Creating table httpconfig_configdirective
Creating table httpconfig_virtualhost
Creating table httpconfig_vhostdirective
Installing index for httpconfig.VHostDirective model
Installing json fixture 'initial_data' from absolute path.
Installed 62 object(s) from 1 fixture(s)
```

You're nearly ready to start managing the object in the administration application; just register all the model classes with the administration interface and restart the Apache web server. As you already know, you have to create the admin.py file in the application directory with contents similar to Listing 5-5.

Listing 5-5. *Basic administration hooks*

```python
from django.contrib import admin
from www_example_com.httpconfig.models import *

class VirtualHostAdmin(admin.ModelAdmin):
    pass

class VHostDirectiveAdmin(admin.ModelAdmin):
    pass

class ConfigDirectiveAdmin(admin.ModelAdmin):
    pass


admin.site.register(VirtualHost, VirtualHostAdmin)
admin.site.register(ConfigDirective, ConfigDirectiveAdmin)
admin.site.register(VHostDirective, VHostDirectiveAdmin)
```

If you navigate to the administration console, which you can find at http://www.example.com/admin/, you will be provided with the login screen. You can log in with the user account that you created during the first syncdb call. Once logged in, you'll be presented with the standard administration interface, which lists all model classes and allows you to create the individual entries. Now, you must appreciate how much work this has already spared you from—you don't need to deal with user management, model object discovery, or any other housekeeping tasks. However, the admin interface is generic and has absolutely no knowledge about the purpose behind your data models and what fields are important to you.

Let's take our model as an example. The main entity for you is the Virtual Host. However, if you navigate to it in the administration interface, you'll only see one column in the listing view. If you have added any entries you'll see that it's the description field that is displayed. Click the Add button to add a new Virtual Host. All property fields are displayed, but what about the configuration directives? These need to be created separately on a different screen, and then you have to link each directive to the appropriate Virtual Host. That's not very useful, is it?

Luckily, the Django administration module is very flexible and can be customized to accommodate most of the requirements that you can think of. We'll improve the look and feel of the administration interface and add more functionality to it in the next sections.

Modifying the Administration Interface

Most of the administration interface tuning is done in the `models.py` and `admin.py` files. The Python community is attempting to separate the model definition files completely from the administration customization files, and a lot of work has already been done to achieve this separation. However, as of this writing, some items affecting the administration interface can still be found in the `models.py` file. In either case, I will always indicate which file you need to make changes in, but unless instructed otherwise always assume the application directory: `/srv/app/www_example_com/httpconfig/`.

Improving the Class and Object Lists

There's only so much that the administration application can guess about your data model, its properties, and the information you'd like to be presented with. Therefore, if you don't make any modifications or adjustments, you'll just get the standard object representation string displays, just as the strings are returned by the `__unicode__()` method of the class. In the following sections, I'll show you how to change the default layout.

Customizing the Class Names

By default, Django attempts to guess the name of the class. Usually the administration framework gets reasonably close results, but sometimes you may end up with strange names. For example, our three classes will be listed as:

- Config directives
- V host directives
- Virtual hosts

The "V host directives" name may look a bit cryptic in this situation. Another issue is the plural form of the class name. The examples we have resolved quite nicely, but should we have a class called "HostEntry," for example, we'd end up with the automatically generated plural form "Host Entrys," which obviously isn't correct.

In situations like this, you may want to set the class name and the plural form of the name yourself. You don't need to set both, just the one that you want to modify. This setting is done in the model definition file, `models.py`. Listing 5-6 shows the additions to the class definition we created earlier.

Listing 5-6. *Changing the class names*

```
class ConfigDirective(models.Model):
    class Meta:
        verbose_name = 'Configuration Directive'
        verbose_name_plural = 'Configuration Directives'
    [...]

class VirtualHost(models.Model):
    class Meta:
        verbose_name = 'Virtual Host'
        verbose_name_plural = 'Virtual Hosts'
    [...]

class VHostDirective(models.Model):
    class Meta:
        verbose_name = 'Virtual Host Directive'
        verbose_name_plural = 'Virtual Host Directives'
    [...]
```

Make the modifications and reload the Apache web server. Now you will be presented with more readable options:

- Configuration Directives

- Virtual Host Directives

- Virtual Hosts

Adding New Fields to the Object List

Let's start by modifying the virtual hosts listing. If you haven't created any virtual hosts yet, you can do that now. It doesn't really matter what properties you're going to use in the configuration; at this stage we're only interested in getting the layout right. Also assign some configuration directives to the Virtual Hosts that you've created.

One of the most important attributes of any Virtual Host is ServerName, which defines the hostname this particular Virtual Host is responding to. As you know, the Apache web server identifies the Virtual Host by the HOST HTTP header value. It takes that value from the HTTP request and tries to match it against all ServerName or ServerAlias fields in the configuration file. When it finds a match, it knows which Virtual Host is supposed to serve that particular request. So these two directives are the ones you would probably want to see in the Virtual Host listing.

How do you include them in the list where only the string representation of the object is displayed? You can use the ModelAdmin class property list_display to specify the properties you want to have displayed, but there is no such property as a list of server names in the Virtual Host class. Therefore we'll have to write our own method that returns every associated ServerName and ServerAlias. Extend your VirtualHost class with the method shown in Listing 5-7.

Listing 5-7. *Listing the associated ServerNames and ServerAliases*

```
def domain_names(self):
    result = ''
    primary_domains = self.vhostdirective_set.filter(directive__name='ServerName')
    if primary_domains:
        result = "<a href='http://%(d)s' target='_blank'>%(d)s</a>" %
                                        {'d': primary_domains[0].value}
    else:
        result = 'No primary domain defined!'
    secondary_domains =
self.vhostdirective_set.filter(directive__name='ServerAlias')
    if secondary_domains:
        result += ' ('
        for domain in secondary_domains:
            result += "<a href='http://%(d)s' target='_blank'>%(d)s</a>, " %
                                            {'d': domain.value}
        result = result[:-2] + ')'
    return result
domain_names.allow_tags = True
```

This code fetches all `VHostDirective` objects that point to the `ConfigDirective` object whose name is either `'ServerName'` or `'ServerAlias'`. The value of such a `VHostDirective` object is then appended to the result string. In fact, this value is used to construct an HTML link, which should open in a new browser window when clicked. The intention here is that all the links of the Virtual Host are presented in the listing and are clickable, so you can immediately test them.

Let's take a closer look at the instruction that retrieves the `VHostDirective` objects (the highlighted lines in Listing 5-7). As you know from the model definition, the `VirtualHost` class, which we're modifying now, does not link to the `VHostDirective` class. The link is reversed; the `VHostDirective` class has a foreign key that points back to the `VirtuaHost` class. Django allows you to create reverse lookups as well by using the special attribute name `<lowercase_class_name>_set`. In our case the name is `virtualhostdirective_set`. This attribute implements standard object selection methods, such as `filter()` and `all()`. Now, using this `virtualhostdirective_set` attribute, we're actually accessing the instances of the `VHostDirective` class, and therefore we can specify a forward filter that matches the corresponding `Directive` object name against our search string: `directive__name='ServerName'`.

Let's add another method that returns a link to the object representation URL. We are also going to display this in the listing, so that users can click on it and the code snippet just for this VirtualHost will appear in a new browser window. This `VirtualHost` class method is defined in the `models.py` file:

```
def code_snippet(self):
    return "<a href='/%i/' target='_blank'>View code snippet</a>" % self.id
code_snippet.allow_tags = True
```

Have you noticed that in both cases we modify the method's `allow_tags` property by setting it to `True`? This prevents Django from parsing the HTML codes and replacing them with "safe" characters. With the tags enabled, we can place any HTML code in the object listing; for example, we can include links to external URLs, or include images.

Finally, let's list all the properties that we want to see in the object list. This includes the class attributes as well as the names of the two functions that we've just created. Add the following property to the `ModelAdmin` class definition in the `admin.py` file:

```
class VirtualHostAdmin(admin.ModelAdmin):
    list_display = ('description', 'is_default', 'is_template',
                    'bind_address', 'domain_names', 'code_snippet')
```

Now when you navigate to the Virtual Host object list, you should see something similar to Figure 5-2. It may not be obvious, but the listed domain names and the code snippet text are clickable and should open the URL in a new browser window.

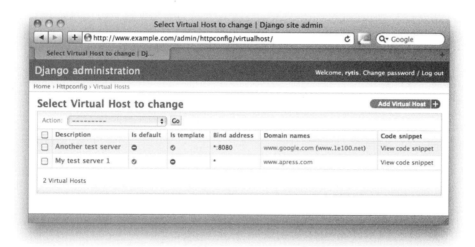

Figure 5-2. *The modified object list view*

Reorganizing the Form Fields

If you tried adding the Virtual Host instances using the current administration interface, you probably noticed how unfriendly and confusing the process is. First you have to create a new `VirtualHost` object; then you have to navigate away from it and create one or more `VHostDirective` objects by picking the newly created Virtual Host object. Wouldn't it be nicer if you could create all that from one form? Luckily this is very easy thing to do. In Django terms this is called an *inline formset* and allows you to edit models on the same page as the parent model.

In our case, the parent model is the `VirtualHost` and we want to edit the instances of the `VHostDirective` inline. This can be accomplished in only two steps. First you create a new administration class that inherits from the `admin.TabularInline` class. Add the following code to the `admin.py` file. The properties of this class indicate which child model we want to include and how many extra empty lines we want to have in the formset:

```
class VHostDirectiveInLine(admin.TabularInline):
    model = VHostDirective
    extra = 1
```

The second step is to instruct the administration class that you want to have this inline form included in the main model edit form:

```
class VirtualHostAdmin(admin.ModelAdmin):
    inlines = (VHostDirectiveInLine,)
    [...]
```

This simple manipulation results in a rather nice looking formset that includes the entry fields for both the parent and the child models, as shown in Figure 5-3.

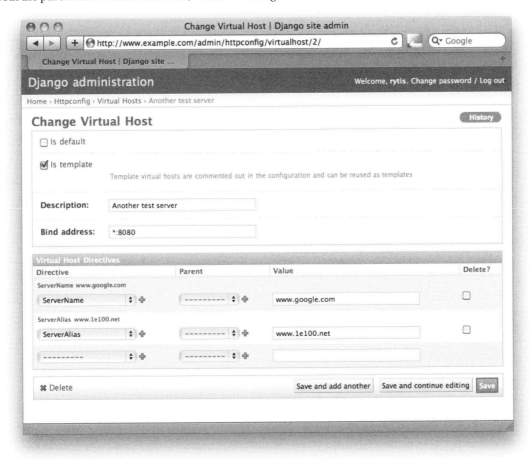

Figure 5-3. *Including the child model editing form*

If you don't like the way the fields are organized in the form, you can change their order and also group them into logical groups. You group the fields by defining the *fieldsets*. Each fieldset is a tuple of two elements: a fieldset name and a dictionary of fieldset properties. One dictionary key is required, the list of fields. The other two keys, `classes` and `description`, are optional. Following is an example of the `ConfigDirective` model administration form, which has two fieldset groups defined:

```
class ConfigDirectiveAdmin(admin.ModelAdmin):
    fieldsets = [
                (None,     {'fields': ['name']}),
                ('Details', {'fields': ['is_container', 'documentation'],
                        'classes': ['collapse'],
                        'description': 'Specify the config directive details'})
            ]
```

The first group contains only one field and has no name. The second group is labeled `'Details'`. It has a short description below the label, contains two fields, and has a show/hide capability.

The `'classes'` property defines the CSS class name and depends on the class definitions. The standard Django administration CSS defines two useful classes: the `'collapse'` class allows you to show/hide the whole group and, the `'wide'` class adds some extra space for the form fields.

Adding Custom Object Actions

We're nearly ready with the application, but there are two more functions that we need to implement. In the Virtual Host model we have a Boolean flag that indicates whether the host is the default. This information is also conveniently displayed in the listing. However, if we want to change it, we have to navigate to the object's edit page and change the setting there.

It would be nice if this could be done from the object-list screen, by just selecting the appropriate object and using an action from the drop-down menu in the top-left corner of the list. However, the only action that is currently available there is Delete selected Virtual Hosts. Django allows you to define your own action functions and add them to the administration screen menu. There are two steps to get a new function in the actions list. Firs you define a method in the administration class and second you must identify the administration class in whose actions list this method should be listed as an action.

The custom action method is passed three parameters when called. The first is the instance of the `ModelAdmin` class that called the method. You can define the custom methods outside of the `ModelAdmin` class, in which case multiple `ModelAdmin` classes can reuse them. If you define the method within a particular `ModelAdmin` class, the first parameter will always be the instance of that class; in other words, this is a typical class method `'self'` property.

The second parameter is the HTTP request object. It can be used to pass the message back to the user once the action is complete.

The third argument is the query set that contains all objects that have been selected by the user. This is the list of objects you will be operating on. Because there can be only one default Virtual Host, we have to check whether multiple objects have been selected and if so, return an error indicating that. Listing 5-8 shows the modifications to the model administration class that create a new custom object action.

Listing 5-8. *A custom action to set the default Virtual Host flag*

```
class VirtualHostAdmin(admin.ModelAdmin):
    [...]
    actions = ('make_default',)

    def make_default(self, request, queryset):
        if len(queryset) == 1:
            VirtualHost.objects.all().update(is_default=False)
            queryset.update(is_default=True)
            self.message_user(request,
                "Virtual host '%s' has been made the default virtual host" %↵
queryset[0])
        else:
            self.message_user(request, 'ERROR: Only one host can be set as the↵
default!')
    make_default.short_description = 'Make selected Virtual Host default'
```

The second custom action that we're going to define is object duplication. This action takes the selected objects and "clones" them. The clones are going to have the same settings and the same set of the configuration directives with the same values, but the following exceptions will apply:

- The virtual host description will get the "(Copy)" string appended to its description.

- The new virtual host will not be the default.

- The new virtual host will not be a template.

The challenge here is to resolve all parent-child dependencies of the VHostDirective objects correctly. In the Apache Virtual Host definition, you can have only one level of encapsulation, so we don't need to do any recursive discovery of the related objects. The duplication method can be split into the following logical steps:

- Create a new instance of the VirtualHost class and clone all properties.

- Clone all directives that do not have any parents.

- Clone all directives that are containers and therefore may potentially contain child directives.

- For each container directive, find all its child directives and clone them.

Listing 5-9 shows the duplication function code.

Listing 5-9. *The action to duplicate the Virtual Host objects*

```
def duplicate(self, request, queryset):
    msg = ''
    for vhost in queryset:
        new_vhost = VirtualHost()
        new_vhost.description = "%s (Copy)" % vhost.description
        new_vhost.bind_address = vhost.bind_address
```

```
        new_vhost.is_template = False
        new_vhost.is_default = False
        new_vhost.save()
        # recreate all 'orphan' directives that aren't parents
        o=vhost.vhostdirective_set.filter(parent=None).↵
filter(directive__is_container=False)
        for vhd in o:
            new_vhd = VHostDirective()
            new_vhd.directive = vhd.directive
            new_vhd.value = vhd.value
            new_vhd.vhost = new_vhost
            new_vhd.save()
        # recreate all parent directives
        for vhd in vhost.vhostdirective_set.filter(directive__is_container=True):
            new_vhd = VHostDirective()
            new_vhd.directive = vhd.directive
            new_vhd.value = vhd.value
            new_vhd.vhost = new_vhost
            new_vhd.save()
            # and all their children
            for child_vhd in vhost.vhostdirective_set.filter(parent=vhd):
                msg += str(child_vhd)
                new_child_vhd = VHostDirective()
                new_child_vhd.directive = child_vhd.directive
                new_child_vhd.value = child_vhd.value
                new_child_vhd.vhost = new_vhost
                new_child_vhd.parent = new_vhd
                new_child_vhd.save()
    self.message_user(request, msg)
duplicate.short_description = 'Duplicate selected Virtual Hosts'
```

Generating the Configuration File

We've finished adjusting the administration interface, so it is now ready for adding new Virtual Hosts and managing the existing database entries. Now we need to finish writing the view method that will display the information. There is one issue though—the "parent" directives mimic the XML syntax. That is, they have opening and closing elements. The default string representation that we've written for the VHostDirective model class takes care of the opening element, but we also need to write a function that generates an XML-like closing tag. These two tags will be used to enclose the "child" configuration directives.

Add the following method to the VHostDirective class in the models.py file. This function converts the <tag> to </tag> if the directive is marked as a container directive:

```
def close_tag(self):
    return "</%s>" % self.directive.name.strip('<>') if self.directive.is_container↵
else ""
```

Once you've done that, extend the previously created empty view method with the code from Listing 5-10. This code iterates through all available objects if no arguments were supplied. If an integer is supplied as an argument, it will select only the object with the matching ID. For all objects in the list, a dictionary structure is created. This structure contains the virtual host object and the corresponding directive objects. The orphan and the containers are stored separately, so it's easier to distinguish between them in the template. The return object sets the MIME type of the response to "text/plain", which allows you to download the URL directly to the configuration file.

Listing 5-10. *The view method*

```python
from www_example_com.httpconfig.models import *
from django.http import HttpResponse, HttpResponseRedirect
from django.shortcuts import render_to_response, get_object_or_404

# Create your views here.

def full_config(request, object_id=None):
    if not object_id:
        vhosts = VirtualHost.objects.all()
    else:
        vhosts = VirtualHost.objects.filter(id=object_id)
    vhosts_list = []
    for vhost in vhosts:
        vhost_struct = {}
        vhost_struct['vhost_data'] = vhost
        vhost_struct['orphan_directives'] = \
vhost.vhostdirective_set.filter(directive__is_container=False).filter(parent=None)
        vhost_struct['containers'] = []
        for container_directive in \
          vhost.vhostdirective_set.filter(directive__is_container=True):
            vhost_struct['containers'].append({'parent': container_directive,
                                               'children': \
            vhost.vhostdirective_set.filter(parent=container_directive),
                                              })
        vhosts_list.append(vhost_struct)
    return render_to_response('full_config.txt',
                              {'vhosts': vhosts_list},
                              mimetype='text/plain')
```

▦**Note** Please note that the backslash character in the examples is used to wrap the long lines of code. This is a valid Python language syntax that allows you to format your code for a greater readability. If you are re-typing these examples, please maintain the same code structure and layout. Do not confuse the backslash characters with the line wrapping symbol (↵), which indicates that the line was too long to fit on a page and has been wrapped. You must join the lines split by this symbol when reusing the examples.

As you know from Chapters 3 and 4, the templates are stored in the `templates` subdirectory in the application folder. Listing 5-11 shows the `full_config.txt` template.

Listing 5-11. *The Virtual Host view template*

```
# Virtual host configuration section
# automatically generated - do not edit

{% for vhost in vhosts %}

##
## {{ vhost.vhost_data.description }}
##
{% if vhost.vhost_data.is_template %}#{% endif %} <VirtualHost {{↵
vhost.vhost_data.bind_address }}>
{% if vhost.vhost_data.is_template %}#{% endif %}     {% for orphan_directive in ↵
vhost.orphan_directives %}
{% if vhost.vhost_data.is_template %}#{% endif %}      {{ orphan_directive }}
{% if vhost.vhost_data.is_template %}#{% endif %}     {% endfor %}
{% if vhost.vhost_data.is_template %}#{% endif %}     {% for container in
vhost.containers %}
{% if vhost.vhost_data.is_template %}#{% endif %}      {{ container.parent|safe }}
{% if vhost.vhost_data.is_template %}#{% endif %}       {% for child_dir in ↵
container.children %}
{% if vhost.vhost_data.is_template %}#{% endif %}        {{ child_dir }}
{% if vhost.vhost_data.is_template %}#{% endif %}       {% endfor %}
{% if vhost.vhost_data.is_template %}#{% endif %}      {{
container.parent.close_tag|safe }}
{% if vhost.vhost_data.is_template %}#{% endif %}     {% endfor %}
{% if vhost.vhost_data.is_template %}#{% endif %}  </VirtualHost>
```

After you've made all the modifications you should be able to navigate to the web site URL (in our example this would be `http://www.example.com/`), and the result should be a section of the automatically generated Apache configuration file that contains the Virtual Host definitions, as shown in Listing 5-12. Note that the templates are also included, but are commented out and thus will be ignored by the web server.

Listing 5-12. *A sample configuration file*

```
# Virtual host configuration section
# automatically generated - do not edit
##
```

```
## My test server 1
##
  <VirtualHost *>
      ServerName www.apress.com
      <Directory />
          AcceptPathInfo Off
          AddDefaultCharset Off
      </Directory>
  </VirtualHost>
##
## Another test server
##
#  <VirtualHost *:8080>
#
#      ServerName www.google.com
#
#      ServerAlias www.1e100.net
#
#
#  </VirtualHost>
```

Summary

In this chapter we discussed how to modify the default Django administration application to make it more user-friendly and suit your object models. Key points to remember:

- The object listing can include any model properties as well as custom-defined functions.
- The custom-defined functions in the object list can also generate HTML output.
- You can add custom actions to the object list administration page.
- If your model has many fields, they can be rearranged into logical groups.
- You can include the child model in the parent edit page as an inline fieldset.

CHAPTER 6

■ ■ ■

Gathering and Presenting Statistical Data from Apache Log Files

This chapter covers the architecture and implementation of plug-in based applications. As an example, we're going to build a framework for analyzing Apache log files. Rather than creating a monolithic application, we'll use the modular approach. Once we have a base framework, we'll create a plug-in for it that performs the analysis based on the geographical location of the requestor.

Application Structure and Functionality

In the data mining and statistics gathering area, it is difficult to come up with a single application that suits the requirements of multiple users. Let's take the analysis of Apache web server logs as an example. Each request that is received by the web server is written to a log file. There are several different data fields written in each log line, along with the timestamp when the request came in.

Let's imagine you've been asked to write an application that analyzes the log files and produces a report. This is the extent of a typical request that comes from the users who are interested in the statistical information. Obviously, there is not much you can do with this request, so you ask for more information, such as what exactly the users want to see on their report. Now the hypothetical users are getting more involved in the design phase, and they tell you that they want to see the total amount of downloads for a particular file. Well, that's easy to do. But then you get another request that asks for per-hour statistics of the site hits. You script that in. Then there's a request to correlate the time of the day with the browser type. And the list goes on and on. Even if you're writing the tools for one particular organization, the requirements are too diverse and impossible to capture at the requirement-gathering phase. So what should you do in this situation?

Wouldn't it be nice to have a generic application that could be extended with modules that specialize in extracting and processing the information? Each module would be responsible for performing the specific calculations and producing the reports. These modules could be added and removed as and when required, without affecting the functionality of other modules, and more important, without requiring any changes to the main application. This type of modular structure is often referred to as the *plug-in architecture*.

A plug-in is a small piece of software that extends the functionality of the main application. This technique is very popular and used in many different applications. A good example is the web browser. Most of the popular web browsers on the market support plug-ins. A web page may contain an embedded Adobe Flash movie, but the browser itself doesn't know (and doesn't need to know) how to handle this type of file. So it looks for a plug-in that has the *capability* to process and display the Adobe Flash file. If it finds such a plug-in, it passes the file object to it for processing. If it can't find a plug-in, the object is simply not displayed to the end user. The absence of the appropriate plug-in does not prevent the web page from being displayed.

We'll use this approach to build the application for analyzing Apache logs. Let's begin with the requirements for the particular statistical analysis tasks for the application.

Application Requirements

We need to implement two main requirements in our application:

- The main application will be responsible for parsing the Apache log files and extracting the fields from each log line. The log line format may differ between web server installations, so the application should be configurable to match the log file format.

- The application should be able to discover the installed plug-in modules and pass the extracted fields to the appropriate plug-in module for the further processing. Adding new plug-in modules should not have any effect on the functionality of the existing modules and the functionality of the main application.

Application Design

The requirements imply that the application should be split into two parts:

Main application: The application will parse the log files from the list of directories supplied as a command-line argument to it. Each log file will be processed one line at a time. The application does not guarantee that the files are processed in chronological order. Each log line is split in word boundaries, and the field separator is the space character. It is possible that some fields are will have space characters in their contents; such fields must be enclosed in double quotes. For ease of use, the fields will be identified by the corresponding log format field codes, as described in the Apache documentation.

Plug-in manager component: The plug-in manager is responsible for discovering and registering the available plug-in modules. Only the special Python classes will be treated as plug-in modules. Each plug-in exposes the log fields it's interested in. When the main application parses the log files, it will check the subscribed plug-in table and pass the required information to the relevant plug-ins.

Next, let's look at how we can implement the plug-in framework in Python.

Plug-in Framework Implementation in Python

There's good and bad news when it comes to the plug-in framework implementation in Python. The bad news is that there is no standard approach in implementing the plug-in architecture. There are several different techniques, as well as commercial and open source products to use, but they each approach the problem differently. Some are better in one area, but may fall short in other areas. The way you choose to implement this architecture largely depends on what you want to achieve.

The good news is that there is no de facto standard for implementing the plug-in framework, so we get to write our own! As we write the implementation, you'll learn several new things about the Python language and programming techniques, such as class type inspection, duck typing, and dynamic module loading.

Before we dive into the technical details, let's establish exactly what a plug-in is and how it is related to the main, or host, application.

The Mechanics of a Plug-in Framework

The host application processes the data it receives—whether it's a log file for the log-parsing engine, an HTML file for a web browser, or another type of file. Its work is completely unaffected by the presence of the plug-ins or their functionality. However, the host application provides a service to the plug-in modules.

In the case of the log-processing application, its sole responsibility is reading the data from the files, recognizing the log format, and converting that data into the appropriate data structures. This is the service that it provides to the plug-in modules. The main application does not care whether the data it has produced is used by any of the modules or how it is used.

The plug-in modules largely depend on the host application. Let's take the plug-in that counts the number of requests as an example. This plug-in cannot perform any counting unless it receives the data. So the plug-in is rarely useful without the main application.

You may wonder why you should bother with this separation at all. Why can't the plug-in modules read the data files and do whatever they need to do with the data? As we discussed, there might be many different applications performing different calculations with the same data. Having each of those modules implement the same data reading and parsing functionality would be inefficient from the development perspective—it takes time to redevelop the same process again and again.

Obviously, this is a rather simplistic example. Quite often, the end user does not notice this separation between the main application and the plug-in modules. The user experiences the application as the combined result of the application and the plug-in.

Let's consider the web browser example again. The HTML page is rendered by the browser engine and presented to the user. The plug-in modules render the various components within the page. For example, the Adobe Flash movie is rendered by the Flash plug-in, and the Windows Media files are rendered by the Windows Media plug-in module. The user sees only the end result: the rendered web page. Adding new plug-ins to the system simply extends the functionality of the application. After deploying a new plug-in, users can start visiting web sites that did not display correctly (or at all) before the plug-in was installed.

Another great example of the plug-in based application is the Eclipse project (`http://eclipse.org/`). It started as a Java development environment, but has grown into a platform that supports multiple languages, integrates with various version control systems, and provides for modeling and reporting—all thanks to its plug-in architecture. The basic application doesn't do a lot, but you can extend it and tailor it to your needs by installing the appropriate plug-ins. So the same "application" might do completely different things. To me, it's a Python development platform; to someone else, it's a UML modeling tool.

Interface Model

As you might have already guessed, the host application and the plug-in modules are typically very loosely coupled entities. Therefore, a protocol must be defined for the interaction between those two entities. Usually, the host application exposes the well-documented service interfaces, such as function names. The plug-in methods call them whenever they need anything from the host application.

Similarly, the plug-ins also expose their interface, so that the host application can send the data to them or notify them about some occurring events. This is where matters get slightly more complicated. The plug-in modules usually implement functionality that the host application may not be aware of. Therefore, the plug-ins may announce their capabilities, such as a capability to display a Flash movie file. The capability type is usually associated with the module function name, so that the main application knows which method implements the capability.

As an example, let's consider a simplistic browser model. We have a basic host application that receives the HTML page and also downloads all linked in resources. Each resource has a MIME type associated with it. The Flash objects have the `application/x-shockwave-flash` type. When the browser comes across such an object, it will look in its plug-in registry and search for a plug-in that claims to have a capability to process this type of file. Once the plug-in and the method name are found, the host application calls that method and passes the file object to it.

Plug-in Registration and Discovery

So what exactly is this plug-in registry that the host application checks? In simple terms, it's a list of all the plug-in modules that have been found and loaded together with the main application. This list usually contains the object instances, their capabilities, and the functions that implement these capabilities. The registry is a central location to store all plug-in instances, so that the host application can find them during runtime.

The plug-in registry is created during the plug-in discovery process. The discovery process varies between the different implementations, but usually involves finding the appropriate application files and loading them into memory. Typically, there is a separate process within the host application that deals with the plug-in management tasks, such as the discovery, registration, and control. Figure 6-1 shows an overview of all the components and their relationships.

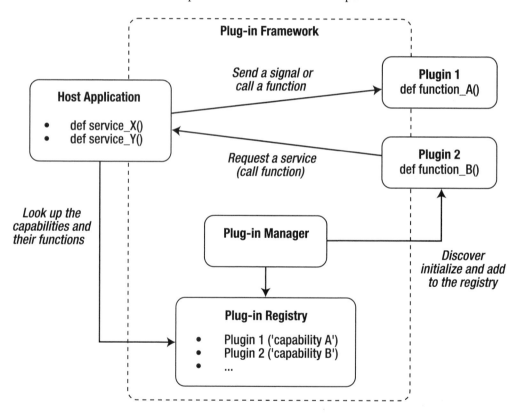

Figure 6-1. *Typical plug-in architecture*

Creating the Plug-in Framework

As I've mentioned, there are several ways of implementing the plug-in based architecture in Python. Here, I'm going to discuss one of the simplest methods, which is flexible enough to suit the needs of most small applications.

■**Note** Dr André Roberge has made a very descriptive presentation at PyCon 2009 comparing several different plug-in mechanisms. You can find his presentation, titled "Plugins and monkeypatching: increasing flexibility, dealing with inflexibility," at `http://blip.tv/file/1949302/`. If you decide that you need a more sophisticated implementation, take a look at the implementations provided by the Zope (`http://zope.org/`), Grok (`http://grok.zope.org/`), and Envisage (`http://code.enthought.com/projects/envisage/`) frameworks. These products are enterprise-grade plug-in frameworks that will allow you to build extensible applications. The downside of using them is that they are usually too big and complicated for simple applications.

Discovery and Registration

The discovery process is based on the fact that the base class can find all its child classes. Here's a simple example:

```
>>> class Plugin(object):
...   pass
...
>>> class MyPlugin1(Plugin):
...   def __init__(self):
...     print 'plugin 1'
...
>>> class MyPlugin2(Plugin):
...   def __init__(self):
...     print 'plugin 2'
...
>>> Plugin.__subclasses__()
[<class '__main__.MyPlugin1'>, <class '__main__.MyPlugin2'>]
>>>
```

This code creates a base class and then defines two more classes that inherit from the base class. We now can find all classes that have inherited from the main class by calling the base class built-in method __subclasses__(). This is a very powerful mechanism for finding classes without knowing their names, or even the names of the module from which they have been loaded.

Once the classes have been discovered, we can create the instances of each class and add them to a list. This is the registration process. After all the objects have been registered, the main program can start calling their methods:

```
>>> plugins = []
>>> for cls in Plugin.__subclasses__():
...   obj = cls()
...   plugins.append(obj)
```

```
...
plugin 1
plugin 2
>>> plugins
[<__main__.MyPlugin1 object at 0x10048c8d0>, <__main__.MyPlugin2 object at
0x10048c910>]
>>>
```

So the discovery and registration process flow is as follows:

- All plug-in classes inherit from one base class that is known to the plug-in manager.

- The plug-in manager imports one or more modules that contain the plug-in class definitions.

- The plug-in manager calls the base class method __subclasses__() and discovers all loaded plug-in classes.

- The plug-in manager creates instances.

We now have several problems to resolve. First, the plug-in classes need to be stored in a separate location, preferably in separate files. This allows for deploying new plug-ins and removing obsolete ones without worrying that you might accidentally overwrite the application files. So we need a mechanism to import arbitrary Python modules that contain the plug-in class definitions. You can use the Python built-in method __import__ to load any module by its name at runtime, but the module file needs to be in the system search path.

For the sample application. we'll use the following directory and file structure:

```
http_log_parser.py                <-- host application
manager.py                        <-- plug-in manager module
plugins/                          <-- directory containing all plug-in modules
          plugin_<name>.py        <-- module containing one or more plug-in
classes
logs/                             <-- directory containing the log files
          <any name>              <-- any file is assumed to be a log file
```

This directory structure is assumed to be the default, but we'll allow the paths to be modified, so you can change them to better suit your requirements. The plug-in modules follow this particular naming convention, so that it is easier to distinguish them from the normal Python scripts. Each module must import the Plugin class from the manager.py module.

Let's start with the manager class initialization method. We're going to allow the host application to pass any optional initialization parameters to the plug-in objects, so that they can perform any runtime initialization they need. There is one issue, however. We don't know what those parameters can be, and if there are any at all. So instead of defining the exact argument list structure, we'll pass only the keyword arguments. The manager's __init__() method takes a dictionary as an argument, and passes this on to the plug-in method initialization function.

We also need to discover the location of the plug-in files. It can be passed as an argument to the manager's constructor, in which case, it should be an absolute path; otherwise, we'll assume a subdirectory called /plugins/ relative to the location of the script:

```
class PluginManager():
    def __init__(self, path=None, plugin_init_args={}):
        if path:
            self.plugin_dir = path
        else:
            self.plugin_dir = os.path.dirname(__file__) + '/plugins/'
        self.plugins = []
        self._load_plugins()
        self._register_plugins(**plugin_init_args)
```

The next step is to load all plug-in files as modules. Each Python application can be loaded as a module, so all its functions and classes become available to the main application. We cannot use the conventional `import` statement to import the files, because their names become known to us only during runtime. So we'll use the built-in method `__import__`, which allows us to use a variable containing the module name. Otherwise, this method is identical to the `import` method, which means that the module it's trying to load should be located in a search path. Obviously, this is not the case. Therefore, we need to add the directory containing the plug-in modules to the system path. We can do this by appending the directory to the `sys.path` array:

```
def _load_plugins(self):
    sys.path.append(self.plugin_dir)
    plugin_files = [fn for fn in os.listdir(self.plugin_dir) if↵
fn.startswith('plugin_') and fn.endswith('.py')]
    plugin_modules = [m.split('.')[0] for m in plugin_files]
    for module in plugin_modules:
        m = __import__(module)
```

Finally, we discover the classes that inherit from the base class using the `__subclasses__` method and append the initialized objects to the plug-in list. Note how we pass the keyword arguments to the plug-ins:

```
def _register_plugins(self, **kwargs):
    for plugin in Plugin.__subclasses__():
        obj = plugin(**kwargs)
        self.plugins.append(obj)
```

We're using the keyword argument list here because we don't know yet what, if any, parameters will be required or used by the plug-in classes. Furthermore, the modules may use or recognize different arguments. By using the keyword arguments, we allow the modules to respond to only those arguments that interest them. Listing 6-1 shows the full listing of the plug-in manager.

Listing 6-1. *Plug-in Discovery and Registration*

```
#!/usr/bin/env python

import sys
import os
```

```
class Plugin(object):
    pass


class PluginManager():
    def __init__(self, path=None, plugin_init_args={}):
        if path:
            self.plugin_dir = path
        else:
            self.plugin_dir = os.path.dirname(__file__) + '/plugins/'
        self.plugins = []
        self._load_plugins()
        self._register_plugins(**plugin_init_args)

    def _load_plugins(self):
        sys.path.append(self.plugin_dir)
        plugin_files = [fn for fn in os.listdir(self.plugin_dir) if \
                            fn.startswith('plugin_') and fn.endswith('.py')]
        plugin_modules = [m.split('.')[0] for m in plugin_files]
        for module in plugin_modules:
            m = __import__(module)

    def _register_plugins(self, **kwargs):
        for plugin in Plugin.__subclasses__():
            obj = plugin(**kwargs)
            self.plugins.append(obj)
```

This is all we need to initialize all plug-in modules. As soon as we create an instance of the
PluginManager class, it will automatically discover the available modules, load them, initialize all
plug-in classes, and put the initialized objects in the list:

```
plugin_manager = PluginManager()
```

Defining the Plug-in Modules

So far, we have only two requirements that the plug-in classes must satisfy: each class must inherit
from the base Plugin class, and their __init__ method must accept the keyword arguments. The class
may choose to completely ignore what has been passed to it during the initialization, but it still must
accept the arguments; otherwise, we'll get the invalid argument list exception when the main
application passes the arguments we don't expect to receive.

The plug-in module skeleton looks like this:

```
#!/usr/bin/env python

from manager import Plugin

class CountHTTP200(Plugin):
```

```
def __init__(self, **kwargs):
    pass
```

This plug-in obviously doesn't do much yet. We now need to define the interfaces between the main application and the plug-in. In our log-parsing application example, the communication is going to be only one way: the application sends the messages (log information) to the plug-ins for further processing. In addition, the application may send other commands or signals that inform the plug-in objects about the current state of the application. So now we need to create the host application.

Log-Parsing Application

As we've discussed, the host application does not and should not depend on the functionality and the presence of the accompanying plug-ins. It provides a set of services that can be consumed by the plug-ins. In our example, the main application is responsible for handling the Apache access log files. In order to understand the best way to handle the log information, let's first look at the way Apache logs the request data.

Format of Apache Log Files

The format of a log file is defined by the `LogFormat` directive in the Apache configuration file, which is typically either `/etc/apache2/apache2.conf` or `/etc/httpd/conf/httpd.conf`, depending on your Linux distribution. Here is an example:

```
LogFormat "%h %l %u %t \"%r\" %>s %b \"%{Referer}i\" \"%{User-Agent}i\"" combined
```

This configuration line is split into three parts. First is the directive name. The second part is the format string that defines the structure of the log line. We'll come back to the format string definitions shortly. The last part is the name of the logging format.

You can define as many different logging line formats as you like, and then assign them to the logging file definitions as necessary. For example, you can add the following directive to a virtual host definition section, which instructs the Apache web server to write the log lines in the format described by the `combined` log format directive, into a log file called `logs/access.log`:

```
CustomLog logs/access.log combined
```

You can have multiple `CustomLog` directives, each with a different file name and the format directive.

■**Note** Refer to the official Apache documentation for more information about the log files. You can find it at `http://httpd.apache.org/docs/2.2/logs.html`.

The format string that is used with the `LogFormat` configuration statement contains one or more directives that start with the % character. When a log line is written to the log file, the directives are replaced with the corresponding values. Table 6-1 lists some of the most commonly used directives.

Table 6-1. *Commonly Used Log Format Directives*

Directive	Description
%a	IP address of the remote host.
%A	IP address of the local host.
%B	The response size in bytes. HTTP header size is not included.
%b	Same as %B, but the - sign is used instead of 0 if the response is empty.
%{cookie_name}C	The value of the *cookie_name* cookie.
%D	The request processing time in microseconds.
%h	The remote host.
%H	The request protocol (HTTP 1.0, 1.1, etc.).
%{header_field}i	The contents of the HTTP request field. These are commonly used HTTP request headers: Referer: If present, identifies the referring URL User-Agent: The string identifying the user client software Via: List of the proxies through which the request was sent Accept-Language: List of language codes accepted by the client Content-Type: Request MIME content type
%l	Remote *logname* from the remote identd process, if running. This is usually -, unless the mod_ident module is installed. [a]
%m	The request method (POST, GET, etc.).
%{header_field}o	The contents of the HTTP header variable in the response. See the %{ }I definition for more details.
%P	The process ID of the Apache web server child that served the request.
%q	The query string (only for GET requests), if it exists. The string is prepended with the ? character.
%r	The first line of the request. This usually includes the request method, the request URL, and the protocol definition.
%s	The status of the response, such as 404 or 200. This is the status of the original (!) request. If there are any internal redirects configured, this will be different from the final status that is sent back to the requestor.

Directive	Description
%>s	The last status of the request. In other words, this is what the client receives.
%t	The timestamp of when the request was received. This is a standard English format, which looks like [20/May/2010:07:26:23 +0100]. You can modify the format. See the %{*format*}t directive definition for details.
%{*format*}t	The timestamp as defined by the *format* string. The format is defined using the strftime directives.
%T	The request serving time, in seconds.
%u	The remote user if authenticating using the auth module.
%U	The URL part of the request. The query string is not included.

aEven if both the remote process and the Apache module are present, I would not recommend relying on this information, as the identd protocol is considered insecure.

Log File Reader

As you can see, the log format can vary depending on the log format definition in the Apache configuration. We need to accommodate the differences in the formats. To make it easier to communicate with the plug-in modules, we will map the values extracted from the log lines into a data structure that can be passed on to the plug-in code.

First, we need to map the Apache log format directives to the more descriptive strings that can be used as the dictionary keys. Here is the mapping table that we will use:

```
DIRECTIVE_MAP = {
                  '%h': 'remote_host',
                  '%l': 'remote_logname',
                  '%u': 'remote_user',
                  '%t': 'time_stamp',
                  '%r': 'request_line',
                  '%>s': 'status',
                  '%b': 'response_size',
                  '%{Referer}i':   'referer_url',
                  '%{User-Agent}i': 'user_agent',
                }
```

When we initialize the log reader object, we give it two optional arguments. The first argument sets the log format line as it is defined in the Apache configuration. The default will be assumed if no argument string is supplied. The other argument indicates the location of the log files. Once we have identified the log line format, we will create a list of the alternative directive names as defined in our mapping table. The keywords in the list will be in exactly the same order as the directives appear in the log format string.

The following initialization function performs all the steps described:

```
class LogLineGenerator:
    def __init__(self, log_format=None, log_dir='logs'):
        # LogFormat "%h %l %u %t \"%r\" %>s %b \"%{Referer}i\" \"%{User-Agent}i\""↵
combined
        if not log_format:
            self.format_string = '%h %l %u %t %r %>s %b %{Referer}i %{User-Agent}i'
        else:
            self.format_string = log_format
        self.log_dir = log_dir
        self.re_tsquote = re.compile(r'(\[|\])')
        self.field_list = []
        for directive in self.format_string.split(' '):
            self.field_list.append(DIRECTIVE_MAP[directive])
```

The log strings usually follow a simple pattern, with fields separated by space characters. If a field value contains space characters, it will be surrounded by the quote characters. Examples are the %r and %t fields, as you can see from the following sample log lines:

```
220.181.7.76 - - [20/May/2010:07:26:23 +0100] "GET / HTTP/1.1" 200 29460 "-"↵
"Baiduspider+(+http://www.baidu.com/search/spider.htm)"
220.181.7.116 - - [20/May/2010:07:26:43 +0100] "GET / HTTP/1.1" 200 29460 "-"↵
"Baiduspider+(+http://www.baidu.com/search/spider.htm)"
209.85.228.85 - - [20/May/2010:07:26:49 +0100] "GET /feeds/latest/ HTTP/1.1" 200
45088 "-"\
                                "FeedBurner/1.0 (http://www.FeedBurner.com)"
209.85.228.84 - - [20/May/2010:07:26:57 +0100] "GET /feeds/latest/ HTTP/1.1" 200
45088 "-"\
                                "FeedBurner/1.0 (http://www.FeedBurner.com)"
```

▪**Note** Remember that the \ symbol indicates that the contents of the line have been wrapped. In the real log file, the contents are on a single line.

We are going to use the built-in Python module for parsing comma-separated values (CSV) format files. Although the file format implies that the values are separated by commas, the library is flexible enough to allow you to specify any character as a separator. In addition to the separator, you can specify the quote character. In our case, the separator is the space character, and the quote character (used to wrap the request and user agent strings) is the double quote character.

I'm guessing that you've already noticed a problem here. The time field contains a space, but it is not surrounded by double quotes. Instead, it is surrounded by square brackets. Unfortunately, the CSV library does not allow specifying a selection for multiple quote characters, so we'll need to use a regular expression to replace all occurrences of the square brackets with double quotes. The regular expression that matches the square brackets has been defined in the class constructor method. We'll use the precompiled regular expression later in the code:

```
self.re_tsquote = re.compile(r'(\[|\])')
```

Now let's write a simple file reader that does on-the-fly character translation, replacing the square brackets with the double quotes. This is a generator function that you can iterate through. We'll talk about the generator function in more detail in the next chapter.

```
def _quote_translator(self, file_name):
    for line in open(file_name):
        yield self.re_tsquote.sub('"', line)
```

We also need to have a function that lists all the files it finds in the specified log directory. The following function lists all the files and returns each file name that it finds along with the directory name. This function lists only the file objects, ignoring any directories.

```
def _file_list(self):
    for file in os.listdir(self.log_dir):
        file_name = "%s/%s" % (self.log_dir, file)
        if os.path.isfile(file_name):
            yield file_name
```

Finally, we need to extract all fields from the log lines that we read in and create a dictionary object. The dictionary keys are the directive names from the mapping table we created earlier, and the values are the fields extracted from the log line. This may sound like a complicated task, but it actually isn't, because the CSV library provides this functionality for us. The initialized `csv.DictReader` class returns an iterator object that iterates through all lines returned by the first argument object. In our case, this object is the file reader method (`_quote_translator`) that we wrote earlier.

The next argument to the `DictReader` class is the list of the dictionary keys. The extracted fields will be mapped to those names. The two additional parameters specify the separator and the quote symbols.

```
reader = csv.DictReader(self._quote_translator(file),
                        fieldnames=self.field_list,
                        delimiter=' ',
                        quotechar='"')
```

Now we can iterate through the resulting object, which will return a new dictionary of the mapped values. Listing 6-2 shows the full listing of the log reader class, along with the required modules.

Listing 6-2. *The Log File Reader Class*

```
class LogLineGenerator:
    def __init__(self, log_format=None, log_dir='logs'):
        # LogFormat "%h %l %u %t \"%r\" %>s %b \"%{Referer}i\" \"%{User-Agent}i\""↵
combined
        if not log_format:
            self.format_string = '%h %l %u %t %r %>s %b %{Referer}i %{User-Agent}i'
```

```
        else:
            self.format_string = log_format
        self.log_dir = log_dir
        self.re_tsquote = re.compile(r'(\[|\])')
        self.field_list = []
        for directive in self.format_string.split(' '):
            self.field_list.append(DIRECTIVE_MAP[directive])

    def _quote_translator(self, file_name):
        for line in open(file_name):
            yield self.re_tsquote.sub('"', line)

    def _file_list(self):
        for file in os.listdir(self.log_dir):
            file_name = "%s/%s" % (self.log_dir, file)
            if os.path.isfile(file_name):
                yield file_name

    def get_loglines(self):
        for file in self._file_list():
            reader = csv.DictReader(self._quote_translator(file),
                                    fieldnames=self.field_list,
                                    delimiter=' ', quotechar='"')
            for line in reader:
                yield line
```

We now can create an instance of the generator class and iterate through all log lines from all the files in the specified directory:

```
log_generator = LogLineGenerator()
for log_line in log_generator.get_loglines():
    print "-" * 20
    for k, v in log_line.iteritems():
        print "%20s: %s" % (k, v)
```

This will produce a result similar to the following:

```
--------------------
              status: 200
         remote_user: -
        request_line: GET /posts/7802/ HTTP/1.1
      remote_logname: -
         referer_url: -
          user_agent: Mozilla/5.0 (compatible; Googlebot/2.1;
+http://www.google.com/bot.html)
       response_size: 26507
          time_stamp: 20/May/2010:11:57:55 +0100
         remote_host: 66.249.65.40
```

```
--------------------
          status: 200
     remote_user: -
    request_line: GET / HTTP/1.1
  remote_logname: -
      referer_url: -
       user_agent: Sogou web
spider/4.0(+http://www.sogou.com/docs/help/webmasters.htm#07)
    response_size: 26130
       time_stamp: 20/May/2010:11:58:47 +0100
      remote_host: 220.181.94.216
--------------------
          status: 200
     remote_user: -
    request_line: GET /posts/7803/ HTTP/1.1
  remote_logname: -
      referer_url: -
       user_agent: Mozilla/5.0 (compatible; Googlebot/2.1;
+http://www.google.com/bot.html)
    response_size: 29040
       time_stamp: 20/May/2010:11:59:00 +0100
      remote_host: 66.249.65.40
```

Calling the Plug-in Methods

We now need to define a way to pass this information to the plug-in modules. We have two problems to resolve:

- We need to know which methods of the plug-in object we can call.

- We need to know when to call them. For example, some plug-ins may not implement the methods.

We need to be able to identify the type of a plug-in, because the type defines what a plug-in is capable of doing. Knowing the plug-in capabilities, we will know when to call the appropriate plug-in methods. Going back to the web browser example, some plug-ins are able to handle the image files; others can handle the video content. It would be pointless to send the video content to the image-processing plug-ins, because they wouldn't know what to do with it. In other words, they are not *capable* of handling that request.

We'll begin by tackling the second problem. In the log-processing application, we'll allow the plug-ins to expose the keyword list to the plug-in manager. These keywords identify what type of requests the plug-in is interested in receiving. This does not mean that it can handle those requests, but at least the plug-in expresses its interest in them. Each request that is made from the host application is also marked with a list of keywords. If the keyword sets overlap, then the request is forwarded to the plug-in object. Otherwise, we don't bother calling the plug-in, because it clearly is not interested in receiving any requests of that type.

Tagging the Plug-in Classes

The tagging on the plug-in class is simple. We'll just add a property to the class definition, which is a list of the tags. We may leave this list empty, in which case the plug-in will receive only the untagged calls:

```
class CountHTTP200(Plugin):
    def __init__(self, **kwargs):
        self.keywords = ['counter']
```

We also need to modify the manager class, so that the keywords are registered along with each plug-in object. So we'll replace the plug-in registry list with the dictionary object, where the keys are the plug-in objects and the values are their tag lists. If the plug-in does not define the keyword list, we'll assume the list is empty:

```
class PluginManager():
    def __init__(self, path=None, plugin_init_args={}):
        [...]
        self.plugins = {}

    [...]

    def _register_plugins(self, **kwargs):
        for plugin in Plugin.__subclasses__():
            obj = plugin(**kwargs)
            self.plugins[obj] = obj.keywords if hasattr(obj, 'keywords') else []
```

Plug-in Methods and the Call Mechanism

We now have all the plug-ins tagged, and, in theory, we should know which methods are available on which plug-in objects. However, this approach is not very flexible. We've added the tags so the functions are optimized and the plug-ins are not called unnecessarily. There still might be situations when the plug-in announces its interest in some type of call, but does not implement the functions that the host application associates with that set of keywords.

Since the host application and plug-in software are very loosely coupled and quite often developed by completely different organizations, it is practically impossible to synchronize the development progress of the two. For example, suppose that a host application is designed to call the function_A() method on all plug-ins that announce their interest in the keyword foobar. Then the host application is modified so that it calls the two methods function_A and function_B on all plug-ins marked with the same keyword. However, some of the plug-ins may not be maintained, or they simply may not be interested in implementing the new function—it's sufficient to implement just the single function for their purposes.

This may seem to be a problem, but it actually isn't. The host application is going to call the method without checking whether it's available. If the plug-in implements that method, it will execute it. If the method is not implemented and not defined, that's fine—we simply ignore the exception. This technique is called *duck typing*.

We'll give the manager class the following new method, which will be responsible for calling the plug-in methods. The main application will call this method with the name of the function that it wants the plug-ins to run. Optionally, it can also pass the list of arguments and keywords. If the keywords are defined, the call will be dispatched only to the plug-ins that are marked with one or more keywords from that list:

```
def call_method(self, method, args={}, keywords=[]):
    for plugin in self.plugins:
        if not keywords or (set(keywords) & set(self.plugins[plugin])):
            try:
                getattr(plugin, method)(**args)
            except:
                pass
```

Now we can finish writing our host application. Let's replace the print statement that prints the log line structure with the actual call to the plug-in manager call dispatcher method. We'll call the process() method in the main loop and pass in the log line structure as an argument. All plug-ins that implement this method will receive the function call along with the keyword arguments. At the end of the loop, we'll call the report() function. The plug-ins that have anything to report now have an opportunity to do so. If the plug-in is not designed to produce any reports, it will simply ignore the call.

```
def main():
    plugin_manager = PluginManager()
    log_generator = LogLineGenerator()
    for log_line in log_generator.get_loglines():
        plugin_manager.call_method('process', args=log_line)
    plugin_manager.call_method('report')
```

WHAT IS DUCK TYPING?

The term *duck typing* comes from James Whitcomb Riley's quote, "When I see a bird that walks like a duck and swims like a duck and quacks like a duck, I call that bird a duck."

In object-oriented programming languages, duck typing means that the behavior of an object is determined by the set of its available methods and properties, not its inheritance. In other words, we're not worried about the type of the object class, as long as the methods and properties we're interested in are present and available. Therefore, duck typing does not rely on object type tests.

When you need something from the object, you simply ask for it. If the object doesn't know what you want from it, an exception will be raised. This means that the object doesn't know how to "quack" and therefore it is not a "duck." This method of "test and see what happens" is sometimes referred to as the Easier to Ask for Forgiveness Than Permission (EAFP) principle. It's best illustrated in the following sample code:

```
>>> class Cow():
...   def moo(self):
...     print 'moo..'
...
```

```
>>> class Duck():
...   def quack(self):
...     print 'quack!'
...
>>> animal1 = Cow()
>>> animal2 = Duck()
>>>
>>> for animal in [animal1, animal2]:
...   if hasattr(animal, 'quack'):
...     animal.quack()
...   else:
...     print animal, 'cannot quack'
...
<__main__.Cow instance at 0x100491a28> cannot quack
quack!
>>>
>>> for animal in [animal1, animal2]:
...   try:
...     animal.quack()
...   except AttributeError:
...     print animal, 'cannot quack'
...
<__main__.Cow instance at 0x100491a28> cannot quack
quack!
>>>
```

In the first iteration, we explicitly check for the availability of the method (we ask for permission) before we call the method. In the second iteration, we call the method without checking if it's available. We then catch the possible exception (we ask for forgiveness) and handle the absence of the method accordingly, if at all.

Plug-in Modules

We're now in the position to start writing the plug-in modules and using the scripts to analyze the Apache web server log files. In this section, we'll create a script that counts all requests and sorts them by the country from which they originated. We will use the GeoIP Python library to perform the IP-to-country-name mappings.

■**Note** The GeoIP data is produced by the MaxMind company, which provides the databases for individual (free) and commercial (paid for) use. You can find more information about MaxMind's products and services at `http://maxmind.com/app/ip-location`.

The GeoIP database attempts to provide the geographical information (such as country, city, and coordinates) of the location where the IP address is located. This is useful for various purposes. For example, it allows you to provide localized ad service, where you can display advertisements to users depending on their location.

Installing the Required Libraries

The GeoIP database libraries are written in C, but there are Python bindings available as well. The packages are available on most Linux platforms. For example, on a Fedora system, run the following command to install these libraries:

```
$ sudo yum install GeoIP GeoIP-python
```

This will install the C libraries along with the helper tools and the Python bindings. The package may include the initial database that contains the IP-to-country mapping data, but most likely, this data will be out of date, as the database is normally updated every three to four weeks. There are two databases that are free for personal use: the Countries database and the Cities database. I suggest updating those two databases regularly if you want to have up-to-date information. The tools that can fetch the latest version of the database are provided in the base package. Here's how you fetch the databases after you install the packages:

```
$ sudo touch /usr/share/GeoIP/GeoIP.dat
$ sudo touch /usr/share/GeoIP/GeoLiteCity.dat
$ sudo perl /usr/share/doc/GeoIP-1.4.7/fetch-geoipdata.pl
Fetching GeoIP.dat from
http://geolite.maxmind.com/download/geoip/database/GeoLiteCountry/GeoIP.dat.gz
GeoIP database updated. Old copy is at GeoIP.dat.20100521
$ sudo perl /usr/share/doc/GeoIP-1.4.7/fetch-geoipdata-city.pl
Fetching GeoLiteCity.dat from
http://geolite.maxmind.com/download/geoip/database/GeoLiteCity.dat.gz
GeoIP database updated. Old copy is at GeoLiteCity.dat.20100521
```

The reason for the touch command at the beginning is that if the .dat files are not present, the tools will fail to download the new version, so you must create those files first.

Using the GeoIP Python Bindings

When the libraries are installed, they will look for the data files in the standard location (typically in /usr/share/GeoIP/), so you don't need to specify the location. You need to specify only the access method:

```
import GeoIP

# the data is read from the disk every time it's accessed
# this is the slowest access method
gi = GeoIP.new(GeoIP.GEOIP_STANDARD)
# the data is cached in memory
gi = GeoIP.new(GeoIP.GEOIP_MEMORY_CACHE)
```

Once you initialize the data access object, you can start looking up the information:

```
>>> import GeoIP
>>> gi = GeoIP.new(GeoIP.GEOIP_MEMORY_CACHE)
>>> gi.country_name_by_name('www.apress.com')
'United States'
>>> gi.country_code_by_name('www.apress.com')
'US'
>>> gi.country_name_by_addr('4.4.4.4')
'United States'
>>> gi.country_code_by_addr('4.4.4.4')
'US'
>>>
```

If you want to retrieve the city information, you need to open the specific data file. You then can perform the city data lookups as well:

```
>>> import GeoIP
>>> gi = GeoIP.open('/usr/share/GeoIP/GeoLiteCity.dat', GeoIP.GEOIP_MEMORY_CACHE)
>>> gir = gi.record_by_name('www.apress.com')
>>> for k, v in gir.iteritems():
...   print "%20s: %s" % (k, v)
...
                city: Emeryville
         region_name: California
              region: CA
           area_code: 510
           time_zone: America/Los_Angeles
           longitude: -122.289703369
          metro_code: 807
       country_code3: USA
```

```
        latitude: 37.8342018127
     postal_code: 94608
        dma_code: 807
    country_code: US
    country_name: United States
>>>
```

Writing the Plug-in Code

We need to decide which methods we're going to implement. We need to receive the information about each log line that is being processed. Therefore, the plug-in must implement the process() method, which will perform the country lookup and increase the appropriate counters. At the end of the loop, we need to print a simple report that lists all the countries and sorts the list by the number of requests.

As you can see in Listing 6-3, we use only one field from the data structure and just ignore the rest of the data.

Listing 6-3. *The GeoIP Lookup Plug-in*

```python
#!/usr/bin/env python

from manager import Plugin
from operator import itemgetter
import GeoIP

class GeoIPStats(Plugin):

    def __init__(self, **kwargs):
        self.gi = GeoIP.new(GeoIP.GEOIP_MEMORY_CACHE)
        self.countries = {}

    def process(self, **kwargs):
        if 'remote_host' in kwargs:
            country = self.gi.country_name_by_addr(kwargs['remote_host'])
            if country in self.countries:
                self.countries[country] += 1
            else:
                self.countries[country] = 1

    def report(self, **kwargs):
        print "== Requests by country =="
        for (country, count) in sorted(self.countries.iteritems(),
                                       key=itemgetter(1), reverse=True):
            print " %10d: %s" % (count, country)
```

Save this file as plugin_geoiplookup.py in the plugins/ directory. (Actually, any name with the plugin_ prefix and .py suffix will be recognized as a valid plug-in module.) Now if you run the main application, you'll get the result similar to the one in the following example, provided that you have a sample log file in the logs/ directory.

```
$ ./http_log_parser.py
== Requests by country ==
      382: United States
      258: Sweden
      103: France
       42: China
       31: Russian Federation
        9: India
        8: Italy
        7: United Kingdom
        7: Anonymous Proxy
        6: Philippines
        6: Switzerland
        2: Tunisia
        2: Japan
        1: Croatia
```

Summary

In this chapter, we wrote a simple yet extensible and powerful plug-in framework in Python. We also implemented a simple Apache web server log parser and wrote a plug-in to count the number of requests and group them by the country from which they originated.

Key points to remember:

- The plug-ins allow decoupling the main application from its extensions—plug-in modules.

- The plug-in architecture typically consists of three components: the host application, the plug-in framework, and the plug-in modules.

- The plug-in framework is responsible for finding and registering the plug-in modules.

- Any Python class can find the other classes that inherited from it, and this mechanism can be used to find and group the classes. This property of the class can be used to find all plug-in classes.

- You can use the MaxMind GeoIP database to find the physical location of an IP address.

## CHAPTER 7

Performing Complex Searches and Reporting on Application Log Files

System administration duties often include installing and supporting various applications. These may be either produced by open-source communities or developed in-house. There are also a wide variety of languages used when developing those applications; common languages found these days would be Java, PHP, Python, Ruby and (yes, some still are using it) Perl. In this chapter I am going to talk about applications developed in Java as this seems to be the most common language selected by large enterprises for their web applications. Java applications commonly run within the application server container, such as Tomcat, Jetty, Websphere, or JBoss. You as a system administrator need to know whether the application is running correctly. Every well-organized and structured application is supposed to write its status to one or more log files; in the Java world, this is usually done via the log4j adapter. By observing the log file, a system administrator can detect any faults and failures within the application, which are commonly logged as exception stack traces. The logging of a full exception stack trace usually indicates an unrecoverable error—an error that the application was not able to handle itself. If you do not happen to have many requests, and the application is merely doing anything, catching these exceptions and analyzing them can be done by hand. However, if you need to manage hundreds of servers and there are tens of GBs of information produced, you surely need some automated tools to gather and analyze the data for you. In this chapter I am going to explain how I developed the open-source tool called *Exctractor* (no, this is not a typo, the name is constructed by joining two words: *exception* and *extractor*) and how it functions.

Defining the Problem

Before proceeding let's review the problem that this application will be trying to resolve. Every program writes its running status to a log file. What exactly is being logged is up to developer who created the application. There are no enforced standards on what to log, and even the format of the logging is somewhat undefined. Although it's not required, most log entries have time stamps and include a severity level to indicate the importance of the message along with the actual text of the status message. This is not enforced, and you may find that the log files you are dealing with have more attributes or maybe even less. For example, some applications that I have come across don't even bother logging a time stamp.

Generally, well-developed Java applications follow more or less the same standard when logging their status messages. Normally the messages are status reports written by the application that indicate what the application is doing at the moment. In situations when the application runs into an undefined state it will generate an exception, which will normally be logged with full execution status information— the call stack.

I have created a simple web application that I'm going to use throughout this chapter to illustrate various aspects of exception raising and analyzing different types of exceptions. Listing 7-1 is the source code of this application. You can compile it with the javac tool and run it from within the Tomcat application container. Beware that this application is to be used only as an example, as it potentially allows any user to access any file on your system; the only limitation is your file system's access rights mechanism.

Listing 7-1. *A Java program to illustrate application behavior*

```java
import java.io.*;
import java.util.*;
import java.text.*;
import javax.servlet.*;
import javax.servlet.http.*;

public class FileServer extends HttpServlet {

    public void doGet(HttpServletRequest request, HttpServletResponse response)
    throws IOException, ServletException
    {
        response.setContentType("text/html");
        PrintWriter out = response.getWriter();

        String fileName = request.getParameter("fn");
        if (fileName != null) {
            out.println(readFile(fileName));
        } else {
            out.println("No file specified");
        }

    }

    private String readFile(String file) throws IOException {
        StringBuilder stringBuilder = new StringBuilder();
        Scanner scanner = new Scanner(new BufferedReader(new FileReader(file)));

        try {
            while(scanner.hasNextLine()) {
                stringBuilder.append(scanner.nextLine() + "\n");
            }
        } finally {
            scanner.close();
        }
        return stringBuilder.toString();
    }
}
```

Listing 7-2 is an example of a Java stack trace, which has been generated by the web application running in the Tomcat application container.

Listing 7-2. *An example of a Java stack trace*

```
Jan 18, 2010 8:08:49 AM org.apache.catalina.core.StandardWrapperValve invoke
SEVERE: Servlet.service() for servlet FileServer threw exception
java.io.FileNotFoundException: /etc/this_does_not_exist_1061 (No such file or
directory)
    at java.io.FileInputStream.open(Native Method)
    at java.io.FileInputStream.<init>(FileInputStream.java:137)
    at java.io.FileInputStream.<init>(FileInputStream.java:96)
    at java.io.FileReader.<init>(FileReader.java:58)
    at FileServer.readFile(FileServer.java:30)
    at FileServer.doGet(FileServer.java:21)
    at javax.servlet.http.HttpServlet.service(HttpServlet.java:690)
    at javax.servlet.http.HttpServlet.service(HttpServlet.java:803)
    at org.apache.catalina.core.ApplicationFilterChain.internalDoFilter⏎
(ApplicationFilterChain.java:269)
    at org.apache.catalina.core.ApplicationFilterChain.doFilter⏎
(ApplicationFilterChain.java:188)
    at
org.apache.catalina.core.StandardWrapperValve.invoke(StandardWrapperValve.java:210)
    at
org.apache.catalina.core.StandardContextValve.invoke(StandardContextValve.java:172)
    at org.apache.catalina.core.StandardHostValve.invoke(StandardHostValve.java:127)
    at org.apache.catalina.valves.ErrorReportValve.invoke(ErrorReportValve.java:117)
    at
org.apache.catalina.core.StandardEngineValve.invoke(StandardEngineValve.java:108)
    at org.apache.catalina.connector.CoyoteAdapter.service(CoyoteAdapter.java:151)
    at org.apache.coyote.http11.Http11Processor.process(Http11Processor.java:870)
    at org.apache.coyote.http11.Http11BaseProtocol$Http11ConnectionHandler.⏎
processConnection(Http11BaseProtocol.java:665)
    at
org.apache.tomcat.util.net.PoolTcpEndpoint.processSocket(PoolTcpEndpoint.java:528)
    at org.apache.tomcat.util.net.LeaderFollowerWorkerThread.runIt⏎
(LeaderFollowerWorkerThread.java:81)
    at
org.apache.tomcat.util.threads.ThreadPool$ControlRunnable.run(ThreadPool.java:685)
    at java.lang.Thread.run(Thread.java:636)
```

If you take a closer look at the exception, you may notice that the application code tried to open a file, but the file did not exist. Obviously, a well-written application should handle a simple case like a missing file more gracefully than throwing an exception, but sometimes it is not feasible to build a check for every possible scenario into the application logic. In the case of more complex applications, this may not be possible at all.

Why We Use Exceptions

Language constructs such as events and signals are part of a normal program flow. Exceptions, by contrast, indicate that something has gone wrong while executing the program, such as a function called with wrong parameters so that the result cannot be calculated. For example, suppose we have a function that divides two numbers and accepts them as parameters. Naturally, division by zero is not possible, and should such a function receive an instruction to divide by zero it would have no idea what to do. So a seemingly simple function becomes rather complicated; it has to check whether it can divide the two numbers it is given and also return two values instead of one. One value is to indicate whether the operation completed successfully, and the other holds the actual result. Alternatively, it could return either a number if the operation was successful or a null object otherwise. In either case, the code that called this function now has to be able handle both numbers and null objects as a result, rendering simple arithmetic constructs into more complicated `if ... else` logic flows.

This is where exceptions come in. Instead of returning a special code that indicates the error, functions that cannot complete their normal operation will simply raise an exception. At the moment when an exception is raised, the program execution stops and the Java environment proceeds with the exception-handling procedure. Exceptions can be "caught" by the application. Going back to the division example, the whole calculation code can be wrapped in Java's `try ... catch` construct. Then, regardless of the point at which the code failed, and the specific function (such as division), the code would catch any arithmetical exceptions and would know than the calculation couldn't have been completed.

Are Exceptions Always a Bad Sign?

The short answer is "no" and the slightly longer answer is "it depends." The reason for an exception to be raised is that something unexpected happened. Let's say we have a web application that serves files from our server. All files are linked from external pages, and the general assumption is that whoever creates the listing would only list files that do exist. But, being human, we all make mistakes, and the operator of the listing may have made a typo, so the resulting link would point to a file that does not exist. Now if a user clicks on the link, the application tries to do exactly what it is told to—retrieve the file. But the file does not exist and so the code that is responsible for reading in the file would fail and throw an exception saying that the file does not exist.

Should the application check for the missing files and react appropriately? In this example probably the answer is yes, but in more complicated situations it is not always possible to predict and write code for every possible outcome. Even with simple applications like my file retriever service, it's not always possible to think about every possibility of what can wrong. As an example, let's run the application as a Tomcat user and assume that all files being written to the file system have permissions set such that Tomcat users have read access to them. It's been like that for a long time, and the application works flawlessly. One day a new system administrator joins the crew and without knowing deploys a file with different user permissions, and suddenly there's a file access error. The file is not missing, but the process that runs with Tomcat user permissions cannot read it. The developer has not thought of this situation and so there's no code to handle it. This is where exception handling is really helpful; the application would encounter a situation that is different from a normal program flow and cannot handle it, so the code raises an exception and either the system administrator or the developer can examine why things have gone wrong.

Why We Should Analyze Exceptions

Now that we know exceptions in the logs aren't always a bad sign, does that mean we should leave them unhandled? Generally my point of view is that the logs files should contain as few exceptions as possible. An occasional exception means that something *exceptional* has happened and we should investigate, but if there are similar exceptions over a period of time that means that the event is not exceptional anymore and is something commonplace. Therefore the application needs to be changed so that handling such events becomes part of the normal program flow rather than an exceptional event.

Going back to my file reader example, the developer initially thought that there might be one possible error that he needs to check for and that was a missing parameter. So he built the check into the application logic:

```
if (fileName != null) {
    out.println(readFile(fileName));
} else {
    out.println("No file specified");
}
```

That's a good strategy, as it may sometimes happen that the external references do not specify any file name, but the application happily handles the situation.

Now let's pretend for a moment that this has been running for a long time and no one has reported any issues. But one day you decided to have a look at the application log file and noticed some unusual exception stack traces that have never been logged before:

```
Jan 18, 2010 8:08:35 AM org.apache.catalina.core.StandardWrapperValve invoke
SEVERE: Servlet.service() for servlet FileServer threw exception
java.io.FileNotFoundException: /etc/this_does_not_exist_2 (No such file or
directory)
    at java.io.FileInputStream.open(Native Method)
...
```

This indicates that users are trying to reach a file that does not exist. You know that the only link to your web service is from another page, so you go and fix it. How do you prevent this from happening again? There's nothing wrong with your application, but you might want to check and improve the process of adding the new links to the external page so that it only points to the files that do exist. Whether to build in a case for handling files that do not exist is entirely up to you, as there are no hard rules defined about when and what should be handled in the application logic. My view is that if the exception is highly unlikely to happen, it's best to keep the application logic as simple as possible.

Now some time later you encounter yet another exception:

```
Jan 18, 2010 8:07:59 AM org.apache.catalina.core.StandardWrapperValve invoke
SEVERE: Servlet.service() for servlet FileServer threw exception
java.io.FileNotFoundException: /etc/shadow (Permission denied)
    at java.io.FileInputStream.open(Native Method)
...
```

This time it's indicating that the file is present but with the wrong permissions. Again it's time to investigate why this is happening and fix the root cause of the issue, which isn't always the application but might well be something external to it. In this situation a new system administrator changed the file permissions, and that broke the application.

As you can see from this simple real-life scenario, exceptions in the application log files do not necessarily mean issues with the application that is generating them. To find the root cause of the issues that are either directly or indirectly indicated by the exception logs you as a system administrator need to know as much as possible about the various indicators. Having exception stack tracing is very useful, but you also want to know when the exception first started to appear in the log files. What is the extent of the problem—how many of the exceptions are you getting? If you are receiving a large number of them it is probably not really an exceptional situation, and the application needs to be modified to handle it as part of the application logic.

Parsing Complex Log Files

Parsing log files (or any other unstructured set of data) is a rather challenging task. Unlike structured data files like XML or JSON, plain log text files do not follow any strict rules and may change without any warning. It is completely up to the person who has developed the application to decide what gets logged and in what format. The format of the log entries might even change between different releases of the software. As a system administrator you may need to negotiate some sort of approval procedure so that if you automate log parsing you will not get caught by surprise when the format of the file changes. It is best to engage developers as well, so they use the same tools as you are. If they are using the same tools as you are, they are less likely to break them.

In this chapter I'm going to use the `catalina.out` file generated by the Tomcat application server. As you can see, the application itself is not writing any log messages at all, so the only log entries you will find there are from the JVM and Tomcat. Obviously if you are using different application containers, such as Jetty or JBoss your log entries may look different. Even if you are using Tomcat, you can override default behavior and the way messages are formatted, so look at the log files that you are dealing with and adjust the examples in this chapter accordingly, so that they match your environment.

What Can We Find in a Typical Log File?

Before proceeding with writing the analyzer code or changing any configuration for it, take a look and identify the types of messages you have in the log files and how you can unambiguously identify them. Look for common attributes that make them distinguishable. Typically you will see standard messages generated by either the application itself or the application container.

These messages are meant to inform you about the state of the application. Because these messages are generated by the application they most likely indicate expected behavior and each state they inform you about is part of the normal application flow. As I'm going to investigate exceptions I'm not really interested in that type of message. Listing 7-3 is a snippet from Tomcat's log file that shows what "normal" log messages look like.

Listing 7-3. *Standard logging messages in catalina.out*

```
Jan 17, 2010 8:18:24 AM org.apache.catalina.core.AprLifecycleListener lifecycleEvent
INFO: The Apache Tomcat Native library which allows optimal performance in
production↵
 environments was not found on the java.l
ibrary.path: /usr/lib/jvm/java-1.6.0-openjdk-
1.6.0.0/jre/lib/i386/client:/usr/lib/jvm/↵
java-1.6.0-openjdk-1.6.0.0/jre/lib/i386:
/usr/lib/jvm/java-1.6.0-openjdk-
1.6.0.0/jre/../lib/i386:/usr/java/packages/lib/i386:/lib:/↵
usr/libJan 17, 2010 8:18:24 AM org.apache.coyote.http11.Http11BaseProtocol↵
initINFO:Initializing Coyote HTTP/1.1 on http-8081Jan 17, 2010 8:18:24 AM↵
org.apache.catalina.startup.Catalina load
INFO: Initialization processed in 673 ms
Jan 17, 2010 8:18:24 AM org.apache.catalina.core.StandardService start
INFO: Starting service Catalina
```

```
Jan 17, 2010 8:18:24 AM org.apache.catalina.core.StandardEngine start
INFO: Starting Servlet Engine: Apache Tomcat/5.5.23
Jan 17, 2010 8:18:24 AM org.apache.catalina.core.StandardHost start
INFO: XML validation disabled
Jan 17, 2010 8:18:25 AM org.apache.catalina.core.ApplicationContext log
INFO: ContextListener: contextInitialized()
Jan 17, 2010 8:18:25 AM org.apache.catalina.core.ApplicationContext log
INFO: SessionListener: contextInitialized()
Jan 17, 2010 8:18:25 AM org.apache.catalina.core.ApplicationContext log
INFO: ContextListener: contextInitialized()
Jan 17, 2010 8:18:25 AM org.apache.catalina.core.ApplicationContext log
INFO: SessionListener: contextInitialized()
Jan 17, 2010 8:18:25 AM org.apache.catalina.core.ApplicationContext log
INFO: org.apache.webapp.balancer.BalancerFilter: init(): ruleChain:↵
 [org.apache.webapp.balancer.RuleChain: [org.apache.webapp.
balancer.rules.URLStringMatchRule: Target string: News / Redirect URL:↵
 http://www.cnn.com], [org.apache.webapp.balancer.rules.
RequestParameterRule: Target param name: paramName / Target param value:↵
 paramValue / Redirect URL: http://www.yahoo.com], [or
g.apache.webapp.balancer.rules.AcceptEverythingRule: Redirect URL:↵
 http://jakarta.apache.org]]
```

You can see that all log entries start with a date stamp. This is one of the attributes I will use to detect the log entry. Also notice that log entries may span multiple lines. So each long entry starts with a line that begins with has a time stamp and finishes when another line with a time stamp is detected. Write this down, as this is going to become one of the design decisions for your application.

The Structure of an Exception Stack Trace Log

Listing 7-4 is an example of a stack trace that has been generated by the JVM. This stack trace is from the Tomcat application that failed to load my web application due to a malformed web.xml. As you can see, such things cannot be predicted; hence they are exceptions to normal operation.

Listing 7-4. *An example of an exception stack trace*

```
Jan 17, 2010 10:07:04 AM org.apache.catalina.startup.ContextConfig
applicationWebConfig
SEVERE: Parse error in application web.xml file at jndi:/localhost/test/WEB-
INF/web.xml
org.xml.sax.SAXParseException: The element type "servlet-class" must be terminated↵
 by the matching end-tag "</servlet-class>".
    at org.apache.xerces.parsers.AbstractSAXParser.parse(Unknown Source)
    at org.apache.xerces.jaxp.SAXParserImpl$JAXPSAXParser.parse(Unknown Source)
    at org.apache.tomcat.util.digester.Digester.parse(Digester.java:1562)
```

```
    at org.apache.catalina.startup.ContextConfig.applicationWebConfig↵
(ContextConfig.java:348)
    at org.apache.catalina.startup.ContextConfig.start(ContextConfig.java:1043)
    at
org.apache.catalina.startup.ContextConfig.lifecycleEvent(ContextConfig.java:261)
    at org.apache.catalina.util.LifecycleSupport.fireLifecycleEvent↵
(LifecycleSupport.java:120)
    at org.apache.catalina.core.StandardContext.start(StandardContext.java:4144)
    at org.apache.catalina.startup.HostConfig.checkResources(HostConfig.java:1105)
    at org.apache.catalina.startup.HostConfig.check(HostConfig.java:1203)
    at org.apache.catalina.startup.HostConfig.lifecycleEvent(HostConfig.java:293)
    at org.apache.catalina.util.LifecycleSupport.fireLifecycleEvent↵
(LifecycleSupport.java:120)
    at
org.apache.catalina.core.ContainerBase.backgroundProcess(ContainerBase.java:1306)
    at org.apache.catalina.core.ContainerBase$ContainerBackgroundProcessor.↵
processChildren(ContainerBase.java:1570)
    at org.apache.catalina.core.ContainerBase$ContainerBackgroundProcessor.↵
processChildren(ContainerBase.java:1579)
    at org.apache.catalina.core.ContainerBase$ContainerBackgroundProcessor.run↵
(ContainerBase.java:1559)
    at java.lang.Thread.run(Thread.java:636)
```

Like "normal" log entries, this starts with a time stamp showing when the entry was created. It also spans a few lines; in fact, most stack traces are rather lengthy and may contain over a hundred lines, depending on the application structure. A stack trace effectively is a call stack and prints out the entire function hierarchy down to the one that has encountered the exceptional situation.

The structure of a Java exception stack trace log is not formal in any way; I'm just splitting it for my own convenience, as this will help me to organize these log entries later in the parser code. You should be able to apply the same structure without much trouble.

The first line of the log entry I'm going to call the *logline*. This line contains a timestamp of when the log entry was created and also the module name and the function where the exception occurred:

```
Jan 17, 2010 10:07:04 AM org.apache.catalina.startup.ContextConfig
applicationWebConfig
```

The following line I'm going to call the *headline*. This line is not really part of the actual stack trace, but is printed out by the application code that "caught" the exception:

```
SEVERE: Parse error in application web.xml file at jndi:/localhost/test/WEB-
INF/web.xml
```

And finally, the third section contains the "body" of the exception. This includes all the following lines and is the last part of the log entry. Usually the last line is a Java thread run method.

```
org.xml.sax.SAXParseException: The element type "servlet-class" must be terminated
by the matching end-tag "</servlet-class>".
    at org.apache.xerces.parsers.AbstractSAXParser.parse(Unknown Source)
    at org.apache.xerces.jaxp.SAXParserImpl$JAXPSAXParser.parse(Unknown Source)
```

```
    at org.apache.tomcat.util.digester.Digester.parse(Digester.java:1562)
...
at java.lang.Thread.run(Thread.java:636)
```

I've defined the structure of an exception log entry, but how do I know that this is an exception and not a normal log entry? So far they both look the same: they both have timestamp, and they both span across one or more lines. To a human it's a rather obvious difference, and you immediately spot the exception, but are there any other fingerprints in the exception stack trace that I could use to identify it as a genuine exception and not the lengthy log entry?

If you look and compare different exception stack traces you'll notice one commonality: each exception stack trace mentions the exception class name. Some examples include `org.xml.sax.SAXParseException` and `java.io.FileNotFoundException`. This occurs because each exception is effectively an instance of the exception class. Again, class name could be anything, but it is an accepted practice to append the word "`Exception` to the class name. So I'm going to use this as one of my classifiers. Another classifier is the word `java`. Because I'm dealing with Java programs in most cases I will have one or more methods from native Java libraries. So I'm going to work on the assumption that if my exception candidate contains these two words, it is likely to be an actual exception. But I don't want to be limiting myself, so I have to make sure that my application structure allows me to change or plug in another validation method.

Now I have something to operate on—I know how my log entries should look. I also know what the exception looks like, as well as what makes it different from the normal log entry. That should be enough to implement the log parser.

Handling Multiple Files

Before diving into the actual parsing, I need to read the data in first. This may sound trivial, but if you want to do this efficiently, there are some tricks you might want to know about.

First you need to decide where you will get the data from. While this may seem obvious, remember that log files come in different shapes and sizes. I want to have the tool flexible enough so it can be applied to different situations. To make things simple and remove guesswork at the implementation phase, I'll start with listing some requirements and assumption that I'm going to rely on:

- Log files can be either plain text or compressed with bzip2.

- Log files have the extension `.log` for a plain text file or `.log.bz2` for a bzip2 file.

- I need to be able to process just a subset of log files based on their name. For example, I need to be able to use the file pattern `webserver`; all files that match this will be processed, but not other files.

- The results from all files processed should be combined into one report.

- The tool should operate on all files found in a specified directory or list of different directories. Log files from all subdirectories should also be included.

Handling Multiple Files

Given the requirements just stated, I define two variables that represent the patterns for file search calls:

```
LOG_PATTERN = ".log"
BZLOG_PATTERN = ".log.bz2"
```

The filename pattern is stored in the global variable OPTIONS.file_pattern. By default this is set to an empty string and so it will match all file names. This variable is controlled by the command-line parsing class, which I'm going to talk about later in the chapter. For the time being, just note that it can be set to any value by using the -p or --pattern option.

I need to create a list of directories and all subdirectories recursively so that I can search for the log files in them. Users are going to supply me with a list of top-level directories, which I need to explode into a full tree of all sub- and sub-sub directories.

The list of arguments is going to be stored in the ARGS variable by the OptionParser class. There is a really handy function in Python's os library called walk. It recursively builds a list of files in each directory and all subdirectories.

Let's set up a simple directory structure and see how the os.walk function works:

```
$ mkdir -p top_dir_{1,2}/sub_dir_{1,2}/sub_sub_dir
```

This will produce a three-level directory structure:

```
$ ls -1R
top_dir_1
top_dir_2

./top_dir_1:
sub_dir_1
sub_dir_2

./top_dir_1/sub_dir_1:
sub_sub_dir

./top_dir_1/sub_dir_1/sub_sub_dir:

./top_dir_1/sub_dir_2:
sub_sub_dir

./top_dir_1/sub_dir_2/sub_sub_dir:

./top_dir_2:
sub_dir_1
sub_dir_2

./top_dir_2/sub_dir_1:
sub_sub_dir

./top_dir_2/sub_dir_1/sub_sub_dir:

./top_dir_2/sub_dir_2:
sub_sub_dir

./top_dir_2/sub_dir_2/sub_sub_dir:
```

Now we can use `os.walk` to generate the same output], as shown in Listing 7-5.

Listing 7-5. *Recursively retrieving a list of directories with os.walk*

```
$ python
Python 2.6.1 (r261:67515, Jul  7 2009, 23:51:51)
[GCC 4.2.1 (Apple Inc. build 5646)] on darwin
Type "help", "copyright", "credits" or "license" for more information.
>>> import os
>>> for d in os.walk('.'):
...   print d
...
('.', ['top_dir_1', 'top_dir_2'], [])
('./top_dir_1', ['sub_dir_1', 'sub_dir_2'], [])
('./top_dir_1/sub_dir_1', ['sub_sub_dir'], [])
('./top_dir_1/sub_dir_1/sub_sub_dir', [], [])
('./top_dir_1/sub_dir_2', ['sub_sub_dir'], [])
('./top_dir_1/sub_dir_2/sub_sub_dir', [], [])
('./top_dir_2', ['sub_dir_1', 'sub_dir_2'], [])
('./top_dir_2/sub_dir_1', ['sub_sub_dir'], [])
('./top_dir_2/sub_dir_1/sub_sub_dir', [], [])
('./top_dir_2/sub_dir_2', ['sub_sub_dir'], [])
('./top_dir_2/sub_dir_2/sub_sub_dir', [], [])
>>> os.walk('.')
<generator object walk at 0x1004920a0>
>>>
```

As you can see, a call to `os.walk` returns a generator object. I will talk about generators in more detail later in this chapter, but for now, note that they are objects that you can iterate through just like any normal Python list or tuple object.

The return result is a three-tuple with the following entries:

> The directory path: The current directory whose contents are exposed in the next two variables.

> Directory names: A list of directory names in the directory path. This list excludes '.' And '..' directories.

> File names: A list of the file names in the directory path.

By default `os.walk` will not follow symbolic links that point to directories. To follow symbolic links, you can set the `followlinks` parameter to True, which will instruct `os.walk` to follow all symbolic links that it comes across while scanning the directory tree.

I'm only interested in the directory listing, as I'm going to use a different function to filter out the files that will be processed and analyzed. Collecting only the first element of the three-tuple result, I can build the list of directories. So to build a recursive list of all directories from the list of top-level directories that are supplied as an argument list, I would write the following:

```
DIRS = []
for dir in ARGS:
    for root, dirs, files in os.walk(dir):
        DIRS.append(root)
```

Now the DIRS list contains all directories that I will need to search for log files. I need to go through this list and search for all files that have a name satisfying two search patterns: either LOG_PATTERN or BZLOG_PATTERN and OPTIONS.file_pattern.

I'm going to use one of the simplest ways of obtaining the list, which is to traverse through the list of directories, create a simple listing of contents, and then match the result against search patterns and use only files that satisfy both. The following code does just that and opens matched files for reading:

```
for DIR in DIRS:

    for file in (DIR + "/" + f for f in os.listdir(DIR) if
                     f.find(LOG_PATTERN) != -1 and f.find(OPTIONS.file_pattern)
!= -1 ):
        if file.find(BZLOG_PATTERN) != -1:
            fd = bz2.BZ2File(file, 'r')
        else:
            fd = open(file, 'r')
```

Take a closer look at the list construct, which is called *list comprehension*. This is a very powerful mechanism for creating lists of objects that you want to iterate through. With list comprehension you can quickly and elegantly apply some validation or transformation to an existing list and get the new list immediately.

For example, here's what you'd do to quickly generate a list of all even numbers squared from 1 to 10:

```
>>> [x**2 for x in range(10) if x % 2 == 0]
[0, 4, 16, 36, 64]
```

The basic structure for list comprehension is

```
[ <operand> /operation/ for <operand> in <list> /if <check  condition>/ ]
```

where <operand> is a variable used to generate a list, /operation/ is an optional operation that you might need to perform on each element of the resulting list, <list> is the list of items you're iterating through, and /<check condition>/ is the validation filter that filters out unwanted elements from the resulting list.

With this in mind, if I dissect my file list construct, here's what I have:

- Each element of the resulting array will be constructed as DIR + "/" + f, where DIR is the directory name and f is gathered from the os.listdir().

- The variable f is assigned in sequence to all elements of a list returned by calling os.listdir().

- Only those values are accepted that satisfy the condition (f.find(LOG_PATTERN) != -1 and f.find(OPTIONS.file_pattern) != -1), which requires them to match both LOG_PATTERN and OPTIONS.file_pattern.

Also note that you can use list comprehension to generate either a list object or a generator. If you create a generator, the next element value will be derived only when requested, for example in a for loop. Depending on the use, this may be much quicker and more memory-efficient than generating and holding the whole list in memory.

Using the Built In Bzip2 Library

You may have noticed that there are two statements that create a file descriptor object. One is for flat text log files and the other one is for files compressed with bzip2. The differentiator is the log file extension, which in case of bzip2 compression is .bz2.

Python includes a bzip2-handling module as part of a standard set of packages. The most useful class in the module is BZ2File, which implements a full interface for handling compressed files. You can use it just as you would use the standard Open function. The returned object is a file descriptor object that implements standard file-handling operations: read, readline, write, writeline, seek and close.

Since the only difference is in how the file descriptor object is created, even though I'm using a different function to get the object, the result is assigned to the same fd variable that will be used later in the code.

Traversing Through Large Data Files

If I have to read and process large amounts of data, I cannot use the simplistic approach of loading everything into memory and then processing it. And I will most definitely be dealing with large volumes of data here. Depending on your situation this might be different, but busy systems are likely to have gigabytes of log data generated on an hourly basis. Obviously all this data cannot be loaded into memory at once.

The solution to this problem is to use generators. The generator function allows you to produce output (reading the lines from a file) without actually loading the whole file into memory. If you just simply need to read the file line by line, you don't really need to encapsulate the readline() function, as you can simply write:

```
f = open('file.txt', 'r')
for line in f:
    print line
```

However, if you need to manipulate the file data and use the result, it might be a good idea to write your own generator function that performs required calculations and produces the results. For example, you might want to write a generator that searches for a particular string in the file and prints the string plus few lines before that string and few lines after it. This is where generators come in handy.

What Are Generators, And How Do We Use Them?

Simply put, a Python generator is a function that potentially can return many values, and it is also able to maintain its own state between the returns. This means that you can call the function multiple times and it will return a new result every time. Each time you call it subsequently, it knows its last location and will continue from that point.

The following example function generates Fibonacci numbers:

```
def f():
    x, y = 0, 1
    while 1:
        yield y
        x, y = y, y+x
```

When this function is called for the first time, it will initiate x and y and enter the infinite loop. The first statement in the loop is to return the value of y (note that in generators you must use the yield statement). The next time you call this function it'll start from the point where it stopped execution and returned a value—the yield statement. The next statement is to reassign x and y with new values, where x becomes the old y and the new y is a sum of old y and x. It is important to note that calling the generator function does not return the values the function is meant to calculate—it returns the actual generator object. You can then either iterate through it as you would normally do with a list or call next() method, which will get you the next value:

```
>>> g = f()
>>> for i in range(10):
...   g.next()
...
1
1
2
3
5
8
13
21
34
55
>>>
```

As you can see, generators are actually functions and not lists, but they can be used as lists. Sometimes, as in the Fibonacci example, the virtual lists can be infinite. When the generator has a limited set of results, such as lines in a file or rows in a database query, it must raise a StopIteration exception, which will signal the caller that there are no more results available.

You can use generators to go through all lines in the file. This will effectively return the next line whenever you call the next() function without actually loading the whole file into memory. Once it is defined as a generator, you can just iterate through it.

In my code I have a get_suspect() function, which is effectively a generator that returns excerpts of text from the log file that potentially might be an exception stack trace. This function accepts a generator as its argument and iterates through it, therefore retrieving all the lines.

First of all I create a generator that returns all lines in the file:

```
g = (line for line in fd)
```

And then I use this generator to retrieve the lines in my function:

```
def get_suspect(g):
    line = g.next()
    next_line = g.next()
    while 1:
        <do something with line and next_line>
        yield result
        try:
            line, next_line = next_line, g.next()
        except:
            raise StopIteration
```

I enclose the call to next() in the try: ... except: clause because when the last line of the file has been reached, the generator will raise an exception. Therefore, when the file cannot be read anymore, I simply raise the StopIteration exception, which acts as a signal to the iterator that the generator has exhausted all its values.

Detecting Exceptions

The majority of the log entries contain only one line. So my approach in detecting exception log entries is this:

- Ignore all one-line entries. These are most likely to be from the application and will not have a stack trace because it is simply not possible to put a full stack trace into one line.

- All log entries that have multiple lines are considered to contain an exception stack trace.

- An exception stack trace log entry must contain the words java and exception in the log text body.

The reason for having this two-phase detection is that a simple check like "does it have more than one line?" is very inexpensive and can eliminate a significant number of log entries.

Detecting Potential Candidates

In abstract language the algorithm for this function would look like the following:

- Read in two lines from a file.

- If the second line does not match the date stamp pattern, add it to the result string.

- Keep reading lines in and appending until the date stamp pattern is matched.

- Return the result.

- Repeat until there is no more data in the file.

As you can see in Listing 7-6, using a generator function here is an obvious choice, because I need to preserve the internal function state after the function returns the resulting string that contains a potential exception stack trace. The function itself accepts another generator function, which it uses to retrieve the lines of text. Using this approach it is possible to replace a file-reading generator with any other generator that is capable of generating log lines. For example, this might be a database-reading function, or even a function that listens and accepts syslog service messages.

Listing 7-6. *A generator function to detect potential exceptions*

```
def get_suspect(g):
    line = g.next()
    next_line = g.next()
    while 1:
        if not (TS_RE_1.search(next_line) or TS_RE_2.search(next_line)):
            suspect_body = line
            while not (TS_RE_1.search(next_line) or TS_RE_2.search(next_line)):
                suspect_body += next_line
                next_line = g.next()
            yield suspect_body
        else:
            try:
                line, next_line = next_line, g.next()
            except:
                raise StopIteration
```

Obviously this can be replaced with a function that has more advanced logic and a better hit-to-miss ratio, but it is equally effective and lightweight.

Here are a couple of ideas you might want to experiment with:

- Instead of using two predefined patterns for time stamp detection, try defining a list with precompiled patterns that would match the majority of popular formats. Then, as the function runs, it would count successful matches and rearrange the list on the fly so that most popular match gets match first.

- If you have a large number of multiple-line log entries, this simple approach will fail. Try generating hashes of the first line in the log body and store them in a separate data structure. The real exception validator function would update this table with True/False values depending on whether the guess was correct. This function can then check hashes against this table, so it will know which repeating log entries are not really exceptions although they may look like ones.

Filtering Legitimate Exception Traces

Up until now all the code is in standard functions. This is mostly because the code was dealing with selecting the files and doing some initial validation. Neither of those tasks have anything to do with the actual exception-handling code. Now, for the exception parsing and analyzing tasks, I am going to define a class with appropriate methods. This way I can distribute and use it as a completely independent module. For example, let's say I wanted to implement a web-based application where my users could submit their exception logs and get some statistics, and I want to be able to reuse this code. Functions that open files and deal with file patterns become obsolete, because there are simply no files to deal with—all data comes from a web server. Similarly, you may also want to analyze data stored in a database, in which case you would have to write an interface to retrieve this data. However, you still can reuse the code that deals with exception stack trace text. So always try to keep your code logically separated.

As I have mentioned, my exception detection mechanism (Listing 7-7) is somewhat naïve—I check for the words `exception` and `java` in the stack trace body.

Listing 7-7. *Validating exceptions*

```
def is_exception(self, strace):
        if strace.lower().find('exception') != -1 and \
            strace.lower().find('java')        != -1:
            return True
        else:
            return False
```

This is easy to change, and should you need anything more sophisticated than this simple test, you can rewrite this function to use a more appropriate algorithm for your situation.

Listing 7-8 shows how this detection mechanism fits together with other parts of the class.

Listing 7-8. *The basic structure of the exception container class*

```
class ExceptionContainer:
    def __init__(self):
        <initialise the object>

    def insert(self, suspect_body, f_name=""):
        lines = suspect_body.strip().split("\n", 1)
        log_l = lines[0]
        if self.is_exception(lines[1]):
            <update exceptions statistics and couners>
```

For every suspect log line detected, the `insert` method will be called. That method will then call the validation function, which checks whether the text supplied is actually a stack trace and should be counted.

Storing Data in Data Structures

The main goal of my application is to gather statistics about the exceptions that occur in the log file. Therefore I need to think about how to store this data as well as where to store it. There are two alternatives—I can either hold this data in memory or dump it into a database. When choosing between those two options I need to ask whether I need to do either of the following:

- Maintain this data in the same structure after the program has terminated

- Hold lots of records for a long period of time and access them from any other tools

If the answer to either of those questions were positive, I probably would need to use an external database to hold the statistical data. However I do not anticipate that the log files are going to have a large number of *different* types of exceptions. There might be hundreds of thousands of exceptions, but most likely there will be just a few hundred types of them. It is really hard to think of an application that would generate the whole range of exceptions.

Additionally, storing statistical data is not part of the lifecycle of this application. It is up to an external process to gather and analyze this data, so for the purposes of this application, this data needs to be "live" only during the calculation phase.

Therefore I am going to use Python's list data structure to keep the data and later for reporting, but it will all be lost when the application finishes its execution.

The Structure of Exception Stack Trace Data

There is no need to hold every single exception that I come across, only a counter of all occurrences of any particular type of exception along with details for that type. As previously discussed, an exception stack trace can be dissected into these parts:

- The log line (the line with the time stamp).

- The exception head line (the first line of the exception stack trace).

- The exception body (the stack trace).

In addition to this information, I also need to have the following:

- A counter to count the number of occurrences of each particular type.

- A description for a quick reference.

- A group that can be used to organize different types of exceptions. For example, you might want to have a group that counts all exception related to missing files; but because they might be generated by different parts of the application, or even different libraries, you may need to use different rules altogether to match them. Grouping here is the only convenient way to maintain the same counter for all those exceptions.

- A filename so that users know in which file the exception has been found. This is useful if you are analyzing numerous files that are stored in a single directory.

So every time I insert a new exception, the following dictionary will be appended to a list:

```
{ 'count'    : # counter
  'log_line' : # log line
  'header'   : # header line
  'body'     : # body text with stack trace
  'f_name'   : # file name
  'desc'     : # description
  'group'    : # group
}
```

Generating an Exception Fingerprint for Unknown Exceptions

Assuming that I haven't provided any classification rules yet, the application needs to be able to recognize similar exceptions and group them accordingly. One possibility would be to store an exception body text and compare others against it. If the next exception matches the stored one, increase the counter; otherwise, store that one as well and use it for future comparisons. Figure 7-1 is a flowchart of this process.

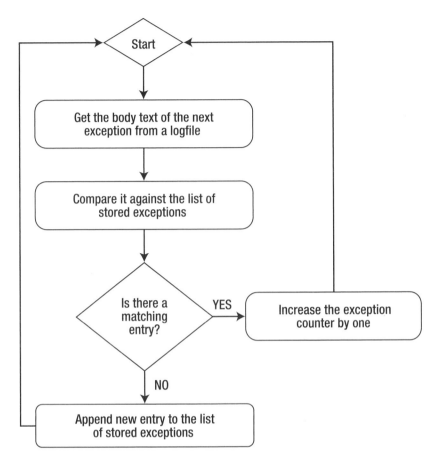

Figure 7-1. *Counting the exceptions*

This would work, but it would be very slow as the string compare operations are really slow and expensive in terms of computing power. So when possible, try to avoid them, especially if you need to compare long strings such as long fragments of text.

A much more efficient way to perform quick text blob comparison is to generate some unique attribute for each text fragment and then compare those attributes. (By *unique*, I mean unique within that particular piece of text.)

Such an attribute can be an MD5 hash function of the data stream. As you may already know, a cryptographic hash function (of which MD5 is a widely used example)is a procedure that accepts any block of data and returns a bit string of a predefined size. This string is generated in a way that if the original data is modified it will change. By definition the output string may be much smaller than the input string, so obviously the information is lost and cannot be restored; but the algorithm guarantees that if the hash values of two strings are the same there is a very high probability that the original stings are the same, too.

Python has a built in MD5 library that can be used to generate MD5 sums for any input data. So I'm going to use this function to generate MD5 hashes for all exceptions that I encounter and compare those strings instead of comparing the full stack traces. Listing 7-9 is an excerpt from the insert method. The following variables are defined at the beginning of the function:

log_l: The exception log line

hd_l: The exception header line

bd_l: The exception body text

f_name: The filename where the exception has been found

self.exception: The dictionary where the key is theMD5 sum of the exception body text and the value is another dictionary that holds the details about the exception stack trace.

Listing 7-9. *Generating MD5 and comparing it against stored values*

```
01:    m = md5.new()
02:    m.update(log_l.split(" ", 3)[2])
03:    m.update(hd_l)
04:    for ml in bd_l.strip().split("\n"):
05:        if ml:
06:            ml = re.sub("\(.*\)", "", ml)
07:            ml = re.sub("\$Proxy", "", ml)
08:            m.update(ml)
09:        if m.hexdigest() in self.exceptions:
10:            self.exceptions[m.hexdigest()]['count'] += 1
11:        else:
12:            self.exceptions[m.hexdigest()] = { 'count'   : 1,
13:                                               'log_line': log_l,
14:                                               'header'  : hd_l,
15:                                               'body'    : bd_l,
16:                                               'f_name': f_name,
17:                                               'desc'    : 'NOT IDENTIFIED',
18:                                         'group' : 'unrecognised_'+m.hexdigest(), }
```

Here is a detailed explanation of what's actually happening in this function:

Lines 1–3: Initialize the md5 object and assign it the third field of the exception log line and the whole exception header line. The reason I'm picking only the last field of the exception log line is that the first two fields are going to contain date and time strings, which are constantly changing, so I don't want them to change the MD5 hash I'm going to generate.

Lines 4–5: Iterate over all lines of the exception body, one at a time.

Lines 6–8: Strip all text between brackets and remove all references to automatically generated Java Proxy objects. If the line numbers are different but otherwise the exception stack traces look identical, there is a high chance that in fact they are the same. Proxy objects are assigned sequential numbers, so they will never have the same name; therefore I need to remove them as well, so that MD5 hash doesn't change.

Line 9: Call the hexdigest method, which will generate an MD5 hash for the text that has been stored using the update function and compare the result against all stored keys.

Line 10: If there is a match, increase its counter.

Lines 11–18: Otherwise, insert a new record.

Detecting Known Exceptions

So far my application can detect unique exceptions and categorize them appropriately. This is quite useful, but there are some issues:

- As with any heuristic algorithm, the current implementation is really naïve in its way of detecting and comparing exceptions. It does a decent job but may struggle even with really simple cases such as a File Not Found exception. If the exception is raised in different parts of your Java application it will produce completely different output, and essentially same type of exception will be logged multiple times. One might argue that this is expected behavior and you really need to know where the exception has been raised, and that would be a valid comment. In other situations you don't really care about these details and would like to combine all File Not Found error messages into one group. At present this is not possible.

- The naming convention is really confusing; all your exception groups are going to have unreadable names such as *unrecognised_6c2dc65d7c0bfb0768ddff8cabaccf68*.

- If the exception details contain time- or request-specific information, this algorithm is going to see those exceptions as different, because there is no way of knowing that "File Not Found: file1.txt" and "File Not Found: file2.txt" are effectively the same exception. To verify this behavior, I generated over a thousand exceptions in which the requested file name is the same and a similar number of error messages with unique filenames. The result of running the application against this sample log file was one group with over a thousand instances and over a thousand different groups with one or two instances in them. The reality is that all exceptions are of the same type.

- Although I am not comparing large pieces of text, calculating an MD5 hash and then comparing has strings is still relatively slow.

In light of those issues, I am going to modify the application so that it allows me to define how I want my exceptions detected and categorized.

As you already know, each exception is split into three parts: log line, header and stack trace body. I am going to allow to users define a regular expression for any of those fields and then use that regular expression to detect exceptions. If any of the defined regular expressions is a match, then the exception will be categorized accordingly; otherwise, it'll go for further processing by the heuristic algorithm I implemented earlier. I am also going to allow users define any grouping name that they like, so it will be more meaningful than the *unrecognised_6c2dc65d7c0bfb0768ddff8cabaccf68* strings.

The Configuration File

There are many ways of storing configuration data for your applications. I prefer to use XML documents for the following reasons:

- Python has built-in libraries for parsing XML and as such, accessing configuration data is simple.

- Syntax validation happens automatically when the configuration file is fed to the XML parser, so I need not worry about checking the syntax of the configuration file.

- XML documents have a clearly defined unambiguous structure that allows me to implement hierarchical structures should I need to.

There is also a practical downside of using XML—it's not really human-friendly. However, by using appropriate editors that can do syntax highlighting we can mitigate this. Nowadays most editors support this functionality. The ViM editor, which is available on nearly all Linux distributions, is also able to highlight XML syntax.

Listing 7-10 is a simple configuration file to catch majority of the File Not Found exceptions.

Listing 7-10. *A configuration file with two rules*

```
<?xml version="1.0"?>
<config>
    <exception_types>
        <exception logline=""
                   headline=""
                   body="java\.io\.FileNotFoundException: .+ \(No such file or↩
directory\)"
                   group="File not found exception"
                   desc="File not found exception"
        />
        <exception logline=""
                   headline=""
                   body="java\.io\.FileNotFoundException: .+ \(Permission denied\)"
                   group="Permission denied exception"
                   desc="Permission denied exception"
        />
    </exception_types>
</config>
```

The configuration file starts with a document identification string that tells the parsers it is an XML version 1.0 document. For basic processing this information isn't strictly required and can be omitted, but for completeness it's best to adhere to the specification.

The root element of the XML configuration files is the <config> tag, which encompasses all other configuration items. Now I have the option of putting exception declarations directly within the <config> tags, and since I have not planned to have anything else in my configuration file it would just be fine. However if I later added any new type of configuration items, for example something that affects reporting, it would not logically fit. So it is always a good idea to create a branch tag and place all elements of a given type within it. Therefore I define a new domain element, which I'm going to call <exception_types>. All declarations for each individual exception type are going to be defined here.

As you can see the actual exception declaration is pretty straightforward. I have three placeholders for regular expressions followed by a description and group name fields.

Parsing XML Files with Python

There are two ways of parsing an XML document. One method is called SAX, or Simple API for XML. Before you process XML with SAX you need to define a callback function for each tag that you are interested in. You then call a SAX method to parse the XML. The parser will then read the XML file one line at a time and call a registered method for each recognized element.

Another method, which I'm going to use in my example, is called the DOM or Document Object Model. Unlike SAX, the DOM parser reads the whole XML document into memory, parses it, and builds an internal representation of that document. By nature, XML documents represent a tree-like structure, with node elements that contain child or branch elements, and so on. So the DOM parser builds a tree-like linked data structure and provides you with methods of traversing through this tree structure.

There are three basic steps in finding the information in an XML document: parse the XML document, find a tree node that contains the elements that interest you, and finally read their values or contents.

Parsing an XML document is really simple and only takes one line of code (two if you count the include statement). The following code reads in the whole configuration file and creates an XML parser object that later can be used to find information.

```
from xml.dom import minidom
config = minidom.parse(CONFIG_FILE)
```

The next step is to find all <exception> elements. I know that their "parent" node is the <exception_types> element, so I need to get a list of those first. This can be done with the getElementsByTagName method, which is available for any XML object. This method accepts one argument, the name of the element you're trying to find. The result is a list of Element objects that have the name you searched for. The search performed by method is recursive, so if I start at the top level (which in my instance is the document object) it will return all elements that have this particular name. In that case I may as well search for the <exception> tag. With this simplistic configuration file that method would work as well, but the name exception is much too generic, and therefore may be used outside exception_types sections. Another important thing to note is that each Element object is also searchable and has the same method available to use. So I can go through the list of <exception_types> elements and drill down further, searching for an <exception> tag in each:

```
for et in config.getElementsByTagName('exception_types'):
    for e in et.getElementsByTagName('exception'):
```

■**Note** The following text might seem slightly confusing, because there is an overlap of terminology. XML elements can have attributes, as in this example: <element attribute="attribute value">element value</element>. Similarly, Python objects or classes also have attributes that you access like this: python_object.attribute. When XML is parsed and the representing Python object is built for your document, you would use *Python class attributes* to access *XML document attributes*.

Now I've reached the elements that I am interested in and need to extract their values. As you can see from the configuration file example, I chose to store data as element attributes. Attributes in each Element object can be accessed using an attribute called attributes. This attribute is an object that acts as a dictionary. Each element of the dictionary has two values: *name* contains name of the XML element attribute, and *value* holds the actual text value of the attribute.

It may sound confusing, but it should become clear if you look at the example in Listing 7-11.

Listing 7-11. *Accessing configuration data in the XML document*

```
for et in config.getElementsByTagName('exception_types'):
    for e in et.getElementsByTagName('exception'):
        print e.attributes['logline'].value
        print e.attributes['headline'].value
        print e.attributes['body'].value
        print e.attributes['group'].value
        print e.attributes['desc'].value
```

As you can see from this example, searching for and accessing attributes of XML document elements is really a trivial task.

Storing and Applying Filters

All exception detection and classification rules are going to be stored in an array. Each array element is a dictionary that contains precompiled regular expressions, both group and description fields ,and finally an ID string, which is just an MD5 hash of regular expression strings. This ID can be used later in referencing particular exception groups and will remain unique as long as the rules are not changed.

Using precompiled regular expressions increases search speed significantly, because they are already validated and converted to bytecode ready for execution.

Configuration parsing and importing are done during the class initialization, as you can see from the example in Listing 7-12.

Listing 7-12. *Class initialisation and configuration import*

```
class ExceptionContainer:
    def __init__(self):
        self.filters = []
        config = minidom.parse(CONFIG_FILE)
        for et in config.getElementsByTagName('exception_types'):
            for e in et.getElementsByTagName('exception'):
                m = md5.new()
                m.update(e.attributes['logline'].value)
                m.update(e.attributes['headline'].value)
                m.update(e.attributes['body'].value)
                self.filters.append({ 'id'   : m.hexdigest(),
                                      'll_re':
                                          re.compile(e.attributes['logline'].value),
```

```
                                    'hl_re':
                                        re.compile(e.attributes['headline'].value),
                                    'bl_re':
                                        re.compile(e.attributes['body'].value),
                                    'group': e.attributes['group'].value,
                                    'desc' : e.attributes['desc'].value, })
```

When the `insert` method (described in detail earlier) is called, it will loop through the list of filters and attempt to search for matching strings. When such a string is found, the exception details are either stored or the running counter for the group is increased, depending on whether this exception has already been encountered in the log file. If no matches were found, the heuristic categorization method will be executed as shown in Listing 7-13.

Listing 7-13. *Code to match custom categorisation rules*

```
def insert(self, suspect_body, f_name=""):
    ...

    if self.is_exception(lines[1]):
        self.count += 1

        ...

        logged = False

        for f in self.filters:
            if f['ll_re'].search(log_l) and
                    f['hl_re'].search(hd_l) and
                    f['bl_re'].search(bd_l):
                logged = True
                if f['id'] in self.exceptions:
                    self.exceptions[f['id']]['count'] += 1
                else:
                    self.exceptions[f['id']] = { 'count'    : 1,
                                                 'log_line' : log_l,
                                                 'header'   : hd_l,
                                                 'body'     : bd_l,
                                                 'f_name'   : f_name,
                                                 'desc'     : f['desc'],
                                                 'group'    : f['group'], }
                break

        if not logged:
            # ... unknown exception, try to automatically categorise
```

The Benefits of a Precompiled Search Over a Plain-Text Search

I've mentioned that MD5 hash calculation and then string comparison can be slow comparing to a precompiled regular expression search, but is that really true? Let me do some experiments and test the theory.

First I am going to run the application against the log file with over 4000 different exceptions and measure execution time. There are four types of exception in the file: several exceptions generated by the Tomcat engine, a few hundred Permission Denied exceptions, over a thousand File Not Found with the same file name, and over a thousand File Not Found with different filenames. The first number in the result indicates the total number of exceptions and the second is the total number of identified groups:

```
$ time ./exctractor.py .
4098, 1070

real    0m1.759s
user    0m1.699s
sys     0m0.047s
```

As you can see, it took nearly two seconds to crawl through the file and count all exceptions. Now let's try with two simple rules that detect both types of File Not Found and Permission Denied exceptions:

```
$ time ./exctractor.py .
4098, 6

real    0m0.789s
user    0m0.746s
sys     0m0.037s
```

So the execution time has been improved significantly and the application finishes its job over twice as fast. Provided that the dataset is relatively small and some of the execution time is spent loading libraries and reading in configuration files, the actual savings can be even greater if applied to larger log files.

Also notice that what had been over a thousand exception groups became just 6. This is much more manageable and informative.

Producing Reports

I now have a fully functioning application that reads in log files, parses them, searches for exceptions, and finally counts similar exceptions, based on either on automatic groups or categories defined by the user. All that is very well and good, but unless someone can read and analyze this data it's still pretty useless.

Let's write a simple reporting function, so that people who are going to use this application can benefit from it.

Grouping Exceptions

If you paid close attention to the previous sections discussing exception grouping, you may have noticed that exceptions are not grouped based on a *group* field.

If the exception is not categorized in the configuration file, it would have been grouped based on its MD5 hash value; however in that case the group name and exception ID would have one-to-one mapping anyway, because the group name is generated from the hash value:

```
if m.hexdigest() in self.exceptions:
    self.exceptions[m.hexdigest()]['count'] += 1
else:
    self.exceptions[m.hexdigest()] = { 'count'    : 1,
                                       'log_line' : log_l,
                                       'header'   : hd_l,
                                       'body'     : bd_l,
                                       'f_name'   : f_name,
                                       'desc'     : 'NOT IDENTIFIED',
                                       'group'    : 'unrecognised_'+m.hexdigest(), }
```

However, if the exception has been "caught" using one of the filters from the configuration file, it would have been categorized based on the filter MD5 hash value and not the 'group' string:

```
if f['ll_re'].search(log_l) and f['hl_re'].search(hd_l) and f['bl_re'].search(bd_l):
    if f['id'] in self.exceptions:
        self.exceptions[f['id']]['count'] += 1
    else:
        self.exceptions[f['id']] = { 'count'    : 1,
                                     'log_line' : log_l,
                                     'header'   : hd_l,
                                     'body'     : bd_l,
                                     'f_name'   : f_name,
                                     'desc'     : f['desc'],
                                     'group'    : f['group'], }
```

This approach allows you to find out how many times each individual filter has been hit and also group the counters based on the 'group' field. So first of all I need to go through the list of all logged exceptions and create distinct categories. The categories dictionary is only going to store the group name and the total count of exceptions in that group. I also use the option key -v (for *verbose*) to tell whether or not to print the exception details. Listing 7-14 shows the code.

Listing 7-14. *Grouping exception IDs into categories*

```
def print_status(self):
    categories = {}
    for e in self.exceptions:
        if self.exceptions[e]['group'] in categories:
            categories[self.exceptions[e]['group']] += self.exceptions[e]['count']
        else:
            categories[self.exceptions[e]['group']] = self.exceptions[e]['count']
```

```
if OPTIONS.verbose:
    print '-' * 80
    print "Filter ID                :", e
    print "Exception description    :", self.exceptions[e]['desc']
    print "Exception group          :", self.exceptions[e]['group']
    print "Exception count          :", self.exceptions[e]['count']
    print "First file               :", self.exceptions[e]['f_name']
    print "First occurrence log line :", self.exceptions[e]['log_line']
    print "Stack trace headline     :", self.exceptions[e]['header']
    print "Stack trace              :"
    print self.exceptions[e]['body']
```

Producing Differently Formatted Output for the Same Dataset

If there are no options supplied for detailed reporting, the application only prints two numbers, which indicate the total number of exceptions found and the total number of different groups. You can use this information to quickly check the current status and also accumulate the records over a period of time and import that data into Excel or other tools to draw pretty graphs.

If you're planning to import report data to some other application it needs to comply with a format accepted by that application. If you're using Excel to create graphs, the most convenient file type for import would be CSV or Comma Separated Values, but if you just want to display this information on the screen you most likely want it to be more informative than just a pair of numbers separated by comma.

So I introduced an option that allows users to set a format they want to get the result in: either CSV or plain text. I then created two template strings that reference the same variables but provide different formatting:

```
TPL_SUMMARY['csv']  = "%(total)s, %(groups)s"
TPL_SUMMARY['text'] = "="*80 + "\nTotal exceptions: %(total)s\nDifferent groups: %(groups)s"
```

Then, depending on the format key supplied by the user, the print statement will select the appropriate formatting string and pass variables to it:

```
print TPL_SUMMARY[OPTIONS.format.lower()] % {'total': self.count, 'groups': len(categories)}
```

Note how you can pass variables to a formatted sting referencing them by name. This technique is really useful when you need to produce differently formatted output using the same set of variables.

Calculating Group Statistics

Finally, I wanted to produce a more detailed report on how many different groups were found and the number of exceptions in each, both relative (as a percentage) and absolute (the total number of occurrences).

I already have all the details in the dictionary, including the group name and total number of exceptions in the group. But the dictionaries are not sorted, and it would be nice to have a list presented in descending order, where the worst "offenders" are at the top.

Python has a very useful built-in function for sorting any iterable objects: sorted(). This function accepts any iterable object such as list or dictionary and returns a new sorted list. The tricky part is that when iterating through a dictionary, you are only iterating though its keys, so calling sorted() with a dictionary as its parameter, you'd only get a list of sorted keys!

```
>>> d = {'a': 10, 'b': 5, 'c': 20, 'd': 15}
>>> for i in d:
...   print i
...
a
c
b
d
>>> sorted(d)
['a', 'b', 'c', 'd']
>>>
```

Obviously this isn't really what you want—you need both values in your result. Dictionaries have a built-in method that returns key/value pairs as iterable objects—iteritems(). If you use this instead, you'll get a slightly better result, showing both the key and value of each pair, but still sorted on the key value, which isn't what you want either:

```
>>> for i in d.iteritems():
...   print i
...
('a', 10)
('c', 20)
('b', 5)
('d', 15)
>>> sorted(d.iteritems())
[('a', 10), ('b', 5), ('c', 20), ('d', 15)]
>>>
```

The *sorted()* function accepts an argument that allows you specify a function that will be used to extract a comparison key from the list elements when the elements are composite, such as value pairs. In other words, this function should return a second value from each pair. You need a special function from the operator library: itemgetter(). I will use this function to extract the second value from each pair, and this value will be used by the sorted() function to sort the list:

```
>>> from operator import itemgetter
>>> t = ('a', 20)
>>> itemgetter(1)(t)
20
>>> sorted(d.iteritems(), key=itemgetter(1))
[('b', 5), ('a', 10), ('d', 15), ('c', 20)]
>>>
```

And the final touch is telling `sorted()` to sort the list in reverse order, so that the list starts with the item that has the largest value:

```
>>> sorted(d.iteritems(), key=itemgetter(1), reverse=True)
[('c', 20), ('d', 15), ('a', 10), ('b', 5)]
>>>
```

Similarly I am generating and printing the list of exception groups. I also add a statistical calculation, just to show the relative size of each group:

```
for i in sorted(categories.iteritems(), key=operator.itemgetter(1), reverse=True):
    print "%8s (%6.2f%%) : %s" % (i[1], 100 * float(i[1]) / float(self.count), i[0]
)
```

Summary

In this chapter I explained in detail how the open-source tool *Exctractor* was written and what each functional part is doing. This chapter shows how to apply your Python knowledge to build a relatively complex command line tool to analyze large text files. Although Python is not a text-processing language as such, it still can be successfully used for this purpose. Important points to keep in mind:

- Start by defining a problem and what you want your application to achieve.

- Analyze the data structures you will be working with and make design decisions based on that information.

- If you're dealing with large datasets try to minimize the amount of memory required, by using *generators*, Python functions that generate values on-the-fly.

- If you need to read and search information in large data files, use generator constructs to read them one line at a time.

- Python has built-in support for reading and writing compressed files such as bzip2 archives.

- Keep configuration in a structured format such as XML, especially if it tends to contain many items.

CHAPTER 8

A Web Site Availability Check Script for Nagios

In this chapter we are going to build a custom check script for one of the standard NMS (network monitoring systems) available today—Nagios. We will be monitoring a simple web site by using an HTML parsing library, which allows us to check the operational side of the site. The check script attempts to navigate through unsecured pages and then reach some protected pages, too, by simulating a user login action. All action will be recorded and fed back into the Nagios system, which can be configured to do reporting and alerting if required.

Requirements for the Check System

The main requirement for the system we are going to implement is the ability to monitor a remote web site. However, the check should go beyond a simple HTTP GET or POST request, and it must allow the user to specify a navigation path. For example, it should be able to perform some action that simulates the standard user behavior—get to the main web site page and then browse to the products list or navigate to the news web site and select the top story.

As a variation of that scenario, the system also needs to be able to simulate a login process whereby the check submits the user details to the remote web site. These details are then validated by the system and the security token is returned (usually in the form of a browser cookie value).

Unlike a simple HTTP check, which is readily available with the default Nagios distribution, this mechanism actually triggers the web application logic and acts as a more sophisticated check. Combined with the timing parameters, you may implement sophisticated checks that monitor the user logon time and alert if the login process is successful but is taking too long.

We are going to use Python's standard urllib and urllib2 libraries for accessing the web sites. As a web page parser we are going to use the Beautiful Soup HTML parsing library.

Every web site is unique, or at least is trying to stand out from the crowd. Therefore making a universal check system may be a complicated task, so for the sake of simplicity I am going to set some constraints on the system that we'll build in this chapter:

- The navigation (or user journey) path will be coded in the script and not available as a configuration.

- The login check works only on sites that use cookie-based authentication mechanisms.

The Nagios Monitoring System

Nagios is one of the most popular network monitoring systems. It is used to monitor a wide variety of network-attached components using different access protocols such as HTTP, SNMP, FTP, SSH, and so on. The capabilities are endless because Nagios has a plug-in based architecture, which allows you to extend the base functionality to meet your monitoring needs. You can also run the checks remotely by using the Nagios Remote Plugin Executor (NRPE) utility.

In addition to the monitoring tasks, Nagios is also capable of graphing the collected data, such as the system response times or CPU utilization. When problems occur, Nagios has the ability to alert via email or SMS notifications.

Nagios packages (the base application and plug-ins) are available on most Linux platforms, so check your Linux distribution documentation for the installation details. Alternatively, you can download the source code from the Nagios web site at http://www.nagios.org/download. On a typical Fedora system you can install the Nagios base system along with the basic set of plug-ins (or checks) using the following command:

```
$ sudo yum install nagios nagios-plugins-all
```

To proceed with this chapter, you should have some experience in managing Nagios. If you need more information, please refer to the official documentation that you can find online at http://www.nagios.org/documentation/.

Nagios Plug-In Architecture

The power of Nagios NMS is in its plug-in architecture. All check commands are external utilities that can be written in any language—C, Python, Ruby, Perl and so on. The plug-ins communicate with the Nagios system by means of OS return codes and the standard input/output mechanism. In other words, Nagios has a predefined set of return codes that the check scripts must return. The return code dictates what the new service state should be set to. All return codes and the corresponding service states are listed in Table 8-1.

Table 8-1. *Nagios Plug-In Return Codes*

Return Code	Service State
0	OK. The service is in a perfectly healthy condition.
1	WARNING. The service is available but is dangerously close to the critical condition.
2	CRITICAL. The service is not available.
3	UNKNOWN. It's not possible to determine the state of the service.

In addition to the return code, a plug-in should also print at least one line to the standard output. This printed string should contain a mandatory status text followed by the optional performance data string. So a simple one-line report example can be:

```
WebSite OK
```

This text will be appended to the status report message in the Nagios GUI. Similarly, with the performance data appended, it would look like this:

```
WebSite OK | response_time=1.2
```

The performance data part then is available through the built-in Nagios macros and can be used to plot the graphs. More information about using the performance data parameter is available at `http://nagios.sourceforge.net/docs/3_0/perfdata.html`.

When you write a new plug-in, you must provision it first in the configuration files, so that Nagios knows where to find it. Conventionally, all plug-ins are stored in `/usr/lib/nagios/plug-ins`.

Once you've written a check script you must define it in the `command.cfg` configuration file, which can be found in `/etc/nagios/objects/`. The actual location may be different depending on how you installed Nagios. Here is an example of a check definition:

```
define command {
        command_name    check_local_disk
        command_line    $USER1$/check_disk -w $ARG1$ -c $ARG2$ -p $ARG3$
}
```

When you define a service or a host, you now can refer to this check with the `check_local_disk` name. The actual executable is `$USER1$/check_disk` and accepts three arguments. Following is an example of the service definition that uses this check and passes all three parameters to it:

```
define service {
        use                     local-service
        host_name               localhost
        service_description     Root Partition
        check_command           check_local_disk!10%!5%!/
}
```

The `$USER1$` macro that you've seen earlier in the command-line definition simply refers to the plug-ins directory and is defined in `/etc/nagios/private/resource.cfg` as `$USER1$=/usr/lib/nagios/plugins`.

If you want, you can define a new macro and use it with your check scripts. This way, you'll separate the packaged scripts from your own, and it becomes easier to maintain. I recommend doing this for check scripts that have a complicated structure with external configuration files or other dependencies.

The Site Navigation Check

As you know, each site is unique and although usually the same navigation and implementation principles apply, you still have to do a lot of manual work to reverse-engineer it, so that you can successfully simulate the user actions. Matters get much simpler if you know how the site is built and don't have to guess. In this example check we're going to build a script that navigates to the BBC UK web site at `http://news.bbc.co.uk/`, selects the top front-page story, and follows that link.

This check is a good example of a monitor that simulates one of the user behavior patterns and also tests the internal web site logic for at least two functions: the ability to generate the front page and the ability to generate the top story content. We'll also monitor the execution time, and if it exceeds the preconfigured threshold, we'll alert on that as well.

Installing the Beautiful Soup HTML Parsing Library

Before proceeding, you need to install the Beautiful Soup library. Beautiful Soup is a Python module designed to parse HTML and XML documents and extract information from them. This library is ideal for processing the real-world HTML pages, as it ignores the malformed HTML syntax with missing end tags and other errors that a web page may potentially contain.

Because Beautiful Soup is a really popular library, its packages are available for the majority of Linux distributions. For example, on a Fedora system you can install this library with the following command:

```
$ sudo yum install python-BeautifulSoup
```

You can also install it from the Python Package Index (PyPI):

```
$ sudo pip install BeautifulSoup
```

Alternatively, the source code is also available for downloading from the application web site at http://www.crummy.com/software/BeautifulSoup/.

Retrieving a Web Page

In its simplest form, the page-retrieving function can be implemented with only two function calls, and in most cases where you're not submitting any information and just retrieving, this is sufficient. The following example uses the urlopen() function, which performs an HTTP GET request if no additional form data is supplied. We'll look at different methods of submitting data to the web applications later in the chapter.

```
>>> import urllib2
>>> r = urllib2.urlopen('http://news.bbc.co.uk')
>>> html = r.read()
>>> len(html)
90881
>>>
```

The result of the read() call is a string containing the web page as it is served by the server. This string, however, is not a full response and does not include extra information such as HTTP protocol headers. The result object returned by the urlopen() call has the info() method, which you can use to retrieve the HTTP headers as they are returned by the server. You need to remember that the object returned by the info() call is an instance of the httplib.HTTPMessage class, which implements the same protocol as the dictionary class, but in fact is not a dictionary itself:

```
>>> r.info()
<httplib.HTTPMessage instance at 0x1005c7ef0>
>>> print r.info()
Expires: Fri, 14 May 2010 07:20:15 GMT
Accept-Ranges: bytes
Set-Cookie: BBC-
UID=444b6e3cefd9cadf2d0a1f38c1d37453cbc43c1fd0a0b13a641bca65f221d5240Python%2durllib
%2f2%2e6; expires=Sat, 14-May-11 07:20:15 GMT; path=/; domain=bbc.co.uk;
```

```
Set-Cookie: BBC-
UID=444b6e3cefd9cadf2d0a1f38c1d37453cbc43c1fd0a0b13a641bca65f221d5240Python%2durllib
%2f2%2e6; expires=Sat, 14-May-11 07:20:15 GMT; path=/; domain=bbc.co.uk;
Cache-Control: max-age=0
Date: Fri, 14 May 2010 07:20:15 GMT
Transfer-Encoding: chunked
Connection: close
Server: Apache
Content-Type: text/html
Keep-Alive: timeout=10, max=788

>>> r.info()['Server']
'Apache'
>>>
```

■**Tip** You can find out more about the HTTP headers, including a short description and a link to the appropriate
RFC specification document, at `http://www.cs.tut.fi/~jkorpela/http.html`.

Another useful method of the response object is `geturl()`. This method returns the actual URL of
the retrieved document. It is possible that the initial URL will respond with an HTTP redirect, and you'll
actually end up retrieving a page from a completely different URL. In that case you may want to check
the origin of the page. One possible cause of a redirect is that you are trying to access restricted content
without prior authentication. In this case you will most likely be redirected to the login page of the web
site.

```
>>> res = urllib2.urlopen('http://www.hsbc.co.uk/')
>>> res.geturl()
'http://www.hsbc.co.uk/1/2/'
>>>
```

The resulting contents can then be passed to Beautiful Soup for the HTML interpretation and
parsing. The result is an HTML document object that implements various methods for searching and
extracting data from the document. The argument supplied to the `BeautifulSoup` constructor is just a
string, which means you can use any string as an argument, not only the one that you've just retrieved
from the web site.

```
>>> from BeautifulSoup import BeautifulSoup
>>> soup = BeautifulSoup(html)
>>> type(soup)
<class 'BeautifulSoup.BeautifulSoup'>
>>>
```

Parsing the HTML Pages with Beautiful Soup

Once the contents are loaded into the `BeautifulSoup` object, we can start dissecting the BBC front web page. To give you an idea of what we need to find on the page, Figure 8-1 illustrates a sample screenshot of the front page, where you can clearly see the position of the top story. The top story on the BBC News UK when I captured the screen was titled "Cameron and Clegg: We are united." The title obviously changes from article to article, but the layout of the web site rarely changes, and the top story is always displayed in the same location on the web page.

Figure 8-1. *The BBC News UK front page*

We now need to find the corresponding HTML code in the web page. Let's look at the web page source, shown in Listing 8-1. (I did a bit of formatting, so you will probably see a slightly different layout of the code if you view the code from your web browser.)

Listing 8-1. *HTML source code for the BBC News UK front page*

```
[...]

<table cellspacing="0" border="0" cellpadding="0" width="786">
  <tr>
    <td valign="top" width="466">
      <div class="wgreylinebottom">
        <div class="splashformat wrapa">
          <div class="mvb">
<a class="tshsplash" href="/1/hi/uk_politics/election_2010/8676607.stm">
Cameron and Clegg: We are united</a>
          </div>
<a href="/1/hi/uk_politics/election_2010/8676607.stm">
<img src="http://newsimg.bbc.co.uk/media/images/47836000/jpg/_47836386_009274560-
1.jpg" align="" width="466" height="260" alt="Nick Clegg and David Cameron"
border="0" vspace="0" hspace="0"></a>
          <div class="widesummary">
New Prime Minister David Cameron says the UK's first coalition in decades marks a
"historic and seismic shift" in British politics.
          </div>

          <div class="sabull">
<a class="tsl" href="/1/hi/uk_politics/election_2010/8678370.stm">Analysis: Dave and
Nick Show</a>
          </div>
          <div class="sabull">
<a class="tsl" href="http://news.bbc.co.uk/1/shared/election2010/liveevent/">Live
coverage: Text and video</a>
          </div>
          <div class="sabull">
<a class="tsl" href="/1/hi/uk_politics/election_2010/8677088.stm">At-a-glance:
Coalition policies</a>
          </div>
          <div class="sabull">
<a class="tsl" href="/1/hi/uk_politics/election_2010/8675705.stm">Who's who:
Cameron's cabinet</a>
          </div>

[...]
```

We can immediately spot two distinct marks that potentially may lead us to the top story URL link. The first one is the <div> tag that belongs to the mvb class. The second mark could be the <a> tag that belongs to the tshsplash class.

There are several ways to access the tags in a Beautiful Soup document. If you know exactly what you are looking for and the exact structure of the web site, you can simply use the tag names as properties of the soup object:

```
>>> import urllib2
>>> from BeautifulSoup import BeautifulSoup

>>> WEBSITE='http://news.bbc.co.uk/'

>>> result = urllib2.urlopen(WEBSITE)
>>> html = result.read()
>>> soup = BeautifulSoup(html)
>>> print soup.html.head.title
```

This code will print the title HTML string:

```
<title>BBC NEWS | News Front Page</title>
```

This is a convenient and quick method of accessing individual tags, but it does not work very well if the tag encapsulation structure is complicated. For example, the `<div>` tag we're trying to get to is already five levels deeper than the `<table>` tag that encapsulates it, and we don't even know where that particular `<table>` tag is in relation to the document's root element. Also, confusion arises if there are multiple tags at the same level. For example, soup.html.body may contain multiple `<table>` tags, in which case, Beautiful Soup would not know which one of those tags you are trying to access.

For situations like that, Beautiful Soup provides find methods, which allow you to search for the elements regardless of where they are in the document tree. In other words, the search is recursive. There are two find methods: findAll, which returns a list of all tags that match the search string, and find, which returns the first occurrence of the matching tag.

Also bear in mind that each document element implements the same search methods that are available for the main soup object. So if you want to get every `<div>` that is enclosed in a particular `<table>`, you'd first search for a `<table>` tag, and then run another search query starting only from that object, as illustrated here:

```
>>> tables = soup.findAll('table')
>>> len(tables)
24
>>> divs = tables[0].findAll('div')
>>> len(divs)
1
>>> divs[0]
<div class="wideav">
<a href="http://news.bbc.co.uk/1/hi/uk/7459669.stm">
<img src="http://newsimg.bbc.co.uk/nol/shared/img/v4/icons/video_live.gif"
align="left" width="50" height="13" alt="" border="0" vspace="2" hspace="0" />
                    BBC NEWS CHANNEL


            </a>
<br clear="all" />
</div>
>>>
```

Clearly this is not what we wanted. First, there are 24 (!) tables in this document. Second, the first table contained only one <div> tag, which is not what we were searching for. So how do we find that particular tag in this "soup"? To help us, Beautiful Soup allows specifying the tag attributes, such as class, id, or any other attribute that might be included in the tag definition. Each attribute must be accompanied with its value (or a regular expression, if you are searching for a set of values). All attributes with their corresponding values should be passed on as a dictionary argument, attrs.

For example, let's search for all <div> tags that belong to the mvb class:

```
>>> divs = soup.findAll('div', attrs={'class': 'mvb'})
>>> len(divs)
9
>>>
```

This is obviously a much better result, as we're now limited to only nine elements, but it's still not good enough, as we don't know which of them represents the top story. Let's try searching for the <a> tag that belongs to the "tshsplash" class. This time we'll use the shortcut syntax to specify the tag's class, which you can do just by passing a second string instead of a list of attributes:

```
>>> a_tags = soup.findAll('a', 'tshsplash')
>>> len(a_tags)
1
>>> a_tags[0]
<a class="tshsplash" href="/1/hi/uk_politics/election_2010/8676607.stm">Cameron and
Clegg: We are united</a>
>>>
```

Bingo! We've found the URL we were looking for. If you want to access the particular attribute in a tag object, just try accessing it as a dictionary element. It's always a good idea to check whether the dictionary key actually exists; otherwise, you will get the KeyError exception. However, because you're not accessing the "real" Python dictionary object, you cannot use the IS IN construct, as it will give you an incorrect result:

```
>>> 'href' in a_tags[0]
False
>>> a_tags[0].has_key('href')
True
>>> a_tags[0]['href']
u'/1/hi/uk_politics/election_2010/8676607.stm'
>>>
```

The next step is to load this page. Just loading this page successfully is enough to confirm that the web site is working, so we will not do any HTML parsing of this page. The check script also needs to measure the time spent in retrieving both web pages. If the time exceeds defined thresholds, the script will return an error code stating that. Listing 8-2 shows the complete check code.

Listing 8-2. *The site navigation script*

```python
#!/usr/bin/env python

import sys
import urllib2
import time
from BeautifulSoup import BeautifulSoup
from optparse import OptionParser

NAGIOS_OK = 0
NAGIOS_WARNING = 1
NAGIOS_CRITICAL = 2
WEBSITE_ROOT = 'http://news.bbc.co.uk/'

def fetch_top_story():
    status = []
    try:
        result = urllib2.urlopen(WEBSITE_ROOT)
        html = result.read()
        soup = BeautifulSoup(html)
        a_tag = soup.find('a', 'tshsplash')
        story_heading = a_tag.string
        topstory_url = ''
        if a_tag.has_key('href'):
            topstory_url = "%s/%s" % (WEBSITE_ROOT, a_tag['href'])
        else:
            status = [NAGIOS_CRITICAL, 'ERROR: Top story anchor tag has no link']
        result = urllib2.urlopen(topstory_url)
        html = result.read()
        status = [NAGIOS_OK, story_heading]
    except:
        status = [NAGIOS_CRITICAL, 'ERROR: Failed to retrieve the top story']
    return status


def main():
    parser = OptionParser()
    parser.add_option('-w', dest='time_warn', default=1.8,
                      help="Warning threshold in seconds, default: %default")
    parser.add_option('-c', dest='time_crit', default=3.8,
                      help="Critical threshold in seconds, default: %default")
    (options, args) = parser.parse_args()
```

```
    if options.time_crit < options.time_warn:
        options.time_warn = options.time_crit

    start = time.time()
    code, message = fetch_top_story()
    elapsed = time.time() - start
    if code != 0:
        print message
        sys.exit(code)
    else:
        if elapsed < float(options.time_warn):
            print "OK: Top story '%s' retrieved in %f seconds" % (message, elapsed)
            sys.exit(NAGIOS_OK)
        elif elapsed < float(options.time_crit):
            print "WARNING: Top story '%s' retrieved in %f seconds" % (message,
elapsed)
            sys.exit(NAGIOS_WARNING)
        else:
            print "CRITICAL: Top story '%s' retrieved in %f seconds" % (message,
elapsed)
            sys.exit(NAGIOS_CRITICAL)


if __name__ == '__main__':
    main()
```

As you can see, the script accepts two optional arguments that allow you setting the thresholds for both the warning and critical conditions. Let's test the check script with various settings, just to trigger all possible conditions, before deploying it as a Nagios check:

```
$ ./check_website_navigation.py  -w 1.2
OK: Top story 'Cameron and Clegg: We are united' retrieved in 0.923599 seconds
$ echo $?
0
$ ./check_website_navigation.py  -w 0.6
WARNING: Top story 'Cameron and Clegg: We are united' retrieved in 0.867163 seconds
$ echo $?
1
$ ./check_website_navigation.py  -c 0.6
CRITICAL: Top story 'Cameron and Clegg: We are united' retrieved in 0.871813 seconds
$ echo $?
2
$
```

Adding the New Check to the Nagios System

Now it's time to provision this check in Nagios and start monitoring the BBC News web site. First we will add the new section in the command-list file, which is commands.cfg in the /etc/nagios/objects/ directory. The following code makes the check available to use under the name check_website_navigation and instructs that two parameters need to be supplied with the command:

```
define command {
    command_name    check_website_navigation
    command_line    $USER2$/check_website_navigation -w $ARG1$ -c $ARG2$
}
```

You then need to create a configuration file that contains at least a host and a service definition. Listing 8-3 shows how to create a simple configuration file that defines a host template, from which the host then inherits the basic settings. This host is then put into a separate host group. Similarly, a service with the new check command is defined and grouped into a separate service group. We will expand this configuration when we add another check later in the chapter. Once you create the configuration file, you will have to add a cfg_file statement to the nagios.cfg file that points to this configuration file.

Listing 8-3. *Nagios host and service definitions*

```
define host {
    name            template-website-host
    use             generic-host
    register        0
    max_check_attempts    5
    contacts        nagiosadmin
    parents             localhost
    check_command       check-host-alive
}

define host {
    use             template-website-host
    host_name       news.bbc.co.uk
    address             news.bbc.co.uk
    notes           BBC News UK
}

define hostgroup {
    hostgroup_name          InternetWebsites
    alias               Internet Websites
    members             news.bbc.co.uk
}
```

```
define service {
    use             generic-service
    hostgroup_name        InternetWebsites
    service_description   SiteNavigation
    check_command         check_website_navigation!1.5!2.5
}

define servicegroup {
    servicegroup_name   InternetWeb
    alias               Internet Websites
    members             news.bbc.co.uk,SiteNavigation
}
```

If you allow some time for Nagios to recheck all defined services, and then navigate to the service check screen, you should see a result similar to Figure 8-2.

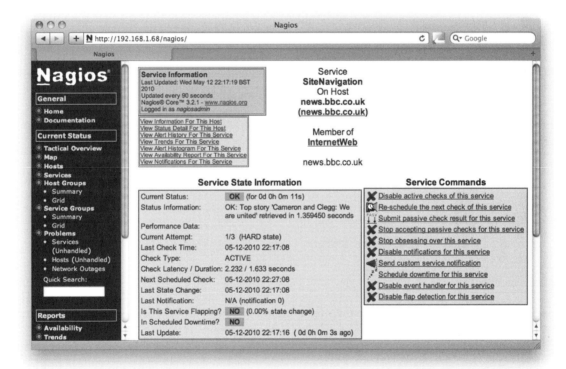

Figure 8-2. *Checking script status in Nagios*

Emulating the User Login Process

The next check we are going to implement is the user login action. As an example web site I'm going to use http://www.telegraph.co.uk/. This site allows users to participate in different promotions and subscribe to mailing lists and email notifications. Obviously, these options need to allow users to identify themselves to the web site.

When the user clicks the Log In link, which is available on the top-right corner of the web page, he or she will be redirected to a log in landing page. This page contains a web page form with two fields: one for the user email address and one for the password. Listing 8-4 shows the form definition in the web page source code.

Listing 8-4. *The telegraph.co.uk login form*

```
<form id="user" class="basicForm" action="./login.htm" method="post">
  <label for="email" >Email address</label>

  <input id="email" name="email" type="text" value=""/>

  <label for="password" >Password</label>

  <input id="password" name="password" type="password" value=""
autocomplete="off"/>

  <div class="cl"></div>
  <a href="forgotpassword.htm" class="noLabel">Forgotten password?</a><br/>
  <a href="http://www.telegraph.co.uk/topics/about-us/3489870/Contact-us.html"
class="noLabel">Need help?</a>
  <div class="bottomButtons">

    <input type="submit" value="Log in" />

  </div>
  <div class="cl"></div>
  <p class="noLabel">Or<a href="registration.htm">register now</a>
    if you do not have a Telegraph.co.uk profile
  </p>
</form>
```

When you fill in the values and hit the Submit button, the web browser encodes the values by combining all fields (including the field names and their new values) into one string and sends that information as an HTTP POST request. The HTTP method is usually specified in the form definition, and as you can see from our example is currently set to POST.

If we want to achieve the same result, we first need to encapsulate the data we are going to submit. Unfortunately, urllib2 does not provide this functionality and we have to use the urllib method to encode the form data. The formatted string containing the form data should be supplied as an optional argument to the urlopen() method. If the additional data is supplied, the method will automatically send the POST request instead of the default GET request.

■**Note** What is the difference between the POST and GET requests? The main difference is in the way these two requests submit additional data to the web services. If you are sending a GET request, the data is contained within the URL string. The URL would then have the syntax similar to this: `http://example.com/some_page?key=value&key2=value2`. Whereas if you send the POST request, the URL will be `http://example.com/some_page`, and the data will be encapsulated in the HTTP request headers.

Web sites usually manage user sessions with HTTP cookies. An HTTP cookie is a protocol message field, which is included in the communication messages sent from the web browser application to the web server. The HTTP protocol by nature is stateless. The HTTP requests do not carry any information that could help identifying the request sender. Keeping track of user activities is essential for the web shopping services or any other service that needs to provide personalized results. This activity is referred to as "maintaining a web session." One of the ways to maintain this session is by using HTTP cookies. Here's an example of an HTTP cookie:

```
Set-Cookie: BBC-
UID=444b6e3cefd9cadf2d0a1f38c1d37453cbc43c1fd0a0b13a641bca65f221d5240Python%2durllib
%2f2%2e6; expires=Sat, 14-May-11 07:20:15 GMT; path=/; domain=bbc.co.uk;
```

There can be multiple cookies set in the HTTP header message. Each cookie has a name and a value along with some extra properties such as the domain that is supposed to receive it, the expiration time, and the URL portion. So how do cookies help to maintain sessions? When the web server receives a request, it sends the initial response back to the web browser. Along with the other HTTP header fields, it inserts the cookie field. The web client in turn saves the cookie in its internal database. When it makes another request it scans the database for cookies that both belong to the same domain it is currently sending the request to and have the matching path property. The web client then includes all matching cookies in its subsequent requests. Now the web server receives requests that are "marked" with the cookies and therefore knows that these requests are part of the same "conversation," or in other words belong to the same web session.

I've described the behavior of a typical web browser that handles the cookie storing and management activities automatically. The default URL processor (or the opener in urllib2 terms) does not process cookies. Luckily, all classes for handling cookies are included in the urllib2 module and you just need to replace the default opener with the custom opener object. The HTTPCookieProcessor class that we are going to use in constructing the new opener object is responsible for storing the HTTP cookies received from the server and then injecting them into all HTTP requests going to the same web site:

```
>>> import urllib, urllib2
>>> url = 'https://auth.telegraph.co.uk/sam-ui/login.htm'
>>> data = urllib.urlencode({'email': 'user@example.com', 'password': 'secret'})
>>> opener = urllib2.build_opener(urllib2.HTTPCookieProcessor())
>>> urllib2.install_opener(opener)
>>> result = opener.open(url, data)
>>> html = result.read()
>>> print html
```

```
[...]
    <h2>
        Welcome, Rytis<br/>
        <span class="subText">
            You are able to update your Telegraph.co.uk profile from this page
        </span>
    </h2>
[...]
```

The HTML page that has been retrieved shows that I have successfully logged on to the system, and the web page that has been returned to me is the user-profile/account-management page. Now let's try visiting the log-off page, which is supposed to log us out from the site, effectively invalidating the session cookie that we retrieved earlier:

```
>>> url_logon = 'https://auth.telegraph.co.uk/sam-ui/login.htm'
>>> url_logoff = 'https://auth.telegraph.co.uk/sam-ui/logoff.htm'
>>> import urllib, urllib2
>>> data = urllib.urlencode({'email': 'user@example.com', 'password': 'secret'})
>>> opener = urllib2.build_opener(urllib2.HTTPCookieProcessor())
>>> urllib2.install_opener(opener)
>>> res = opener.open(url_logon, data)
>>> html_logon = res.read()
>>> res.close()
>>> res = opener.open(url_logoff)
>>> html_logoff = res.read()
>>> res.close()
```

Now let's see if the <span> tag of the class subText is a mark that can be used to distinguish between the registration page (meaning that we have logged on successfully) and the main landing page (meaning we logged off successfully):

```
>>> from BeautifulSoup import BeautifulSoup
>>> soup_logon = BeautifulSoup(html_logon)
>>> soup_logoff = BeautifulSoup(html_logoff)
>>> len(soup_logon.findAll('span', 'subText'))
1
>>> len(soup_logoff.findAll('span', 'subText'))
0
>>>
```

And indeed, this proves to be a reasonably valid test. So we have a way to authenticate ourselves to the web site by submitting the required information in the POST data request. You can use the same method to submit large forms as well. For example, you may want to build an automated check to test the registration functionality of your web site or the comment system.

The check script for Nagios system is quite similar to the one that we wrote for the navigation test. Listing 8-5 shows the complete script.

Listing 8-5. *The site logon/logoff check script*

```python
#!/usr/bin/env python

import sys
import urllib2, urllib
import time
from BeautifulSoup import BeautifulSoup
from optparse import OptionParser

NAGIOS_OK = 0
NAGIOS_WARNING = 1
NAGIOS_CRITICAL = 2
WEBSITE_LOGON  = 'https://auth.telegraph.co.uk/sam-ui/login.htm'
WEBSITE_LOGOFF = 'https://auth.telegraph.co.uk/sam-ui/logoff.htm'
WEBSITE_USER = 'user@example.com'
WEBSITE_PASS = 'secret'

def test_logon_logoff():
    opener = urllib2.build_opener(urllib2.HTTPCookieProcessor())
    urllib2.install_opener(opener)
    data = urllib.urlencode({'email': WEBSITE_USER, 'password': WEBSITE_PASS})
    status = []
    try:
        result = opener.open(WEBSITE_LOGON, data)
        html_logon = result.read()
        result.close()
        result = opener.open(WEBSITE_LOGOFF)
        html_logoff = result.read()
        result.close()
        soup_logon = BeautifulSoup(html_logon)
        soup_logoff = BeautifulSoup(html_logoff)
        if len(soup_logon.findAll('span', 'subText')) == 1 and \
                len(soup_logoff.findAll('span', 'subText')) == 0:
            status = [NAGIOS_OK, 'Logon/logoff operation']
        else:
            status = [NAGIOS_CRITICAL,
                        'ERROR: Failed to logon and then logoff to the web site']
    except:
        status = [NAGIOS_CRITICAL, 'ERROR: Failure in the logon/logoff test']
    return status
```

```python
def main():
    parser = OptionParser()
    parser.add_option('-w', dest='time_warn', default=3.8,
                      help="Warning threshold in seconds, defaul: %default")
    parser.add_option('-c', dest='time_crit', default=5.8,
                      help="Critical threshold in seconds, default: %default")
    (options, args) = parser.parse_args()
    if float(options.time_crit) < float(options.time_warn):
        options.time_warn = options.time_crit
    start = time.time()
    code, message = test_logon_logoff()
    elapsed = time.time() - start
    if code != 0:
        print message
        sys.exit(code)
    else:
        if elapsed < float(options.time_warn):
            print "OK: Performed %s sucessfully in %f seconds" % (message, elapsed)
            sys.exit(NAGIOS_OK)
        elif elapsed < float(options.time_crit):
            print "WARNING: Performed %s sucessfully in %f seconds" % (message,
                                                                       elapsed)
            sys.exit(NAGIOS_WARNING)
        else:
            print "CRITICAL: Performed %s sucessfully in %f seconds" % (message,
                                                                        elapsed)
            sys.exit(NAGIOS_CRITICAL)


if __name__ == '__main__':
    main()
```

You need to add this script to the commands.cfg file and create the appropriate host, hostgroup, service, and service group definitions in the Nagios configuration files, just as we did with the site navigation script. Once you have added this configuration, restart the Nagios process and after a short time you should see the check status appearing in the Nagios console.

Summary

In this chapter we've looked at web site monitoring scripts that go beyond the simple HTTP process check. These tests emulate standard user behavior and actually test the web application logic. Key points to remember:

- You can access web content by using the standard Python `urllib2` module.

- The `urllib2` library provides additional handlers that manage cookies seamlessly.

- You can parse HTML documents with the Beautiful Soup library.

- It is easy to integrate applications with the Nagios monitoring system through the API, which is based on the standard UNIX process communication mechanisms.

- You can find detailed information about the Nagios API in the official documentation, which is available at `http://www.nagios.org/documentation/`.

Management and Monitoring Subsystem

This is the first of three chapters in which I am going to show you how to build a simple distributed monitoring system. In the first part, I demonstrate building a monitoring server component. This component is responsible for sending the queries to all monitoring agents, scheduling the requests, and storing the collected data in the local database. This chapter will discuss three topics: data modeling, interprocess communication, and multithreaded programming. In the data modeling section we will looks at some database design and modeling methods. Later we'll investigate the XML-RPC protocol and the Python libraries that support it. Finally we are going to look at multithreaded programming with Python.

Design

It is important to come up with some sort of design before starting the implementation, especially when coding distributed systems. There are two main areas that I need to establish: the components the monitoring system is going to be made of and the data objects it will operate with.

The Components

From the requirements-gathering exercise I know that the system is going to be centralized—that is, there will be multiple agents reporting to the master monitoring server. Therefore at least two distinct components are needed: a monitoring server and a monitoring agent. The server process is going to communicate with the clients and retrieve the performance and status data from them.

Now there is a question of how smart the agent needs to be. Does it need to know how to perform all checks by itself? Or should it have a pluggable architecture whereby the agent itself only acts as a controller component? I am going to choose the architecture in which the agent relies on plug-ins to perform all checks. The agent process itself will only proxy the server requests to the plug-in code and pass the results back. I'll call these plug-ins the "sensors," because that is effectively what they are doing—measuring the system's parameters.

Figure 9-1 represents a high-level component interaction diagram. The following sections provide a more detailed design description of each component.

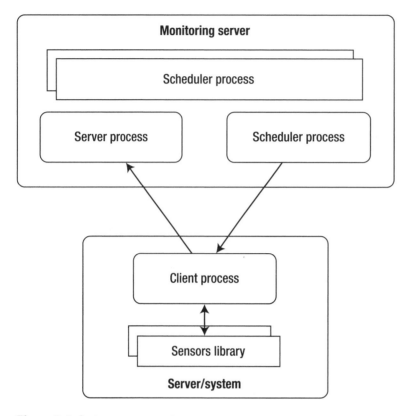

Figure 9-1. *System components*

The Monitoring Server

The monitoring server is responsible for sending out the requests to the client systems and receiving the sensor readings from all clients. There are two options for obtaining the data from the clients: the first is to have the server initiate the connection, and the second is to have the client do so. Each approach has its benefits. When the client initiates the connection there's less overhead on the server side, because it does not need to do any scheduling work. It is also safer, because it is impossible to request the data, and therefore the data will only be received by the system, which is registered on the client—the monitoring server.

However, the biggest disadvantage with the client-initiated connections is that the server has absolutely no control over the incoming information flow, and this can lead to the server being overloaded. Ideally it would be up to the server to decide what information it requires and at what point in time. For example, a really intelligent system disables certain checks if making them doesn't make sense. A good example would be to stop volume usage checks after receiving a hard disk failure alert, because it is obvious that the disk failure will cause all volume checks to fail, so there is no point in reporting symptoms of the underlying issue.

In my simple monitoring system I'm going to use what is effectively a server-initiated control mechanism, but without sacrificing the security model. The server process will be sending out notifications to the client to submit the sensor data. When the client receives such notification it will perform the check and submit the readings back to the server it is registered with. So there is no way of obtaining the data from the client; it's only a one-way communication channel. Only the "trusted" server can receive the results.

Client configuration is done in a similar fashion: the client receives an external signal to update its configuration (either the "trusted" server address or the sensor code) and then it initiates the connection back to the server to get the required details.

The Monitoring Agent

The monitoring agent process is completely passive and acts only when it receives instructions from the server. As described earlier, such instructions can be to submit the sensor readings, update the server address, and retrieve a new sensor code from the server.

When the agent is notified to submit the readings, it will call the external tools to perform the actual reading. It will then read the output from the process and send it back to the monitoring server, along with the process return code.

The server address update command instructs the monitoring agent to connect to the currently registered server and request the new address. The agent will then attempt to connect to the new address. If the operation is successful, the current server address will be replaced with the new address; otherwise the address will not change.

Finally, when the agent receives a command to update the code of one of the sensors, it will connect back to the server and ask for the sensor code archive. The server is going to send the archived copy back to the requesting client. When the archive is received and stored in the temporary location, it is unpacked and a basic sanity check is performed. If the check is successful, the old code is archived and the new code is deployed in to the appropriate location.

The Sensors

Unlike other monitoring systems, where sensors or checks contain some logic (for example, Nagios checks for return OK, WARNING or CRITICAL status messages), I am not going to embed any validation logic into my sensors. After all, the sensor is there to report the status and cannot and should not know whether the situation it's reporting is posing any danger. It's up to the master monitoring server to decide whether the readings are indicating any issues with the systems.

This approach allows further extension of the check logic to perform more advanced and adaptive reporting. For example, instead of simple threshold checks, the system may be expanded with trend checks. Even if the load on the observed system goes beyond the set threshold, it might still be all right because that's how the load pattern goes. Similarly, if the system reports a load much lower than is normal for the given period of time it may indicate issues, which a simple threshold check would fail to detect.

The Data Objects

Naturally, all processes involved are going to consume or produce (or both) some data. The most obvious data is the sensor readings, but there will also be configuration, scheduling settings defined, and so on. So I need to come up with a sound definition and design of what data the monitoring system is going to deal with before writing any code.

There will be four distinctive types of data:

- Configuration data, which describes all monitoring agents, sensors and their parameters

- Site configuration data, which defines what checks need to be performed on each server and where to find the client servers

- Scheduling data, which defines the intervals for the checks
- Performance reading data, which is the data received from the sensors on the client servers

Configuration

The configuration data contains data about sensors, sensor parameters, and monitoring agents. All available agents, along with their names and addresses, are part of the monitoring system configuration. In addition to a simple listing of all hosts and sensors, the configuration also contains information about which sensors are available on what monitoring servers.

The agent servers may be different in their available hardware resources and configuration, so it must be possible to define individual thresholds for each monitoring agent.

Performance Readings

Obviously this is the key data component in the monitoring system. Each performance reading needs to hold the time it was recorded, so that it can be correctly represented on the time line. The numeric value and sensor application return code also need to be recorded, along with the node and the sensor identification information.

Site Configuration

At the moment, site information will hold only the monitoring server address, but the placeholder needs to be put in place so that it allows for future functional expansion. It is important to note that the site information is maintained centrally on the monitoring server, and the agent servers would retrieve this information and update local configuration accordingly.

The reason for storing this information centrally is that it is much easier to control the configuration if it is stored in one location. When the agents need updating, a separate process will issue update commands for the configuration to be automatically updated.

Scheduling

The scheduling configuration defines what sensor commands need to be executed on what monitoring agents and at what intervals. There will be information held for each agent-check combination with appropriate interval setting.

This data is similar to the information defined in UNIX cron files, but it does not have to be as flexible in terms of defining execution time patterns. All time intervals will be of an equal length.

The Data Structures

In the previous section I briefly described the high-level design of the data structures that I'm going to use in the monitoring system. In this section I'm going to create the database layout and relationships between different database tables. Finally, this information will be mapped to the SQL statements that will be used to initialize the database.

The modeling tool I've used to create the diagrams and data model is MySQL Workbench, which is an open-source application you can download from http://wb.mysql.com. MySQL Workbench is a powerful database and entity relationship (ER) visual design tool. You can create new visual designs and generate SQL scripts from the design.

Introduction to Data Normalization

Data normalization is a way of ensuring that data is maintained in a way that prevents loss of data integrity. If the database structures are not normalized, erroneous code actions, user data-entry mistakes, or system or application failure during the update operation can lead to data corruption. The data corruption I am referring to here is the logical one, whereby the database files are correct but the information stored may be logically incorrect. To continue with the data layout section I need to explain few concepts of data normalization, so that you can understand why I'm organizing the data in a particular way.

Let's assume I want to implement one of the configuration section requirements; namely, to store the following information items:

- information about a sensor
- sensor options
- monitoring agent information

So I create a table with the following fields: hostname, address, sensor name, and sensor options. I then enter a few checks I want to perform on two monitoring agents:

```
hostname          address           sensor            options
--------------    --------------    --------------    --------------
my laptop         127.0.0.1         disk_check        free_space
my laptop         127.0.0.1         memory_check      total
remote server     192.168.0.1       disk_check        free_space
remote server     192.168.0.1       memory_check      total
```

Now let's say I want to update the address field of the remote server. Because the information is stored in two different rows, I need to make sure that all rows are going to be updated. If for some reason the application that attempts to update the database fails to identify all rows and update accordingly, I may end up with the following data in my table:

```
hostname          address           sensor            options
--------------    --------------    --------------    --------------
my laptop         127.0.0.1         disk_check        free_space
my laptop         127.0.0.1         memory_check      total
remote server     192.168.0.1       disk_check        free_space
remote server     192.168.0.2       memory_check      total
```

This data is correct from the database perspective, but it is inconsistent: the remote server now has two addresses, and it is not clear which one is correct.

This is where data normalization comes in handy. Following a few simple rules, you can split the information into different tables and thus eliminate the possibility of data corruption or irregularities. There are three basic data normalization forms, each defining the rules for structuring the data. In addition to these forms, there are a number of higher-degree normalization forms developed, but in most cases they pose only an academic interest.

I'm going to start with the First Normal Form, which defines two important properties for the table structure: rows must be unique, and there should be no repeating groups within columns.

The first rule is pretty obvious and means that there must be a way of uniquely identifying each row. The unique key can be either one column or a combination of columns.

The second rule means that I cannot define multiple columns that carry what is logically the same information. For example, if I wanted to have multiple checks for each server and added these checks as additional columns to store that information, it would violate the second rule, as in this example:

```
hostname    address     sensor1      options1      sensor2         options2
----------  ----------  -----------  -----------   --------------  -----------
my laptop   127.0.0.1   disk_check   free_space    memory_check    total
```

It is also not allowed to have grouped data in the single column; for example, listing options as a string like free_space,swap_space would also violate this rule.

The data is considered to be in the Second Normal Form when it satisfies all the rules of the First Normal Form and also satisfies the requirement that all fields that are not part of the primary key depend on all fields of the key. Consider the following example:

```
address          sensor            default option
---------------  ---------------   ---------------
127.0.0.1        disk_check        free_space
127.0.0.1        memory_check      total
192.168.0.1      disk_check        free_space
192.168.0.2      memory_check      total
```

Neither address nor sensor fields alone can be unique keys for each row, but the combination address-sensor can be considered a unique key for each row. So the table conforms to the first normal form. The default option field, however, only depends on the sensor and has no relation to the address column, therefore this table is not in the Second Normal Form.

I need to split the data into two tables so that each table satisfies the Second Normal Form rules. The first table lists default options for each sensor, and the unique key is the sensor field.

```
sensor           default option
---------------  ---------------
disk_check       free_space
memory_check     total
```

The second table lists all checks on each node, where unique key is the combination of both columns.

```
address          sensor
---------------  ---------------
127.0.0.1        disk_check
127.0.0.1        memory_check
192.168.0.1      disk_check
192.168.0.2      memory_check
```

■**Note** It's worth noting that if the First Normal Form table has no composite keys, it is automatically in the Second Normal Form.

Finally, the Third Normal Form requires that all nonkey fields depend on the primary key only. In the following example, I record what checks have been performed on each agent. Assume for the purpose of this example that only one check could be performed each minute, so the `address"-"check time` is a unique key.

```
address       check time    sensor          sensor location
----------    ------------  -------------   -----------------
127.0.0.1     10:20         disk_check      /checks/disk
127.0.0.1     10:21         disk_check      /checks/disk
127.0.0.1     10:22         memory_check    /checks/memory
127.0.0.1     10:23         memory_check    /checks/memory
```

This table complies with the rules of the Second Normal Form, but is still not in the Third Normal Form. That's because although all fields depend on a full primary key, some of them also depend on the non-key fields. In particular, the `sensor location` depends on the `sensor` field. In a faulty application it is possible to have a situation where `sensor location` is different for the same sensor. Therefore I need to split `sensor"-"sensor location` into a separate table to comply with the Third Normal Form.

In general, data normalization prevents your data from losing its integrity, so it is usually considered to be a good practice. Sometimes, however, normalizing data can impose serious penalties on the application's performance and code complexity. If you are absolutely sure that no serious issues will occur should the data become irregular, and more importantly, if you have a means to recover from that situation, you can sacrifice the completeness of the data normalization in favor of speed and code simplicity. So always apply your own judgment when designing your data structures.

In the following examples I am going to show a situation in which it is not feasible to follow the normalization rules strictly, and you can make some compromises.

Configuration Data

Let's start with the configuration data, which contains information about all monitoring agents and the sensor checks assigned to them. There are multiple approaches to organizing and designing database tables. One of the formal methods is to write down all columns as one record and start from there applying all rules from the First Normal Form. When you're done and have one or more tables in the First Normal Form, you proceed by applying the Second Normal Form rules until you get the desired result—ideally database tables in the Third Normal Form.

Although this method works perfectly every time, I find it bit tedious, because with some practice you already know how to organize the tables and going through all the formal steps just creates unnecessary work. I find the following method a lot more effective.

Think about the objects in your model that are static and self-contained. Going back to the configuration data I see two objects there: host and sensor. Now create tables for each such object. I'll start with the table for the host entries, Table 9-1.

Table 9-1. *The Host Entries*

Field	Data Type	Description
id	integer	The unique identifier.
name	text	The name of the host.
address	text	The IP address or full domain name of the host.
port	text	The port number on which the client process is running.

As you can see, this table is already in the Third Normal Form and there's absolutely no need to improve anything in it. Each entry is unique, there are no repetition groups in the columns, there's only one primary key field (name), and other fields depend only on that field.

■ **Note** I need to point out that the ID in this table and other tables is not to be treated as a unique field. When normalizing data, fields must carry sensible information, and arbitrary fields such as hidden IDs or timestamps cannot be treated as informational fields, because they do not constitute the dataset. They are used mostly for reference purposes, because it is faster and more efficient to operate on integer values rather than text or keys of other data types.

Now let's proceed to the sensor definition. This is going to be slightly more complicated, because from the sensor design I already know that each sensor can perform several checks. For example, the disk volume sensor can perform multiple checks, such as total space, used space, used inodes, and so on. You might want to add all fields into one table, so that the sensor-check combination becomes a unique key field. This may be fine for small datasets, but if you want to expand and add more fields, this structure becomes inflexible and you'll need to redesign the tables. As a rule of thumb I recommend splitting any data that has the '*contains multiple …*' attribute. Going back to my example I can declare that each *sensor contains multiple checks*. Therefore, if you split this information across two tables, in most cases you'll be spot on. Table 9-2 is the table for the sensor entries.

Table 9-2. *The Sensor Entries*

Field	Data Type	Description
id	integer	The unique identifier
name	text	The name of the sensor

The table for the checks (or the *probes* as I'm going to call them in this book) is shown in Table 9-3; it contains more information and also references the sensor entries.

Table 9-3. *The Probe Entries*

Field	Data Type	Description
id	integer	The unique identifier.
name	text	The name of the probe.
parameter	text	The string to be passed to the sensor check command.
warning	float	The default threshold for this particular probe, at the warning level.
error	float	The default threshold for this particular probe, at the error level.
sensor_id	integer	The ID of the sensor record. As I mentioned, in formal notation this should have been the name of the sensor, but for simplicity and flexibility we use unique row IDs.

Now look really carefully at Tables 9-2 and 9-3 and see if you can spot any violations of the normalization form rules. The sensor table is so simple that no doubt it is in the Third Normal Form, but what about the probe table? At first glance it looks fine, but on closer inspection you'll realize that I have repetitive groups, so this table is not even in the First Normal Form! There are two fields that effectively define similar types of information: the threshold fields, warning and error. I must create a new table to hold threshold definitions, including warning, error, and possibly others such as informational and critical if I ever want to add them. That, however, brings another complication—I cannot put any values in that table, because threshold values are specific to each probe. So I will need to define yet another table that ties the probe and the threshold records together and adds the value column. I now have two choices—restructure the table, introduce two new ones, and also face much more complicated code to deal with this, or accept the limitation of the two threshold levels. Because the monitoring system I'm building here is really simple, and I don't require much granularity in thresholds, I go with the second option.

When you're finished defining static components, proceed to the relations. My monitoring system is going to perform probe readings on all monitored hosts, so I need to define this relation. Obviously not all probes apply to all hosts, so I have to create another table that defines probe-to-host mapping. I'm also going to allow threshold overrides on a per-host basis. It is only going to be a placeholder in the table, and the logic of threshold precedence must be implemented at the code level. See Table 9-4.

Table 9-4. *Probe-to-Host Mapping*

Field	Data Type	Description
id	integer	The unique identifier.
probe_id	integer	The ID of the probe record.
host_id	integer	The ID of the host record on which the probe must be executed.
warning	float	The placeholder for the warning threshold override entry. Must not be a required field, because if left empty the default will be assumed.
error	float	The placeholder for the error threshold override entry. Must not be a required field, because if left empty the default will be assumed.

Performance Data

The only additional information in the performance data table is the reading returned by the monitoring agent and the time stamp when the measurement has been performed. The remaining information can be found from the host-to-probe mapping table (Table 9-4). The probe readings table (Table 9-5) contains details about the host where the measurement has been made, the type of the sensor, and the exact check parameters.

Table 9-5. *Probe Readings*

Field	Data Type	Description
id	Integer	The unique identifier
hostprobe_id	Integer	The ID of the record in the host-to-probe mapping table
timestamp	Text	The timestamp indicating the time when the measurement was made
probe_value	Float	The value returned by the probe code
ret_code	Integer	The return code of the sensor code

Scheduling

The scheduling data consists of two distinct components that are not related to each other: the scheduling data that defines what probes need to be executed at specific intervals and the ticket queue, which is used to hold instructions for the ticket scheduler process. Let's take a closer look at each of them.

The probing schedule table (Table 9-6) holds static data that references individual records in the probe-to -host map table. This is needed to find the information about the sensor name and specific probe parameters that need to be executed. It also indicates which monitoring agent (or host) needs to be contacted. In addition to this information, the scheduling table contains the interval parameter, which indicates the time period between probe readings.

Table 9-6. *Probe Scheduling*

Field	Data Type	Description
id	Integer	The unique identifier
hostprobe_id	Integer	The ID of the record in the host to probe mapping table
probeinterval	Integer	The interval between probe checks expressed in minutes

The ticket queue table (Table 9-7) contains dynamic data about the probes to be executed. This table is populated either by the scheduler process or by any other process that needs to obtain performance data from the agents. The dispatcher process reads all entries from the table and sends requests to the monitoring agents. Once the request is sent, the record is updated as dispatched. This is done to prevent duplicate requests. Finally, when the monitoring server process receives the sensor data along with the ticket number it removes the record from the table.

Table 9-7. *The Probe Tickets Queue*

Field	Data Type	Description
id	Integer	The unique identifier.
hostprobe_id	Integer	The ID of the record in the host-to-probe mapping table. This record contains all information needed to perform the sensor query call.
timestamp	Text	The timestamp record indicates when the ticket has been placed in the queue. Useful to detect situations when the request has been dispatched, but the result never came back.
dispatched	Integer	A flag indicating whether the ticket has been dispatched to the corresponding monitoring agent.

Site Configuration

The site configuration information is organized into two tables: system-wide parameters and host-specific parameters. I wanted to have the flexibility of defining new custom parameters as I develop the application, so instead of fixing settings to table columns, therefore each setting is defined as a key-value pair in the table. The *key* column uniquely identifies the parameter name and the value is the default value, which can be overridden in the second table that maps parameters to specific hosts. This approach allows me to have a two-level inheritance system, just as I have with the sensor threshold entries.

So the first table contains the key-value records as shown in Table 9-8.

Table 9-8. *System Parameters*

Field	Data type	Description
id	Integer	The unique identifier.
name	Text	The unique name of the system parameter setting.
value	Text	The default value for the key, which can either be used as a system-wide setting or be overridden if required for each specific host entry. All values are stored as text and must be type converted to appropriate types at the run time.

The second table (Table 9-9) references the system parameters table and allows overriding the settings.

Table 9-9. *Host-Specific Parameters*

Field	Data type	Description
id	integer	The unique identifier.
param_id	integer	The ID of the record in the parameters table.
host_id	integer	The ID of the host table record. This allows applying specific settings for every particular host.
dispatched	text	The host specific parameter value.

Representing the Information in an ER Diagram

I now have defined all the tables that I will be using on the monitoring server. Each field is defined, along with the relations between the tables. Even though I have only a few tables, it is still sometimes confusing to find and visualize the relation between different tables. To make things easier, especially when writing SQL queries, it is a good idea to draw an entity relationship (ER) diagram, a concept introduced in Chapter 5.

Figure 9-2 is the ER diagram I drew for the tables defined earlier.

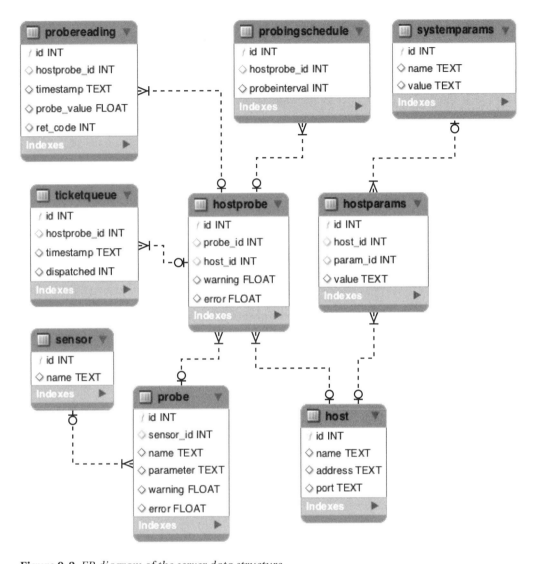

Figure 9-2. *ER diagram of the server data structure*

Communication Flows

The monitoring that I am building here is effectively a distributed computational system. It has most of the distributed system attributes—the controller process (the scheduler component) is responsible for sending job requests to the processing nodes (monitoring agents), and finally the information is supplied back to the data processing component (the monitoring server).

As with any distributed system it is crucial to define communication flows and the methods of exchanging the information. There are many methods to implement process communication—SOAP (discussed in detail in Chapter 2), REST (REpresentational State Transfer), XML-RPC, and so on. I am going to use the XML-RPC method of exchanging information and calling remote methods, because it is relatively simple to use and Python comes with built-in XML-RPC client and server libraries.

XML-RPC for Information Exchange

XML-RPC is a method of performing remote procedure calls, whereby one process sends a message to a remote system and causes it to execute a particular function. The XML-RPC protocol is similar to the SOAP protocol but has a much simpler structure. In fact, the original XML-RPC was a predecessor of the SOAP protocol. The XML-RPC messages are encoded using XML and uses HTTP as a transport mechanism.

Structure

The XML-RPC call messages have a relatively simple structure and allow only one method of data serialization. Following is an example of an XML-RPC procedure call message:

```
<methodCall>
<methodName>cmd_get_sensor_code</methodName>
<params>
<param>
<value><string>disk</string></value>
</param>
</params>
</methodCall>
```

Although in this example only one parameter is passed on to the remote procedure, the XML-RPC allows multiple parameters nested into arrays or lists, which means it allows transporting complex objects and structures as request or response parameters. The XML-RPC protocol supports major data types such as arrays, base64 encoded data streams, Booleans, datetime objects, double-precision floating point numbers, integers, strings, structures and null objects.

Following is an example of a response to the sensor update request, and the response object is a binary data object encoded in base64 so that it can be encapsulated in an XML message:

```
<methodResponse>
<params>
<param>
<value><base64>
```
QlpoOTFBWSZTWbXv/NUAAad/hP6YQIB+9v/vOw5fCv/v3+4AAQAIQAIdVWSrWEoknonqmYpoOwmT
TEANBoPUGIONB6nqMmnqCVNBMSaGp6Jp6I9IAAGgAZNABoADhppghkNNMjJhANNAGEOaZMACBoJJ
Knp6JPJNlDOT1PUObUADQAaGQABoDT1Mfhn03axWSSsQghGnU545FVUO8YoQcAwgFBiiK7+M3lmm
9b2lcEqqqb5TUIVrK2vGUFTK6AEqDJIMQwCK7At2EVF6xHAj3e5I33xZm8d8+FQEApNQvgxJEflD
nwilZzqaPMelGNtGl27o7Ss51FloebZuhJZOQ5aVjg6gZIyrzq6MNttwJpbNuJHGMzNiJQ4RMSkQ
23GVRwYVCyti8yqZ1ppjGGBr6lG4QY328gCTLALIZNlYNqO1p8U48MsCHPFLznOVKisKYsE7nubL
K1tdUnEQ4XKbibYRsVQSsDnwYtshI+I1gkr2DWoihkgeB4fejEhqPRLzISHihEnOF5Ge4sqCpMgt
8IAyfCEqEyEetRVc/QnBQOrV6dA18m9GHtJOGkikwdjGTpgGdAMTw5FqKHHMHT1ucTvZcRWOurze
q2ndOEjXSliyjqWyXlD5/aWSwKy5UhjUKjbGhyRbVUHIEZQSekThXKgZNUq1Mi7eXZddjBdKRigi
F+RgMBo1LwT5iqJoUSZtCokLR/T5dLx2ySEQZA+ZaARBHaPwlDRNtiF25NTtoLgTsWpDJQRoKwSI

```
UKYILTRv2giFmqLzY1KOawTkMRrztnSqDbUNsKeNQ8UpddfLkXFdEA/xdyRThQkLXv/NUA==
</base64></value>
</param>
</params>
</methodResponse>
```

Python Support

Python has built-in support for the XML-RPC protocol and allows you to write simple client and server applications without needing to install any additional packages.

The client library is called `xmlrpclib` and provides basic functions for accessing the services and creating the XML-RPC call messages. In order to access the server, you first need to create a proxy object and then use it to call the remote procedures. In most cases you must know the names of the procedures you will be using, because XML-RPC does not use a formal service definition language such as WSDL. Some servers may provide a list of available procedures if you call the reserved method `systems.listMethods()`, so it's worth trying, but do not rely on this method. When initializing the remote connection, you also need to specify an endpoint URL, such as `/xmlrpc/` used in the example below:

```
>>> import xmlrpclib
>>> proxy = xmlrpclib.ServerProxy('http://192.168.1.65:8081/xmlrpc/')
>>> url = proxy.cmd_get_new_monitor_url('myhost')
>>> print url
http://localhost:8081/xmlrpc/
>>>
```

Python also has a basic XML-RPC server, which allows you to write functions and make them available to remote clients. The workflow of creating an XML-RPC server is extremely straightforward—you need to import the server class, create a server object, initialize it with the server address and port number you wish it listen to, register your function with the server, and finally run the server:

```
>>> from SimpleXMLRPCServer import SimpleXMLRPCServer as s
>>> def hello(name):
... return "Hello, %s!" % name
...
>>> server = s(('localhost', 8080))
>>> server.register_function(hello, 'hello')
>>> server.serve_forever()
```

Then you can connect and use the exposed functions using the client library:

```
>>> import xmlrpclib
>>> proxy = xmlrpclib.ServerProxy('http://localhost:8080/')
>>> print proxy.hello('John')
Hello, John!
>>>
```

CherryPy

Although the built-in XML-RPC server is really simple to use, I needed a solution that was more scalable in case I had to support widely distributed systems with hundreds of monitoring agents submitting their results. The SimpleXMLRPCServer library by default starts only a single process and therefore is not multithreaded, which means only one connection can be established to it and all other clients will have to wait. This is where *CherryPy* comes in.

In a nutshell CherryPy is a web application framework that allows rapid development and deployment of web applications. It is written in Python, and not surprisingly the web development language that it supports is also Python.

In addition to being the web application framework, CherryPy is also a web server that complies with RFC2616, which defines the HTTP 1.1 protocol. CherryPy can be used as highly configurable and customizable web server on its own, or in combination with any web server that supports the WSGI interface.

The reason I chose CherryPy to use as an HTTP server and a simple framework for exposing my XML-RPC functions is that it supports multiple socket connections and multithreading out of the box, so I don't have to write any additional code. In addition to that, the framework provides an easy way of configuring it.

It is very simple to use CherryPy. Here is a simple example of a web application that just prints out a static message:

```
import cherrypy
from datetime import datetime

class CurrentTime(object):
def index(self):
return str(datetime.now())
index.exposed = True

cherrypy.quickstart(CurrentTime())
```

This is all you need for a web service that displays the current time. Things are not very different if you want to serve XML-RPC procedures. You just have to inherit your main class from the _cptools.XMLRPCController class and use the @cherrypy.expose decorator function, which effectively registers each function with the framework and also makes it available as a remote procedure.

Let's rewrite the hello RPC service using CherryPy:

```
import cherrypy
from cherrypy import _cptools

class Root(_cptools.XMLRPCController):
@cherrypy.expose
def hello(self, name):
return "Hello, %s" % name

cherrypy.quickstart(Root(), '/')
```

As you can see, the framework adds a very little overhead to the default built-in implementation, but in exchange it provides a multithreaded fully configurable web server and the ability to use it behind enterprise-grade web servers such as Apache.

You can install the latest CherryPy package using Python installer `pip` with the following command:

```
pip install cherrypy
```

The Server Process

The server process does not initiate any connection; it only accepts incoming requests. The communication in fact is initiated by the scheduler process or other tools that instruct the clients that they need to perform some actions and then report back to the server or request additional details from it. Because the server process is manipulating large datasets—it stores probe readings, and maintains client configuration data—it is going to make use of a lightweight database engine: SQLite3.

Storing Data in a SQLite3 Database

SQLite3 is a lightweight database management system. It is fully self contained and in fact is merely a set of libraries that together allow the applications to use SQL syntax to store and manipulate data, which means that you don't need to set up and configure any database server. SQLite3 does not need to be configured—you "connect" directly to the database file. Python has built-in support for SQLite3; you just need to import the library and start using it.

Initializing the Database File

You can either create a database from a Python application or write a file with SQL instructions and initialize the database from the command line. Alternatively, SQLite3 provides a command-line tool to interact with the database.

Listing 9-1 shows the complete sequence of initialization SQL statements; this will make further reading easier, as the server code is going to contain lots of SQL statements and you really need to have the table schema and initial data at hand.

Listing 9-1. *Initialisation SQL commands for the server database*

```
-- *****************************************
-- Table: SENSOR
-- Description: List of all available sensors

DROP TABLE IF EXISTS sensor;

CREATE TABLE sensor (
    id INTEGER PRIMARY KEY,
    name TEXT
);

INSERT INTO sensor VALUES (1, 'cpu_load');
INSERT INTO sensor VALUES (2, 'memory');
INSERT INTO sensor VALUES (3, 'processes');
```

```
-- ****************************************
--        Table: PROBE
-- Description: Adds parameter list to sensor command
--              and defines default thresholds

DROP TABLE IF EXISTS probe;

CREATE TABLE probe (
    id INTEGER PRIMARY KEY,
    sensor_id INTEGER,
    name TEXT,
    parameter TEXT,
    warning FLOAT,
    error FLOAT,
    FOREIGN KEY (sensor_id) REFERENCES sensor(id)
);

INSERT INTO probe VALUES ( 1, 1, 'Idle CPU %', 'idle', NULL, NULL);
INSERT INTO probe VALUES ( 2, 1, 'Used CPU %', 'used', NULL, NULL);
INSERT INTO probe VALUES ( 3, 1, 'User CPU %', 'user', NULL, NULL);
INSERT INTO probe VALUES ( 4, 1, 'System CPU %', 'system', NULL, NULL);
INSERT INTO probe VALUES ( 5, 1, 'IO Wait CPU %', 'iowait', NULL, NULL);
INSERT INTO probe VALUES ( 6, 2, 'Free memory, %', 'free_pct', NULL, NULL);
INSERT INTO probe VALUES ( 7, 2, 'Free memory, in bytes', 'free', NULL, NULL);
INSERT INTO probe VALUES ( 8, 2, 'Used memory, %', 'used_pct', NULL, NULL);
INSERT INTO probe VALUES ( 9, 2, 'Used memory, in bytes', 'used', NULL, NULL);
INSERT INTO probe VALUES (10, 2, 'Used swap, %', 'swap_used_pct', NULL, NULL);
INSERT INTO probe VALUES (11, 3, '1 min load average', 'load1', NULL, NULL);
INSERT INTO probe VALUES (12, 3, '5 min load average', 'load5', NULL, NULL);
INSERT INTO probe VALUES (13, 3, '15 min load average', 'load15', NULL, NULL);
INSERT INTO probe VALUES (14, 3, 'Running processes', 'running', NULL, NULL);
INSERT INTO probe VALUES (15, 3, 'Total processes', 'total', NULL, NULL);

-- ****************************************
--        Table: HOST
-- Description: List of all monitoring agents

DROP TABLE IF EXISTS host;

CREATE TABLE host (
    id INTEGER PRIMARY KEY,
    name TEXT,
    address TEXT,
    port TEXT
);
```

```
INSERT INTO host VALUES (1, 'My laptop', 'localhost', '8080');

-- *******************************************
--         Table: HOSTPROBE
-- Description: Maps available probes to the hosts
--                   overrides thresholds if required

DROP TABLE IF EXISTS hostprobe;

CREATE TABLE hostprobe (
    id INTEGER PRIMARY KEY,
    probe_id INTEGER,
    host_id INTEGER,
    warning FLOAT,
    error FLOAT,
    FOREIGN KEY (probe_id) REFERENCES probe(id),
    FOREIGN KEY (host_id) REFERENCES host(id)
);


INSERT INTO hostprobe VALUES ( 1, 1, 1, NULL, NULL);
INSERT INTO hostprobe VALUES ( 2, 2, 1, NULL, NULL);
INSERT INTO hostprobe VALUES ( 3, 3, 1, NULL, NULL);
INSERT INTO hostprobe VALUES ( 4, 4, 1, NULL, NULL);
INSERT INTO hostprobe VALUES ( 5, 5, 1, NULL, NULL);
INSERT INTO hostprobe VALUES ( 6, 6, 1, NULL, NULL);
INSERT INTO hostprobe VALUES ( 7, 7, 1, NULL, NULL);
INSERT INTO hostprobe VALUES ( 8, 8, 1, NULL, NULL);
INSERT INTO hostprobe VALUES ( 9, 9, 1, NULL, NULL);
INSERT INTO hostprobe VALUES (10, 10, 1, NULL, NULL);
INSERT INTO hostprobe VALUES (11, 11, 1, NULL, NULL);
INSERT INTO hostprobe VALUES (12, 12, 1, NULL, NULL);
INSERT INTO hostprobe VALUES (13, 13, 1, NULL, NULL);
INSERT INTO hostprobe VALUES (14, 14, 1, NULL, NULL);
INSERT INTO hostprobe VALUES (15, 15, 1, NULL, NULL);

-- *******************************************
--         Table: TICKETQUEUE
-- Description: Holds all pendiing and sent tickets
--                   tickets are removed when the sensor reading arrive
```

```
DROP TABLE IF EXISTS ticketqueue;

CREATE TABLE ticketqueue (
    id INTEGER PRIMARY KEY,
    hostprobe_id INTEGER,
    timestamp TEXT,
    dispatched INTEGER,
    FOREIGN KEY (hostprobe_id) REFERENCES hostprobe(id)
);

-- *******************************************
--        Table: PROBEREADING
-- Description: Stores all readings obtained from the monitoring agents

DROP TABLE IF EXISTS probereading;

CREATE TABLE probereading (
    id INTEGER PRIMARY KEY,
    hostprobe_id INTEGER,
    timestamp TEXT,
    probe_value FLOAT,
    ret_code INTEGER,
    FOREIGN KEY (hostprobe_id) REFERENCES hostprobe(id)
);

-- *******************************************
--        Table: PROBINGSCHEDULE
-- Description: Defines execution intervals for the probes

DROP TABLE IF EXISTS probingschedule;

CREATE TABLE probingschedule (
    id INTEGER PRIMARY KEY,
    hostprobe_id INTEGER,
    probeinterval INTEGER,
    FOREIGN KEY (hostprobe_id) REFERENCES hostprobe(id)
);

INSERT INTO probingschedule VALUES (1, 11, 1);
INSERT INTO probingschedule VALUES (2, 15, 1);
INSERT INTO probingschedule VALUES (3, 8, 5);
INSERT INTO probingschedule VALUES (4, 10, 5);
```

```
-- ******************************************
--       Table: SYSTEMPARAMS
-- Description: Defines system configuration parameters

DROP TABLE IF EXISTS systemparams;

CREATE TABLE systemparams (
    id INTEGER PRIMARY KEY,
    name TEXT,
    value TEXT
);

INSERT INTO systemparams VALUES (1, 'monitor_url', 'http://localhost:8081/xmlrpc/');

-- ******************************************
--       Table: HOSTPARAMS
-- Description: Assigns system parameters to the hosts
--             allows to override the default values

DROP TABLE IF EXISTS hostparams;

CREATE TABLE hostparams (
    id INTEGER PRIMARY KEY,
    host_id INTEGER,
    param_id INTEGER,
    value TEXT,
    FOREIGN KEY (host_id) REFERENCES host(id),
    FOREIGN KEY (param_id) REFERENCES systemparams(id)
);

INSERT INTO hostparams VALUES (1, 1, 1, 'http://localhost:8081/xmlrpc/');
```

Save these commands into a text file, or download the code from the book's source-code repository on http:Apress.com and run the following command to create the initial database file:

```
sqlite3 -init monitor_db_init.sql monitor.db
```

This will create a new database file, or open the existing file if it exists, and run the SQL commands from the file.

■**Caution** I'm using the DROP TABLE command, so effectively running this command wipes out any data that you might have collected in your database file. Use it with caution.

Accessing the data in SQLite3 database is really simple from the Python application:

```
>>> import sqlite3
>>> con = sqlite3.connect('monitor.db')
>>> for e in con.execute('select * from hostprobe'):
... print e
...
(1, 1, 1, None, None)
(2, 2, 1, None, None)
(3, 3, 1, None, None)
(4, 4, 1, None, None)
(5, 5, 1, None, None)
(6, 6, 1, None, None)
(7, 7, 1, None, None)
(8, 8, 1, None, None)
(9, 9, 1, None, None)
(10, 10, 1, None, None)
(11, 11, 1, None, None)
(12, 12, 1, None, None)
(13, 13, 1, None, None)
(14, 14, 1, None, None)
(15, 15, 1, None, None)
>>>
```

You need to note, however, that if you run the `update` or `insert` statements, you must call the `commit()` function after you've run the `execute()` statement to finish the transaction; otherwise, the transaction will be rolled back and all changes will be lost.

Actions

The main purpose of the server process is to accept the data submitted by the monitoring agents. However, in addition to that, it also provides automatic configuration and sensor code upgrade services. The server also implements a dummy service that always returns a string containing the text "OK". The main purpose of this service is so that clients can test the health of the server before changing their configuration.

Accepting Sensor Readings

The function that implements sensor data storage requires three arguments to be supplied: the ticket number, the probe reading along with the sensor application return code, and the timestamp when the reading was made.

When the call is received it is important to validate the ticket against the ticket queue. If the ticket number is not in the queue, that means the supplied reading is not valid and might indicate an attempt to forge the data by some malicious application. It is also possible that the client took a really long time to respond and the ticket has aged in the queue, so that we're not interested in this data anymore.

Because we need to record the sensor reading time accurately, it is best to record this at the client side and submit it along with the reading data instead of time-stamping the data at the server side.

Also note that the code removes the ticket from the ticket queue, and this effectively finishes the probe-reading request cycle. Listing 9-2 shows the code.

Listing 9-2. *The sensor data store function*

```
@cherrypy.expose
def cmd_store_probe_data(self, ticket, probe, tstamp):
    # probe - [ret_code, data_string]
    self.store_reading(ticket, probe, tstamp)
    return 'OK'

def store_reading(ticket, probe, tstamp):
    con = sqlite3.connect('monitor.db')
    res = [r[0] for r in con.execute('SELECT hostprobe_id FROM ticketqueue WHERE
id=?',
                                     (ticket,) )][0]
    if res:
        con.execute('DELETE FROM ticketqueue WHERE id=?', (ticket,) )
        con.execute('INSERT INTO probereading VALUES (NULL, ?, ?, ?, ?)',
                    (res, str(tstamp), float(probe[1].strip()), int(probe[0])))
        con.commit()
    else:
        print 'Ticket does not exist: %s' % str(ticket)
```

Supplying a New Configuration

As you know from the database section, the server database has two tables that contain system configuration properties. Although I have created a data structure that allows for future expansion and is capable of holding a virtually unlimited number of configuration parameters, at this time it is going to serve only one purpose: to define the monitoring server address. The entry that is responsible for this parameter has the key value of 'monitor_url'. It is possible to override this setting for each individual node, and this is basically a way of distributing the load between multiple monitoring servers.

When the client gets an instruction to retrieve new data, it will connect back to the server and supply its hostname. The server code (Listing 9-3) first tries to look up its own address and port number from the CherryPy configuration class. To read the CherryPy configuration, you call the following function and provide the configuration item key as a parameter:

```
cherrypy.config.get('server.socket_port')
```

Bear in mind that you will get the result back only if it is defined in the configuration; therefore I have fallback statements that assume the default values.

The next step is to find the host specific settings and if they are not found, use the system-wide or default values. It is also possible that they are not defined; if so, we will send either the CherryPy configuration or, failing that, the assumed defaults.

Listing 9-3. *Supplying a new server address*

```
@cherrypy.expose
def cmd_get_new_monitor_url(self, host):
    port = cherrypy.config.get('server.socket_port') if
                        cherrypy.config.get('server.socket_port') else 8080
    host = cherrypy.config.get('server.socket_host') if
                        cherrypy.config.get('server.socket_host') else '127.0.0.1'
    server_url = "http://%s:%s/xmlrpc/" % (host, str(port))
    con = sqlite3.connect('monitor.db')
    res = con.execute("""SELECT hostparams.value
                            FROM hostparams, host, systemparams
                           WHERE host.id = hostparams.host_id
                             AND systemparams.name = 'monitor_url'
                             AND hostparams.param_id = systemparams.id
                             AND host.address = ?""", (host,) ).fetchone()
    if not res:
        res = con.execute("""SELECT value FROM systemparams WHERE name =

'monitor_url'""").fetchone()
    if res:
        server_url = res[0]
    return server_url
```

Providing New Sensor Code

When instructed to do so, the clients may request an update of the sensor check application. Chapter 10 talks in detail about the structure and logic of sensor applications; for now, just note that the code is stored as a compressed TAR archive in a preconfigured directory. You will notice that the configuration of the sensor code directory is not stored in the database. This is done to make it easier for users to change it to any other location. Chapter 10 also discusses how to access configuration data stored in the plain text files.

When sending binary data via an XML-RPC link, you must use a special function of the Python xmlrpclib library: Binary(), which encapsulates the binary data and converts it to a format conforming to HTTP and XML requirements. The binary data is converted to the base64 character set so it can be accepted by the client, which expects to receive only a certain range of available characters. Listing 9-4 shows the code.

Listing 9-4. *Sending binary data via an XML-RPC link*

```
@cherrypy.expose
def cmd_get_sensor_code(self, sensor):
    with open("%s/%s.tar.bz2" % (self.cm.sensor.source_dir, sensor), 'rb') as f:
        return xmlrpclib.Binary(f.read())
```

The Server Health Check

The final action in the server process is the system health check call, which at the moment simply returns a predefined string. You can extend it to perform more a elaborate self health check, for example testing that the database is present and can be read and written to.

```
@cherrypy.expose
def healthcheck(self):
    return 'OK'
```

The Scheduler

Since the monitoring clients are completely passive and will not perform any actions unless told to. I need some sort of scheduling mechanism that sends instructions to the clients to perform monitoring checks.

There are several approaches to implementing this scheduling mechanism. The simplest way is to write a script that sends request for sensor check to all nodes at regular intervals and run this script as a UNIX cron job. This would be easy to implement, but it lacks flexibility—I would probably end up needing to add a new cron entry for each polling interval, and therefore changing the polling schedule would mean changing all cron entries.

Another solution is to write a standalone daemon process that would run in the background and send check requests at defined periods. Because the polling schedule is defined in the database, it could easily adapt to it without needing to change cron configuration. An additional benefit is that it can also run where the cron daemon is not available.

Actions

The request scheduler should implement several actions, which I'll describe in this section.

The primary function of the scheduler daemon is to send sensor reading requests. This process will look at the *pending tickets queue* in the database and send requests for the tickets that have not been sent out yet. I am going to call this process *Ticket Dispatcher*.

Obviously the tickets must be somehow generated and injected into the pending-ticket queue. So I need another process that does exactly that. This process will look at the scheduling table to see what checks need to be run and at what intervals. When it finds ones that are meant to be executed at the present time, it will insert a corresponding ticket into the pending-ticket table. I will name this process *Ticket Scheduler*. You may notice that I've already implied scheduling logic—generate tickets at the given intervals of time. However, this modular structure allows me to use any scheduling algorithm; for example, I can increase time periods for less important checks if the load on the system increases. Also, because all tickets are in the database queue, they can be injected by external processes as well, such as command-line tools.

Running Multiple Processes

It is clear that I need to run two or even more separate processes for my scheduler implementation. I can either write separate scripts and run them in parallel or write a multithreaded application that spawns several processes. The first approach is easier to implement, because I don't have to deal with process management in my scripts, but it lacks maintainability—I could easily end up running and maintaining lots of scripts.

Another approach is to spawn multiple threads or processes from within my application. This is a bit more complicated, as I have to take care of starting and stopping processes from my application, but it also gives more flexibility and results in better code, because all functions are maintained within the same script and can share common object and class definitions.

Multithreading, Multiprocessing, and GIL

Python has supported multiple threads for long time now. In fact, there are two libraries that implement multithreading. First is the `thread` library, which provides low-level primitives; I would advise avoiding this module unless you really have a specific requirement to control threading activities at a low level. The other is the `threading` library, which provides high-level classes to deal with multiple threads and also helper classes, such as `Lock`, `Queue`, `Semaphore`, `Event`, and so on.

Thread implementations vary from system to system, but in general they can be seen as lightweight processes. Usually threads are started from within a process and share the same memory address space. Because they share the memory it is very easy for them to communicate—they can easily access the same variables. Therefore, developers must take extra care when using multiple threads—shared variables must be locked before updating, so that other threads do not get inconsistent results. This is not necessarily a bad thing, but you need to keep it in mind when using threads.

A bigger issue when using threads is the Python interpreter implementation. Because Python memory management is not thread-safe, it is not possible to (safely) run multiple native threads that interpret Python bytecode. The mechanism to stop multiple threads executing at once, called *Global Interpreter Lock* (GIL), ensures that only one Python interpreter thread is running at any given point in time. So although each Python thread maps to a dedicated native system thread, only one is running at a time; therefore, effectively your multithreaded application becomes single-threaded, with additional overhead imposed by GIL and thread-scheduling and context-switching mechanisms.

You may wonder why the threading library provides various locking primitives if there's only one thread running at a time. Well, the main goal for GIL is to prevent multiple threads from accessing the same Python object structures. So it protects the internal memory structures of the interpreter, but not your application data, which you have to take care of by yourself.

This situation with the locking threads is quite specific to the original Python implementation and is unlikely to change. The current Python interpreter—CPython—is heavily optimized, and rewriting it without GIL would impact the performance of those single-threaded Python applications. There are other Python implementations, such as IronPython, that do not have GIL and therefore are more efficient in using multiple CPU cores.

An alternative to the threads is to use processes in the application. The major difference between a thread and a process is that the process has its own completely isolated memory segment and stack. Therefore multiple processes cannot share the same objects, which eliminates all the issues with object data being updated by multiple threads at the same time. This comes at a price, though—there is a lot more additional overhead involved when creating a new process, because the main process needs to be copied and a new memory segment allocated. Another issue is that developers cannot reference the same object from two different processes. So processes need different methods of communication, such as queues and pipes.

Support for multiprocessing has been implemented in Python starting with version 2.6. Python has a library called `multiprocessing`, whose API very closely matches the threading library calls, so porting existing multithreaded applications is a relatively simple task.

So as you can see, "true" multiprocessing in Python can be achieved by running your code within the processes rather than the threads. In some cases this approach is more advantageous, because the processes do not share anything and are completely independent from each other, which allows decoupling of the processes even further and running them on different servers. Processes share data using the queue and pipe primitives, which can use TCP/IP to send data from one process to another.

Basic Usage Patterns and Examples

As mentioned earlier, the multiprocessing library API is very similar to the threading library. The listings and code snippets in this section provide several examples of how to create multiple processes and exchange data between them.

You can define the code you want to run in a separate process either as a function or a class that inherits from the multiprocessing.Process class. There are no hard rules about which approach to use and when; it largely depends on the task size and complexity of the code. I prefer to use classes instead of functions because it allows me to extend the code base more easily; also, the new classes can be extended, so the application code can be used as a base library for the new applications that extend functionality.

Listing 9-5 demonstrates creating processes with the multiprocessing library.

Listing 9-5. *Creating processes with the multiprocessing library*

```
import multiprocessing
import time

def sleeper(timeout):
    print "function: I am a sleeper function and going to sleep for %s seconds" %
timeout
    time.sleep(timeout)
    print "function: I'm done!"

class SleeperClass(multiprocessing.Process):
    def __init__(self, timeout):
        self.timeout = timeout
        print "Class: I am a class and can do initialisation tasks before starting"
        super(SleeperClass, self).__init__()

    def run(self):
        print "Class: I have been told to run now"
        print "Class: So I'm going to sleep for %s seconds" % self.timeout
        time.sleep(self.timeout)
        print "Class: I'm done."

p1 = multiprocessing.Process(target=sleeper, args=(5,))
p2 = SleeperClass(10)
p1.start()
p2.start()
p1.join()
p2.join()
```

As you can see, if you're using classes you have the advantage of running some initialization tasks before the process is started. Running the example code will produce the following results:

```
Class: I am a class and can do initialisation tasks before starting
function: I am a sleeper function and going to sleep for 5 seconds
Class: I have been told to run now
```

```
Class: So I'm going to sleep for 10 seconds
function: I'm done!
Class: I'm done.
```

When you develop applications that spawn multiple processes, and especially if they are going to be long-running processes, such as services, you have to handle interrupts, so that all processes are terminated gracefully. Now let's do a quick experiment and see what happens if you hit Ctrl-C when the program is running:

```
Class: I am a class and can do initialisation tasks before starting
function: I am a sleeper function and going to sleep for 5 seconds
Class: I have been told to run now
Class: So I'm going to sleep for 10 seconds
^CTraceback (most recent call last):
  File "./example_processes.py", line 26, in <module>
    p1.join()
  File "/System/Library/Frameworks/Python.framework/Versions/2.6/lib/python2.6/↵
multiprocessing/process.py", line 119, in join
Process Process-1:
Traceback (most recent call last):
Process SleeperClass-2:
  File "/System/Library/Frameworks/Python.framework/Versions/2.6/lib/python2.6/↵
multiprocessing/process.py", line 231, in _bootstrap
Traceback (most recent call last):
  File "/System/Library/Frameworks/Python.framework/Versions/2.6/lib/python2.6/↵
multiprocessing/process.py", line 231, in _bootstrap
    res = self._popen.wait(timeout)
  File "/System/Library/Frameworks/Python.framework/Versions/2.6/lib/python2.6/↵
multiprocessing/forking.py", line 117, in wait
    self.run()
  File "./example_processes.py", line 19, in run
    self.run()
  File "/System/Library/Frameworks/Python.framework/Versions/2.6/lib/python2.6/↵
multiprocessing/process.py", line 88, in run
    self._target(*self._args, **self._kwargs)
  File "./example_processes.py", line 7, in sleeper
    time.sleep(timeout)
    return self.poll(0)
    time.sleep(self.timeout)
  File "/System/Library/Frameworks/Python.framework/Versions/2.6/lib/python2.6/↵
multiprocessing/forking.py", line 106, in poll
    pid, sts = os.waitpid(self.pid, flag)
KeyboardInterrupt
KeyboardInterrupt
KeyboardInterrupt
```

As you can see, this is pretty poor behavior—both of the processes have received the KeyboardInterrupt exception and terminated abnormally. Also, if you try this experiment multiple times, you may get different results each time. The actual result depends on where the processes were in the CPU execution queue at the time they received the keyboard interrupt signal.

To resolve this issue, I need to catch and handle the interrupts in each of my processes, so that when the interrupt arrives, the process finishes what it was doing and exits gracefully. I am going to wrap both functions into `try: ... except KeyboardInterrupt: ...` clauses, which allows me to catch all interrupts received by the processes. It is also important to know that the main process also receives the interrupt signal and therefore needs to handle it as well. But what is the main process doing while the child processes are running? It is just waiting for them to finish, so basically it is "stuck" at the `p1.join()` statement. If there is nothing else for the main process to do, it is best to make it check for the number of running child processes and join them back once all have finished their work. You can see this in Listing 9-6.

Listing 9-6. *Multiple processes handling interrupts*

```
import multiprocessing
import time

def sleeper(timeout):
    try:
        print "function: I am a sleeper function and going to sleep for %s↵
seconds" %
 timeout
        time.sleep(timeout)
        print "function: I'm done!"
    except KeyboardInterrupt:
        print "function: I have received a signal to stop, exiting..."

class SleeperClass(multiprocessing.Process):
    def __init__(self, timeout):
        self.timeout = timeout
        print "Class: I am a class and can do initialisation tasks before starting"
        super(SleeperClass, self).__init__()

    def run(self):
        try:
            print "Class: I have been told to run now"
            print "Class: So I'm going to sleep for %s seconds" % self.timeout
            time.sleep(self.timeout)
            print "Class: I'm done."
        except KeyboardInterrupt:
            print "Class: I must stop now, exiting..."

p1 = multiprocessing.Process(target=sleeper, args=(5,))
p2 = SleeperClass(10)
p1.start()
p2.start()
```

```
try:
    while len(multiprocessing.active_children()) != 0:
        time.sleep(1)
except KeyboardInterrupt:
    p1.terminate()
    p2.terminate()
p1.join()
p2.join()
```

In this example I am calling the `multithreading.active_children()` function, which returns a list of active processes running. If the list is not empty, the main process just sleeps for one second before checking the list again. When the keyboard interrupt is received, the main process will attempt to terminate the child processes. When you press Ctrl-C, all processes are going to receive this interrupt and will therefore stop their execution. However if you send a SIGINT signal to the main process, it will terminate because the SIGINT will actually raise the `KeyboardInterrupt`, but unlike with the Ctrl-C combination this signal is not cascaded to the child processes. Therefore, you must either send a signal to the child processes or simply terminate them.

Running Methods at Equal Intervals

As you know, one of the processes in my application is the Ticket Scheduler process. This process will look at the scheduling configuration and inject request tickets into the ticket queue; they will then be dispatched by the Ticket Dispatcher process. What I want to do here is basically implement a process that behaves like the UNIX cron daemon, processing tickets at predefined intervals of time.

So, for example, I may have a sensor check that I want to probe every 5 minutes. I then need this process to inject the appropriate ticket into the queue every 5 minutes. The algorithm that I am going to implement has the following steps:

- Wake up at predefined intervals of time. In our example the shortest interval is 1 minute.

- Find all rules that are supposed to be triggered at the minute.

- Insert appropriate records into the tickets queue.

I therefore need a mechanism to "wake-up" at a given interval of time. I could use the `time.sleep()` function, which allows me to pause execution for any number of seconds, but that would sacrifice accuracy, because the other code (finding rules and inserting tickets) also takes some time, so if I set my thread to sleep for 60 seconds, and the execution time is 1 second, the total time period will be 61 seconds. I might measure the execution time and then call the sleep function only for 60 seconds minus the execution-time interval, but measuring and subtraction calls are also going to consume time, so that will not be as accurate, either.

What I need is a mechanism that sends a signal to my process, and the process waits for the signal. When the signal is received, the process performs whatever is needed and then waits for the signal again.

A Simple Clock Implementation

First I need an oscillator process, whose main purpose is to generate events at predefined intervals of time. Any other processes that require timed execution can listen for the events and react accordingly.

The oscillator process uses the `time.sleep()` function to measure intervals between the events. Because there is not much else to do apart from setting and resetting the event, the timer is pretty accurate. Listing 9-7 shows the code that implements the oscillator class.

Listing 9-7. *The oscillator class generates events at defined intervals.*

```
class Oscillator(multiprocessing.Process):

    def __init__(self, event, period):
        self.period = period
        self.event = event
        super(Oscillator, self).__init__()

    def run(self):
        try:
            while True:
                self.event.clear()
                time.sleep(self.period)
                self.event.set()
        except KeyboardInterrupt:
            pass
```

The oscillator class accepts a proxy object, which is referenced in the example as the event variable. This proxy object is an instance returned by the multiprocessing.Manager class. The Manager class is a mechanism of sharing state and data between different processes and supports other data types as well, such as: list, dict, NameSpace, Lock, RLock, Semaphore, Condition, Event, Queue, Value, and Array. Apart from the list, dict, and NameSpace, all other types are clones of the corresponding primitives in the threading library.

Let's define a simple class that will listen to the events and perform some actions when they are received. The code in Listing 9-8 simply prints the current time.

Listing 9-8. *The Scheduler class listens to periodic events.*

```
class Scheduler(multiprocessing.Process):

    def __init__(self, event):
        self.event = event
        super(Scheduler, self).__init__()

    def run(self):
        try:
            while True:
                self.event.wait()
                print datetime.now()
        except KeyboardInterrupt:
            pass
```

261

Now let's see how it all comes together. In the main process code in Listing 9-9 I am creating an instance of the Manager class. I will then use it to return a proxy to the Event instance. The same object will be passed to both the Oscillator and the Scheduler processes. The Oscillator will set and clear the event state, and the Scheduler will wait for the event to clear before it prints the time and goes back to the wait state again.

Listing 9-9. *Passing a shared event object to the two processes*

```
mgr = multiprocessing.Manager()
e = mgr.Event()
o = Oscillator(e, 60)
s = Scheduler(e)
o.start()
s.start()
try:
    while len(multiprocessing.active_children()) != 0:
        time.sleep(1)
except KeyboardInterrupt:
    o.terminate()
    s.terminate()
o.join()
s.join()
```

If you run this code, you'll get the output generated every minute. You can use as many "subscriber" objects as you need here, all waiting for the event generated by the Oscillator instance.

```
2010-02-28 18:35:09.243200
2010-02-28 18:36:09.244793
2010-02-28 18:37:09.246509
2010-02-28 18:38:09.248229
2010-02-28 18:39:09.249935
2010-02-28 18:40:09.251436
2010-02-28 18:41:09.253154
```

It is important to note that this implementation, although quite accurate, is not ideal and the interval is actually slightly longer than the predefined 60 seconds. This is because some time is spent resetting the event object. However, given the interval size (60 seconds), this error is really negligible (approximately 2000 milliseconds) and is only approximately 0.003% of the total oscillation period. For a simple scheduling system this is acceptable.

A Cron-Like Scheduler

Let's go back to the ticket scheduler implementation. As you remember, the scheduling information is stored in the `probingschedule` table, which has the following fields:

Table 9-10. *The probing schedule table fields*

Field	Data Type	Description
id	Integer	The unique identifier.
hostprobe_id	Integer	Points to the corresponding host probe entry. This field contains the ID of the host probe row.
probeinterval	Integer	The probing interval in minutes.

My implementation of the scheduler is slightly different from the logic that the cron application is using. The cron configuration allows you to specify exactly when something should happen, such as "5 minutes past the hour, every Tuesday" or "every 10 minutes, between 9 and 17 every day", whereas my scheduler understands only the time periods such as "every X minutes."

The algorithm I'm going to use to calculate whether something needs to happen is this:

- Take the number of seconds since the epoch, or arbitrary starting point (1970-01-01).

- Divide it by 60, so it is expressed in minutes.

- The recording is scheduled to happen at this time if the current time expressed in minutes is divisible by the probing interval value; in other words, current time modulus probe interval should equal zero.

This may sound rather complicated, but the SQLite3 SQL language allows me to perform all those checks within one SQL statement. I am using `strftime('%s', 'now')` built-in function to get the number of seconds since the epoch, which is converted into minutes and the modulus of the probing interval checked in the same statement. Listing 9-10 shows the full code of the Ticket Scheduler class.

Listing 9-10. *The TicketScheduler class inserts probing tickets into the ticket queue.*

```
class TicketScheduler(multiprocessing.Process):

    def __init__(self, event):
        self.event = event
        self.con = sqlite3.connect('monitor.db')
        super(TicketScheduler, self).__init__()
```

```
def run(self):
    try:
        from datetime import datetime
        while True:
            self.event.wait()
            res = [r[0] for r in self.con.execute("""SELECT hostprobe_id
                                         FROM probingschedule
                                        WHERE (strftime('%s', 'now')/60) %
                                probingschedule.probeinterval = 0;""")]
            for probe_id in res:
                self.con.execute("INSERT INTO ticketqueue VALUES
                            (NULL, ?, datetime('now'), 0)", (probe_id,))
            self.con.commit()
    except KeyboardInterrupt:
        pass
```

Therefore the result stored in the res array is going to contain the ID numbers of all host probes that need to be executed that minute. The next for loop inserts corresponding records into the ticket queue. Each record contains the probe ID and the timestamp, and the dispatched flag is set to zero, which means the ticket hasn't been sent to the target host yet.

Ticket Dispatcher

Once the tickets are placed in the pending tickets queue, there is another process called the ticket dispatcher that searches for pending tickets and sends requests to the client hosts. Each client implements the cmd_submit_reading XMLRPC call that expects to find the following information in the request:

- Ticket number
- Sensor name
- Sensor parameters

Additionally, I also need to know the hostname and port number of the XML-RPC server.

All this information is scattered across multiple tables and needs to be pulled together. Figure 9-3 is an ER diagram of the tables that contain this information and how they are related to each other. This will help define the SQL query.

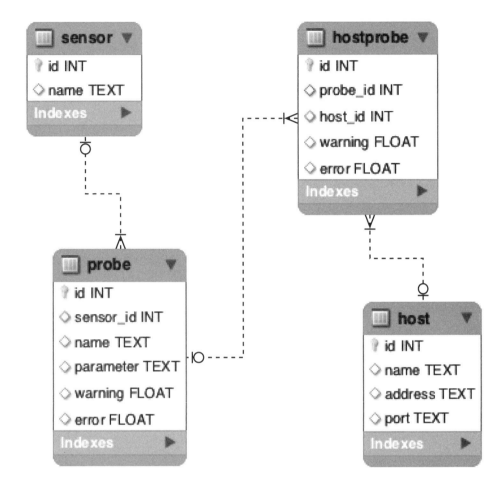

Figure 9-3. *ER diagram of the tables and relations for the ticket dispatcher component*

As you already know, the ticket queue contains ticket IDs and the hostprobe row IDs, so I have to start by requesting all entries that have not been dispatched yet:

```
pending_tickets = [r for r in self.con.execute("""SELECT id, hostprobe_id
                                                  FROM ticketqueue
                                                  WHERE dispatched = 0""")]
```

Once I have a list of the hostprobe row IDs, I need to find out the sensor name from the sensor table. This entry is referenced from the probe table, which contains parameters specific to this particular sensor. The probe is directly referenced from the host probe entry. XML-RPC server information is in the host table, which is also referenced directly from the host probe table. I now need to combine all that data into a single SQL statement. The simplest way is to use implicit join notation, which lists all fields that need to match. Because I'm using primary key fields when referencing the rows, it is a matter of comparing them in the select statement.

In Listing 9-11 you see the part of the ticket dispatcher code that uses the previously generated list of pending tickets. The for loop will iterate through all ticket ID – hostprobe ID pairs and get the information required to make a sensor check call. Once the call is made, the corresponding ticket is marked as dispatched, so it will not show up in the subsequent queries.

Listing 9-11. *Retrieving information from multiple tables*

```
for (ticket_id, hostprobe_id) in pending_tickets:
    res = [r for r in self.con.execute("""SELECT host.address,
                                                  host.port,
                                                  sensor.name,
                                                  probe.parameter
                                           FROM hostprobe, host, probe, sensor
                                           WHERE hostprobe.id=?
                                                  AND hostprobe.host_id = host.id
                                                  AND hostprobe.probe_id = probe.id
                                                  AND probe.sensor_id = sensor.id""",
                                                     (hostprobe_id,) )][0]
    self._send_request(ticket_id, res[0], res[1], res[2], res[3])
    self.con.execute("UPDATE ticketqueue SET dispatched=1 WHERE id=?", (ticket_id,))
    self.con.commit()
```

The comparison operations in the WHERE clause effectively performs a join on the table data, so that only matching records are returned as a result. Obviously, the starting point is the host probe row ID. You may also notice that I call another function, self._send_request, which performs the XML-RPC call to the remote system. The code (Listing 9-12) is pretty self-explanatory; there is just one thing to note: the parameter string is a comma-separated list when stored in the database, and it needs to be converted into an array before it is sent to the remote client.

Listing 9-12. *The function that sends an XML-RPC call to the client nodes*

```
def _send_request(self, ticket, address, port, sensor, parameter_string=None):
    url = "http://%s:%s/xmlrpc/" % (address, port)
    proxy = xmlrpclib.ServerProxy(url, allow_none=True)
    if parameter_string:
        parameter = parameter_string.split(',')
    else:
        parameter = None
    print ticket
    print sensor
    print parameter
    res = proxy.cmd_submit_reading(ticket, sensor, parameter)
    return
```

Summary

This was the first of three chapters in which I show how to implement a simple distributed monitoring system. This chapter was dedicated to the data structures and the monitoring server component; the subsequent chapters will analyze in detail the structure of the monitoring agents and the statistical analyzer. Important points to keep in mind:

- Always start your projects with a sound design.

- Define all the components that your system is made of and the actions they are going to perform.

- Define the data structures that your components are going to use.

- When designing the database tables, try to get as close as possible to the Third Normal Form, but don't forget that simplicity and practicality also have some influence in the decisions you make.

- Although XML-RPC is a rather old protocol, thanks to its simplicity it's still quite useful for small to medium-scale projects.

- Python has built-in support for XML-RPC: `xmlrpclib` for the client implementation and `SimpleXMLRPCServer` for the server implementation.

- CherryPy is useful in automating web framework tasks, and it also has support for the XML-RPC function wrapping.

- Multithreading in Python is not "true" multithreading—even though you run separate threads, only one is active because of the Global Interpreter Lock (GIL) implementation.

- If you need to take full advantage of multiple processors and avoid complex object-locking situations, decouple your components into separate processes that don't have shared data and use the `multiprocessing` library, which uses processes instead of threads.

■ ■ ■

Remote Monitoring Agents

This is the second of a series of three chapters that discuss the implementation details of a simple distributed monitoring system. In the previous chapter I laid out the high-level system design and described in detail the server implementation. This chapter is dedicated to the monitoring agent implementation, interaction with the sensor application, and the security model.

Design

I'm going to expand on the client or monitoring agent design that I briefly touched in the previous chapter. As you already know, the monitoring agent is responsible for accepting the sensor read commands and sending the results back. It relies on external utilities to perform the measurements.

The Passive Component

The monitoring agent component will be a *passive* component, which means that it only reacts to incoming commands to perform actions. This architecture allows us to have fine-grained control over the whole system operation and communication flow. The monitoring server can decide when and what to query, and this behavior may change depending on the previous responses from the agents.

Architecture

The architecture of the monitoring agent is such that it is divided into two distinct components: the agent code, which runs as a daemon process and accepts commands from the monitoring server, and the sensors, which are responsible for checking the system status.

The sensor code can be any application and is invoked by the agent when it receives a command to perform a check. Because the sensors can be written in any programming or scripting language, this provides greater flexibility in the tools that can be used to monitor the system.

Actions

Again, the main purpose of the monitoring agent is to call the sensor code, read in the results, and submit them to the monitoring server. In addition to that it also performs self-configuration and self-update tasks.

Accepting a New Configuration

The security model implies that each monitoring agent must know its monitoring server address and use it for communication. In other words the agent, when queried, does not answer the requestor but initiates the connection to the known server and submits the requested data.

This approach requires the server URL (for the XML-RPC communication) to be stored locally on each agent. Although the server address is unlikely to change, we still need to handle the situations when it does change. One way of changing the configuration is to use some sort of configuration management system, such as Puppet, Chef, or CFEngine to maintain the configuration, but we are going to implement a mechanism whereby the client accepts a request to update its configuration. If you remember, in the previous chapter we created site and node configuration parameters on the server database. So now we're going to use those to update the client configuration.

When the client receives a command to update the configuration, it will initiate the connection back to the currently registered server and request a new URL. Once the new URL is retrieved, it will attempt to connect to the new server. If the connection fails, the configuration will not be updated; otherwise, the new data will overwrite the existing settings, and going forward the new URL will be used for the communication.

Upgrading the Sensors

The sensor code can change when new functionality is introduced, such as adding new parameters or improving existing checks. Therefore, the agents must be able to update their sensors' base with the new code.

This functionality is similar to the configuration update—the agent upon receiving the command to update its sensor application initiates the connection back to the server requesting the new code. The server sends the archive containing the new code from its repository.

When the code transfer is complete, the agent unpacks the code into a temporary location, runs a simple check command to ensure that the executable is not corrupted, and, if this operation is successful, replaces the existing code with the new application.

The same mechanism can be used to deploy brand-new sensors as well; there simply won't be existing code to replace, so it's just the new code being deployed.

Submitting Sensor Readings

This is the primary function of the monitoring agent: submit the readings to the main server. Each sensor produces two values—the application return code and a single floating-point value that represents this particular reading. If there are multiple values to be returned, they must be split into two separate checks and each check must be called separately.

The agent receives an instruction to run the check, and each instruction contains two parameters: the sensor name and the options string. The sensor name is used to find the sensor code; the directory containing the sensor application must have the same name as the sensor. In addition to this convention, the sensor application name must match the name defined in the client configuration file. When the agent receives the instruction, it starts the sensor application and passes the option string to it as additional parameters.

The Security Model

This approach may pose some security concerns, because theoretically anyone could send a query to the agent process and obtain the readings. There are several possible solutions to this problem. One would be to use some sort of authentication mechanism whereby the requestor identifies itself and the agent responds only to the authorized parties. Another approach, much simpler to implement, is to decouple the request-response dialog into two distinct parts: the request or command phase and the response, which in fact is the action initiated by the agent component.

Therefore, we're not going to enforce any restrictions on who can connect and send requests for actions to the agents. That would add another layer of security, but it would bring some complications as well. If you're interested in improving the security model, you may want to consider adding a two-way SSL certificate, so only the applications that possess the SSL key and have their key deployed on the agent can connect.

When the command is transmitted, the agent will respond with the default confirmation message, saying that the command is accepted and terminate the session. It will then go and perform all the actions that are associated with the received command.

If the action implies that a connection has to be made to a central server, the agent will use server details that are stored locally in the configuration file. This ensures that only the registered and trusted parties will receive the data.

To keep track of all commands, the server stamps each command with a ticket number and sends it along with the command request. When the agent finishes processing the command and sends the results back, it will include the same ticket number in the response. This mechanism serves two purposes. First, the server knows what has been requested and from whom, so it minimizes the data that needs to be transferred. It also acts as an additional security mechanism, whereby only the responses with valid tickets are accepted, so no one will be able to inject wrong data into the master server without knowing the ticket numbers.

Configuration

In the previous chapter I briefly mentioned the use of the Python library for managing and parsing configuration files—the `ConfigParser` module. In this chapter I'm going to show you in more detail how to read and write configuration files using this module. As part of this exercise, we're also going to build a simple wrapper class to hide all the read and write methods—you'll access all configuration file attributes as if you were accessing the attributes of a regular Python object.

This approach simplifies the coding process and also leaves you an opportunity to replace the `ConfigParser` module with other means of reading and writing the configuration; for example, you might want to store it in XML or JSON format files.

The ConfigParser Library

The `ConfigParser` library defines several classes that you can use to parse the Windows INI style configuration files. I'll describe the format in more detail later in this section. The basic configuration class in the library is called `RawConfigParser`, which implements a basic configuration file syntax parser with methods to read and write the configuration files. It is possible to use this class directly, but it is more convenient to use two other classes that extends its functionality and provides some convenience methods for accessing the data.

These descendant classes are called `ConfigParser` and `SafeConfigParser`; the former extends the `.get()` and `.items()` methods and the later extends the `.set()` method.

The File Format

Before we proceed with the description of how to use the class methods for accessing the configuration data, let's look at the file format supported by the ConfigParser library. You have probably come across Windows INI-style configuration files. Although they are known as the "Windows configuration files," a similar (or the same) format is used by many Linux applications as well, thanks to its simplicity.

The configuration file is divided into sections, each containing any number of key-and- value pairs. Each key can be assigned a value using one of the two available assignment formats: *key: value* or *key=value*. Comments are also allowed and must start with either the ; or the # symbol. When one or the other is found, everything to the end of the line is ignored. Consider the following example:

```
[user]
# define a user
name=John
location=London
[computer]
name=Jons-PC   ; network name
operatingsystem=OS X
```

The ConfigParser library also allows specifying the references to other configuration items. For example, you can set a variable to some value and then, when setting another variable, you can re-use the value of the first one. This allows us to define common entries in one place. In Listing 10-1 we define the database table names and have a custom table name prefix controllable by the end user.

Listing 10-1. *An example configuration file*

```
[database]
ip=192.168.1.1
name=my_database
user=myuser
password=mypassword

[tables]
use_prefix=no
prefix=mytables
user_table=%(prefix)s_users
mailbox_table=%(prefix)s_mailboxes
```

You may have noticed that the reference syntax is the standard Python string format using the dictionary names: %(*dictionary_key*)s. Although we have defined the item we're referencing before other items that use it, the position has no meaning and the item can appear anywhere within the section.

Using the ConfigParser Class Methods

Now that we know what the configuration files look like, let's see how to access the information in them. In the following examples we will use the configuration file with the contents from Listing 10-1; the file name is example.cfg.

Let's start with opening and reading in the configuration file:

```
>>> import ConfigParser
>>> c = ConfigParser.RawConfigParser()
>>> c.read('example.cfg')
```

■**Tip** You can also use the `feadfp()` method if you need to use a file pointer rather than a file name. This can be useful in situations where you've just written to a file object and now need to parse it as a configuration file.

Once the file has been read and parsed, you can access the values directly with the `get()` method, which requires you to specify the section and key names as the required arguments. The following code also demonstrates one of the convenience methods, `getboolean()`, which converts the value of the specified key to the Boolean representation. The accepted values that represent the `True` value are 1, yes, on and `true`, whereas the representation of `False` can be one of the following: 0, no, off and `false`. Two other convenience functions are `getint()` and `getfloat()`, which convert the values to the integer and floating-point representations accordingly. The `get()` method always returns a string value:

```
>>> c.get('database', 'name')
'my_database'
>>> c.get('tables', 'use_prefix')
'no'
>>> c.getboolean('tables', 'use_prefix')
False
>>>
```

Those methods are good if you know the names of the sections and keys beforehand, but what should you do if the sections are dynamic and you cannot know the exact names and number of them? In this case you can use the `sections()` method, which returns the names of all sections in the configuration file as a list. Similarly, you can find out all keys within each section by using the `options()` method:

```
>>> for s in c.sections():
...     print "Section: %s" % s
...     for o in c.options(s):
...       print " Option: %s" % o
...
Section: tables
 Option: mailbox_table
 Option: use_prefix
 Option: prefix
 Option: user_table
Section: database
 Option: ip
 Option: password
 Option: user
 Option: name
>>>
```

The previous example also illustrates one important property of the ConfigParser classes—the results are not returned in the same order as they appear in the configuration file. Keep that in mind, especially if it is important for your script to maintain this order. A simple real-world case might be when the keys within a section represent steps that the application needs to perform and they need to happen in a specific order.

Let's assume the following example of a configuration file where users can add any number of arithmetical operations that are applied to an internal variable in the application:

```
[tasks]
step_1="+10"
step_2="*5"
step_3="-12"
step_4="/3"
step_5="+45"
```

All these operations are going to be evaluated and applied to a variable called x. Effectively, the intention of this configuration is to calculate a value of the following expression:

$$((x + 10) * 5 - 12) / 3 + 45$$

If the initial value of x is 11, then the expected result should be 76. Let's parse the configuration file, evaluate all operations, and see what we get:

```
>>> import ConfigParser
>>> c.read('example2.cfg')
['example2.cfg']
>>> x = 11.0
>>> for o in c.options('tasks'):
...   print "Operation: %s" % c.get('tasks', o)
...   x = eval("x %s" % c.get('tasks', o).strip('"'))
...
Operation: "+10"
Operation: "-12"
Operation: "*5"
Operation: "+45"
Operation: "/3"
>>> x
30.0
>>>
```

This is clearly wrong, and the reason is that the operations were applied in the wrong order. This can lead to unexpected results, and it might be difficult to identify where the problem lies. Just by applying the operations in the wrong order we ended up evaluating the following formula:

$$((x + 10 - 12) * 5 + 45) / 3$$

So if you require the sections and/or keys to appear in a specific order, make sure to name them so that it allows for a simple string sort and then sort the list before using it:

```
>>> x = 11.0
>>> for o in sorted(c.options('tasks')):
...   print "Operation: %s" % c.get('tasks', o)
...   x = eval("x %s" % c.get('tasks', o).strip('"'))
...
Operation: "+10"
Operation: "*5"
Operation: "-12"
Operation: "/3"
Operation: "+45"
>>> x
76.0
>>>
```

■**Caution** In my example I'm using a string with an appended integer. This is the easiest way; just don't forget to extend the index numbers with zeroes if you go beyond 9. So make sure that you use key (or section) names similar to: *step_01, step_02, ..., step_83,* and so on. Apply a similar strategy for indexes of three or more digits. The reason for this approach is that the strings are what will be sorted, not the integer values of the appended numbers, in which case 'step_9' is actually greater than 'step_11'.

The ConfigParser classes also provide two convenience methods that allow you to quickly check the presence of either a section or a key within a section: has_section() and has_option(), respectively. These methods are really useful as they allow you to have optional parameters, which if not defined would assume some default setting (if required, obviously) or can be overridden in the configuration file.

```
>>> import ConfigParser
>>> c = ConfigParser.RawConfigParser()
>>> c.read('example.cfg')
['example.cfg']
>>> c.has_section('tables')
True
>>> c.has_section('doesnotexist')
False
>>> c.has_option('tables', 'prefix')
True
>>> c.has_option('tables', 'optional')
False
>>>
```

So far all we have done are the read-only operations with the configuration data. We've examined the available sections and their contents, and we also know how to check whether the section or the key exists. The ConfigParser module also provides a means to change the contents of the configuration file. This can be achieved with one of the available methods that allow you to add or remove a section and also update the value of any given key. To add a section you should use the `add_section()` method. Changing a key value is done with the `set()` method, which if the key does not exist will also create a new one:

```
>>> c.add_section('server')
>>> c.set('server', 'address', '192.168.1.2')
>>> c.set('server', 'description', 'test server')
>>> c.sections()
['tables', 'server', 'database']
>>> c.options('server')
['description', 'address']
>>>
```

You can also remove either a key from the section or the section as a whole (in which case all the keys contained within that section will also be removed) with the `remove_option()` and `remove_section()` methods, respectively:

```
>>> c.options('server')
['description', 'address']
>>> c.remove_option('server', 'description')
True
>>> c.options('server')
['address']
>>> c.remove_section('server')
True
>>> c.sections()
['tables', 'database']
>>>
```

Finally, once you've made all the modifications to the configuration file, you can save it to a file object by using the `write()` function. Once saved, the file can be read in again with the `read()` method that you're already familiar with:

```
>>> import ConfigParser
>>> c = ConfigParser.RawConfigParser()
>>> c.add_section('section')
>>> c.set('section', 'key1', '1')
>>> c.set('section', 'key2', 'hello')
>>> c.write(open('example3.cfg', 'w'))
>>> ^D
$ cat example3.cfg
[section]
key2 = hello
key1 = 1
$
```

The Configuration Class Wrapper

We now know enough about the ConfigParser library to start using it, but before proceeding I'd like to show you how to hide all library methods and represent them as class methods. If you look at the configuration file, it is simply a set of parameters. So why not hide the complexity of the get and set methods and represent all of the data contained in the configuration file as class variables? There are a few reasons for doing this. First, it simplifies access to the variables; for example instead of writing var = c.get('section', 'key'), we could simply use the var = c.section.key construct (similarly for the set() operation). The second reason is that because the implementation is hidden from the rest of the code, we can easily replace the ConfigParser library with other methods of storing and retrieving configuration data.

So before going ahead, let's understand what we need from the wrapper class. The basic requirements are listed below:

- When the class is initiated, the configuration file must be read and all items must be mapped into the corresponding attributes of the class instance.

- When the attribute is set to a value but does not yet exist, it must be created dynamically and the new value assigned to it.

- The class instance must provide a means of saving the configuration back to the file if it has been modified.

We will use the built-in methods getattr() and setattr() to create and access the attributes of the instance. These methods allow access to the attributes by the attribute name stored in the variable. Listing 10-2 shows the complete wrapper class, individual parts of which I'll discuss in more detail further in the section.

Listing 10-2. *The configuration wrapper class*

```
01 class ConfigManager(object):
02
03     class Section:
04         def __init__(self, name, parser):
05             self.__dict__['name'] = name
06             self.__dict__['parser'] = parser
07
08         def __setattr__(self, option, value):
09             self.__dict__[option] = str(value)
10             self.parser.set(self.name, option, str(value))
11
12     def __init__(self, file_name):
13         self.parser = SafeConfigParser()
14         self.parser.read(file_name)
15         self.file_name = file_name
16         for section in self.parser.sections():
17             setattr(self, section, self.Section(section, self.parser))
18             for option in self.parser.options(section):
19                 setattr(getattr(self, section),
                            option, self.parser.get(section, option))
20
```

```
21      def __getattr__(self, section):
22          self.parser.add_section(section)
23          setattr(self, section, Section(section, self.parser))
24          return getattr(self, section)
25
26      def save_config(self):
27          f = open(self.file_name, 'w')
28          self.parser.write(f)
29          f.close()
```

Let's start with the constructor method, which is defined in lines 12–19. In the first three lines of code (13–15), we create a new instance of the `ConfigParser` class and read in the configuration file, the filename of which is passed to us in the constructor parameter.

In line 16 we iterate through all available section names; each name is stored in the variable named `section`. The attribute name was not known until we read in the configuration file, and thus couldn't be defined in the class definition. To create an attribute in any object by using its name we use the built-in function `setattr()`. This method accepts three parameters: a reference to the object, the name of the attribute we are either accessing or creating, and the value we want to assign to the attribute. If translated to a code representation, the statement `object.attribute = value` has the same meaning as `setattr(object, 'attribute', value)`. If the attribute does not exist, it will be created and the value assigned to it:

```
>>> class C:
...   pass
...
>>> o = C()
>>> dir(o)
['__doc__', '__module__']
>>> setattr(o, 'newattr', 10)
>>> dir(o)
['__doc__', '__module__', 'newattr']
>>> o.newattr
10
>>>
```

Thus, we're creating a new attribute with the name of the section from the configuration file. The value we are assigning is a new instance of another class—the `Section` class, which is defined in lines 3–10. We'll come back to this class a bit later; for now, just note that you can assign values to any attribute names in that class as instances.

Once the attribute with the section name is created, we go through all options (or the keys, as I have been referring to them) in that section and create attributes with the same names as the keys. We also assign values from the configuration file to those attributes. All this is happening in the rather lengthy line 19, where we use the `setattr()` function. The first argument to the function, as we already know, is the reference to an object, but how do we get that reference if the variable name is not known at the time when we wrote the application? Well, we've just created the attribute by using a name, and the name is still stored in another variable as a string, so similarly we can use that string name to access it. The function to access an object's attributes by their names is called `getattr()`, which accepts two parameters—a reference to an object and the name of the attribute we're accessing. Therefore, the statement `val = object.attribute` is functionally equal to `val = getattr(object, 'attribute')`, as we can see from the following example:

```
>>> dir(o)
['__doc__', '__module__', 'newattr']
>>> o.newattr
10
>>> getattr(o, 'newattr')
10
>>>
```

We now have functionality that covers our first requirement—when an instance of the configuration manager class is created, the constructor method opens the configuration file, reads all the data, and creates corresponding object attributes. This allows us to read values of all attributes in the configuration file and also modify them. The second part of this exercise is to make the model accept new attributes and assign values to them. We already know how to create object attributes during initialization, but that is a controlled process, whereby when the class is initiated the constructor method __init__() is called. What happens if we try to access an attribute that does not exist? Well, normally we would get an `AttributeError` exception raised by the Python interpreter if we do that:

```
>>> class C:
...    attribute = 'value'
...
>>> o = C()
>>> o.attribute
'value'
>>> o.does_not_exist
Traceback (most recent call last):
  File "<stdin>", line 1, in <module>
AttributeError: C instance has no attribute 'does_not_exist'
>>>
```

But we can override this behavior, or to be more accurate, intercept the processing and do something in cases where the attribute does not exist. For example, instead of raising an exception we could always return some default value:

```
>>> class C:
...    attribute = 'value'
...    def __getattr__(self, attr):
...      return 'default value for %s' % attr
...
>>> o = C()
>>> o.attribute
'value'
>>> o.does_not_exist
'default value for does_not_exist'
>>>
```

We do this by overriding the built-in object method __getattr__(). When you request an attribute of an object, the interpreter checks whether it exists and if so, returns its value. If the attribute does not exist, the interpreter checks whether the __getattr__() method is defined and if so, calls it. This method should either return the attribute value or raise an AttributeError exception.

So when is our __getattr__() method going to be called? It will be called when we try to access a section object that hasn't been defined yet, for example when we try to assign a value to a nonexistent section, like this:

```
config_manager.new_section.option = value
```

In this situation the __getattr__() method will be called and the attribute parameter will be set to the string new_section. We then need to create a new section in the parser instance and a new attribute in the object instance, just as we did when we initiated the object. All this happens in lines 22–23. Finally, in line 24, we return a reference to our section object. But wait, we've created a section object, but not the attributes within it! In other words, we've created the config_manager.new_section attribute, but not the config_manager.new_section.option.

Finally we've reached the Section class. To begin, let's see what we need to define for each section object. First we define the section name, and then we need to have a reference to the parser object, so whenever we write to the section object attributes (which effectively are the configuration file section keys) we need to call the parser set() method to set the key's value. The remaining attributes are just the keys from the configuration file.

I also need to mention that each Python object has a built-in dictionary of all attributes that belong to that object, and the dictionary is called __dict__. You can use this dictionary to access and modify the object attributes:

```
>>> class C:
...   def __init__(self):
...     self.a = 1
...
>>> o.a
1
>>> o.__dict__['a']
1
>>> o.b
Traceback (most recent call last):
  File "<stdin>", line 1, in <module>
AttributeError: C instance has no attribute 'b'
>>> o.__dict__['b'] = 2
>>> o.b
2
>>>
```

Just as each class instance has the built-in class method __getattr__(), it also has the __setattr__() function. This function, if defined, is called by the Python interpreter before it attempts to modify the object attribute directly. This allows you to override default behavior and intercept all assignment calls, even the initialization ones:

```
>>> class C:
...   def __init__(self):
```

```
...     self.attr = 'default'
...   def __setattr__(self, attr, value):
...     self.__dict__[attr] = 'you cannot change it'
...
>>> o = C()
>>> o.attr
'you cannot change it'
>>>
```

So we define (in lines 8–10) our custom __setattr__() method, which does two things—it creates a new attribute in the Section class instance and also calls the parser method to create a configuration entry. But why do we have to use the dictionary in the initialization method? Could we not initialize the class instance as in the following example?

```
def __init__(self, name, parser):
    self.name = name
    self.parser = parser
```

Well, if we did that, the new __setattr__() method would get called. And it would reference the name attribute (line 10, self.name), which we are trying to create! So to bypass the call to the __setattr__() method we need to modify the __dict__ dictionary directly in our constructor method.

■**Note** Keep in mind that the __getattr__() and __setattr__() calls are asymmetrical. The __getattr__() function is called after the lookup for the attribute has been performed (and failed). So if the attribute exists, this method will never be called. The __setattr__() function is called *before* the lookup in the internal dictionary is performed.

And finally, in lines 26–29, we define a helper function that saves all our changes to the same configuration file. There is no automatic change detection, so we need to make sure to call this function when the changes have been made to the configuration object.

The Sensor Design

We must agree on some structure in the sensor application, so that the agent knows how to control it. Therefore we need to make sure that each sensor application conforms to the following criteria: the sensor name must be the same across all installed sensors. The default application name is check, which can be changed in the configuration.

Each application must also report its options if called with the options command-line parameter The output is free-form text but must contain clear and concise information about the accepted parameters. Here's an example:

```
$ disk/check options
percent <vol> - free space %
used <vol> - used in KB
free <vol> - free in KB
```

The result must always be a single floating-point number or an integer. No extra spaces or characters are allowed, as the result will be assumed to be a number and treated as such. If the application is not capable of producing results in the required format, you can write a wrapper shell script to remove extra characters. The output of an example check command looks like this:

```
$ disk/check used /
432477328
```

Finally, the return code after the application finishes is recorded. The following assumptions are made about the return code: if the code is 0,it means that the application did not encounter any errors. If the return code is not equal 0, it means that the application could not perform its check properly and the result produced by it should not be trusted.

All sensors must be stored in a preconfigured directory; by default it is in sensors/'. The backup copies of the updated sensors must be placed in a separate directory, the default name for which is sensors_backup/'.

You can set all these options in the configuration file, which must be present and shall be named client.cfg. Following is a sample of the configuration file containing the default values:

```
[sensor]
executable = check
help = options
path = sensors/
backup = sensors_backup/
[monitor]
url = http://localhost:8081/xmlrpc/
```

Running External Processes

One of the most important functions of the monitoring agent is to run external processes and read the data they produce. Calling external utilities and commands is very useful, and you may find yourself doing that a lot in your applications. Therefore it is essential to understand and explore all options provided by the Python libraries.

Up until Python version 2.4 there were a number of different libraries that provided means of invoking external processes, such as os.system, os.spawn, os.popen, popen2, and commands. With version 2.4 a new library has been introduced, and it aims to replace the functionality of the older libraries. The new library is called subprocess and provides functionality to spawn new processes, send and receive information from their input, output, and error pipes, and also obtain the process return codes.

Using the subprocess Library

The subprocess module defines one class, which is used to spawn new processes—the Popen class. The name of an external program is passed as the first argument to the Popen class constructor. You have two options when passing the command name: use a string or use an array. These are treated differently depending on whether you use the shell to execute the command or not.

The default setting is not to use the shell. In that case, the Popen class expects the first argument to be the name of the executable. If it finds a list passed to it, the first element in the list will be treated as a command name and the remaining elements of the list will be passed as command-line arguments to the process:

```
>>> import subprocess
>>> subprocess.Popen('date')
<subprocess.Popen object at 0x10048ca90>
Wed 17 Mar 2010 22:29:24 GMT
>>> subprocess.Popen(('echo', 'this is a test'))
<subprocess.Popen object at 0x10048ca10>
this is a test
>>>
```

Therefore, if you attempt to specify a command to execute along with its arguments in the same string it will fail, because the Popen class looks for the executable name as it is specified in the string, and that obviously fails:

```
>>> subprocess.Popen('echo "this is a test"')
Traceback (most recent call last):
  File "<stdin>", line 1, in <module>
  File "/System/Library/Frameworks/Python.framework/Versions/2.6/lib/python2.6/↩
subprocess.py", line 595, in __init__
    errread, errwrite)
  File "/System/Library/Frameworks/Python.framework/Versions/2.6/lib/python2.6/↩
subprocess.py", line 1106, in _execute_child
    raise child_exception
OSError: [Errno 2] No such file or directory
>>>
```

Another alternative is to run commands using the shell. You have to instruct Popen to use the shell by setting the shell variable to True:

```
>>> subprocess.Popen('echo "this is a test"', shell=True)
<subprocess.Popen object at 0x10048cb10>
this is a test
>>>
```

As you can see, this time the example works as expected. If you're using the shell and the command is a string, it will be passed to the shell in the exact form, so make sure that you format the string exactly as you would if you were typing the command at the shell prompt directly; that includes adding backslashes to escape space characters in the filenames.

Executing a command with the shell is effectively equivalent to spawning the shell executable and passing the command and its arguments, as in this example:

```
>>> import subprocess
>>> subprocess.Popen(('/bin/sh', '-c', 'echo "this is a test"'))
<subprocess.Popen object at 0x10048cc10>
this is a test
>>>
```

The default shell used to run commands is /usr/sh on Unix/Linux systems. The Python documentation says that you can specify any other shell of your choice by setting the executable argument to a different binary; however, that does not work properly and in fact only uses the other shell to spawn the default shell. Following is an excerpt from the subprocess library that is responsible for setting an alternative executable:

```
if shell:
    args = ["/bin/sh", "-c"] + args

if executable is None:
    executable = args[0]

[...]

os.execvp(executable, args)
```

As you can see from this code snippet, if the shell variable is set, the argument list is extended with the default shell binary location and the argument -c, which instructs the shell to treat anything after it as a command string. The next check is to verify whether the executable argument is not empty. If it is, then it will be set to the first item in the argument list, which will be either the default shell or /bin/sh. And finally, the os.execvp function is called with two arguments: executable, which is the filename of the program to load, and the arguments list.

Let's say we only specified shell=True, so the default shell should be used because args[0] (containing /bin/sh) gets assigned to the executable variable. However, if we tried to use both the shell and executable arguments at the same time, we would end up calling the same default shell from within another executable, contrary to what the manual is saying! We can confirm this by performing a simple experiment:

```
>>> import subprocess
>>> subprocess.Popen('echo $0', shell=True)
<subprocess.Popen object at 0x10048ca50>
/bin/sh
>>> subprocess.Popen('echo $0', shell=True, executable='/bin/csh')
<subprocess.Popen object at 0x10048ca90>
/bin/sh
>>>
```

In both cases the result is the same, which means the effective shell that runs our commands is the same /bin/sh. The easiest and most concise way to overrule the default shell is to use the "shell-less" Popen call and specify the shell executable as the command name:

```
>>> subprocess.Popen(('/bin/csh', '-c', 'echo $0'))
<subprocess.Popen object at 0x10048cad0>
/bin/csh
>>>
```

If you use the Popen command with shell=None (which is the default setting) but don't want to construct the array every time you call the external utility, you might want to consider the following pattern: create a string that looks like a command you'd use on a shell prompt, and then use the string split() method to create an array that contains the name of the program and its arguments:

```
>>> import subprocess
>>> cmd = "echo argument1 argument2 argument3"
>>> subprocess.Popen(cmd.split())
argument1 argument2 argument3
<subprocess.Popen object at 0x10048cad0>
>>>
```

One of the useful parameters to the Popen command is the preexec_fn argument, which allows you to run any function before the new process is started. It is important to note that this code is called after the system fork() call but before the exec() call, which means the new process is already created and in memory but hasn't started yet. A typical situation where you might want to use this functionality is to change the effective user ID of the new process, as shown in Listing 10-3.

Listing 10-3. *Changing the user ID when running an external process*

```
#!/usr/bin/env python

import subprocess
import os

print "I am running with the following user id: ", os.getuid()
subprocess.Popen(('/bin/sh', '-c',
                  'echo "I am an external shell process with effective user id:";
                   id'),
                  preexec_fn=os.setuid(501))
```

Running this code as the root user will produce results similar to the following, which shows that the new process got a new user ID assigned to it:

```
$ sudo ./setsid_example.py
Password:
I am running with the following user id:  0
I am an external shell process with effective user id:
uid=501(rytis) gid=20(staff)
```

You can also change the current directory of the running process by setting the cwd argument to the new path:

```
>>> import subprocess
>>> import os
>>> print os.getcwd()
/home/rytis/
>>> subprocess.Popen('pwd', cwd='/etc')
<subprocess.Popen object at 0x10048cb50>
/etc
>>>
```

It is also possible to override the default shell environment variables. These are inherited from the current process, but should you wish to create a new set of variables, you can do so by assigning a mapping to the env argument:

```
>>> import subprocess, os
>>> os.environ['PATH']
'/usr/local/sbin:/usr/local/bin:/usr/sbin:/usr/bin:/sbin:/bin:/usr/games'
>>> subprocess.Popen('echo $PATH', shell=True, env={'PATH': '/bin/'})
<subprocess.Popen object at 0x2b461ac0dd90>
/bin/
>>>
```

If you only want to change one variable and leave the others intact, make a copy of the os.environ dictionary and then modify the entry that you want to change. It's best to use the dict function when you define a new dictionary, which makes a copy of the existing one instead of just creating a reference to it:

```
>>> import os
>>> new = dict(os.environ)
>>> new['PATH'] = '/bin/'
>>> os.environ['PATH']
'/usr/local/sbin:/usr/local/bin:/usr/sbin:/usr/bin:/sbin:/bin:/usr/games'
>>> new['PATH']
'/bin/'
```

Controlling the Running Processes

You have to keep in mind that the processes may not terminate instantaneously. Therefore, you need to be able to check whether the process is still running, what its process ID is, and what the return code was when it finished running, and you even need to terminate the process explicitly.

Listing 10-4 demonstrates how to start a new process and then wait for it to finish. The Popen class also has a pid attribute, which contains the process ID of the started process.

Listing 10-4. *Waiting for the process to terminate*

```
import subprocess
import time
from datetime import datetime

p = subprocess.Popen('sleep 60', shell=True)

while True:
    rc = p.poll()
    if rc is None:
        print "[%s] Process with PID: %d is still running..." % (datetime.now(), p.pid)
        time.sleep(10)
```

```
    else:
        print "[%s] Process with PID: %d has terminated. Exit code: %d" %
                                              (datetime.now(), p.pid, rc)
        break
```

If you run this example you'll get results similar to the following:

```
[2010-03-18 20:56:33.844824] Process with PID: 81203 is still running...
[2010-03-18 20:56:43.845769] Process with PID: 81203 is still running...
[2010-03-18 20:56:53.846158] Process with PID: 81203 is still running...
[2010-03-18 20:57:03.846568] Process with PID: 81203 is still running...
[2010-03-18 20:57:13.846975] Process with PID: 81203 is still running...
[2010-03-18 20:57:23.847360] Process with PID: 81203 is still running...
[2010-03-18 20:57:33.847819] Process with PID: 81203 has terminated. Exit code: 0
```

Alternatively, you can use the Popen class method wait(), which blocks and waits for the process to finish before returning control to your application. In most situations it is very useful and frees you from writing your own wait loop, but beware of the fact that wait() may go into a deadlock if the process that you run generates a lot of output:

```
>>> import subprocess
>>> from datetime import datetime
>>> def now():
...   print datetime.now()
...
>>> p = subprocess.Popen('sleep 60', shell=True, preexec_fn=now)
2010-03-18 21:06:14.767768
>>> p.wait()
0
>>> now()
2010-03-18 21:07:20.119642
>>>
```

Let's modify the previous example and insert a kill() command, which forcefully terminates the running process. Listing 10-5 shows the code.

Listing 10-5. *Terminating the running process*

```
import subprocess
import time
from datetime import datetime

p = subprocess.Popen('sleep 60', shell=True)
```

287

```
while True:
    rc = p.poll()
    if rc is None:
        print "[%s] Process with PID: %d is still running..." % (datetime.now(), p.pid)
        time.sleep(10)
        p.kill()
    else:
        print "[%s] Process with PID: %d has terminated. Exit code: %d" %
                                            (datetime.now(), p.pid, rc)

        break
```

Now if you run this script you'll see the following results:

```
[2010-03-18 21:11:45.146796] Process with PID: 81242 is still running...
[2010-03-18 21:11:55.147579] Process with PID: 81242 is still running...
[2010-03-18 21:12:05.148198] Process with PID: 81242 has terminated. Exit code: -9
```

Notice that the return code changes to a negative value. The negative return value indicates that the process has been terminated and did not finish the execution by itself. The numeric value will indicate the signal number that terminated the process. Table 10-1 lists the most popular signals and their numerical representations.

Table 10-1. *Signal Numeric Values*

Signal Name	Numeric Value	Description
SIGHUP	1	Hangup
SIGINT	2	Terminal interrupt, usually from keyboard
SIGQUIT	3	Terminal quit, usually from keyboard
SIGABRT	4	Abort signal
SIGKILL	9	Kill signal, cannot be caught
SIGUSR1	10	User-defined signal 1
SIGUSR2	12	User-defined signal 2
SIGTERM	15	Termination signal
SIGSTOP	19	Stop execution, cannot be caught

Communicating with External Processes

It is good to know how to call external processes, but if you can't communicate with them they are of little use. Most shell processes have three communication channels: standard input, standard output, and standard error, usually referenced as `stdin`, `stdout` and `stderr`. When you create a new instance of the `Popen` class, you can define any of those channels and set them to one of the following:

- An existing file descriptor
- An existing file object
- A special value of `subprocess.PIPE`, which indicates that a pipe to a standard stream should be created
- A special value of `subprocess.STDOUT`, which can be used to redirect error messages to standard output stream

Using File Descriptors

Before we continue, let me remind you what file descriptors are. File descriptors are the integer numbers corresponding to the files opened by the running process. In Linux there are usually three file descriptors assigned for every process that is running: 0 for standard input, 1 for standard output, and 2 for standard error. Any other file, socket, or pipe opened during runtime will get subsequent numbers assigned, starting with 3.

In Python you would use file descriptors for low-level I/O operations, so they are not frequently used. This is because Python provides an additional abstraction level and most of the file operations can be performed using the Python *file* objects, which provide multiple file manipulation operations. File descriptors are returned by either the `os.open()` or the `os.pipe()` method. Consider the following example, in which a new file is created and then the output of the command is redirected to it. If you run this example, you will not see any output displayed on the terminal, but the date string will be written to the `out.txt` file instead.

```
import subprocess
import os

f = os.open('out.txt', os.O_CREAT|os.O_WRONLY)
subprocess.Popen('date', stdout=f)
```

Using File Objects

The previous example used low-level file I/O operators that work with file descriptors. The built-in Python function `open()` is easier to use and provides a higher-level API to the file operations, such as `read()` and `write()`. The object is also an iterator in itself, so you can use convenient Python language constructs, such as `for ... in ...:` to iterate through the contents of the file.

There is absolutely no difference in passing the file objects to the `Popen` constructor, and the result is effectively the same as when using the file descriptors:

```
import subprocess
import os

f = open('out.txt', 'w')
subprocess.Popen('date', stdout=f)
```

Using the Pipe Objects

The methods described earlier allow you to redirect a program's input/output to a file, but how do you access that data from within the Python application? One option would be to wait until the program finishes and then read the file, but that would be inefficient and also requires you to have read/write access to the current directory where the application is executed. Alternatively, you can create a pipe and assign read and write file descriptors to different communication channels in the Popen call, but this option appears too complicated and convoluted.

The subprocess library provides an easier way to achieve this—by assigning stdin, stdout and/or stderr arguments a special variable: subprocess.PIPE. You then have two options: either use the object's communicate() method or read and write directly from the file objects that will be associated with the I/O channels.

The communicate() method returns a tuple of two strings containing the data returned from the process:

```
>>> import subprocess
>>> p = subprocess.Popen(('echo', 'test'), stdout=subprocess.PIPE)
>>> out_data, err_data = p.communicate()
>>> print out_data
test
>>> print err_data
None
>>>
```

You can also use the optional argument input to pass any data you need to the process:

```
>>> import subprocess
>>> p = subprocess.Popen(('wc', '-c'), stdout=subprocess.PIPE,
stdin=subprocess.PIPE)
>>> out_data, err_data = p.communicate(input='test string')
>>> print out_data
      11
>>>
```

■**Caution** This function buffers all data in memory and as such is not suitable to be used with large datasets. For example, if your application is expected to produce huge amounts of data, it may cause unexpected results. The size of "safe" data is undefined and largely depends on the exact Python version, the Linux version, and the amount of memory you have available in your system.

An alternative to using communicate() is to read and write directly from the file objects that are available through the Popen class instance:

```
>>> import subprocess
>>> p = subprocess.Popen('cat /usr/share/dict/words', shell=True,
stdout=subprocess.PIPE)
>>> i = 0
>>> for l in p.stdout:
...   i += 1
...
>>> print i
234936
>>>
```

Similarly you can write to the process, using the stdin variable that is associated with the standard input file object. The advantage of this approach is that the data can be accessed as and when needed and is not loaded into memory all at once.

An added benefit is that you can monitor the process activity over a long time and process the output as it becomes available. The following example shows how to read lines from the tail command. After I started the Python application, I generated a few log lines and they appeared in the Python output. If you want to replicate this exercise, use the Linux logger "message" command to get some logging messages written to the system log file:

```
>>> import subprocess
>>> p = subprocess.Popen('tail -f /var/log/messages', shell=True,
stdout=subprocess.PIPE)
>>> while True:
...   print p.stdout.readline()
...
Mar 8 21:43:14 linux -- MARK --
Mar 8 22:03:15 linux -- MARK --
Mar 8 22:16:54 linux rytis: this is a test
Mar 8 22:17:01 linux rytis: this is a test 2
```

In more complex scenarios, you might want to have a separate thread running; this would watch the output from the command being generated and pass that data on to other processes or threads for further processing.

Redirecting Standard Error

Applications usually differentiate between error messages and normal output by writing error messages to the standard error file descriptor. Sometimes all you really need is all output generated by the application in one piece, regardless of whether it's the normal output from the application or the error messages.

To handle such situations, the subprocess library provides the special variable subprocess.STDOUT, which you can assign to the stderr argument. This redirects all output from the error file descriptor to standard output:

```
>>> import subprocess
>>> p = subprocess.Popen('/bin/sh -c "no_such_command"', shell=True, ↵
 stdout=subprocess.PIPE, stderr=subprocess.PIPE)
>>> out_data, err_data = p.communicate()
>>> print out_data

>>> print err_data
/bin/sh: no_such_command: command not found

>>> p = subprocess.Popen('/bin/sh -c "no_such_command"', shell=True, ↵
 stdout=subprocess.PIPE, stderr=subprocess.STDOUT)
>>> out_data, err_data = p.communicate()
>>> print out_data
/bin/sh: no_such_command: command not found

>>> print err_data
None
>>>
```

Automatically Updating Sensor Code

Finally, we have to implement a mechanism in the agent application that allows us to update any of the sensors from a central location. When you're in charge of thousands of servers, the last thing you want to do is manually copy, unpack, replace, and validate the package you're updating on each of those servers. So one of the functions that we are going to add to our agent code is to retrieve a package automatically (in this example it will be just a compressed TAR archive) and deploy it on top of the existing one. So when needed we can replace the package with the newer one on the master server and then instruct all agents to retrieve it and update accordingly.

Sending and Receiving Binary Data with XML-RPC

All the communication flows so far have been happening over the XML-RPC protocol, and it has coped rather well with the simple data structures, such as strings, integers, arrays and so on, but with binary data the data transfer is not trivial anymore. As you already know, XML-RPC is a text-based protocol, so encapsulating raw binary data into an XML-RPC message is not an option.

What we need to do is to represent the binary data using only the characters that are considered to be text and are allowed by the XML-RPC protocol. There is a special encoding scheme developed just for that purpose, known as Base64. The number 64 represents the number of characters that are used in encoding. In the most popular variation of the Base64 encoding scheme, the following characters are used: lowercase and uppercase letters a-z and A-Z, numbers 0–9, and two extra characters: + and /. Because there are 64 characters, they can be represented by 6-bit numbers. So when the encoding of the binary data is performed, all 8-bit bytes in the binary data are represented in a continuous stream of bits, which is then divided into the 6-bit chunks. Each 6-bit number is mapped to one of the 64 characters from the Base64 table, and we end up with data constructed from the 64 characters that are valid to include as a string in the XML-RPC message. Because each character is still represented by the 8-bit byte, we have a roughly 33 percent increase in the data volume ($8/6 = 1.3(3)$) after the encoding.

When we receive the data, we need to convert it back to its binary representation. The process is the opposite of the first conversion: we first get the 6-bit numbers from the encoding/decoding table and put all 6-bit chunks into one continuous bit stream, which is then divided into 8-bit bytes.

Luckily for us we don't need to worry about any of that, because the XML-RPC library provides a class for encoding and decoding binary data. So on the monitoring server side, which will be transmitting the binary files, we have the following XML-RPC method exposed:

```
@cherrypy.expose
def cmd_get_sensor_code(self, sensor):
    with open("%s/%s.tar.bz2" % (self.cm.sensor.source_dir, sensor), 'rb') as f:
        return xmlrpclib.Binary(f.read())
```

As you can see, this code returns an instance of the xmlrpclib.Binary class, which accepts one argument—a bit stream that need to be encoded. When the client receives such an object it can directly write it to a file handle, and the decoding is automatically performed and stored in the object's attribute called data. So on the client side, the request for data and its writing to a file are achieved by the following code:

```
proxy = xmlrpclib.ServerProxy(self.cm.monitor.url)
tmp_dir = tempfile.mkdtemp(dir='.')
dst_file = "%s/%s.tar.bz2" % (tmp_dir, sensor)
with open(dst_file, 'wb') as f:
    f.write(proxy.cmd_get_sensor_code(sensor).data)
    f.close()
```

Working with Files and Archives (TAR and BZip2)

I briefly touched on file operations when we read and wrote to a file in the data transmission functions. Let's examine more closely the common file operations that you might need to perform and the tools provided by the Python libraries that can make your life easier.

Listing 10-6 shows the function from the monitoring agent code that is responsible for retrieving a new sensor package, unpacking it, testing it, and finally replacing the original package with it.

Listing 10-6. *The automatic package update function*

```
01 @cherrypy.expose
02 def cmd_update_sensor_code(self, sensor):
03     # get the new file
04     proxy = xmlrpclib.ServerProxy(self.cm.monitor.url)
05     tmp_dir = tempfile.mkdtemp(dir='.')
06     dst_file = "%s/%s.tar.bz2" % (tmp_dir, sensor)
07     with open(dst_file, 'wb') as f:
08         f.write(proxy.cmd_get_sensor_code(sensor).data)
09         f.close()
10     # unpack it
11     arch = tarfile.open(dst_file)
12     arch.extractall(path=tmp_dir)
13     arch.close()
14     # check it
```

```
15      cmd = ["%s/%s/%s" % (tmp_dir, sensor, self.cm.sensor.executable), "options"]
16      p = subprocess.Popen(cmd, stdout=subprocess.PIPE)
17      p.communicate()
18      if p.returncode != 0:
19          # remove if fails
20          shutil.rmtree(tmp_dir)
21      else:
22          # back up the existing package
23          sens_dir = "%s/%s" % (self.cm.sensor.path, sensor)
24          bck_dir = "%s/%s_%s" % (self.cm.sensor.backup, sensor,
                                    datetime.strftime(datetime.now(),
'%Y-%m-%dT%H:%M:%S'))
25          try:
26              shutil.move(sens_dir, bck_dir)
27          except:
28              pass
29          os.remove(dst_file)
30          # replace with new
31          shutil.move("%s/%s" % (tmp_dir, sensor), sens_dir)
32          os.rmdir(tmp_dir)
33      return 'OK'
```

You are probably already familiar with basic file operations such as open(), read(), write() and close() from the previous examples, so I'll just quickly remind you what they do and then concentrate on the functions that are not as widely known but are very useful if you do not want to rely on the external utilities and tools provided by the operating system.

Any file operation starts with the open() command, which accepts two arguments: the name of the file you're accessing and the access mode. The access mode argument can be either r (the default if omitted) for a read operation, w for a write operation, or a for an append operation. Bear in mind that w mode truncates the file if it already exists. You can also append an optional b parameter to the mode argument, which indicates whether the file contains binary data. It is good practice to indicate whether the file contains any binary data, because that dictates how the newline characters are treated. The default is to use text mode, which in some cases may convert the newline characters to the platform-specific representation (for example \n may be converted to the sequence \n\r). Specifying the binary mode where appropriate will both improve the readability of the code and also make it more portable between different platforms. The open() function returns a file object if the operation was successful.

Once the file is open, you can read and write data to it using the read() and write() methods of the file object. If you're dealing with a text file, you can also use the readline() function, which reads in the next line from the file, or readlines() to read all lines into an array. When you're done with the file operations, don't forget to call the close() method to finish all the operations that may have been buffered and actually release the file handle.

Sometimes you need to create either a temporary file or a directory. In the example above we want to deploy the sensor code into a temporary location before we test it. If we replaced the existing code immediately and the new code was faulty, we'd be in trouble. Not only is there no backup to restore from, but the code would be immediately become available for execution. To deal with the temporary file and directory creation, Python provides a module called tempfile. Line 5 uses the mkdtemp() function, which creates a temporary directory. You can also pass an optional argument dir, which specifies where the directory should be created. If this argument is omitted, the directory location is determined from one of the following environment variables: TMPDIR, TEMP, or TMP, which are operating-system specific. The result is a directory name:

```
>>> import tempfile
>>> d = tempfile.mkdtemp()
>>> d
'/var/folders/7X/7XBjCSfXGbOoJog2bNb3uk+++TI/-Tmp-/tmpPBCHIc'
```

Similarly, you can create a temporary file by calling the mkstemp() method. This method also accepts the same dir parameter to indicate the location where the file should be created. When opening a temporary file, you should also indicate whether the file is a binary (the default) or text file by setting another optional argument, text, to either False (the default) or True. The function returns a tuple: a file descriptor number and a file name. Do not mix the file descriptor (which is just an integer) with the file object, though. If you want to use higher-level read() and write() operations, you'll have to create a corresponding file object first:

```
>>> import tempfile
>>> f = tempfile.mkstemp()
>>> f
(3, '/var/folders/7X/7XBjCSfXGbOoJog2bNb3uk+++TI/-Tmp-/tmpFsBEXt')
>>> import os
>>> fo = os.fdopen(f[0], 'w')
>>> fo.write('test')
```

Both the temporary directory and the file will be created in the most secure manner and will only be readable and writable by the user that created them.

■**Note** It is also important to mention that the deletion of the temporary files and directories are the responsibility of the process, and the library will not take care of that matter for you.

Use the os.remove() function (line 29) to remove a file and os.rmdir() to remove a directory:

```
>>> os.remove(f[1])
>>> os.rmdir(d)
```

You have to bear in mind that os.rmdir() only removes empty directories. Luckily, Python has another useful built-in module, shutil, which provides a number of high-level operations for managing files and directories. One useful function is rmtree() (line 20), which removes the directory tree recursively with all its contents. You can also move the whole tree structure with the move() function (lines 26 and 31).

Finally, I'm going to introduce you to yet another built-in Python library—tarfile, which is used to work with TAR, BZip2, and GZip archives. As you can see in lines 11–13, it is extremely simple to use this library for unpacking the archives. When opening an archive with the open() function, you don't need to specify the format, as it will be automatically detected. You could specify it by providing an optional mode parameter, which has the same syntax as the built-in function open() mode argument; however, in this case it is extended with one of the following compression arguments: :bz2 for BZip2 compression or :gz for GZip compression. By default the archive is opened in read mode. If you need to write to an archive (add new files) you have to specify write mode:

```
$ ls -l
total 8
-rw-r--r--  1 rytis  rytis  26  1 Apr 14:35 test.txt
$ python
Python 2.6.1 (r261:67515, Feb 11 2010, 00:51:29)
[GCC 4.2.1 (Apple Inc. build 5646)] on darwin
Type "help", "copyright", "credits" or "license" for more information.
>>> import tarfile
>>> t = tarfile.open('archive.tar.bz2', 'w:bz2')
>>> t.add('test.txt')
>>> t.close()
>>> ^D
$ ls -l
total 16
-rw-r--r--  1 rytis  rytis  147  1 Apr 14:36 archive.tar.bz2
-rw-r--r--  1 rytis  rytis   26  1 Apr 14:35 test.txt
$ tar jtvf archive.tar.bz2
-rw-r--r--  0 rytis  rytis        26  1 Apr 14:35 test.txt
$
```

Summary

In this chapter we looked at the architecture of the monitoring agent component and how it is interacting with the operating system. We also investigated various technologies provided by the different Python libraries that abstracted some of the file and process operations, and we reviewed basic file operations such as open(), read(), write(), and close. We will continue working on the monitoring system in the next chapter, where we'll add the statistics calculation and graphing functions.

Important points to note:

- The ConfigParser library allows you to use the INI type of configuration files.

- Python provides high-level libraries for operations on files and archives: shutil and tarfile.

- Use the subprocess library to run external commands and communicate with external processes.

CHAPTER 11

■ ■ ■

Statistics Gathering and Reporting

This is the third and final chapter in the series dedicated to the development of a monitoring system. In the previous chapters, we created two components: a monitoring server and a monitoring agent component that can collect and store the statistical data from various sources. To make this data really useful, we need to analyze it, derive some conclusions, and present the results to the end users. In this chapter, we'll create a simple web-based application that performs statistical analysis on the data and also generates some reports.

Application Requirements and Design

The statistical representation system should be fairly simple and easy to use. The following is the basic functionality it needs to provide:

- The system should provide a list of all available hosts that are being monitored.

- For each available host, there should be a list of all probes (a *probe* is a simple check script running on the remote server) available for that host.

- The probes should be grouped into two criteria: probe name and data timescale.

- The data should be presented on different timescales, such as readings obtained in the last 24 hours, last 7 days, and last 30 days.

- The system should report on the number of times the set thresholds have been reached. This information can be expressed as a percentage from the number of all requests that have been made in a timescale period.

- The system should provide basic statistical analysis of the data, such as the average values, data trending, and so on.

The system will be a script that reads the data from the monitoring database, and then generates the static HTML pages along with the required data graph images. This script can be run on a regular basis using system scheduling tools such as cron.

The graphing and statistical analysis will be performed by using the NumPy and matplotlib libraries.

Using the NumPy Library

Statistical analysis is something scientists have been doing for a long time. Therefore, a plethora of scientific libraries are available for nearly every computer language. Perhaps the most popular libraries for the Python programming language are NumPy (formerly known as Numeric), which provides high-level mathematical functions, and SciPy, which provides more than 15 different scientific modules (with various scientific algorithms for optimizations, linear algebra, signal processing and analysis, and statistical analysis).

Most of that functionality may be overkill for what we're going to do here. However, the convenience of calling just a single function and knowing that the result can be trusted outweighs the burden of installing a few additional packages on your system. I recommend spending some time getting acquainted with these two libraries (and also the graphic plotting library, matplotlib, which we'll discuss later in the chapter), as they provide useful tools for analysis and reporting.

Installing NumPy

Availability of the NumPy package largely depends on which Linux distribution you're using. Some distributions, such as Fedora and Ubuntu, which try to keep up to date with the latest versions of applications, will provide the binary package. In that case, you can use the operating system package manager (like yum or aptitude) to install the package for you. For example, here is how to install NumPy on a Fedora system:

```
$ yum install numpy
```

Some distributions, especially the enterprise-grade ones like Red Hat Enterprise Linux and CentOS, are more conservative in the package selection, and may not provide the precompiled packages. For these distributions, it's best to download the source packages and build the library from the source code. You can find the NumPy source code at http://sourceforge.net/projects/numpy/.

NumPy Examples

Most NumPy functions are optimized to work efficiently with arrays. These arrays can have one or more dimensions. In most of our examples, we'll be operating on single-dimension arrays, where the data in the array is the scalar readings of the sensors over a time period.

Working with Arrays

The NumPy array is not the same as the regular Python array datatype. The array structure is specifically crafted to be efficient when used by the NumPy functions. The type implementation is specific to the NumPy C code. It provides some compatibility in terms of the access methods, but not all functions are duplicated, as you can see from this example:

```
>>> import numpy
>>> array_py = [1, 4, 5, 7, 9]
>>> array_np = numpy.array([1, 4, 5, 7, 9])
>>> type(array_py)
<type 'list'>
>>> type(array_np)
<type 'numpy.ndarray'>
>>> array_np.append(2)
```

```
Traceback (most recent call last):
  File "<stdin>", line 1, in <module>
AttributeError: 'numpy.ndarray' object has no attribute 'append'
>>>
```

Since we're going to use NumPy arrays extensively, let's take a closer look at their basic functionality. As you already noticed, the arrays are created by calling NumPy's array constructor. The scientific nature of this datatype is obvious when you look at the exposed methods of the array object. It lacks a rather simplistic method of appending new values, but provides some of the most common statistical functions:

```
>>> a1 = numpy.array([1, 4, 5, 7, 9])
>>> a1.mean()   # calculate a mean value of the array
5.2000000000000002
>>> a1.std()    # calculate the standard deviation
2.7129319932501073
>>> a1.var()    # calculate the variance
7.3599999999999994
>>>
```

Let's first find out how to append another element to a list. As you've seen, the standard list method append() doesn't work here. However, the NumPy library has its own version of the append function that you can use to append elements:

```
>>> a1 = numpy.array([1, 2, 3])
>>> numpy.append(a1, [4])
array([1, 2, 3, 4])
>>>
```

Another difference from the normal Python lists is how you access multidimensional arrays:

```
>>> a1 = numpy.array([[1, 2, 3], [4, 5, 6]])
>>> a1[1, 1]    # second element of the second row
5
>>>
```

Multidimensional arrays must have the same number of entries in each row, because effectively, they are the matrix elements. You can always change the shape of the array, as long as you have enough elements in the array:

```
>>> a = np.arange(16)
>>> a
array([ 0,  1,  2,  3,  4,  5,  6,  7,  8,  9, 10, 11, 12, 13, 14, 15])
>>> a.reshape(2, 8)
array([[ 0,  1,  2,  3,  4,  5,  6,  7],
       [ 8,  9, 10, 11, 12, 13, 14, 15]])
```

```
>>> a.reshape(4, 4)
array([[ 0,  1,  2,  3],
       [ 4,  5,  6,  7],
       [ 8,  9, 10, 11],
       [12, 13, 14, 15]])
>>> a.reshape(4, 5)
Traceback (most recent call last):
  File "<stdin>", line 1, in <module>
ValueError: total size of new array must be unchanged
>>>
```

So you've seen how to append an element to a list and also how to construct and use multidimensional arrays. Let's try to append another row to a two-dimensional array:

```
>>> numpy.append(a1, [7, 8, 9])
array([1, 2, 3, 4, 5, 6, 7, 8, 9])
>>>
```

This is clearly wrong. We wanted a third row to appear, but instead, we got a single-dimension list with the additional entries appended to it. What's happened is that NumPy flattened the list and appended the new values to it, because that's what the append() operation does—appends new elements, and not sublists.

Fortunately, NumPy has two other functions that allow appending not only new rows, but also new columns to the lists. The vstack() function appends a new row, and the hstack() function appends a new column:

```
>>> numpy.vstack((a1, [7, 8, 9]))
array([[1, 2, 3],
       [4, 5, 6],
       [7, 8, 9]])
>>> numpy.hstack((a1, [[7], [8]]))
array([[1, 2, 3, 7],
       [4, 5, 6, 8]])
>>>
```

Additional convenience functions allow you to iterate through the array:

```
>>> a = numpy.array([[1, 2, 3], [4, 5, 6], [7, 8, 9]])
>>> # simple iterator returns subarrays
>>> for i in a: print i
...
[1 2 3]
[4 5 6]
[7 8 9]
>>> # the following flattens the array
>>> for i in a.flat: print i,
...
1 2 3 4 5 6 7 8 9
```

```
>>> # returns a tuple with the element "coordinates" and the element itself
>>> for i in numpy.ndenumerate(a): print i
...
((0, 0), 1)
((0, 1), 2)
((0, 2), 3)
((1, 0), 4)
((1, 1), 5)
((1, 2), 6)
((2, 0), 7)
((2, 1), 8)
((2, 2), 9)
>>>
```

Obviously, you can do the usual slicing and dicing, as you would with "normal" Python arrays:

```
>>> a = numpy.array([[1, 2, 3, 4, 5], [6, 7, 8, 9, 0]])
>>> # get the middle 3 digits from the first row
... a[0, 1:4]
array([2, 3, 4])
>>> # same but from the second row this time
... a[1, 1:4]
array([7, 8, 9])
>>> # what about making a vertical cut at the third column?
... a[:,2]
array([3, 8])
>>>
```

Finally, let's look at some of the advanced array indexing techniques, which we'll use later in the chapter. You're familiar with the standard Python array indexes, where you either indicate the specific item you want to look at or a range of values. The NumPy array objects can also accept other arrays as indexes:

```
>>> a = np.arange(-10, 1)
>>> a
array([-10,  -9,  -8,  -7,  -6,  -5,  -4,  -3,  -2,  -1,   0])
>>> i = np.arange(0, 9, 2)
>>> i
array([0, 2, 4, 6, 8])
>>> a[i]
array([-10,  -8,  -6,  -4,  -2])
>>>
```

These examples demonstrate the basics of array manipulation. We'll cover other topics, like sorting, searching, and array reshaping, as they are needed for our sample program.

Basic Mathematical and Statistical Operations

So far, you may have gotten the impression that the NumPy library is all about advanced array manipulation. Although it is true that the array datatype is at the core of NumPy, this library is not only about array manipulation. NumPy comes with an extensive set of scientific routines, such as linear algebra, statistics, and financial functions. Here, I will show you some basic examples of the module functions that I find most useful.

The NumPy library provides a wide range of mathematical primitives, such as the sum of all elements, add, multiply, divide, and power functions. Most of them are self-explanatory, as you can see from the following example:

```
>>> import numpy as np
>>> a = np.linspace(1, 11, 8)
>>> a
array([  1.        ,   2.42857143,   3.85714286,   5.28571429,
         6.71428571,   8.14285714,   9.57142857,  11.        ])
>>> # sum of all elements
... np.sum(a)
48.0
>>> # round all elements to the nearest integer
... np.rint(a)
array([  1.,   2.,   4.,   5.,   7.,   8.,  10.,  11.])
>>> # add two elements
... np.add(a, 100)
array([ 101.        ,  102.42857143,  103.85714286,  105.28571429,
        106.71428571,  108.14285714,  109.57142857,  111.        ])
>>> # the second element can also be an array, but the shapes must match
... np.add(np.array([1, 2, 3]), np.array([10, 20, 30]))
array([11, 22, 33])
>>> # similarly you can subtract the elements
... np.subtract(a, 10)
array([-9.        , -7.57142857, -6.14285714, -4.71428571, -3.28571429,
       -1.85714286, -0.42857143,  1.        ])
>>> # multiply
... np.multiply(a, 10)
array([  10.        ,   24.28571429,   38.57142857,   52.85714286,
         67.14285714,   81.42857143,   95.71428571,  110.        ])
>>> # ... or divide
... np.divide(a, 10)
array([ 0.1       ,  0.24285714,  0.38571429,  0.52857143,  0.67142857,
        0.81428571,  0.95714286,  1.1       ])
>>> # ... raise each element to power from the second array
... np.power(a, 2)
array([   1.        ,    5.89795918,   14.87755102,   27.93877551,
         45.08163265,   66.30612245,   91.6122449 ,  121.        ])
>>>
```

The following are two functions that you can use to find the maximum and minimum values in an array:

```
>>> a
array([0, 7, 7, 2, 6, 3, 2, 8, 4, 3])
>>> np.amin(a)
0
>>> np.amax(a)
8
>>>
```

Calculating the Mean and Standard Deviation

Since we are going to build a reporting system that produces statistical reports about the behavior of our system, let's look at some of the statistical functions that we will be using.

Quite possibly, the most commonly used function is for calculating the average value of a series of elements. The NumPy library provides two functions to calculate the average of all numbers in an array: mean() and average().

The mean() function calculates a simple mathematical mean of any given set of numbers.

```
>>> a = np.arange(10.)
>>> a
array([ 0.,  1.,  2.,  3.,  4.,  5.,  6.,  7.,  8.,  9.])
>>> np.mean(a)
4.5
>>>
```

The average() function accepts an extra parameter, which allows you to provide weights that will be used to calculate the average value of an array. Keep in mind that the array of weights must be the same length as the primary array.

```
>>> a = np.array([5., 5., 5., 6., 6.])
>>> np.mean(a)
5.4000000000000004
>>> np.average(a, weights=np.array([1, 1, 1, 5, 10]))
5.833333333333333
>>>
```

You may wonder why you would use a weighted average. One of the most popular use cases is when you want to make some elements more significant than the others, especially if the elements are listed in a time sequence. Using the preceding example, let's assume that the numbers we used initially (5, 5, 5, 6, 6) represent the system load readings, and the readings were obtained every minute. Now we can calculate the average (or the arithmetic mean) by simply adding all the numbers together and then dividing them by the total number of elements in the array (this is what the mean() function does). In our example, that result is 5.4. However, the last readings—the most recent—are usually of greater interest and importance. Therefore, we use weights in the calculation that effectively tell the average() function which numbers are more important to us. As you can see from the result, the last two values of 6 more heavily influenced the end result once we indicated their importance.

The less known and used statistical functions are *variance* and *standard deviation*. Both of these indicators are closely related to each other and are measures of how spread out a distribution is. Simply stated, these are the functions that measure variability of a dataset. The variance is calculated as an average of the square of the distance of each data point from the mean. In mathematical terms, the variance shows the statistical dispersion of data. As an example, let's assume we have a set of random data in an array: [1, 4, 3, 5, 6, 2]. The mean value of this array is 3.5. Now we need to calculate a squared distance from the mean for each element in the array. The squared distance is calculated as ($value - mean$)^2. So, for example, the first value is $(1 - 3.5)^2 = (-2.5)^2 = 6.25$. The rest of the values are as follows: [6.25, 0.25, 0.25, 2.25, 6.25, 2.25]. All we need to do now to get the variance of the original array is calculate the mean of these numbers, which has a value of 2.9 (rounded) in our case. Here's how to perform all those calculations with a single NumPy function call:

```
>>> a
array([ 1.,   4.,   3.,   5.,   6.,   2.])
>>> np.var(a)
2.9166666666666665
>>>
```

We established that this figure indicates the average squared distance from the mean, but because the value is squared, it is a bit misleading. This is because it is not the actual distance, but rather an emphasized value of it. We now need to get the square root of this value to get it back in line with the rest of the values. The resulting value represents the *standard deviation* of a dataset. The square root of 2.9 is roughly equal to 1.7. This means that most elements in the array are not further than 1.7 from the mean, which is 3.5 in our case. Any element outside this range is an exception to the normal expected value. Figure 11-1 illustrates this concept. In the diagram, four out of the six elements are within the standard deviation, and two readings are outside the range. Keep in mind that due to the way the standard deviation is calculated, there are always going to be some values in a dataset that are at a distance from the mean that is greater than the standard deviation of the set.

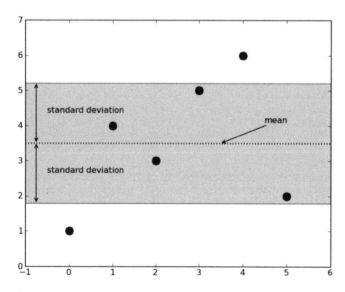

Figure 11-1. *Mean and standard deviation of a dataset*

The NumPy library provides a convenience function to calculate the standard deviation value for any array:

```
>>> a = np.array([1., 4., 3., 5., 6.,2.])
>>> a
array([ 1.,   4.,   3.,   5.,   6.,   2.])
>>> np.std(a)
1.707825127659933
>>>
```

The dataset in our examples so far is reasonably random and has far too few data points. Most real-world data, although seemingly random, follows a distribution known as the *normal distribution*. For example, the average height of people in a nation might be, let's say, 5 feet 11 inches (which is roughly 1.80 meters). The majority of the population would have a height close to this value, but as we go further away, we'll observe that fewer and fewer individuals fall in that range. The distribution peaks at the mean value and gradually diminishes, going to each side from the mean value. The distribution pattern has a bell shape and is defined by two parameters: the mean value of the dataset (the midpoint of the distribution) and the standard deviation (which defines the "sloppiness" of the graph). The bigger the standard deviation, the more "flat" the graph is going to be, and that means that the distribution is scattered more across the range of possible values. Because the distribution is described by the standard deviation value, some interesting observations can be made:

- Approximately 68% of the data fall within one standard deviation distance from the mean.

- Approximately 95% of the data fall within two standard deviation distances from the mean.

- Nearly all (99.7%) of the data falls within three standard deviation distances from the mean.

To bring this into perspective, let's look at the analysis of a much larger dataset. I generated a set of random data that is normally distributed. The mean (in mathematical texts, usually annotated as µ or mu) is 4, and the standard deviation (also known as σ or sigma) is 0.9. The dataset consists of 10,000 random numbers that follow the normal distribution pattern. I then put all these numbers into the appropriate buckets depending on their value, 28 buckets in total. The bucket (or the bar on the graph) value is a sum of all the numbers that fall into the bucket's range. To make it more meaningful, I then normalized the bucket values, so the sum of all buckets is equal to 1. As such, the bucket value now represents the chance or the percentage of the numbers appearing in the dataset.

You can see the resulting histogram of the number distribution in Figure 11-2. The bars are enclosed by the approximation function line, which just helps you to visualize the form of the normal distribution. The vertical line on the horizontal axis at the 4 mark indicates the mean value of all the numbers in the dataset. From that line, we have three standard deviation bands: one sigma value distance, two sigma value distances, and three sigma value distances. As you can see, this visually proves that nearly all data is contained within three standard deviation distances from the mean.

There are few things to bear in mind. First, the graph shape nearly perfectly resembles the theoretical shape of the normal distribution pattern. This is because I've chosen a large dataset. With smaller datasets, the values are more random, and the data does not precisely follow the theoretical shape of the distribution. Therefore, it is important to operate on large datasets if you want to get meaningful results. Second, the normal distribution is designed to model processes that can have any values from –infinity to +infinity. Therefore, it may not be well suited for processes that have only positive results.

Let's say that you want to measure the average car speed on a highway. Obviously, the speed cannot be negative, but the normal distribution allows for that. That is to say that the theoretical model allows, albeit with extremely low probability, a negative speed. However, in practice, if the mean is further than four or five standard deviation distances from the 0 value, it is quite safe to use the normal distribution model.

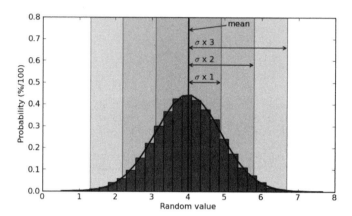

Figure 11-2. *Normal distribution and the standard deviation bands*

We've spent a lot of time discussing and analyzing one scientific phenomenon, but how does that relate to system administration, the subject of this book? As I've mentioned, most of the natural processes are random events, but they all usually cluster around some values. Take the average speed of the cars on a highway. There is a speed limit, but that does not mean that all cars are going to travel at that speed—some will go faster, and some will go slower. But there is a good chance that the average speed will be at or below the speed limit. Also, most cars will be traveling at speeds close to the average. The further you go to each side of this average, the fewer cars will be traveling at those speeds. If you measure the speed of a reasonably big set of cars, you will get the speed distribution shape, which should resemble the ideal pattern of the normal distribution graph.

This model also applies to system usage. Your server or servers are going to perform work only when users request them to do something. Similar to the car speeds on a highway, the system load will average around some value.

I've chosen the distribution function parameters (the mean and standard deviation) so that they model a load pattern on an imaginary four-CPU server. As you can see in Figure 11-2, the load average peaks at 4, which is fairly normal for a busy, but not overloaded, system. Let's assume that the server is constantly busy and does not follow any day/night load-variation patterns. Although the load is pretty much constant, there will always be some variation, but the further you go from the mean, the less chance you have of hitting that reading. For example, it's rather unlikely (32% chance to be precise) that the next reading will be either less than (roughly) 3 or greater than (roughly) 5. Similarly, this rule applies to readings below and above 2 and 6, respectively—actually, the chances of hitting those readings are less than 5%.

What does this tell us? Well, knowing the distribution probabilities, we can *dynamically* set the alert thresholds. Obviously, we're not too concerned about the values going too low, as this wouldn't do any harm to the system (although indirectly, it might indicate some issues). Most interesting are the upper values in the set. We know that two out of every three readings will fall in the first band (one standard deviation distance from the mean to each side). A much higher percentage falls into the second band; in fact, it will be the majority of the readings—more than 95%. You may make a decision that all those readings are normal, and the system is behaving normally. However, if you encounter a reading that theoretically happens only 5% of the time, you may want to get a warning message. Readings that occur only 0.3% of the time are of concern, as they are far from normal system behavior, so you should start investigating immediately.

In other words, we just learned how to define what is "normal" system behavior and how to measure the "abnormalities." This is a really powerful tool to determine the warning and error thresholds for any monitoring system (such as Nagios) that you may be using in your day-to-day job. We will use this mechanism in our application, which will update thresholds automatically.

The complementary function to the standard deviation and variance functions is the histogram calculation function. It is used to sort the numbers into buckets according to their value. I used this function to calculate the size of the bars in the normal distribution pattern in Figure 11-2. This function accepts the an array of the values that it needs to sort, and optionally, the number of bins (the default is 10) and whether the values should be normalized (the default is not to normalize). The result is a tuple of two arrays: one containing the bin size and the other the bin boundaries. Here is an example:

```
>>> a = np.random.randn(1000)
>>> h, b = np.histogram(a, bins=8, normed=True, new=True)
>>> h
array([ 0.00238784,  0.02268444,  0.12416748,  0.30444912,  0.37966596,
        0.26146807,  0.08834994,  0.01074526])
>>> b
array([-3.63950476, -2.80192639, -1.96434802, -1.12676964, -0.28919127,
        0.5483871 ,  1.38596547,  2.22354385,  3.06112222])
>>>
```

The function numpy.random.randn(<count>) is used to generate a normal distribution set with the mean of 0 and the standard deviation of 1.

Finding the Trend Line of a Dataset

The sample application we'll build in this chapter should report on and help us visualize the trends of various readings. For example, let's say that we're collecting data about the CPU load. How can we find out if the load is gradually increasing over time? An obvious way is to look at the graph of the readings, and the really pronounced trends will be visible immediately. But we don't want to need to look at all the possible graphs ourselves and try to spot a trend. If the increase in load is not very obvious, it may be impossible to tell whether the values generally tend to go up or down on the graph, because they will be randomly scattered around some mean value.

Fortunately, a well-developed process known as *regression* or *curve fitting* allows us to find a function that best fits any given dataset. The resulting curve is an approximation of the supplied values that usually are some generic function or trend heavily influenced by random noise. One of the most popular and computationally efficient methods for curve fitting is called the *method of least squares*. This method assumes that the best-fit curve is the one that has a minimal sum of the deviations squared from a given set of data. In other words, the curve should be as close as possible to all data points.

The most common way of defining such curves is using polynomials. A *polynomial* is a function that can be expressed with a fixed-length function using only addition and multiplication operations. As a way of expressing multiplication operations, exponents are also allowed, as long as they are not negative and use whole numbers.

An example of a polynomial function is $y = 2 * x^2 + x + 4$. The largest exponent defines the degree of a polynomial function. In this example, the largest exponential is 2; therefore, this is a second-degree polynomial. So, by using the method of least squares, we can find a polynomial that is the best fit for a given dataset. To keep things simple, we'll be calculating only the first-degree polynomials, which define a straight-line function. The slope of this function shows whether the trend is going up, going down, or not changing significantly over time. The slope degree is defined by the constant multiplier. For example, for $y = a * x + b$, the slope of the line is defined by the value of a. If this value is positive, the line goes upward; if it is negative, the line goes downward. The second constant, b, defines the position of the line on a vertical axis.

As you can see, the first-degree polynomial is defined by two constants: the slope and position. In our function, these are the constants a and b, respectively. Now the question is how to find those constants from any given array of seemingly random data. The actual calculation procedure is somewhat lengthy, and I'm not going to describe it here. Fortunately, NumPy provides a function that accepts two arrays of coordinates (x and y) for the data points and returns the polynomial constants as a result. You can also specify the degree of the desired polynomial function, but we'll stick with the first-degree polynomial calculation. The following example generates some random data, then artificially introduces a slope in the sequence, and then calculates the resulting first-degree polynomial constants:

```
>>> x = np.arange(100)
>>> y = np.random.normal(4., 0.9, 100)
>>> for i in range(100):
...     y[i] = y[i] + i/40
>>> a, b = np.polyfit(x, y, 1)
```

■**Note** You can find more details about polynomial functions and how the constants are derived on the Wikipedia page at http://en.wikipedia.org/wiki/Polynomial.

In Figure 11-3, you can see the raw data (shown as dots) along with the best-fit, or trend, line. Although there are some values that are much larger than the rest of the dataset, the actual trend isn't as steep as you may have expected. The trend function constants also give us a good indication of what's going to happen in the future. For example, after observing 100 values, we established that the polynomial function for this dataset is $y = 0.024 * x + 3.7$. Therefore, with a certain degree of confidence, we can make an assumption that the average value after another 100 measurements will be 0.024 * 200 + 3.7 = 8.5. If we assume that this is the load average reading of our system, we'll have a clear idea of what the average load is going to be in the near future. This is a powerful methodology that you can employ for capacity planning.

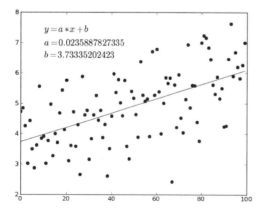

Figure 11-3. *Best-fit trend line for random data*

Reading and Writing Data to Files

In some situations, you may need to write data to a file and then later read it in for further processing. NumPy provides several input/output procedures you can use for this purpose. In the following example, the data is stored to a text file, and the comma character is used as a delimiter.

```
>>> a = np.arange(16).reshape(4,4)
>>> a
array([[  0,   1,   2,   3],
       [  4,   5,   6,   7],
       [  8,   9,  10,  11],
       [ 12,  13,  14,  15]])
>>> np.savetxt('data.txt', a, fmt="%G", delimiter=',')
>>> b = np.loadtxt('data.txt', delimiter=',')
>>> b
array([[  0.,   1.,   2.,   3.],
       [  4.,   5.,   6.,   7.],
       [  8.,   9.,  10.,  11.],
       [ 12.,  13.,  14.,  15.]])
>>>
```

Many popular tools, such as Excel, understand this format, so you can use this method to export your data and exchange files with others who may be using different tools.

Representing Data with matplotlib

You may be were wondering what program I used to generate the graphs shown in figures you've seen in this chapter. I used a tool available as another Python library, called matplotlib. The primary use for this library is to create and plot various scientific diagrams. It allows you to generate and save image files, but also comes with a graphical interface with zooming and panning options. The library provides functions for producing both 2D and 3D plots.

matplotlib is a sophisticated piece of software, which offers functionality similar to commercial products such as MATLAB. Here, we'll just look at generating simple 2D graphs and adding annotations to them.

■**Note** For more detailed information about using matplotlib, see *Beginning Python Visualization: Crafting Visual Transformation Scripts*, by Shai Vaingast (Apress, 2009).

Installing matplotlib

Generally, you have two options for installing matplotlib: use the Python Package Index (PyPI) installer (pip) tool or build the package from the source code. Here's a command to install the library from PyPI:

```
$ sudo pip install matplotlib
```

■**Caution** If you use the `pip` tool, make sure to check which version is installed. I've come across situations where the `matplotlib` release on PyPI was much older than the latest release.

I recommend the other option: building the library from the latest source code package. This way, you'll be sure that you're getting the latest release. The process isn't complicated. First, download the source code from the SourceForge repository at `http://sourceforge.net/projects/matplotlib/files/matplotlib/`. Then unpack it and run the following commands to build and install the `matplotlib` module:

```
$ python setup.py build
$ sudo python setup.py install
```

Depending on your Linux installation, you may also need to install some additional packages that `matplotlib` depends on and that are not included in the default installation. For example, you may need to install the FreeType development libraries and header files (the `freetype-devel` package for Red Hat Linux) and development tools for programs to manipulate PNG image format files (the `libpng-devel` package for Red Hat Linux). Consult your Linux distribution documentation for the specific details, such as the installation procedure and package names.

When you are finished installing the library, you can check that it is functioning correctly by issuing the following commands:

```
$ python
Python 2.6.2 (r262:71600, Jan 25 2010, 18:46:45)
[GCC 4.4.2 20091222 (Red Hat 4.4.2-20)] on linux2
Type "help", "copyright", "credits" or "license" for more information.
>>> import matplotlib
>>> matplotlib.__version__
'0.99.1.1'
>>>
```

Understanding the Library Structure

The `matplotlib` API is organized into three layers of responsibility:

- The first layer is the `matplotlib.backend_bases.FigureCanvas` object, which represents the area onto which the figure is drawn.

- The second layer is the `matplotlib.backend_bases.Renderer` object, which knows how to draw on the `FigureCanvas` object.

- The third layer is the `matplotlib.artist.Artist` object, which knows how to use the `Rendered` object.

Generally, the first two layers are responsible for talking to the system graphic libraries, such as the wxPython and PostScript engines, and the `Artist` is used to handle the higher-level primitives, such as lines and text. Most of the time, you will be using just the `Artist` object.

The Artist is split into two different types: drawing primitives and containers. The primitives are the objects that represent the objects you want to plot, such as lines, text, rectangles, and so on. The containers are the objects that contain primitives. The standard pattern of creating a graph using matplotlib is to create a main contained object (instance of the Figure class), add one or more Axes or Subplot instances, and then use the helper methods of those instances to draw the primitives. For my graphs, I usually use Subplot, as it is a subclass of Axes and provides higher-level access control.

Plotting Graphs

One of the mostly widely used methods of the Subplot class is the plot() function. It is used to draw lines or markers on the Subplot (or Axes). Listing 11-1 demonstrates how to draw a sine function graph.

Listing 11-1. *Drawing a Simple Graph*

```python
import matplotlib.pyplot as plt
import numpy as np

fig = plt.figure()
ax = fig.add_subplot(1, 1, 1)
x = np.arange(100)
y = np.sin(2 * np.pi * x / 100)
ax.plot(y)
plt.show()
```

If you run this script on a system with an X window manager running, you will see a graph plotted in a separate window, as shown in Figure 11-4. You'll be able to use the window functions such as panning and zooming, as well as save and print the file.

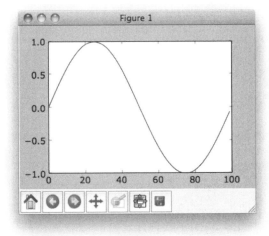

Figure 11-4. *An example of matplotlib window instance*

Changing the Appearance of the Plot Primitives

The more complete syntax for the `plot()` function is to include two arrays of coordinates, x and y, and specify the plot formatting, such as the plot color and style. The following code plots the same graph as Listing 11-1, but using a red dotted line instead, which is specified by the r shortcut for the color and the : shortcut for the line type.

```
x = np.arange(100)
y = np.sin(2 * np.pi * x / 100)
ax.plot(x, y, 'r:')
```

You can also use the keyword arguments to specify the formatting of the graph and the drawing color.

```
ax.plot(x, y, linestyle='dashed', color='blue')
```

Table 11-1 lists the most commonly used formatting string characters and their keyword argument alternatives.

Table 11-1. *Graph Style Formatting Characters and Keyword Arguments*

Style Shortcut	Keyword Argument	Description
-	`linestyle='solid'`	Solid line
- -	`linestyle='dashed'`	Dashed line
:	`linestyle='dotted'`	Dotted line
-.	`linestyle='dash_dot'`	Dashed and dotted line
o	`marker='circle'`	Circle marker (not connected with a line)
.	`marker='dot'`	Dot marker (not connected with a line)
*	`marker='star'`	Star marker (not connected with a line)
+	`marker='plus'`	Plus marker (not connected with a line)
x	`marker='x'`	X marker (not connected with a line)

When you use a shortcut style string, a limited set of colors is available, as shown in Table 11-2. When you use a keyword argument to specify the color, you have a lot more choices.

Table 11-2. *Graph Color Shortcuts*

Style Shortcut	Color
k	Black
w	White
b	Blue
g	Green
r	Red
c	Cyan
m	Magenta
y	Yellow

If you are using only shades of gray, you can set the color keyword argument to a string that represents a floating-point number in the range of 0 to 1, where 0 indicates black and 1 indicates white. Make sure it is set to a string; do not assign the float directly.

```
ax.plot(x, y, linestyle='dashed', color='0.5')  # good
ax.plot(x, y, linestyle='dashed', color=0.5)    # bad
```

You can also use HTML hex strings, such as #aa11bb. Yet another way to specify colors is to pass a tuple of three floating-point numbers in the range of 0 to 1 that represent the red, green, and blue components, as in this example:

```
ax.plot(x, y, linestyle='dashed', color=(0.2, 0.7, 0.3))
```

Drawing Bars and Using Multiple Axes

Another commonly used plotting method uses bar primitives, created with the bar() method. Listing 11-2 demonstrates creating a plot with two graphs. The first graph is also placed on a polar coordinate system. Both plots use bar primitives to display the data.

Listing 11-2. *Plotting Bars Using Cartesian and Polar Coordinates*

```
import matplotlib.pyplot as plt
import numpy as np

fig = plt.figure()

ax = fig.add_subplot(2, 1, 1, polar=True)
x = np.arange(25)
```

```
y = np.sin(2 * np.pi * x / 25)
ax.bar(x * np.pi * 2/ 25, abs(y), width=0.3, alpha=0.3)

ax2 = fig.add_subplot(2, 1, 2)
x2 = np.arange(25)
y2 = np.sin(2 * np.pi * x2 / 25)
ax2.bar(x2, y2)

plt.show()
```

Notice that we now have two Axes objects. They are automatically arranged, but you must specify where on the grid each one goes. So when you initialize each of the Axes objects. you need to specify how many rows and columns there will be on the canvas—two rows and one column in the example in Listing 11-2. Then for the each Axes object, you need to give the sequence number, which will be used to place them accordingly on the canvas grid. The example uses 1 and 2, respectively:

```
ax = fig.add_subplot(2, 1, 1, polar=True) # rows, columns, id
...
ax2 = fig.add_subplot(2, 1, 2)                # rows, columns, id
```

The polar keyword argument indicates whether the axis will have the Cartesian coordinate system or polar coordinates. If you set the coordinate system to polar, keep in mind that the full circle range is from 0 to 2*π.

The bar() method uses two optional keyword arguments: width, which sets the bar width, and alpha, which controls the transparency of the primitive. You can see the resulting plot in Figure 11-5.

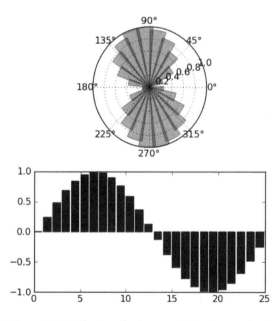

Figure 11-5. *Plotting the bars on Cartesian and polar coordinates*

Working with Text Strings

You've probably noticed that there has been very little text on the graphs shown so far. `matplotlib` conveniently adds values to both of axes, but that is as far as it can guess. Adding text like axis annotations, figure titles, and various labels is our responsibility. Fortunately, `Axes` objects have multiple helper functions that can assist us in adding the text to our plots. You can place text as follows:

- Add text to the x and y axes.
- Add a plot title.
- Arbitrarily place text anywhere on the plot surface.
- Annotate specific points on the graph.

The title and annotations for both axes are set during the axis (or the subplot) initialization by using the appropriate keyword arguments. The arbitrary text string can be placed using the `text()` method and specifying the coordinates and the text string. Similarly, an annotation can be created with the `annotate()` function. The `annotate()` function accepts the keyword arguments that indicate where the text should be placed (the `xytext` argument) and where the arrow should point to (the `xy` argument). An optional `arrowprops` dictionary allows you to extensively configure the look and feel of the annotation arrows, but the simplest configuration is the `arrowstyle` dictionary item, which you can use to set the direction of the arrow.

Listing 11-3 demonstrates adding all four types of text.

Listing 11-3. *Adding Text to a Graph*

```
import matplotlib.pyplot as plt
import numpy as np

fig = plt.figure()
ax = fig.add_subplot(1, 1, 1,
                     title="Fourth degree polynomial",
                     xlabel='X Axis',
                     ylabel='Y Axis')
x = np.linspace(-5., 3)
y = 0.2 * x**4 + 0.5 * x**3 - 2.5 * x**2 - 1.2 * x - 0.6
ax.plot(x, y)
ax.grid(True)

ax.text(-4.5, 6, r'$y = 0.2 x^4 + 0.4 x^3 - 2.5 x^2 - 1.2 x - 0.6$', fontsize=14)
ax.annotate('Turning point',
            xy=(1.8, -7),
            xytext=(-0.8, -12.6),
            arrowprops=dict(arrowstyle="->",)
            )

plt.show()
```

Notice how the text string has been formatted. Listing 11-3 uses the Python raw string notation (just a reminder that it is defined as `r'anystring'`) and encloses the whole expression within $ characters.

This instructs the `matplotlib` text-rendering engine that the text will contain the subset of TeX markup instructions.

Figure 11-6 shows the plot generated by Listing 11-3.

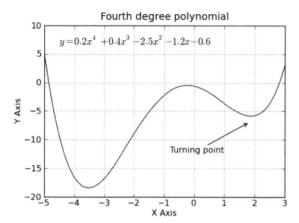

Figure 11-6. *Adding text to a graph*

Saving Plots to a File

So far, we've looked at the various aspects of plot generation. You've seen that the plots that you generate are displayed in an interactive window within your GUI. This is perfectly acceptable if you just need to quickly check the results, but it also means that you need to perform the full calculation every time you want to see the graph. You have an option of saving the graph from the plot display window, but this is manual process and not suitable for automated reporting systems.

`matplotlib` uses imaging back-end processes that generate the images. For the majority of us who just want to use the most popular formats—such as PNG, PDF, SVG, PS, and EPS—`matplotlib` offers the Anti-Grain Geometry (Agg) back end, which uses the C++ anti-grain image-rendering engine behind the scenes. By default, `matplotlib` uses one of the GUI engines (for example, wxPython) when you import the `pyplot` module. To change this behavior, you must first instruct it to use the Agg back end, and then import `pyplot`.

Listing 11-4 shows an example of how to initialize `matplotlib` with the Agg back end and generate two files in different formats.

Listing 11-4. *Saving Images to Files*

```
#!/usr/bin/env python

import matplotlib
matplotlib.use('Agg')
import matplotlib.pyplot as plt
import numpy as np

fig = plt.figure()
```

```
ax = fig.add_subplot(1, 1, 1)
x = np.arange(100)
y = np.sin(2 * np.pi * x / 100)
ax.plot(y)
plt.savefig('sin-wave.png')
plt.savefig('sin-wave.pdf')
```

Notice that you don't need to specifically tell the Agg engine the file type. It is smart enough to figure that out from the file name extension. If you must use a nonstandard extension, or no extension at all, you can use an optional keyword argument to force the file type:

```
plt.savefig('sin-wave', format='png')
```

Graphing Statistical Data

We have spent a great deal of time discussing various statistical methods of data analysis. You know how to check if there are any trends in the dataset and whether the trend is positive or negative. You also know how to calculate the average value of the dataset and the likelihood of the data fitting within the predefined boundaries (standard deviation). Now let's see how to apply this knowledge in practice. We'll build a simple application that runs periodically and generates status pages. These pages are static pages that will be served by the Apache web server.

Collating Data from the Database

Chapter 9 provided the details of the various database tables we're using for our monitoring system and how they are related to each other. Because we're interested in reporting on the probe readings for this chapter's example, of most interest to us here is the probereading table, which contains the raw data obtained from the sensors. The values for this table need to be filtered before processing, so we need to know to which sensor—or to be more precise, which probe—this reading belongs. We also need to group the probe readings by the host from which they have been read. In other words, we need to iterate through all entries in the host table, then for each host we find, we need to check which probes are running on it. Once we establish the entire host-to-probe combinations, we need to obtain the sensor readings over the time.

In the test database that I am using for this example, I have two hosts (called My laptop and My server) in the host table and two probes (called Used CPU % and HTTP requests). Both hosts are reporting their CPU usage figures, but only the server is serving the web pages and therefore is monitoring the number of incoming HTTP requests. You can download the database file with the data along with the rest of the source code for this book. The database is preloaded with sample performance data that has been randomly generated, but attempts to follow real-world usage patterns.

Before we proceed with the implementation, let's quickly outline the basic structure of the site generator script.

Displaying Available Hosts

First, we need to find all the hosts that are present in the database. Once we have that list, we'll use the host ID to search for all probes associated with this host. We need to gather the probe name, the warning and error threshold values, and the host probe ID, which we'll use to search for the probe readings. Listing 11-5 shows the code used to gather this information.

Listing 11-5. *Retrieving All Hosts and the Associated Probes*

```
class SiteGenerator:
    def __init__(self, db_name):
        self.db_name = db_name
        self.conn = sqlite3.connect(self.db_name)
        self.hosts = []
        self._get_all_hosts()

    def _get_all_hosts(self):
        for h in self.conn.execute("SELECT * FROM host"):
            host_entry = list(h)
            query_str = """ SELECT  hostprobe.id,
                                    probe.name,
                                    COALESCE(hostprobe.warning, probe.warning),
                                    COALESCE(hostprobe.error, probe.error)
                            FROM    probe,
                                    hostprobe
                            WHERE   probe.id = hostprobe.probe_id AND
                                    hostprobe.host_id = ?
                        """
            probes = self.conn.execute(query_str, (h[0],)).fetchall()
            host_entry.append(probes)
            self.hosts.append(host_entry)
```

In this code, notice the COALESCE() function, which returns the first non-null result from the list. Remember that we can define the site-wide threshold in the probe table, but we also allow overruling this setting in the hostprobe table. This allows us to set thresholds on a per-host basis. So the logic is to check whether the host-specific threshold setting is not set to NULL and fall back to the default if it is. Here is a simplified example to illustrate the behavior of this function:

```
sqlite> select coalesce(1, 2);
1
sqlite> select coalesce(NULL, 2);
2
sqlite> select coalesce(NULL, NULL);

sqlite>
```

Drawing Timescale Graphs

Now we have all the information required for further data processing: the hosts and the associated host probes. There are many different ways to represent the statistical information that we've gathered. In this example, we'll sort the information by one of the two parameters: the probe names and the timescale. To simplify the implementation, we'll use the predefined list of available timescales: 1 day, 7 days, and 30 days.

I find it easier to develop the templates and the corresponding code if I visualize the web site structure that I'm developing. Figure 11-7 represents the structure of our web site, along with the sample HTML file names (IDs to be replaced with the actual values) and the corresponding Jinja2 templates.

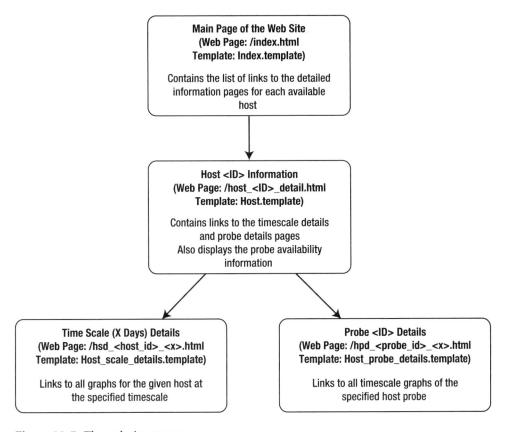

Figure 11-7. *The web site structure*

The Index Page

The index page is the simplest page on our web site. It requires a minimum amount of code to generate, because we don't need to do any calculations. We just pass in the list of hosts, which we've already generated in the class initialization method.

The private class method loads the template and passes the host list to it:

```
def _generate_hosts_view(self):
    t = self.tpl_env.get_template('index.template')
    f = open("%s/index.html" % self.location, 'w')
    f.write(t.render({'hosts': self.hosts}))
    f.close()
```

The template iterates through the list of hosts and generates links to the host details page:

```
<h1>Hosts</h1>
<ul>
{% for host in hosts %}
    <li><a href="host_{{ host[0] }}_details.html">{{ host[1] }}</a>
        ({{ host[2] }}:{{ host[3] }})</li>
{% endfor %}
</ul>
```

We'll use the host list and the host probe list quite a lot in this example. Table 11-3 shows the details of each field, so you don't need to memorize what each field contains.

Table 11-3. *The Host and Probe List Fields*

Element	Element Field	Description
self.hosts	0	Host ID
self.hosts	1	Name of the host
self.hosts	2	Address of the host
self.hosts	3	Port number of the monitoring agent
self.hosts	4	List of the probe elements (following fields)
host[4]	0	Host probe ID
host[4]	1	Name of the probe
host[4]	2	Warning threshold (or None if not defined)
host[4]	3	Error threshold (or None if not defined)

Host Details Page

For the host details page, we need to calculate the service availability figures and display them on a web page for each host. Each page will have two sections: one to display the service availability statistics and the other to list the links to the pages containing graphs for each timescale/host probe combination.

Listing 11-6 shows the two private methods that perform the calculations and also generate the web site pages.

Listing 11-6. *Generating the Host Details Web Page*

```
def _generate_host_toc(self, host):
    probe_sa = {}
    for probe in host[4]:
        probe_sa[probe[1]] = {}
        for scale in TIMESCALES:
            probe_sa[probe[1]][scale] =
            self._calculate_service_availability(probe, scale)
    t = self.tpl_env.get_template('host.template')
    f = open("%s/host_%s_details.html" % (self.location, host[0]), 'w')
    f.write(t.render({ 'host': host,
                       'timescales': TIMESCALES,
                       'probe_sa': probe_sa,
                     }))
    f.close()


def _calculate_service_availability(self, probe, scale):
    sa_warn = None
    sa_err  = None
    sampling_rate = self.conn.execute("""SELECT probeinterval
                                            FROM probingschedule
                                            WHERE hostprobe_id=?""",
                                      (probe[0],)).fetchone()[0]
    records_to_read = int(24 * 60 * scale / sampling_rate)
    query_str = """SELECT count(*)
                     FROM (SELECT probe_value
                             FROM probereading
                            WHERE hostprobe_id=?
                            LIMIT ?)
                    WHERE probe_value > ?"""
    if probe[2]:
        warning_hits = self.conn.execute(query_str,
                                         (probe[0], records_to_read, probe[2],)
                                         ).fetchone()[0]
        sa_warn = float(warning_hits) / records_to_read
    if probe[3]:
        error_hits   = self.conn.execute(query_str,
                                         (probe[0], records_to_read, probe[3],)
                                         ).fetchone()[0]
        sa_err  = float(error_hits) / records_to_read
    return (sa_warn, sa_err)
```

The first function, _generate_host_toc(), will be called for every host found in the list. As a
parameter, the _generate_host_toc() function receives a host structure, which also contains the list

of all probes associated with it (see Table 11-3). The function then iterates through all host entries and all timescale values, calling the second function, _calculate_service_availability().

The _calculate_service_availability() function calculates the number of times each threshold has been breached for each host probe in a given timescale. To do that, it needs to figure out how many records to analyze. This depends on the sampling rate. For example, if we're reading a probe every minute, we'll have 24 * 60 = 1440 records made every day. However, if we are performing a check every 5 minutes, that will be 24 * (60/5) = 288 records. The sampling rate is stored in the database, so we'll just need to fetch that value and calculate the number of records to analyze.

The next step is to count the number of records whose value is above the threshold settings. The database query we are going to use is the same for both value checks. So we construct it once and then use it when needed in the connection.execute() calls, with the appropriate threshold setting. Let's look at the SQL query:

```
SELECT count(*)
  FROM (SELECT probe_value
          FROM probereading
          WHERE hostprobe_id=?
          LIMIT ?)
  WHERE probe_value > ?
```

This is actually two nested queries. The first query that will be executed by the SQLite3 engine is the inner SELECT statement, which selects the last *x* records from the list for a specified host probe. The outer SELECT statement counts the number of records from the list that have a probe_value above the specified threshold value. You may notice that we don't order the list in any way in the inner SELECT statement. So how sure are we that we're actually going to get the *last* records, and not a random or semi random selection of records from the database? In SQLite, each row has an associated ROWID value, and all rows are sorted by their row IDs. If we don't specify the order in our SELECT statement, it will be sorted by the row IDs automatically. Since we're only adding rows into the database, all our row IDs will be in the sequence. Therefore, a simple LIMIT SQL statement guarantees that we'll get the last rows selected.

■**Note** You can find more information about the row ID field in the official SQLite3 documentation, located at http://sqlite.org/lang_createtable.html#rowid. Note that other database engines, such as PostgreSQL and MySQL, may behave differently.

The SQL query will be executed only if the threshold value is available; otherwise, the function returns None as a result. Once the calculations have been performed, we load the template and pass the variables to it. The template is responsible for displaying the availability statistics and also generating links to the pages containing the graphs. Listing 11-7 shows the host details template.

Listing 11-7. *Host Details Template*

```
<h1>Host details: {{ host[1] }}</h1>
  <h2>Views grouped by the timescales</h2>
    <p>Here you'll find all available probes for this host on the same↩
timescale.</p>
      <ul>
      {% for scale in timescales %}
        <li><a href="hsd_{{ host[0] }}_{{ scale }}.html">{{ scale }} day(s)↩
view</a></li>
      {% endfor %}
      </ul>
  <h2>Views grouped by the probes</h2>
    <p>Here you'll find all available time scale views of the same probe</p>
      <ul>
      {% for probe in host[4] %}
        <li><a href="hpd_{{ probe[0] }}.html">{{ probe[1] }}</a></li>
      {% endfor %}
      </ul>
  <h2>Host statistics</h2>
    <h3>Service availability details</h3>
      {% for probe in probe_sa %}
      <h4>Availability of the "{{ probe }}" check</h4>
        <ul>
        {% for scale in probe_sa[probe] %}
          <li>On a {{ scale }} day(s) scale:
            <ul>
              <li>Warning: {{ probe_sa[probe][scale][0]|round(3) }}%</li>
              <li>Error: {{ probe_sa[probe][scale][1]|round(3) }}%</li>
            </ul>
          </li>
        {% endfor %}
        </ul>
      {% endfor %}
```

Graph Collection Pages

The graph collection pages are linked from the detailed host information pages. As you can see from the diagram in Figure 11-7, we'll have two types of graph collection pages: ones that contain the graphs with the same timescale but plotting data from different probes, and those that plot all available timescale graphs for a single host probe.

Although these functions are quite similar, I have separated them into two function calls, mostly to keep the modular structure of the code. Listing 11-8 shows both functions.

Listing 11-8. *Generating the Graph Collection Pages*

```
def _generate_host_probe_details(self, host_struct, probe_struct):
    t = self.tpl_env.get_template('host_probe_details.template')
    f = open("%s/hpd_%s.html" % (self.location, probe_struct[0]), 'w')
    images = []
    for scale in TIMESCALES:
        images.append([ scale,
                        "plot_%s_%s.png" % (probe_struct[0], scale),
                      ])
    f.write(t.render({'host': host_struct,
                      'probe': probe_struct,
                      'images': images,
                     }))
    f.close()

def _generate_host_scale_details(self, host_struct, scale):
    t = self.tpl_env.get_template('host_scale_details.template')
    f = open("%s/hsd_%s_%s.html" % (self.location, host_struct[0], scale), 'w')
    images = []
    for probe in host_struct[4]:
        images.append([ probe[1],
                        "plot_%s_%s.png" % (probe[0], scale),
                      ])
    f.write(t.render({'host': host_struct,
                      'scale': scale,
                      'images': images,
                     }))
    f.close()
```

The _generate_host_probe_details() function is responsible for linking to all host probe images for all available timescales. The following is the template code for this function:

```
<h1>Host: {{ host[1] }}</h1>
  <h2>Probe: {{ probe[1] }}</h2>
    {% for image in images %}
    <h3>Time scale: {{ image[0] }} day(s)</h3>
      <img src="{{ image[1] }}" />
    {% endfor %}
```

The template simply iterates through the dataset generated by the function. The dataset includes the image file names.

The _generate_host_scale_details() function links to all host probes from a specified timescale. Similar to the first function, this function generates the image file names, and this list is used from within the template. The following is the template code for this function:

```
<h1>Host: {{ host[1] }}</h1>
  <h2>Scale: {{ scale }} day(s)</h2>
    {% for image in images %}
    <h3>{{ image[0] }}</h3>
      <img src="{{ image[1] }}" />
    {% endfor %}
```

Plotting Performance Graphs

We've been referencing the images, but we haven't created any graphs yet. In this section, we'll look at the function that reads the data from our database and generates individual images for every possible host probe/timescale combination. As you've seen, these images can be combined by multiple criteria. In this example, we group them by their timescale value and probe name.

In addition to the simple data plotting, our function will also calculate some statistical parameters for the dataset: the trend function for the given data and the standard deviation value, which will give us the suggestion for the new warning and error threshold values. This can be especially useful when you are just starting to monitor a new entity and have no idea what these values should be.

Listing 11-9 shows the function for plotting the performance data. You should recognize the numerical and plotting functions from the earlier discussions of the NumPy and matplotlib modules.

Listing 11-9. *Plotting the Performance Data*

```
def _plot_time_graph(self, hostprobe_id, time_window, sampling_rate, plot_title,
                     plot_file_name, warn=None, err=None):
    records_to_read = int(time_window / sampling_rate)
    records = self.conn.execute("""SELECT timestamp, probe_value
                                   FROM probereading
                                   WHERE hostprobe_id=?
                                   LIMIT ?""",
                               (hostprobe_id, records_to_read)).fetchall()
    time_array, val_array = zip(*records)

    mean = np.mean(val_array)
    std = np.std(val_array)
    warning_val = mean + 3 * std
    error_val = mean + 4 * std

    data_y = np.array(val_array)
    data_x = np.arange(len(data_y))
    data_time = [dateutil.parser.parse(s) for s in time_array]
    data_xtime = matplotlib.dates.date2num(data_time)
    a, b = np.polyfit(data_x, data_y, 1)
    matplotlib.rcParams['font.size'] = 10
    fig = plt.figure(figsize=(8,4))
    ax = fig.add_subplot(1, 1, 1)
```

```
        ax.set_title(plot_title + "\nMean: %.2f, Std Dev: %.2f, Warn Lvl: %.2f, Err Lvl:
                                  %.2f" %
                              (mean, std, warning_val, error_val))
        ax.plot_date(data_xtime, data_y, 'b')

ax.plot_date(data_xtime,
             data_x * a + b,
                  color='black', linewidth=3, marker='None', linestyle='-', alpha=0.5)
        fig.autofmt_xdate()
        if warn:
            ax.axhline(warn, color='orange', linestyle='--', linewidth=2, alpha=0.7)
        if err:
            ax.axhline(err, color='red', linestyle='--', linewidth=2, alpha=0.7)
        ax.grid(True)
        plt.savefig("%s/%s" % (self.location, plot_file_name))
```

The _plot_time_graph() function starts with a SQL query that selects the timestamp and probe_value fields that belong to an appropriate host probe. Once again, here we are using the LIMIT statement to retrieve the latest results from the table.

Bear in mind that this is guaranteed to work only if you're using the SQLite3 database, as the records are automatically ordered by their ROWID value. The other databases may behave differently. Also, this assumption relies on the fact that we never delete any records from the database; therefore the row IDs are guaranteed to be sequential.

If you're using a different database engine, or if you're updating any of the records in this table and you suspect that the row ID may change and the ordering may be altered, you can force the ordering by the timestamp field. This ensures that all records will be sorted by their timestamp before the LIMIT instruction chops off the last section from the results list. However, this may have a significant impact on the performance, which can be improved by adding an index on the required field:

```
sqlite> .timer ON
sqlite> SELECT timestamp, probe_value FROM probereading WHERE hostprobe_id=1 LIMIT
5;
2009-12-16T21:30:20|0.0
2009-12-16T21:31:20|0.000431470294632392
2009-12-16T21:32:20|0.000311748085651205
2009-12-16T21:33:20|0.000777994331440024
2009-12-16T21:34:20|0.00475251893721452
CPU Time: user 0.000139 sys 0.000072
sqlite> SELECT timestamp, probe_value FROM probereading WHERE hostprobe_id=↵
1 ORDER BY timestamp LIMIT 5;
2009-12-16T21:30:20|0.0
2009-12-16T21:31:20|0.000431470294632392
2009-12-16T21:32:20|0.000311748085651205
2009-12-16T21:33:20|0.000777994331440024
2009-12-16T21:34:20|0.00475251893721452
```

```
CPU Time: user 0.192693 sys 0.018909
sqlite> CREATE INDEX idx_ts ON probereading (timestamp);
CPU Time: user 0.849272 sys 0.105697
sqlite> SELECT timestamp, probe_value FROM probereading WHERE hostprobe_id=↵
1 ORDER BY timestamp LIMIT 5;
2009-12-16T21:30:20|0.0
2009-12-16T21:31:20|0.000431470294632392
2009-12-16T21:32:20|0.000311748085651205
2009-12-16T21:33:20|0.000777994331440024
2009-12-16T21:34:20|0.00475251893721452
CPU Time: user 0.000169 sys 0.000136
sqlite>
```

The data we are plotting is time-sensitive, so it would make more sense to have it plotted against the corresponding timestamp values on the x axis. matplotlib has a function to plot timed data called time_plot(). Its syntax is identical to that of the plot() function, but the data argument (either only X or both, X and Y data) must be floating-point numbers representing the number of days since 0001-01-01, with the fraction part defining hours, minutes, and seconds. To achieve this, we need to perform two operations: convert the text strings to the Python datetime type and then convert that into the floating-point numbers. This is done by the following piece of code:

```
    import dateutil
...
    data_time = [dateutil.parser.parse(s) for s in time_array]
    data_xtime = matplotlib.dates.date2num(data_time)
```

If available, we also plot the warning and error threshold lines. Each plot title includes the statistical parameters of the dataset along with the suggested values for the warning and error thresholds. Figure 11-8 shows a sample plot.

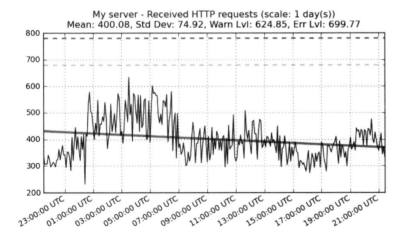

Figure 11-8. *A plot of performance data*

Summary

In this chapter, we looked at basic statistical analysis using the NumPy library. The statistical functions in this library can provide you with better insight into the systems you are monitoring especially if you remember these key points:

- Most real-life data, although seemingly random, follows the normal distribution pattern.

- The standard deviation tells you how far on average each value is from the mean value of the dataset.

- You can use standard deviation to determine the optimum values for the warning and error thresholds.

- The first-degree polynomial function parameters can be used to identify the general trend of a dataset.

- Using the data trend function, you can predict the future behavior of the system.

CHAPTER 12

■■■

Automatic MySQL Database Performance Tuning

In this chapter, we are going to extend the plug-in framework that we built in Chapter 6. As you may remember, the plug-in framework allows us to extend an application's functionality by implementing new methods outside the main application code. The new framework will allow for the plug-ins to generate data and submit it back to the application, so the other plug-ins are able to reuse it. Based on the new framework, we will build an application that inspects the MySQL database configuration and live statistics and makes performance-tuning suggestions. We'll look at some of the tuning parameters and write a few plug-ins.

Requirements Specification and Design

As a system administrator, you probably have been asked to improve the performance of a MySQL database server. This is a creative and challenging task, but at the same time, it can be quite daunting. The database software in itself is a complex piece of software, and you also must account for external factors such as the running environment—the number of CPU cores and the amount of memory. On top of that, the actual table layout and the SQL statement structure play very important roles.

You may have already developed your own strategy for how to approach this problem. The reason I mention "your own strategy" is that, unfortunately, there is no universal solution to tuning the MySQL database. Each installation is unique and requires an individual approach. Various solutions are available to help you identify the most common issues within the database, including commercial options such as MySQL Enterprise Monitor (`http://mysql.com/products/enterprise/monitor.html`) and open source tools such as MySQLTuner (`http://blog.mysqltuner.com/`). The main purpose of such tools is to automate the tuning process by providing insight into the system configuration and behavior.

Assuming that SQL statement tuning is a job for the software developers, you, as a system administrator, are effectively juggling with two parameters: the database configuration and the operating environment configuration. The feedback is provided to you in the form of internal database counters, such as the number of slow queries or the number of connections.

To put all this into perspective, MySQL Community Server 5.1.46 has 291 status variables and 287 configuration variables. I'm not even considering listing the operating environment variables, because that would be nearly impossible. So, it is humanly impossible to correlate all the variables and make meaningful observations at the larger scale.

The available tools attempt to inspect the configuration and, based on the observed status variables, make some suggestions for how to improve the configuration. This works well for basic tuning, but as you dig deeper, you probably will find that you need to modify the tool so that it is tuned to your needs, rather than is based on some generic observations. This is where you need a tool that is extensible and easy to adjust.

Basic Application Requirements

In Chapter 6, we discussed the advantages of the plug-in based architecture. In this architecture, the main (host) application provides some generic service to the plug-ins, which either extend the functionality of the main application or actually provide the services. From the user perspective, the system acts as one entity.

This brings us to the basic requirements list for the application that we're going to build in this chapter:

- The application should be easy to extend, modify, and enhance with new functionality.

- The application should focus on collecting and processing the performance observations from the MySQL database.

- The performance-tuning rules should be easy to transfer and exchange between different instances of the application.

System Design

As a basis for the application, we'll take the plug-in framework we created in Chapter 6. We could take it as is, replace the log-line-reading part with the MySQL data collection function, and start writing the plug-in modules that consume the data. This approach would serve us well in the short term, but may not be the most extensible solution in the long run. The problem is that although we could immediately identify the MySQL configuration parameters and status variables, we would struggle with the operating system status parameters. This is because there is no definite source for this information. Each system is different and may require different tools to report the status.

The solution to this problem is to move the task of producing the information from the host application to the plug-in modules. In other words, some plug-ins will produce the data, which the other plug-ins will rely on for their calculations and, ultimately, their suggestions for performance improvements. In this scenario, the host application acts merely as a dispatcher, and the only service it provides is the connectivity to the database server. The rest of the functionality is provided by the plug-ins. Figure 12-1 shows a schematic diagram of the producer/consumer plug-in architecture.

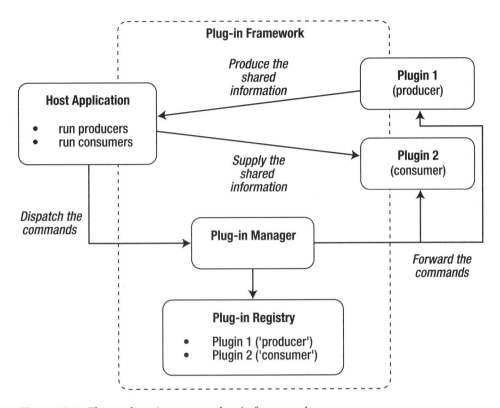

Figure 12-1. *The producer/consumer plug-in framework*

As you can see, the host application still issues the commands via the plug-in manager object. The result is also passed back through the plug-in manager, but for clarity, the figure shows a direct link back to the host application. Once the data is collected from the producer plug-in modules, it is then passed back to the consumer modules. So the host application is responsible for providing the connectivity details to the plug-ins and also maintaining the correct order of producer-first, consumer-last calls.

In addition to these changes to the plug-in framework, we're going to provide three basic producer plug-ins:

- A plug-in to provide the MySQL system variables

- A plug-in to provide the configuration details

- A plug-in to provide the details of the physical and virtual memory available on the system, as well as the number of CPU cores

This will be the basic set of information, upon which we'll build our advisor plug-ins. The advisor plug-ins will perform some calculations based on the results received and provide suggestions on how to improve the server performance.

■**Note** MySQL tuning is a very broad topic. If you would like to learn more, I recommend starting with the MySQL Performance Blog (`http://mysqlperformanceblog.com/`), which includes a wealth of performance-tuning tips and articles.

Modifying the Plug-in Framework

The information sharing between different components can quickly become complicated. The following are some potential problems you may need to resolve:

- Which plug-ins have access to which information? You may want to hide some information from a certain set of plug-ins.

- What if the producer plug-ins are also consumers? Some plug-ins may require information produced by other plug-ins to finish their tasks.

- How do you share large amounts of data between the plug-ins? For example, when the amount of data produced does not fit into physical memory and needs to be stored on disk.

For the sake of simplicity, we are going to have a flat-access model, where the consumer modules can access all the information generated by the producer plug-ins. We will not implement the hierarchical producer layout, and we will assume that the producers are self-sufficient.

Changes to the Host Application

The responsibilities of the host application are limited to the following three tasks:

- Reading the MySQL database credentials from a configuration file

- Establishing the initial connection to the server

- Running the plug-in modules in three stages: run the producers and collect the data, run the producers' process methods, and then run the producers' report module

We will use the Python's ConfigParser library to access the configuration from the Windows INI-style configuration file, which has the following contents (obviously, you will need to adjust the settings to match your database details):

```
[main]
user=root
passwd=password
host=localhost
```

Listing 12-1 shows the full listing of the host application. As you can see, the code is straightforward. It is logically divided into the three main phases as well as the three plug-in processing stages. Notice that we use keywords to distinguish between the producer and consumer modules.

Listing 12-1. *The Host Application*

```python
#!/usr/bin/env python

import re
import os, sys
from ConfigParser import SafeConfigParser
import MySQLdb
from plugin_manager import PluginManager


def main():
    cfg = SafeConfigParser()
    cfg.read('mysql_db.cfg')

    plugin_manager = PluginManager()
    connection = MySQLdb.connect(user=cfg.get('main', 'user'),
                                 passwd=cfg.get('main', 'passwd'),
                                 host=cfg.get('main', 'host'))

    env_vars = plugin_manager.call_method('generate', keywords=['provider'],
                                          args={'connection': connection})
    plugin_manager.call_method('process', keywords=['consumer'],
                               args={'connection': connection, 'env_vars': env_vars})
    plugin_manager.call_method('report')

if __name__ == '__main__':
    main()
```

If you compare this listing to the examples in the Chapter 6, you'll notice that this time, we actually expect something back from the call_method function. This function returns the results generated by the producer plug-in modules and stores them in a single variable. This variable is then passed to the consumer plug-ins as a keyword argument called env_vars. The consumer plug-ins expect this argument to be present. We'll look into the structure of this variable in the next section.

Modifying the Plug-in Manager

The host application just handles a single call to the call_method function, because it doesn't know—and doesn't need to know—the exact number and names of the plug-ins. It is the plug-in manager's responsibility to route the request to the appropriate plug-in modules. However, this approach brings up a problem. If a single call to a function actually yields multiple answers from multiple functions, how do we store the result?

To complicate matters even more, we don't know exactly what the plug-in is going to return. It may be a dictionary, a list, or even a custom object. And we shouldn't need to know this. It's up to the consumer to decrypt this information. The people who write the producer plug-ins are expected to provide extensive documentation about the data structures produced by their modules.

In our case, the plug-in manager component will handle the results in a very simple manner. It's going to store them as separate entries in a dictionary. The dictionary keys will be the plug-in class names, and the key values will be whatever objects are returned by the plug-in module calls. This dictionary is then passed as an argument to the consumer plug-in call. This will result in a flat information store, where all information is accessible by all plug-ins. This may bring some security concerns, but for a simple application like the one we're building here, the simplicity plays an important role.

The only modification to the plug-in manager code is the `call_method()` function, as shown in Listing 12-2.

Listing 12-2. *The Plug-in Manager Method Dispatcher Function*

```python
def call_method(self, method, args={}, keywords=[]):
    result = {}
    for plugin in self.plugins:
        if not keywords or (set(keywords) & set(self.plugins[plugin])):
            try:
                name_space = plugin.__class__.__name__
                result[name_space] = getattr(plugin, method)(**args)
            except AttributeError:
                pass
    return result
```

We now have a plug-in framework that is capable of passing the information between the modules.

If you really need to have the multistage producer architecture, just for few levels, you could use keywords to implement it. For example, you may have the keywords `producer1`, `producer2`, and `producer3`. You then can call the `generate()` method three times, passing a different keyword each time and supplying the intermediate results to the `producer2` and `producer3` instances.

Writing the Producer Plug-ins

We need to produce some data for the advisor plug-ins. We'll start by querying the MySQL internal status and configuration tables. First, let's look at how to access the MySQL database from Python applications.

Accessing the MySQL Database from Python Applications

The support for MySQL databases is provided by the `MySQLdb` Python module, which is available as a prebuilt package on most Linux distributions. For example, on a Fedora system, you can install this module with the following command:

```
$ sudo yum install MySQL-python
```

Alternatively, you can download the latest source package from the project's home page at http://sourceforge.net/projects/mysql-python/ and build the library from the source code.

Once you have installed the library, check that it is loading correctly:

```
$ python
Python 2.6.2 (r262:71600, Jan 25 2010, 18:46:45)
[GCC 4.4.2 20091222 (Red Hat 4.4.2-20)] on linux2
Type "help", "copyright", "credits" or "license" for more information.
>>> import MySQLdb
>>> MySQLdb.__version__
'1.2.3c1'
>>>
```

The MySQLdb library is compatible with the Python DB-API Specification version 2. This specification defines the interface, objects, variables, and error-handling rules that the compliant library must implement. This is an attempt to unify the interface of all database access modules. The advantage of this unification is that, as a developer, you don't need to worry much about the specifics of the database module calls, because they are very similar. The code that you wrote to connect to SQLite 3 should work with the MySQL database without major modifications. The main difference between the libraries is perhaps the connect() method, which is used to connect to the database, and therefore very specific to the database software that you're using.

Regardless of which database module you are using, the first method you'll invoke is usually connect(). This method returns an instance of the connect object, which you will use to access the database. The parameters are database-specific. Since we're discussing the MySQL database in this chapter, here's how you establish a connection to the database server:

```
>>> connection = MySQLdb.connect( host='localhost',
...                               user='root',
...                               passwd='password',
...                               db='test')
>>>
```

These four parameters—the hostname, username, password, and database name—are the ones you'll find yourself using most of the time. However, the MySQL server also supports multiple connection options, which you may need to modify. Table 12-1 lists the most important ones. For a full list of parameters, refer to the MySQLdb documentation (http://mysql-python.sourceforge.net/MySQLdb.html).

Table 12-1. *Commonly Used MySQL Connect Options*

Parameter	Description
host	Name of the host to connect to—either a fully qualified domain name or an IP address of the host.
user	Username you use to authenticate to the database server.
passwd	Password you use for the authentication.

Parameter	Description
db	Name of the database you're connecting to. If omitted, no default database will be selected, and you will need to use the USE DATABASE SQL command to connect to a database.
port	Port number on which the MySQL server is running. The default value is 3306.
unix_socket	Location of the UNIX socket of the MySQL server instance. The default location varies between the distributions, but typically is /var/lib/mysql/mysql.sock.
compress	Flag indicating whether the protocol compression should be enabled or disabled. It is disabled by default.
connect_timeout	Number of seconds to wait for the connect operation to complete. If it is not finished within the specified timeframe, the operation raises an error.
init_command	Initialization command that the server must execute immediately after the connection has been established.
use_unicode	If this flag is set to true, the CHAR, VARCHAR, and TEXT fields are returned as Unicode strings. Otherwise, the return results are just the normal strings. Regardless of this setting, you can always write as Unicode to the database.
charset	Connection character set will be set to the character set specified as the value for this argument.

The returned connect object implements four basic methods for managing the connection status. These methods are listed in Table 12-2.

Table 12-2. *The Connect Object Methods*

Method name	Description
.close()	Closes the established connection, which will not be usable from the moment this method is called. All cursor objects derived from this connection will be unusable, too. Bear in mind that all transactions or changes will be rolled back if you close the connection without committing the changes first.
.commit()	Forces the database engine to commit all outstanding transactions.
.rollback()	Rolls back the last noncommitted transaction, if you're using a MySQL database engine that does support transactions (such as InnoDB).
.cursor()	Returns a cursor object, which you will use to execute the SQL commands and read the results. The MySQL database does not support the cursors, but the MySQLdb library provides this wrapper object, which emulates the cursor functionality.

The real work in the database is done using the cursor objects. A cursor object acts as a context for the query execution and, more important, the data-fetching operations. You can have multiple cursors created by a single connection object. The changes made by any cursor will be seen immediately by the other cursors as long as they belong to the same connection. Table 12-3 lists the most commonly used cursor methods. The connection context used in the examples in the table is created as follows:

```
>>> connection = MySQLdb.connect( host='localhost',
...                                user='root',
...                                passwd='password',
...                                db='zm' )
>>>
>>> cursor = connection.cursor()
```

Table 12-3. *Commonly Used Database Cursor Methods*

Method	Description	Example

.execute()	Prepares and executes the SQL query. It accepts two parameters: the SQL statement that needs to be executed (required) and an optional list of parameters. The variables in the SQL string are specified using the %s string only. The second optional argument must be a tuple, even if it is just a single value.	The following two queries are functionally identical:
		
		`>>> cursor.execute("SELECT type↩`
		`FROM ZonePresets WHERE id=1")`
		`1L`
		`>>> cursor.execute("SELECT type↩`
		`FROM ZonePresets WHERE id=%s", (1,))`
		`1L`
		`>>>`

.executemany()	Similar to the .execute() method; accepts a list of options and iterates through them. The results are combined and accessible using the cursor data-fetching methods. The list elements must be tuples, even if they contain just a single value.	The following example runs two SELECT queries in one command:
		
		`>>> cursor.executemany("""SELECT type↩`
		`FROM ZonePresets WHERE↩`
		`id=%s AND type=%s""",`
		`[ (1, 'Active'), (2, 'Active') ] )`
		`2L`
		`>>>`

.rowcount	A read-only attribute (not a method) that indicates the number of rows the last .execute() statement generated.	

Method	Description	Example
.fetchone()	Returns the next row from the result set. If no more data is available. it will return the None object. The result is always a tuple. Elements are in the same order as specified by the query set.	```>>> cursor.execute("SELECT id,↵ type FROM ZonePresets") 6L >>> cursor.fetchone() (1L, 'Active') [...] >>> cursor.fetchone() (6L, 'Active') >>> cursor.fetchone() >>>```
.fetchall()	Returns all rows returned by the query in the form of a tuple of tuples.	```>>> cursor.execute("SELECT id,↵ type FROM ZonePresets") 6L >>> cursor.fetchall() ((1L, 'Active'), (2L, 'Active'),↵ (3L, 'Active'), (4L, 'Active'),↵ (5L, 'Active'), (6L, 'Active')) >>>```
.fetchmany()	Returns the number of rows specified by its argument. If no argument is supplied, the number of rows read depends on the .arraysize setting.	```>>> cursor.execute("SELECT id, type↵ FROM ZonePresets") 6L >>> cursor.fetchmany(2) ((1L, 'Active'), (2L, 'Active')) >>>```
.arraysize	A read/write attribute that controls the number of rows the .fetchmany() method must return.	```>>> cursor.execute("SELECT id, type↵ FROM ZonePresets") 6L >>> cursor.arraysize 1 >>> cursor.arraysize=3 >>> cursor.fetchmany() ((1L, 'Active'), (2L, 'Active'),↵ (3L, 'Active')) >>>```

Querying the Configuration Variables

You don't really need to connect to any of the databases if you want to retrieve the server configuration or the system status variables. It's enough to establish a connection to the database server.

To get the MySQL variables, we will need to use the MySQL SHOW statement. Its syntax is similar to the SELECT statement, where you are allowed to use the LIKE and WHERE modifiers to limit the query set. (Remember that there are 287 configuration settings and 291 status variables!)

We'll start with the configuration variables. These variables indicate how the server is configured. There are three ways to alter these variables:

- Set them at the server start time using the command-line parameters.

- Set them at the server start time using the options file (usually my.cnf).

- Set them while the server is running using the MySQL SET statement.

■**Note** You can find detailed descriptions of all MySQL variables and how they affect the functionality of the server in the official MySQL documentation at http://dev.mysql.com/doc/refman/5.1/en/server-system-variables.html.

The basic syntax of the command is SHOW VARIABLES. The default behavior of this command is to show the settings that are applied to the current session and is equivalent to the extended syntax of the same command: SHOW LOCAL VARIABLES. If you want to find out which settings will be applied to the new connections, you need to use the SHOW GLOBAL VARIABLES command. The result set can be further modified with the LIKE and WHERE clauses, as shown in the following example:

```
>>> connection = MySQLdb.connect( host='localhost',
...                               user='root',
...                               passwd='password' )
>>> cursor = connection.cursor()
>>> cursor.execute("SHOW GLOBAL VARIABLES LIKE '%innodb%'")
37L
>>> for r in cursor.fetchmany(10): print r
...
('have_innodb', 'YES')
('ignore_builtin_innodb', 'OFF')
('innodb_adaptive_hash_index', 'ON')
('innodb_additional_mem_pool_size', '1048576')
('innodb_autoextend_increment', '8')
('innodb_autoinc_lock_mode', '1')
('innodb_buffer_pool_size', '8388608')
('innodb_checksums', 'ON')
('innodb_commit_concurrency', '0')
('innodb_concurrency_tickets', '500')
```

```
>>>
>>> cursor.execute("SHOW GLOBAL VARIABLES WHERE variable_name LIKE '%innodb%' ↵
 AND value > 0")
18L
>>> for r in cursor.fetchmany(10): print r
...
('innodb_additional_mem_pool_size', '1048576')
('innodb_autoextend_increment', '8')
('innodb_autoinc_lock_mode', '1')
('innodb_buffer_pool_size', '8388608')
('innodb_concurrency_tickets', '500')
('innodb_fast_shutdown', '1')
('innodb_file_io_threads', '4')
('innodb_flush_log_at_trx_commit', '1')
('innodb_lock_wait_timeout', '50')
('innodb_log_buffer_size', '1048576')
>>>
```

■**Tip** The columns of the system configuration table are named *variable_name* and *value*. You can use these names in the SHOW command along with the LIKE and WHERE statements.

Let's write a plug-in class that retrieves all the variables from the database and returns the data to the plug-in manager. As you know, by default, the result is a tuple of tuples. To make it more useful, we'll convert it to the dictionary object, where the variable names are the dictionary keys and the variable values are dictionary values, as shown in Listing 12-3.

Listing 12-3. *Plug-in to Retrieve the MySQL Server Variables*

```
class ServerSystemVariables(Plugin):

    def __init__(self, **kwargs):
        self.keywords = ['provider']
        print self.__class__.__name__, 'initialising...'

    def generate(self, **kwargs):
        cursor = kwargs['connection'].cursor()
        cursor.execute('SHOW GLOBAL VARIABLES')
        result = {}
        for k, v in cursor.fetchall():
            result[k] = v
        cursor.close()
        return result
```

Querying the Server Status Variables

The server status variables provide an insight into the server operation by presenting the internal counters. All variables are read-only and cannot be modified.

■**Note** You can find detailed information about each of the 291 MySQL server status variables in the MySQL documentation, which is available at `http://dev.mysql.com/doc/refman/5.1/en/server-status-variables.html`.

The SHOW command syntax is SHOW STATUS. Similar to the SHOW VARIABLES command without the modifier, this command returns the status applicable to the current session and is equivalent to the SHOW LOCAL STATUS command. If you want to retrieve the server-wide status, use the SHOW GLOBAL STATUS command.

This behavior applies only to version 5.0 and later of the MySQL server. The versions prior to this release had an opposite behavior, where SHOW STATUS assumed the global status, and you needed to explicitly run the SHOW LOCAL STATUS if you wanted to retrieve the session-specific counters. This might present a problem if you're developing a plug-in that may be executed on various versions of the MySQL server. There is a simple solution to this problem: specify the version selector in your SHOW statement. The following query correctly uses an appropriate command modifier and can be used across all versions of MySQL server:

```
SHOW /*!50000 GLOBAL */ STATUS
```

You can use the LIKE and WHERE dataset modifiers with this command, too, as in the following example:

```
>>> cursor.execute("SHOW GLOBAL STATUS WHERE variable_name LIKE '%innodb%' AND value
> 0")
16L
>>> for r in cursor.fetchmany(10): print r
...
('Innodb_buffer_pool_pages_data', '19')
('Innodb_buffer_pool_pages_free', '493')
('Innodb_buffer_pool_pages_total', '512')
('Innodb_buffer_pool_read_ahead_rnd', '1')
('Innodb_buffer_pool_read_requests', '77')
('Innodb_buffer_pool_reads', '12')
('Innodb_data_fsyncs', '3')
('Innodb_data_read', '2494464')
('Innodb_data_reads', '25')
('Innodb_data_writes', '3')
>>>
```

Listing 12-4 shows the plug-in to retrieve the system status variables. This plug-in class is similar to the one that queries the system configuration settings.

Listing 12-4. *The Plug-in to Retrieve the System Status Variables*

```
class ServerStatusVariables(Plugin):

    def __init__(self, **kwargs):
        self.keywords = ['provider']
        print self.__class__.__name__, 'initialising...'

    def generate(self, **kwargs):
        cursor = kwargs['connection'].cursor()
        cursor.execute('SHOW /*!50000 GLOBAL */ STATUS')
        result = {}
        for k, v in cursor.fetchall():
            result[k] = v
        cursor.close()
        return result
```

Collecting the Host Configuration Data

It's all very well and good that we were able to retrieve the MySQL configuration and status data, but we still need to put that data into the context of the operating environment to actually make any use of it.

Let's take the key_buffer_size variable from the system configuration list as an example. This variable sets the amount of memory dedicated to the MyISAM table indexes. This setting can have a significant impact on the performance of the MySQL server. If you set it too small, the indexes will not be cached in memory, and for every lookup, the server will be performing the disk-read operation, which is significantly slower than the read-from-memory operation.

If you allocate too much memory to this buffer, you'll limit the memory available for other operations, such as the file system cache. If the file system cache is too small, all read and write operations will not be cached, and thus the disk I/O will be negatively impacted.

The standard recommendation for this buffer variable is to use 30% to 40% of the total memory available on the server. So, to make this deduction, you actually need to know the amount of physical memory on the system!

There are many different aspects you must consider, but the most significant ones are the amount of physical memory, the amount of virtual memory (or the swap size on Linux systems), and the number of CPU cores.

We're going to use the psutil library, which provides the API to query the system memory readings. This library is designed to get the information about the running processes and perform some basic process manipulations. It is not included in the basic Python module set, but is widely available on most Linux distributions. For example, on a Fedora system, you can install this library with the following command:

```
$ sudo yum install python-psutil
```

The source code along with the complete documentation is available on the project web site at http://code.google.com/p/psutil/.

Unfortunately, this library does not provide the information about the number of available CPU cores. We'll need to query the Linux /proc/ file system to get the report about the available CPUs. This is quite easy to do. We just need to count the lines in the /proc/cpuinfo file that start with the keyword processor.

Listing 12-5 shows the plug-in code that collects the system memory readings as well as the CPU information.

Listing 12-5. *The Plug-in to Retrieve the System Information*

```
import psutil

[...]

class HostProperties(Plugin):

    def __init__(self, **kwargs):
        self.keywords = ['provider']
        print self.__class__.__name__, 'initialising...'

    def _get_total_cores(self):
        f = open('/proc/cpuinfo', 'r')
        c_cpus = 0
        for line in f.readlines():
            if line.startswith('processor'):
                c_cpus += 1
        f.close()
        return c_cpus

    def generate(self, **kwargs):
        result = { 'mem_phys_total': psutil.TOTAL_PHYMEM,
                   'mem_phys_avail': psutil.avail_phymem(),
                   'mem_phys_used' : psutil.used_phymem(),
                   'mem_virt_total': psutil.total_virtmem(),
                   'mem_virt_avail': psutil.avail_virtmem(),
                   'mem_virt_used' : psutil.used_virtmem(),
                   'cpu_cores'     : self._get_total_cores(),
                 }
        return result
```

Writing the Consumer Plug-ins

Now we are ready to start writing the advisor plug-ins. These plug-ins will make suggestions based on the information they receive from the information producer modules. So far, we have collected the base information about the database settings and status, as well as some information about the physical hardware and the operating system. Although the information set is not exhaustive, it includes the crucial details needed to make some educated conclusions. Here, we'll look at three examples that should be sufficient to get you up to speed so you can start developing your own advisor plug-ins.

Checking the MySQL Version

The very first check you may need to perform is the MySQL version number. It's quite important to keep your server installation up to date. Every new release fixes server software bugs and potentially introduces performance improvements.

The plug-in that checks the current MySQL version bases its decision on the latest generally available (GA) release version number, which is available on the MySQL download page at http://mysql.com/downloads/mysql/. To extract this information from the web page, we'll use the Beautiful Soup HTML parsing library. The page structure is relatively simple, and the data we require is included in the last occurrence of the <h1> tag:

```
[...]
<div id="page" class="sidebar" >
    <h1 class="page_header">Download MySQL Community Server</h1>
[...]
<div dojoType="dijit.layout.ContentPane" title="Generally Available (GA) Releases"↩
 id="current_pane" selected="true">

<h1>MySQL Community Server 5.1.47</h1>

<div id="current_os_selection">
[...]
```

The plug-in code will extract this information and compare it against the information reported by the ServerSystemVariables module. Four states can be reported:

- If the major version numbers don't match, it might be a serious issue, and therefore is marked as critical.

- If the current major version matches the latest, but the current minor version number is lower than the latest, we'll mark the issue as a warning.

- If the major and minor versions are up to date, it's just a note that the patch might be beneficial.

- Otherwise, we'll conclude that the current installation is up to date.

■**Note** Another possible check is for versions newer than the current GA release, which may potentially cause problems, because the development versions cannot be thoroughly tested. For the sake of code simplicity, we'll exclude this case in our example. Such an additional check should be relatively easy to include in the module.

The full listing of the plug-in that checks the current MySQL version is shown in Listing 12-6.

Listing 12-6. *The Module to Check the Current Version Against the Latest GA Release*

```
class MySQLVersionAdvisor(Plugin):

    def __init__(self, **kwargs):
        self.keywords = ['consumer']
        self.advices = []
        self.installed_release = None
        self.latest_release = None

    def _check_latest_ga_release(self):
        html = urllib2.urlopen('http://www.mysql.com/downloads/mysql/')
        soup = BeautifulSoup(html)
        tags = soup.findAll('h1')
        version_str = tags[1].string.split()[-1]
        (major, minor, release) = [int(i) for i in version_str.split('.')]
        return (major, minor, release)


    def process(self, **kwargs):
        version = kwargs['env_vars']['ServerSystemVariables']['version'].split('-
')[0]
        (major, minor, release) = [int(i) for i in version.split('.')]
        latest_major, latest_minor, latest_rel = self._check_latest_ga_release()
        self.installed_release = (major, minor, release)
        self.latest_release = (latest_major, latest_minor, latest_rel)
        if major < latest_major:
            self.advices.append(('CRITICAL',
                    'There is a newer major release available, you should upgrade'))
        elif major == latest_major and minor < latest_minor:
            self.advices.append(('WARNING',
                    'There is a newer minor release available, consider an upgrade'))
        elif major == latest_major and minor == latest_minor and release <
latest_rel:
            self.advices.append(('NOTE',
                    'There is a newer update release available, consider a patch'))
        else:
            self.advices.append(('OK', 'Your installation is up to date'))

    def report(self, **kwargs):
        print self.__class__.__name__, 'reporting...'
        print "The running server version is: %d.%d.%d" % self.installed_release
        print "The latest available GA release is: %d.%d.%d" % self.latest_release
        for rec in self.advices:
            print "%10s: %s" % (rec[0], rec[1])
```

The following is the output of the report function performed on a system that is running a slightly older version of the server than is currently available:

```
MySQLVersionAdvisor reporting...
The running server version is: 5.1.46
The latest available GA release is: 5.1.47
        NOTE: There is a newer update release available, consider a patch
```

Checking the Key Buffer Size Setting

We've already discussed the meaning of the key_buffer_size configuration parameter and the impact that this setting can have on the MySQL database server performance. The plug-in module, shown in Listing 12-7, assumes that the optimal setting is 40% of the total available amount of physical memory.

Listing 12-7. *Checking the Optimal Setting of the Key Buffer Size*

```python
class KeyBufferSizeAdvisor(Plugin):

    def __init__(self, **kwargs):
        self.keywords = ['consumer']
        self.physical_mem = 0
        self.key_buffer = 0
        self.ratio = 0.0
        self.recommended_buffer = 0
        self.recommended_ratio = 0.4

    def process(self, **kwargs):
        self.key_buffer = \
int(kwargs['env_vars']['ServerSystemVariables']['key_buffer_size'])
        self.physical_mem =↩
int(kwargs['env_vars']['HostProperties']['mem_phys_total'])
        self.ratio = float(self.key_buffer) / self.physical_mem
        self.recommended_buffer = int(self.physical_mem * self.recommended_ratio)

    def report(self, **kwargs):
        print self.__class__.__name__, 'reporting...'
        print "The key buffer size currently is %d" % self.key_buffer
        if self.ratio < self.recommended_ratio:
            print "This setting seems to be too small for the amount of memory \
                                        installed: %d" % self.physical_mem
        else:
            print "You may have allocated too much memory for the key buffer"
            print "You currently have %d, you must free up some memory"
        print "Consider setting key_buffer_size to %d, if the difference is \
                                        too high" % self.recommended_buffer
```

The following is sample output of the report:

```
KeyBufferSizeAdvisor reporting...
The key buffer size currently is 8384512
This setting seems to be too small for the amount of memory installed: 1051463680
Consider setting key_buffer_size to 420585472, if the difference is too high
```

Checking the Slow Queries Counter

Some SQL queries may take a long time to execute, for various reasons. If you have a large dataset, it may be perfectly normal that most of the queries take a considerably long time to finish. In that case, you may need to increase the `long_query_time` setting. Another possibility is that your tables are not correctly indexed. In that case, you should revisit the table structure and settings.

Our last plug-in module reads two status variables: the total number of requests your database server has received and the total number of queries that took a longer time to execute than specified by `long_query_time`. If the ratio is larger than 0.0001% (more than one query in a million is a slow query), the report will indicate it as an issue. Obviously, you may need to adjust this value to fit your specific database environment.

Slow query tracking is not enabled by default on the MySQL server, so you need to set the `log_slow_queries` variable in the MySQL properties file `/etc/my.cnf` to ON before executing the plug-in code. The full module code is shown in Listing 12-8.

Listing 12-8. *The Plug-in to Check the Slow Query Ratio*

```python
class SlowQueriesAdvisor(Plugin):

    def __init__(self, **kwargs):
        self.keywords = ['consumer']
        self.log_slow = False
        self.long_query_time = 0
        self.total_slow_queries = 0
        self.total_requests = 0
        self.long_qry_ratio = 0.0 # in %
        self.threshold = 0.0001   # in %
        self.advise = ''

    def process(self, **kwargs):
        if kwargs['env_vars']['ServerSystemVariables']['log_slow_queries'] == 'ON':
                self.log_slow = True
        self.long_query_time = \
```

```
float(kwargs['env_vars']['ServerSystemVariables']['long_query_time'])
        self.total_slow_queries = \
                    int(kwargs['env_vars']['ServerStatusVariables']['Slow_queries'])
        self.total_requests = \
                    int(kwargs['env_vars']['ServerStatusVariables']['Questions'])
        self.long_qry_ratio = (100. * self.total_slow_queries) / self.total_requests

    def report(self, **kwargs):
        print self.__class__.__name__, 'reporting...'
        if self.log_slow:
            print "There are %d slow requests out of total %d, which is %f%%" % \
                                                    (self.total_slow_queries,
                                                     self.total_requests,
                                                     self.long_qry_ratio)
            print "Currently all queries taking longer than %f are considered \
                                                slow" % self.long_query_time
            if self.long_qry_ratio < self.threshold:
                print 'The current slow queries ratio seems to be reasonable'
            else:
                print 'You seem to have lots of slow queries, investigate them and \
                                            possibly increase long_query_time'
        else:
            print 'The slow queries are not logged, set log_slow_queries to ON for↵
tracking'
```

The following is sample output of this module:

```
SlowQueriesAdvisor reporting...
There are 0 slow requests out of total 15, which is 0.000000%
Currently all queries taking longer than 10.000000 are considered slow
The current slow queries ratio seems to be reasonable
```

Summary

In this chapter, we've discussed how to inspect the MySQL database settings and the current running status. We also modified the plug-in framework we created in Chapter 6 so that it allows exchanging information between various plug-in modules.

- The MySQL server configuration items can be queried with the SHOW GLOBAL VARIABLES query.

- The database status variables can be checked with the SHOW GLOBAL STATUS command.

- You can use the psutil module to get information about the available system memory.

■ ■ ■

Using Amazon EC2/S3 as a Data Warehouse Solution

Virtual computing, or cloud computing, is becoming increasingly popular. There are various reasons for that, but mainly it is the cost saving. Many large vendors provide cloud computing services, such as Amazon, IBM, Google, Microsoft and VMWare. Most of these services provide an API interface that allows controlling the virtual machine instances and the virtual storage devices. In this chapter, we will investigate how to control Amazon Elastic Compute Cloud (EC2) and Amazon Simple Storage System (S3) from your Python applications.

Specifying the Problem and the Solution

First of all, we need to understand in what circumstances this solution is applicable. Although computing on demand is very convenient method and can lead to the great savings in cost, it may not be applicable in all situations. In this section, we'll briefly discuss the situation in which computing on demand can be successfully used.

The Problem

To help you better understand the problem, let's imagine a typical small web startup company. The company provides some services on the Internet. The user base is relatively small but steadily growing and is evenly spread geographically, which means that the system is busy all 24 hours a day.

The system is of a typical two-tier design and consists of two application nodes and two database nodes. The application servers are running an in-house–built Java application deployed on an Apache Tomcat application server and uses the MySQL database to store the data. The web application and the database servers are reasonably busy and therefore not deemed suitable to run on a virtualized platform. All four servers are rented from a server hosting company and hosted in the remote data center.

Now, this setup satisfies most of the present needs, and considering the slow user base growth, should remain unchanged for a considerable amount of time. The expansion strategy for the company is to add more of the application and the database nodes as needed. The application design allows for nearly linear horizontal scalability.

As the company grows, the owners decided to invest more into market research. To better understand the user behavior and do more targeted sales, the company needs to analyze the data stored in the database. However, as we already know, the database servers are already quite busy, and running additional queries will definitely slow the whole application down. Adding the new database servers just for the data analysis task is not cost effective, because it requires the considerable initial investment and adds to the constant monthly maintenance costs. Furthermore, the analysis will be performed very infrequently, and the new systems would spend most of the time idle.

The second problem our company is facing is the lack of back up strategy. At the moment, all data is stored on the database servers, and although the servers are redundant, they are still located in the same premises. This data definitely should be backed up at a remote location.

Our Solution

One of the solutions to these problems is to use a computing on demand solution such as Amazon EC2. Since the company needs the processing power only occasionally, it can create the virtual servers as and when necessary to perform the calculations. When the calculations are finished, the company can safely destroy the virtual server. In this case, it only pays for the time when the server is active. At the time of this writing, the costs of the virtual instances vary from $0.085 to $2.40 per hour depending on the used memory and the number of allocated virtual CPUs.

If the data analysis is performed once every week and takes eight hours, the total monthly cost will not exceed $18 (assuming an extra-large high-memory instance currently priced at $0.50 per hour). This is a lot less than what a typical server would cost the company should it decide to rent one.

The second part of the initial problem is the lack of remote back up. Amazon provides a highly available and scalable storage solution—Simple Storage System. Similarly to the EC2, you only pay for what you use, and there's no limit of how much you can store on the S3. At the time of this writing, the basic S3 pricing is $0.15 per gigabyte per month for the storage and $0.10 per gigabyte for the data transfer.

This is where you have to be careful, because the total price can add up to a considerable amount. A one terabyte worth of information would set you back by $150 every month. This may sound like a lot of money considering the current storage prices, but bear in mind that you not only get the storage device but also the data protection. Currently, the standard Amazon S3 provides "99.999999999% durability and 99.99% availability of objects over a given year" (http://aws.amazon.com/s3/).

Design Specifications

To accommodate all the requirements and constrains that we set out earlier, we are going to build an application that will create a new instance of the virtual machine in the EC2. The virtual machine will have an instance of the MySQL database server running and available to accept external connections. The database files are going to be stored on a separate highly available volume – an Elastic Block Store volume.

The application will operate in three stages: the initialization, processing and de-initialization. During the initialization stage, the application creates a virtual machine, attaches the volume device to it and starts up the MySQL server. The processing phase depends on your processing requirements, typically contains the data transfer and data processing tasks. We are not going to discuss this phase in great detail, because it really depends on your own requirements. And finally, in the de-initialization phase, we'll shut down the remote MySQL instance, detach the volume, create a snapshot, and destroy the virtual machine.

The reason for creating a snapshot is to create a reference point to which you can revert, should you need to check the state of the data at that particular point in time. You can see this as a version control system. Obviously, each snapshot increases the data usage and therefore your costs, so you'll have to manually control the number of snapshot images that you want to maintain.

The Amazon EC2 and S3 Crash Course

At the time of this writing, there aren't many books about Amazon EC2 and S3. The reason is that both technologies (especially EC2) are rapidly evolving, which makes them fast-moving targets that are hard to aim at. There are some good books, but unfortunately, they are already slightly out-dated.

One of the good manuals about the Amazon web services is *Programming Amazon Web Services: S3, EC2, SQS, FPS, and SimpleDB* by James Murty (O'Reilly Media, 2008). This book has a good overview of the technologies along with the detailed API specification. Another text that focuses more on operational aspects is *Cloud Application Architectures: Building Applications and Infrastructure in the Cloud* by George Reese (O'Reilly Media, 2009).

You can also find a lot of information on the documentations pages for each web service:

- *Amazon EC2*: http://aws.amazon.com/documentation/ec2/

- *Amazon S3*: http://aws.amazon.com/documentation/s3/

It would be hard to try to fit all information about these web services in one chapter, so I'm going to describe the basic concepts. Having said that, this chapter will give you enough information to start using the Amazon EC2 and S3 web services, and you can explore more as you get comfortable with the basic principles.

It is important to understand that both systems, the EC2 and S3, are primarily web services and are designed to be controlled using the standard web service protocols, such as the SOAP and REST. Many tools provide a user-friendly interface to these services, but they all use the abovementioned protocols to interact with the AWS (Amazon Web Services).

If you want to use any of those services, you must sign up to them. You can sign up at http://aws.amazon.com/. You don't have to create an account for each service; in fact, you can use your existing Amazon store account, but you have to sign up to each service individually.

Authentication and Security

When you use the EC2 and S3 services, you have to authenticate yourself to the AWS system. There are different methods of doing so, and different services require you to provide slightly different information. Sometimes, this may cause confusion as to which method has to be used where, and more importantly where to obtain this information. So before exploring each individual service, I'll provide basic information about the security and authentication mechanisms used in AWS.

Account Identifier

Each account has a unique *AWS account ID* number, which consists of 12 digits and looks like: 1234-5678-9012. Each account also has an assigned *canonical user ID*, which is a string containing 64 alphanumeric characters.

The AWS account number is used to share the objects between different accounts. For example if you want to grant access to your virtual machine image to someone else, you'll have to know that person's AWS account ID. This ID is used across all AWS services except the S3.

The canonical user ID is used only in the S3 service. Similar to the AWS account ID, its primary purpose is access control.

You can access this information by going to http://aws.amazon.com/account/, clicking "Security credentials", and scrolling right to the bottom of the web page. The section containing the required information is called Account Identifiers.

Access Credentials

The access credentials are used in every REST API call. These keys are also used in the Amazon S3 SOAP calls.

The access credentials are split into two parts. The first part is the *Access Key ID* and is used to identify the requestor identity.

The second part is the *secret access key*. This key is used to create a signature, which is sent with every API request. When the AWS receives the request, it'll validate the signature by using the corresponding secret access key (which is only known to AWS). Only the valid secret access key can create a signature that could be validated by the AWS secret key counterpart. This ensures that the request is sent from the valid requestor.

Both keys are long alphanumeric strings and can be found under the Access Credentials section under "Access keys" tab. It is advisable to rotate the keys regularly. Also make sure not to disclose the secret key to anyone.

X.509 Certificates

The X.509 certificates are used primarily with the SOAP API requests. The certificate consists of two files. The first file is the X.509 certificate and contains your public key and the related metadata. The public key is sent along with the request body and is used to decrypt the signature information contained in the request.

The second part of the certificate is the private key file. This file is used to create the digital signature, which is included with every SOAP request. You must keep this key secret.

When you generate the X.509 certificate, you'll be provided with both files. However, the secret key is not stored on the Amazon systems; therefore if you've lost your private key, you must regenerate the X.509 certificate again. Similarly to the access credential key, it is a good practice to rotate the certificates regularly.

You can generate news certificates or upload your own in the "Access credentials" sections under the X.509 Certificates tab.

EC2 Key Pair

The EC2 key pair allows you to log on to a new virtual machine instance. Each key pair consists of three parts.

The first part is the key pair name. When you create a new instance, you will select the key pair that you want to use on this instance by selecting an appropriate key pair name.

The second part is the *private key file*. "This file is used to establish an SSH (Secure Shell) session to the new virtual machine instance. It is very important that this key is kept secret and safe at all times. Anyone possessing this key will be able to access any of your virtual machines.

The last part is the public key, which is kept on the AWS system. You cannot download this key. When the virtual machine instance is started, the AWS will copy this key to the running system, which allows you to connect to it using your private key file.

You can generate as many key pairs as you like. Unlike the other credentials, the EC2 keys are accessible only from the EC2 management console, which is available at `https://console.aws.amazon.com/ec2/home`.

The Simple Storage System Concepts

From the user perspective there are only two entities in the S3 architecture—the data objects and the buckets.

The most important entity is the data object. The data object is what is actually stored on the S3 infrastructure. Technically, each data object consists of two parts—the metadata and the data payload. The metadata part describes the object and consists of the key- value pairs. As a developer, you can define any number of the key-value pairs. This metadata is sent in the HTTP header of the request. The second part is the data payload, and it is what you actually want to store on the S3. The data payload size can be anything from 1 byte to 5 gigabytes. You can assign any name to the objects as long as it conforms to the URI naming standards. Basically, if you limit the name to alphanumeric characters, dots, forward slashes, and hyphens you should be OK.

The second entity is the bucket object. The *bucket* is the entity that contains the data objects. The buckets cannot contain other buckets. The object name space is within each bucket, however the bucket name is in the global name space. This means that your objects within a bucket must have unique names, but you can have two objects with the same name in different buckets. The buckets must have unique name on the S3 system, so there is a chance that you may try to use a bucket name that is already used by someone else.

There is a limit of 100 buckets per account, but there is no limit on the size of objects stored in each bucket.

Figure 13-1 illustrates the relationship between the buckets and the objects along with some example names for each.

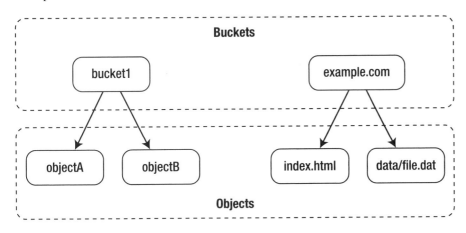

Figure 13-1. *The Amazon S3 buckets and objects*

These names can be mapped to the Amazon S3 resource URLs using the following naming scheme:

```
http://<bucket name>.s3.amazonaws.com/<object name>
```

Therefore, the objects from Figure 13-1 above can be accessed via the following URLs (assuming the public access rights are enabled):

- `http://bucket1.s3.amazonaws.com/objectA`
- `http://bucket1.s3.amazonaws.com/objectB`
- `http://example.com.s3.amazonaws.com/index.html`
- `http://example.com.s3.amazonaws.com/data/file.dat`

I intentionally showed the real web URLs in the second bucket. When you navigate to any website your browser uses the HTTP GET requests to fetch the pages. These are the same as the REST requests used to access the S3 system objects, so you can host complete web sites (or the static parts of the dynamic sites) on the S3.

The Elastic Computing Cloud Concepts

The Amazon EC2 WS is a sophisticated system that interacts with the other services such as Amazon S3 to provide you with the complete computing on demand solution. If you're familiar with any of the virtualization platforms such as Xen, KVM, or VMWare, you will find most of the concepts described here to be quite similar.

Amazon Machine Images and Instances

The Amazon Machine Image (AMI) is the image of the operating system that can be started. The image contains all the packages that are required to run your system. You can have as many AMIs as you need. For example, if you wanted to replicate the two-tier web system that we described earlier, you would create two types of AMIs—a web server AMI and a database AMI. The web server AMI would have the Apache web server and the Apache Tomcat application server packages installed. The database AMI would have a MySQL instance installed.

There are many different AMIs available publically. There are several provided by Amazon as well as other companies. Some of the AMIs are available to use for free, but there are also commercially available AMIs where you have to pay if you want to use them. The easiest way of creating your own AMI is to clone an existing AMI and make your own modification. Make sure that you use an AMI from a trusted source!

■**Note** Try not to base your operations on the publically available AMIs. When the creator of such AMI decides to destroy the AMI, you will not be able to use it again. If you find an AMI that you think is suitable for you, make a copy of it and create a private AMI. Do this even if you don't plan to make any modifications to it. This ensures that you will always be able to find the same AMI every time you need to use it. The typical Linux AMI size on S3 is under 1GB. Assuming the standard $0.15/month fee for a gigabyte of data, maintaining your own AMI would set you back only $1.80 every year.

You cannot run the AMI itself. You must create an instance of the AMI you want to run. The instance is the actual virtual machine that runs the software installed in AMI. An analogue can be a Python class and the class instance (or an object). The class defines the methods and properties (or software packages in Operating System terms). When you want to run the defined methods, you would create an object of that particular class. Similarly an AMI is the contents of the virtual machine and the instance is the actual running virtual machine.

You have two options where you can store the AMIs: you can store them on the Amazon S3 storage, or you can store them on the Amazon Elastic Block Store snapshot (we'll discuss it in the next section). The method of storing an AMI determines how it is created and affects its behavior.

Table 13-1 summarizes the differences between these two methods of storing the AMIs.

Table 13-1. *Comparing S3– and EBS–Backed AMIs*

Aspect	EBS–Backed AMI	S3–Backed AMI
Size limit	An EBS volume is limited to 1TB. This can be convenient for large installations	The S3 backed root partition can be up to 10GB in size. If your root partition needs to be larger than that, you cannot use this method.
Stopping the running instance	You can stop the instance, which means that the virtual machine is not running and you're not charged, but the root partition is not released and still persist as an EBS volume. You can then restart the instance from the same instance volume.	You cannot stop the instance. If you stop the instance it will be terminated and the root partition is destroyed too; therefore, all information stored on that partition would be lost.
Data persistence	The local data storage is attached and can be used to store temporary data. When you stop the instance, the root partition will not be detached, but the local storage will be lost. You can attach any number of EBS volumes to store the data permanently.	The local data storage is attached and can be used to store temporary data. When you terminate the instance, the data from both the root partition and the local storage is lost. You can attach any number of EBS volumes to store the data permanently.
Boot time	The boot time is faster, because the data on root partition is immediately available on the EBS volume. However, the virtual machine will perform slower at the beginning, because the data is gradually fetched form the snapshot.	The boot time is slower, because all data needs to be retrieved from the S3 before it is deployed to the root partition.
Creating a new image	A single API call clones the existing running AMI to a new volume.	You have to create an operating system image with all required packages and then create an image bundle and upload it to the S3. You then register the AMI with the bundled image
Charging	The following charges will apply: • Charge for the volume snapshot (full volume size) • Charge for the volume space used while the instances are in the stopped state (full volume size) • Charge for the running instance	The following charges will apply: • S3 charge for storing the AMI image (compressed) • Charge for the running instance

355

The following figures represent the lifecycles of the S3 backed and EBS backed instances. Figure 13-2 shows the life cycle of a typical S3–backed instance. The instance is created from the AMI image stored on the S3. When the instance is terminated, the volumes are destroyed and all data is lost. You only pay for the S3 store and the running costs of the virtual machine.

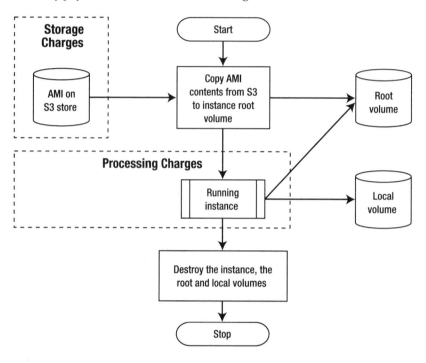

Figure 13-2. *An S3–backed instance life cycle*

Figure 13-3 displays the typical life cycle of an EBS—backed instance. On initial start, the root volume is created from the EBS snapshot. The instance then can have two different states: running and stopped. When the instance is running, you pay the charges for the processing power and the EBS volume charges. When the instance is stopped, you pay for only the EBS volume. If you resume the instance, it'll maintain all data in its root volume; therefore, you pay for it. Finally, if you choose to destroy the instance, the volumes are destroyed too, and you do not pay for the volumes anymore.

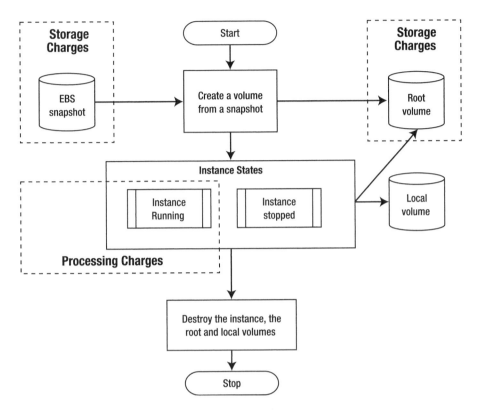

Figure 13-3. *An EBS–backed instance life cycle*

As you can see from the figures, regardless of the instance type, they all get a local storage attached to them. This storage is called an *ephemeral storage*, and its lifetime is limited by the time the instance spends in the running state. It can also survive the operating system restarts (intentional or unintentional), but as soon as you stop the instance, all data on the ephemeral device is lost.

Elastic Block Store

The Elastic Block Store (EBS) is a block-level device that is available to use with the EC2 instances. The volumes are completely independent form the instances and the data is not lost when the instance is terminated and destroyed. The EBS volumes are highly available and reliable storage devices.

Each EBS volume can vary in size from 1GB to 1TB. You can attach multiple volumes to a single running EC2 instance. If you need volumes larger than 1TB, you can use the operating system tools such as LVM (Logical Volume Manager) to combine multiple EBS volumes into a single larger volume.

As I have mentioned, the EBS volumes are block devices, so you have to create a file system before on them before you can use them. Alternatively you can use these as raw devices in the applications that support raw device access.

The Amazon WS also provide functionality to take the volume snapshots. A *volume snapshot* is a point-in-time copy of the volume contents. The copy is backed up to the S3 storage. You can create as many snapshots as you need. The first snapshot is a full copy of the volume, but the sequential snapshots are only recording the differences between the last snapshot and the current volume state.

The operation of taking the snapshot of a volume can be reversed, and you can create a volume from an existing snapshot. This is useful if you have to provide the same data to multiple EC2 instances. You can also share the snapshots between the Amazon WS accounts.

Security Groups

The network access to your instances is controlled using the security groups. The security group is a set of network access rules, like an IPTables rule set. You define the destination network address, the port number and the communication protocol, such as TCP or UDP.

When you start a new instance, you can assign one or more security groups to it. For example, you can have a database security group that allows the TCP access to the port 3306 (MySQL service port). When you create a new database instance, you would select this security group, which will allow the external access to your MySQL server.

Make sure you allow the administration SSH access to your instances; otherwise, you will not be able to connect and manage them.

Elastic IPs and Load Balancers

By default, each instance receives a dynamically allocated public IP address. Obviously, this is not suitable for the servers serving the web content or providing other publically available services. Every time you restart an instance, you may potentially get a different IP address.

You can request an *elastic IP* address, which is always attached to one EC2 instance. This allows you to create one DNS entry for your server, and that entry will not need to change over time. The additional benefit of the elastic IP is that you can assign a failover instance to it. This means that should the primary instance fail, the IP will be relocated to another instance that is capable of serving requests. This method allows you to implement a simple active-standby system configuration.

You can also use the Amazon EC2 load balancing capabilities where the incoming requests are distributed between two or more instances. The virtual load balancer acts similarly to the conventional hardware load balancer such as Alteon or Citrix Netscaler.

Creating a new load balancer instance is relatively simple. You have to select the externally available service port, for example, port 80 for the HTTP traffic. Then, you select the service port on your instances. For example, let's say you are running a Tomcat instance on port 8080 on the EC2 instances, but you want to make this service available via the standard HTTP port 80. In this case, the external service port 80 will be mapped to the internal service port 8080. Last, you assign the EC2 instances to the load balancer.

User Interfaces

As I mentioned, the Amazon WS are designed to be used programmatically. There is no user interface for the S3 system from the Amazon. The EC2 can be controlled from the AWS management console provided by the Amazon, which is available at `https://console.aws.amazon.com/ec2/home`.

There are multiple third-party companies that provide various tools for accessing these services. A simple but powerful S3 management tool is the *S3Fox* add-on to the Firefox browser. You can find it at `http://www.s3fox.net/`. This is not a commercial product and is free to use.

Similarly, there is another Firefox add-on to control the EC2 services. It is called the *ElasticFox* and is available to download at `http://sourceforge.net/projects/elasticfox/`.

Creating a Custom EC2 Image

Now that you have a basic understanding of the EC2 and S3 services, let's put that knowledge to the practical use. As you already know, we need to create an AMI, which we'll use to start our instances. I am going to show you how to create a custom AMI based on already existing image. We'll create a S3–backed AMI image, because in our instance, it will be more cost effective, and we do not require the instance stopping functionality. When the data is transferred and processed, we can destroy the instance.

Reusing Existing Images

Let's start by selecting an existing image from the list of available images. In this exercise I am going to use the standard Amazon AWS management console.

In the Navigation panel on the left-hand–side menu, select the AMIs option. This will display all your own AMIs. You have to switch from "Viewing: Owned by me" to "Viewing: All images" in the drop-down menu. When the view is changed, you'll be presented with the list of all publically available AMIs. I am going to use a CentOS 5.4 AMI made by the company called RightScale. This is a well-known company, which specializes in deploying the mission-critical systems in the cloud environment; therefore, the images produced by them can be trusted. The AMIs ID we are looking for is ami-f8b35e91. You can find this image by entering the IP in the search field.

Figure 13-4 is a screenshot of the AWS management console with the AMI selected.

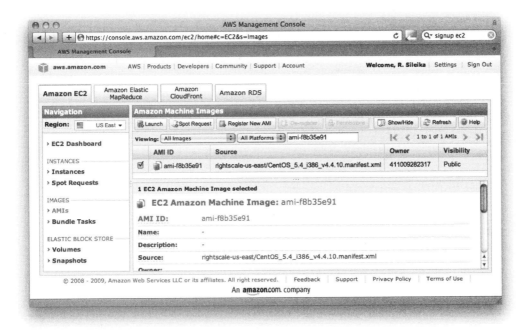

Figure 13-4. *Selecting the AMI to clone*

When you found the AMI, right-click it and select Launch Instance to initiate the instance launch process.

■**Note** Make sure that you have created the security group with the ports 3306 (MySQL) and 22 (SSH) enabled for access from all IPs. You will also need a key pair to be generated and the private key downloaded to your local machine. Save the private key safely, and note its name. We'll refer in this text to this file as `<key-pair name>.pem`.

You can monitor the state of the EC2 instance by clicking the Instances link in the Navigation menu. Once the instance is in the *running* state, you can use SSH to connect to it. Click the instance name, and the details will be displayed on a separate window. Note the instance's public DNS name.

Connect to the instance with the following command:

```
$ ssh -i <key-pair name>.pem root@<instance public DNS>
```

Making Modifications

We're now ready to make modifications to the image. As you remember, our goal is to make this image a MySQL database instance that stores all the files on a dedicated persistent EBS volume.

Install the Additional Packages

First, we need to install the additional packages, the MySQL server in particular. The reason we do this step first is that while mounting the new file system we'll require the MySQL user account to be present, which is created by the package we are going to install now.

Use the Yum installer to install the additional packages:

```
# yum install mysql mysql-server
```

Create and Setup an Elastic Block Store Volume

Second, we are going to setup a new EBS volume. Go back to the AWS management console and select the Volumes menu item from the Navigation menu. The pop-up window appears, where you can select the volume size and it's availability zone.

Make sure that you allocate enough space for your data. The availability zone must match the availability zone of your running instance. You can find out the instance's availability zone by clicking the instance name in the Instances section.

Depending on the volume size, it can take some time for the volume to become available. When the volume becomes available (as indicated by the volume status column), you can attach it to the running EC2 instance. Right-click the volume name, and select Attach Volume menu item. You will then be presented with the list of available running EC2 instances. Select the instance you created earlier. You will also be asked to specify the local device name for the new volume. When selecting a device name (such as `/dev/sdf`), ensure that the name is not in use by any other device.

When the device becomes available (the device file `/dev/sdf` is created on the instance's file system), you can create the file system on it with the following commands:

```
# mke2fs -F -j /dev/sdf
...
# e2label /dev/sdf mysqlvol
```

Now, create a new directory, which will be used to mount the newly created file system and change the ownership so that the MySQL process is able to write to the volume:

```
# mkdir /mysql-db
# chown mysql.mysql /mysql-db
# mount LABEL=mysqlvol /mysql-db
```

Configure the MySQL Instance

Next, we will configure the MySQL instance. You have to change the contents of the MySQL configuration file (located in /etc/my.cnf), so that the socket file and all data files are stored on the EBS volume. This ensures that the data is not lost during the system restarts. The new contents of the MySQL configuration file are presented in Listing 13-1.

Listing 13-1. *Pointing the MySQL Database to the New Location*

```
[mysqld]
datadir=/mysql-db
socket=/mysql-db/mysql.sock
user=mysql
old_passwords=1

[mysqld_safe]
log-error=/var/log/mysqld.log
pid-file=/var/run/mysqld/mysqld.pid
```

Now, let's start the MySQL daemon and set the default password.

■**Caution** Obviously, you'll have to use something more secure and unpredictable than what I'm using in the example below.

```
# chkconfig mysqld on
# service mysqld start
# mysqladmin -u root -S /mysql-db/mysql.sock password 'password'
# mysql -p -S /mysql-db/mysql.sock
[...]
mysql> grant all privileges on *.* to 'root'@'%' identified by 'password' with grant
option;
Query OK, 0 rows affected (0.00 sec)
```

```
mysql> flush privileges;
Query OK, 0 rows affected (0.00 sec)
```

Finally, shut down the MySQL daemon and unmount the volume:

```
# service mysqld stop
# umount /mysql-db
```

Bundling the New AMI

Once you've made all the modifications and are happy with the running instance, you can create a new AMI from it by bundling it.

First of all, you have to prepare your X.509 certificate files and set some environment variables with the access credentials. These will be used in the bundling commands, so make sure you prepare them beforehand to avoid any issues when running the commands. From the account management console, create a new X.509 certificate files (the certificate file and the private key). Save the downloaded files as pk.pem (private key) and cert.pem (certificate) locally. When you have the both files, copy them across to the running instance into the /mnt/ directory.

Go back to the shell prompt on the running EC2 instance, and set the following environment variables to the appropriate values, which you can obtain from the account management web page:

```
export AWS_USER=<12 digit account ID>
export AWS_ACCESS_KEY=<REST access key>
export AWS_SECRET_KEY=<REST secret access key>
```

We're now ready to bundle the running instance. Issue the following command, and wait until it finishes. This is a rather lengthy process and might take up to 10 minutes:

```
# ec2-bundle-vol -u $AWS_USER \
                 -k /mnt/pk.pem \
                 -c /mnt/cert.pem -s 4096 \
                 -p CentOS-5.4-i386-mysql-v2 \
                 -r i386
Copying / into the image file /tmp/CentOS-5.4-i386-mysql-v2...
Excluding:
        /sys
        /proc
        /dev/pts
        /proc/sys/fs/binfmt_misc
        /dev
        /media
        /mnt
        /proc
        /sys
        /tmp/CentOS-5.4-i386-mysql-v2
        /mnt/img-mnt
1+0 records in
```

```
1+0 records out
1048576 bytes (1.0 MB) copied, 0.001929 seconds, 544 MB/s
mke2fs 1.39 (29-May-2006)
Bundling image file...
Splitting /tmp/CentOS-5.4-i386-mysql-v2.tar.gz.enc...
Created CentOS-5.4-i386-mysql-v2.part.00
Created CentOS-5.4-i386-mysql-v2.part.01
[...]
Created CentOS-5.4-i386-mysql-v2.part.62
Created CentOS-5.4-i386-mysql-v2.part.63
Generating digests for each part...
Digests generated.
Unable to read instance meta-data for product-codes
Creating bundle manifest...
ec2-bundle-vol complete.
```

Once the image bundling is complete, you have to upload to the S3 storage. The –b option in the
following command indicates the bucket name. As you know, the bucket name must be unique on the
whole S3 system, so choose it carefully. You don't need to create the bucket beforehand; if the bucket
does not exist, it will be created for you. The upload process is a little bit faster than the bundling
process, but expect it to take a considerable amount of time too:

```
# ec2-upload-bundle -b pro-python-system-administration \
                    -m /tmp/CentOS-5.4-i386-mysql-v2.manifest.xml \
                    -a $AWS_ACCESS_KEY \
                    -s $AWS_SECRET_KEY
Uploading bundled image parts to the S3 bucket pro-python-system-administration ...
Uploaded CentOS-5.4-i386-mysql-v2.part.00
Uploaded CentOS-5.4-i386-mysql-v2.part.01
[...]
Uploaded CentOS-5.4-i386-mysql-v2.part.62
Uploaded CentOS-5.4-i386-mysql-v2.part.63
Uploading manifest ...
Uploaded manifest.
Bundle upload completed.
```

And finally, you have to register the newly created AMI. Once the command is finished executing
you'll be prompted with the AMI ID string. You'll also see the new AMI in your private AMI selection
screen:

```
# ec2-register --name 'pro-python-system-administration/CentOS-5.4-i386-mysql-v2' \
               pro-python-system-administration/CentOS-5.4-i386-mysql-
v2.manifest.xml \
               -K /mnt/pk.pem \
               -C /mnt/cert.pem
IMAGE    ami-2f4fa646
```

Controlling the EC2 Using the Boto Python Module

We finally come to the stage of creating the code to automatically manage the EC2 instances. You can access these services using the SOAP or REST API, but you don't have to do all the heavy lifting yourself, as there are lots of different libraries available. Despite the lack of printed documentation, the subject is well documented on the Internet, and the libraries are available for most of the popular programming languages like Java, Ruby, C#, Perl, and obviously Python.

One of the most popular Python libraries for accessing the Amazon web services is the Boto library. This library provides interfaces to the following AWS:

- Simple Storage Service (S3)

- Simple Queue Service (SQS)

- Elastic Compute Cloud (EC2)

- Mechanical Turk

- SimpleDB (SDB)

- CloudFront

- Virtual Private Cloud (VPC)

The library is available on most of the Linux distributions. For example on a Fedora system, you can install the library with the following command:

```
$ sudo yum install python-boto
```

You can also download the source code from the projects home page at `http://code.google.com/p/boto/`.

Setting Up the Configuration Variables

There will be two types of configuration data.. The account-specific configuration (the REST API access keys) are not specific to our application and can be store in the Boto configuration file called `.boto` in the user directory.

This configuration file contains the access ID key and the secret access key:

```
[Credentials]
aws_access_key_id = <Access key>
aws_secret_access_key = <Secret access key>
```

The application-specific configuration we're going to store in the `backup.cfg` file and access it by using the `ConfigParser` library. The contents of the file are described in the following code:

```
[main]
volume_id=vol-e120af88         # the EBS volume ID which we mount to the EC2 DB
instances
vol_device=/dev/sdf            # the name of the device of the attached volume
mount_dir=/mysql-db            # the name of the mount directory
image_id=ami-2f4fa646          # the name of the custom created AMI image
```

```
key_name=<private key>           # the name of the key pair (and the pem file)
key_location=/home/rytis/EC2/    # the location of the key pair file
security_grp=database            # the name of the security group (with SSH and
MySQL ports)
```

Initializing the EC2 Instance Programmatically

First of all, let's create the skeleton application structure. In Listing 13-2, we start by creating the
BackupManager class. This class will implement the methods of managing our custom EC2 instance. We
also set up a logger object, which we'll use to log the application status.

Listing 13-2. *The Structure of the Application*

```python
#!/usr/bin/env python

import sys
import logging
import time
import subprocess
import boto
import boto.ec2
from ConfigParser import SafeConfigParser
import MySQLdb
from datetime import datetime


CFG_FILE = 'backup.cfg'


class BackupManager:

    def __init__(self, cfg_file=CFG_FILE, logger=None):
        self.logger = logger
        self.config = SafeConfigParser()
        self.config.read(cfg_file)
        self.aws_access_key = boto.config.get('Credentials', 'aws_access_key_id')
        self.aws_secret_key = boto.config.get('Credentials',
                                              'aws_secret_access_key')
        self.ec2conn = boto.ec2.connection.EC2Connection(self.aws_access_key,
                                                         self.aws_secret_key)
        self.image = self.ec2conn.get_image(self.config.get('main', 'image_id'))
        self.volume = self.ec2conn.get_all_volumes([self.config.get('main',
                                                     'volume_id')])[0]
        self.reservation = None
        self.ssh_cmd = []
[...]
def main():
    console = logging.StreamHandler()
    logger = logging.getLogger('DB_Backup')
```

```
    logger.addHandler(console)
    logger.setLevel(logging.DEBUG)
    bck = BackupManager(logger=logger)

if __name__ == '__main__':
    main()
```

As you can see, in the initialization process we're already making the connection to the AWS. The result returned by the EC2Connection() call is the connection object, which we'll use to access the AWS system.

```
self.ec2conn = boto.ec2.connection.EC2Connection(self.aws_access_key,
                                                 self.aws_secret_key)
```

For example, the following two calls return the AMI image and the volume objects:

```
self.image = self.ec2conn.get_image(self.config.get('main', 'image_id'))
self.volume = self.ec2conn.get_all_volumes([self.config.get('main',
'volume_id')])[0]
```

Each of those objects exposes the methods that can be used to control them. For example, the volume object implement the attach method, which can be used to attached the specific volume to an EC2 instance. We'll discover the most frequently used method in the following sections.

Launching the EC2 Instance

Our very first task is to start the instance. This can be accomplished with the run() method, which is available in the image object we created earlier.

The result of this call is a reservation object, which lists all instances started with this call. At the moment, we're starting just one instance, but you can start multiple instances of from the same AMI image.

The run() method requires two parameters to be set: the key pair name and the security group. I'm also specifying the optional placement zone parameter, which indicates in which EC2 zone the instance needs to be started. We don't really care what the zone will be as long as it is the same zone where the volume is created. You cannot attach the volumes from a different zone, so the instance must run in the same zone. You can discover the volume's zone by inspecting the zone attribute of the volume object.

As you know, the instance will not be available immediately; therefore, we have to implement a simple loop that periodically checks the status of the instance and waits until it changes the state to 'running' (see Listing 13-3).

Listing 13-3. *Starting the EC2 Instance*

```
def _start_instance(self):
    self.logger.debug('Starting new instance...')
    self.reservation = self.image.run(key_name=self.config.get('main', 'key_name'),
                        security_groups=[self.config.get('main', 'security_grp')],
                        placement=self.volume.zone)
    instance = self.reservation.instances[0]
```

```
    while instance.state != u'running':
        time.sleep(60)
        instance.update()
        self.logger.debug("instance state: %s" % instance.state)
    self.logger.debug("Instance %s is running and available at %s" % (instance.id,
instance.public_dns_name))
```

Attaching the EBS Volume

Once the instance is running, we can attach the volume to it. As Listing 13-4 shows, the volume can be attached with just a single method call. However, there's a caveat. Even if you wait for the volume to change its state to indicate that it has been successfully 'attached', you still may find out that the device is not ready. I found that an extra 5 seconds wait is usually enough, but just to be on a safe side, we'll wait another 10 seconds.

Listing 13-4. *Attaching the EBS volume*

```
def _attach_volume(self, volume=None):
    if not volume:
        volume_to_attach = self.volume
    else:
        volume_to_attach = volume
    instance_id = self.reservation.instances[0].id
    self.logger.debug("Attaching volume %s to instance %s as %s" %↵
                                    (volume_to_attach.id,
                                     instance_id,
                                     self.config.get('main', 'vol_device')))
    volume_to_attach.attach(instance_id, self.config.get('main', 'vol_device'))
    while volume_to_attach.attachment_state() != u'attached':
        time.sleep(20)
        volume_to_attach.update()
        self.logger.debug("volume status: %s", volume_to_attach.attachment_state())
    time.sleep(10) # give it some extra time
                   # aws sometimes is mis-reporting the volume state
    self.logger.debug("Finished attaching volume")
```

Mounting the EBS Device

The volume is attached, but the file system is not visible to the operating system yet. Unfortunately, there is no API call to mount the file system, because this is the operating system function, and the Amazon WS cannot do anything about it.

So we have to issue the mount command remotely using the ssh command. The ssh command that establishes a remote communication link is always the same, so we construct it one using the method in Listing 13-5, and we'll reuse it every time we need to issue an operating system command on the remote system.

Listing 13-5. *Constructing the ssh Command Paramenters*

```
def _init_remote_cmd_args(self):
    key_file = "%s/%s.pem" % (self.config.get('main', 'key_location'),
                              self.config.get('main', 'key_name'))
    remote_user = 'root'
    remote_host = self.reservation.instances[0].public_dns_name
    remote_resource = "%s@%s" % (remote_user, remote_host)
    self.ssh_cmd = ['ssh',
                    '-o', 'StrictHostKeyChecking=no',
                    '-i', key_file,
                    remote_resource]
```

We have to use the OpenSSH option StrictHostKeyChecking=no, because we will be making the connection to the new host, and by default OpenSSH will warn you that the host key it receives has never been seen before. It will also ask for a confirmation to accept the remote key—behavior you don't want to see in an automated system.

Once the default ssh argument string is constructed, we can issue the remote volume mount command to the running instance, as shown in Listing 13-6.

Listing 13-6. *Mounting the File System on the Remote Host*

```
def _mount_volume(self):
    self.logger.debug("Mounting %s on %s" % (self.config.get('main', 'vol_device'),
                                             self.config.get('main', 'mount_dir')))
    remote_command = "mount %(dev)s %(mp)s && df -h %(mp)s" %    \
                               {'dev': self.config.get('main', 'vol_device'),
                                'mp': self.config.get('main', 'mount_dir')}
    rc = subprocess.call(self.ssh_cmd + [remote_command])
    self.logger.debug('done')
```

Starting the MySQL Instance

Like we did for the mount command, we'll use the same mechanism to start and stop the MySQL daemon on the remote server. We'll be using the standard RedHat distribution /sbin/service command to run the initialization scripts, as shown in Listing 13-7.

Listing 13-7. *Starting and Stopping MySQL Daemon Remotelly*

```
def _control_mysql(self, command):
    self.logger.debug("Sending MySQL DB daemon command to: %s" % command)
    remote_command = "/sbin/service mysqld %s; pgrep mysqld" % command
    rc = subprocess.call(self.ssh_cmd + [remote_command])
    self.logger.debug('done')
```

Transferring the Data

At this point, we have the remote system ready to accept the MySQL database connections. As we've discussed before, the actual data transfer and processing is very specific task, and there are no generic recipes for them. Typically, the steps involved are as follows:

1. Establish a connection to the local database.

2. Establish a connection to the remote database running on an EC2 instance.

3. Find out what local data does not exist on the remote database yet.

4. Read the record set in from the local database and update the remote database accordingly.

5. Delete the old data from the local database if not required.

6. Perform any statistical calculations by using the complex SQL queries or functions on the remote EC2 instance.

But then again, the process largely depends on your requirements, so I will leave the implementation of this task to you. In our example application, we'll use a dummy function that just waits for a brief period of time:

```
def _copy_db(self):
    self.logger.debug('Backing up the DB...')
    time.sleep(60)
```

Destroying the EC2 Instance Programmatically

When we finish updating the remote database and all the data processing tasks are complete, we can start destroying the EC2 instance. The instance will be destroyed, but the database volume will remain along with the data files on it. As a secondary safety measure, we'll also create a snapshot of the volume.

Shutting Down the MySQL Instance

We'll start by shutting down the MySQL database server. You're already familiar with the code, which is shown in Listing 13-7. The only difference is that this time we'll pass the 'stop' argument to the method call.

Unmounting the File System

When the MySQL server is not running, we can safely unmount the file system. Again, we'll do this by issuing the OS command using the ssh connection mechanism, as shown in Listing 13-8.

Listing 13-8. *Unmounting the File System*

```
def _unmount_volume(self):
    self.logger.debug("Unmounting %s" % self.config.get('main', 'mount_dir'))
    remote_command = "sync; sync; umount %(mp)s; df -h %(mp)s" % \
                            {'mp':self.config.get('main', 'mount_dir')}
    rc = subprocess.call(self.ssh_cmd + [remote_command])
    self.logger.debug('done')
```

Detaching the EBS Volume

Technically, you don't need to detach the volume at this point; it'll be detached automatically once the EC2 instance is terminated. However, I would advise you to detach the volume first (as shown in Listing 13-9), because if the EC2 WS behavior changes, assuming the default behavior may cause unnecessary problems in the future.

Listing 13-9. *Detaching the Volume*

```
def _detach_volume(self, volume=None):
    if not volume:
        volume_to_detach = self.volume
    else:
        volume_to_detach = volume
    self.logger.debug("Detaching volume %s" % volume_to_detach.id)
    volume_to_detach.detach()
    while volume_to_detach.attachment_state() == u'attached':
        time.sleep(20)
        volume_to_detach.update()
        self.logger.debug("volume status: %s", volume_to_detach.attachment_state())
    self.logger.debug('done')
```

Taking a Snapshot of the Volume

Once the volume is detached, we will take a snapshot of the current state. Once again, it is just a single method call. We'll also populate the description field with the current timestamp when the snapshot was taken; see Listing 13-10.

Listing 13-10. *Taking a Volume Snapshot*

```
def _create_snapshot(self, volume=None):
    if not volume:
        volume_to_snapshot = self.volume
    else:
        volume_to_snapshot = volume
    self.logger.debug("Taking a snapshot of %s" % volume_to_snapshot.id)
    volume_to_snapshot.create_snapshot(description="Snapshot created on %s" % \

datetime.isoformat(datetime.now()))
    self.logger.debug('done')
```

Shutting Down the Instance

And last, we are going to terminate the EC2 instance. Although unnecessary, we'll wait for the instance to be fully terminated before we continue, as shown in Listing 13-11.

Listing 13-11. *Terminating the Running Instance*

```
def _terminate_instance(self):
        instance = self.reservation.instances[0]
        self.logger.debug("Terminating instance %s" % instance.id)
        instance.stop()
        while instance.state != u'terminated':
            time.sleep(60)
            instance.update()
            self.logger.debug("instance state: %s" % instance.state)
        self.logger.debug('done')
```

The Control Sequence

Although I described the methods in the same order as they should be called, for your convenience, here is the sequence of the method calls that are performed in from the main application function:

```
def main():
    console = logging.StreamHandler()
    logger = logging.getLogger('DB_Backup')
    logger.addHandler(console)
    logger.setLevel(logging.DEBUG)
    bck = BackupManager(logger=logger)
    bck._start_instance()
    bck._init_remote_cmd_args()
    bck._attach_volume()
    bck._mount_volume()
    bck._control_mysql('start')
    bck._copy_db()
    bck._control_mysql('stop')
    bck._unmount_volume()
    bck._detach_volume()
    bck._create_snapshot()
    bck._terminate_instance()
```

The sample output from the running application follows. Please note that the output from the second df command shows the different mount point and the different device because the file system on the EBS volume has been successfully unmounted.

```
$ ./db_backup.py
Starting new instance...
instance state: pending
instance state: running
Instance i-2380bd48 is running and available at ec2-184-73-116-217.compute-
1.amazonaws.com
Attaching volume vol-e120af88 to instance i-2380bd48 as /dev/sdf
volume status: attached
Finished attaching volume
```

```
Mounting /dev/sdf on /mysql-db
Filesystem              Size  Used Avail Use% Mounted on
/dev/sdf               1008M   55M  903M   6% /mysql-db
done
Sending MySQL DB daemon command to: start
Starting MySQL: [  OK  ]
1221
1268
done
Backing up the DB...
Sending MySQL DB daemon command to: stop
Stopping MySQL: [  OK  ]
done
Unmounting /mysql-db
Filesystem              Size  Used Avail Use% Mounted on
/dev/sda1               4.0G  2.2G  1.6G  58% /
done
Detaching volume vol-e120af88
volume status: None
done
Taking a snapshot of vol-e120af88
done
Terminating instance i-2380bd48
instance state: terminated
done
```

Summary

In this chapter, we looked at the Amazon Web Services (AWS) and how Simple Storage System (S3) and the Elastic Computing Cloud (EC2) can be used to perform temporary computational tasks. In addition to the computing on demand task, you discovered how to perform a remote backup of the important data. The simple application we've built in this chapter can serve as a foundation for building your own data warehouse on the virtual computing cloud. Remember these key points from this chapter:

- The EC2 and S3 are primarily the web services designed to be controlled programmatically.

- The main S3 components are the data objects and the buckets containing them.

- The Amazon Machine Images (AMIs) are used as the templates to start the EC2 instances.

- The EC2 instances are the actual running virtual machines

- You can control most of the AWS services using the Python Boto library.

Index

You Need the Companion eBook

Your purchase of this book entitles you to buy the companion PDF-version eBook for only $10. Take the weightless companion with you anywhere.

We believe this Apress title will prove so indispensable that you'll want to carry it with you everywhere, which is why we are offering the companion eBook (in PDF format) for $10 to customers who purchase this book now. Convenient and fully searchable, the PDF version of any content-rich, page-heavy Apress book makes a valuable addition to your programming library. You can easily find and copy code—or perform examples by quickly toggling between instructions and the application. Even simultaneously tackling a donut, diet soda, and complex code becomes simplified with hands-free eBooks!

Once you purchase your book, getting the $10 companion eBook is simple:

❶ Visit **www.apress.com/promo/tendollars/**.

❷ Complete a basic registration form to receive a randomly generated question about this title.

❸ Answer the question correctly in 60 seconds, and you will receive a promotional code to redeem for the $10.00 eBook.

eBookshop

233 Spring Street, New York, NY 10013

Offer valid through 1/11.